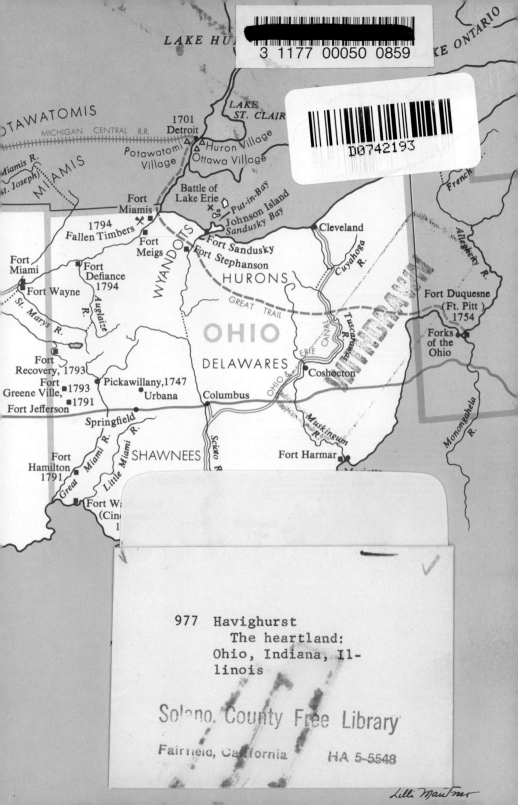

3 1177 00050 0859

D0742193

LAKE HU...
LAKE ONTARIO

OTAWATOMIS
MICHIGAN CENTRAL R.R.
MIAMIS

Miamis R.
St. Joseph

LAKE ST. CLAIR

1701 Detroit
△ Huron Village
Potawatomi Village
△ Ottawa Village

Fort Miamis
Battle of Lake Erie
Put-in-Bay
Johnson Island
Sandusky Bay

French

1794 Fallen Timbers
Fort Meigs
WYANDOTS
Fort Sandusky
Fort Stephanson
Cleveland
Cuyahoga R.
Allegheny R.

Fort Miami
Fort Defiance 1794
Fort Wayne
St. Marys R.
Auglaize R.

HURONS

GREAT TRAIL

WILDERNESS

Fort Duquesne (Ft. Pitt) 1754

OHIO

Forks of the Ohio

ERIE CANAL
Tuscarawas R.
OHIO & ERIE CANAL

Fort Recovery, 1793
Fort Greene Ville, 1793
1791
Fort Jefferson

DELAWARES
Pickawillany, 1747
Urbana
Springfield

Columbus
Coshocton

Monongahela R.

Great Miami R.
Little Miami R.
SHAWNEES
Scioto R.
Muskingum R.

Fort Hamilton 1791
Fort Wa... (Cinc...

Fort Harmar

977 Havighurst
    The heartland:
    Ohio, Indiana, Il-
    linois

Solano County Free Library

Fairfield, California   HA 5-5548

Lilli Mautner

The Heartland:
Ohio, Indiana, Illinois

BOOKS BY WALTER HAVIGHURST

THE HEARTLAND: *Ohio, Indiana, Illinois*
PIER 17
THE QUIET SHORE
UPPER MISSISSIPPI (*Rivers of America*)
THE WINDS OF SPRING
THE LONG SHIPS PASSING
LAND OF PROMISE
SIGNATURE OF TIME
GEORGE ROGERS CLARK: *Soldier in the West*
ANNIE OAKLEY OF THE WILD WEST
WILDERNESS FOR SALE: *The First Western Land Rush*
THE MIAMI YEARS
LAND OF THE LONG HORIZONS

In collaboration with Marion Boyd Havighurst:

SONG OF THE PINES
HIGH PRAIRIE
CLIMB A LOFTY LADDER

REGIONS OF AMERICA

*A series of books that depict our natural regions,
their history, development and character*

Edited by Carl Carmer

THE HEARTLAND: *Ohio, Indiana, Illinois*
by Walter Havighurst

Already published

LOVE SONG TO THE PLAINS
by Mari Sandoz

MASSACHUSETTS: *There She Is—Behold Her*
by Henry F. Howe

SOUTH CAROLINA: *Annals of Pride and Protest*
by William Francis Guess

YANKEE KINGDOM: *Vermont and New Hampshire*
by Ralph Nading Hill

VIRGINIA: *A New Look at the Old Dominion*
by Marshall W. Fishwick

THE
HEARTLAND:
OHIO,
INDIANA,
ILLINOIS

Walter Havighurst

A REGIONS OF AMERICA BOOK

Illustrations by Grattan Condon

HARPER & ROW, PUBLISHERS, NEW YORK AND EVANSTON

Grateful acknowledgment is made for permission to use excerpts from the following publications:

"American Letter" from *Collected Poems of Archibald MacLeish*. Reprinted by permission of Houghton Mifflin Company.

"The Dry Salvages" from *Four Quartets*, copyright 1943 by T. S. Eliot. Reprinted by permission of Harcourt, Brace & World, Inc.

Smoke and Steel and *The People, Yes* by Carl Sandburg. Reprinted by permission of Harcourt, Brace & World, Inc.

"Prairie" from *Cornhuskers* by Carl Sandburg. Copyright 1918 by Holt, Rinehart and Winston, Inc. Copyright renewed 1946 by Carl Sandburg. "Prayers of Steel" from *Chicago Poems* by Carl Sandburg. Reprinted by permission of Holt, Rinehart and Winston, Inc.

"Starved Rock" from *Starved Rock* by Edgar Lee Masters (Macmillan, 1919, 1947). "The Hill," "Dow Kritt," "Willie Metcalf," "Lucinda Matlock," "Joseph Dixon," "Widow McFarlane," "Tom Beatty," and "Fiddler Jones" from *Spoon River Anthology* by Edgar Lee Masters (Macmillan, 1914, 1915, 1942).

"Bryan, Bryan, Bryan, Bryan," "Sew the Flags Together," "The Santa-Fe Trail," "The Eagle That Is Forgotten," "The Congo," "In Praise of Johnny Appleseed," and "Sangamon County Peace Advocate" from *Collected Poems* by Vachel Lindsay. Copyright 1913, 1914, 1920, 1923, 1925 by The Macmillan Company. Copyright 1942, 1948 by Elizabeth C. Lindsay. Reprinted by permission of the publisher.

THE HEARTLAND. *Copyright © 1956, 1962 by Walter Havighurst. Printed in the United States of America. All rights reserved. No part of this book may be used or reproduced in any manner whatsoever without written permission except in the case of brief quotations embodied in critical articles and reviews. For information address Harper & Row, Publishers, Incorporated, 49 East 33rd Street, New York 16, N.Y.*

FIRST EDITION

Excerpts from this book have appeared in *American Heritage* and *The Saturday Evening Post*.

LIBRARY OF CONGRESS CATALOG CARD NUMBER: 62-14531

TO MIRIAM

Death of Pontiac
(Chapter 3)

Contents

Acknowledgments

For help in the gathering of material for this book I am indebted to people in a number of institutions, from the Ministry of the Marine in Paris and the British Museum in London to the Newberry Library in Chicago and the Chicago Historical Society. In particular I should like to thank Dr. James H. Rodabaugh of the Ohio Historical Society, Miss Caroline Dunn of the Indiana Historical Society Library, and Dr. Clyde C. Walton of the Illinois Historical Society. For specific points of information I am grateful to Miss Agnes Hanson of the Cleveland Public Library; Mr. Walter L. Myers, Jr., of the Upper Ohio Development Council; Mr. Hudson Biery, Director of the Ohio Valley Improvement Association; Colonel Edwin C. Higbee of the U.S. Department of Commerce at Cleveland; Mrs. Dorothy E. Powers, curator of the Inland Rivers Library of the Public Library of Cincinnati; and Mr. Brockett R. Bates of the Division of Parks and Memorials, State of Illinois.

Oxford, Ohio   WALTER HAVIGHURST

THE HEARTLAND

OHIO, INDIANA, ILLINOIS

1673-1860

•••••••• Portages

I

THE CURVE
OF A
CONTINENT

Men in the old lands housed by their rivers.
They built their towns in the vales in the earth's shelter.
We first inhabit the world. We dwell
On the half earth, on the open curve of a continent.

—ARCHIBALD MacLEISH

1. Prologue—A Whisper from the Grass

The geography of North America is unlike that of other continents, having broader and simpler lines and enclosing a great central basin between coastal mountain systems. Eastward from the Mississippi stretches a nearly level oblong of land framed by two waterways, the Great Lakes and the Ohio River. These features bound a populous productive region, the states of Ohio, Indiana and Illinois, a region of mingled agriculture and industry, half urban and half rural. Its people came from many backgrounds, from all the American coastal colonies and from every country of Europe. A hundred and sixty years ago the region was an almost empty wilderness. Today it sends products to every part of the world and its population equals that of Austria, Sweden and Greece combined. It is the heartland, the center of America's population and the source of important currents of its political, economic and cultural life.

The Ohio River marks a border; in character and tradition Kentucky is distinct from the states that face it on the north. The Ohio-Indiana and the Indiana-Illinois boundaries are polit-

3

ical only, and quite unapparent even to a careful ear and eye. The land rolls on unchanged; farms, towns and cities repeat the same tempo and impression; people use the same idiom and intonation; they share common attitudes and instincts. This entire region has a common history. It was wrested from the Indians by wars and nominal purchase, and it was tamed and settled by a fifty-year surge of land-seekers. The three states were formed in the first two decades of the 1800's; by 1840 their frontier period was past. A land without barriers, this broad, inviting, immensely productive region became also an avenue through which restless people, many of its own among them, moved on to new frontiers beyond the Mississippi. Even today its highways, railroads and air lines carry America's transcontinental travel. To cross the country one must cross the heartland.

All this movement in an open land has kept the region from developing a self-contained culture. Its energies spill out in various directions and it readily absorbs influences from beyond its borders. Thus it has become open-minded, tolerant, receptive to change, hospitable to new methods, new institutions and ideas. It was the first unfenced "West" in America, and from the receding frontier experience it retains a confident and careless character, with less awareness of the past than of the future.

The heartland is many things—the high-level bridge at Cleveland spanning the smoky gorge of the Cuyahoga and the mysterious earthworks of Fort Ancient above the green gorge of the Little Miami; the big oval racetrack at Indianapolis, with Barney Oldfield blurring by, and a farm boy picking up an arrowhead from the withered grass of an old battlefield on Tippecanoe River; the deep woods of Brown County, Indiana, and the rolling Corn Belt prairies of McLean County, Illinois; the monument to Chief Black Hawk above the Rock River and the graves of the Haymarket martyrs at Waldheim Cemetery in Chicago; the wooded bottoms of the winding Sangamon and the windy lookout of Starved Rock on the Illinois, a string of river barges creeping past Shawneetown and the race of lake-shore traffic on Chicago's Outer Drive.

Looked at from a distance—say from a Spanish island in the Mediterranean where this is being written—the varied land has a large and simple symmetry, like that of the continental nation. It is framed by two commerce-burdened waterways, the Ohio River and the Great Lakes. Along the waterways two bands of industry stretch westward from the upper Ohio and the Great Lakes. The two industrial belts, in turn, frame a central domain of agriculture.

The Ohio River, long a highway of migration and settlement, has become a highway of commerce, with barge tows carrying oil, steel, coal, stone, cement and chemicals between Pittsburgh and the Mississippi. Once a romantic river (the usually caustic Mrs. Trollope said it needed only a few castles to surpass the Rhine), it is now a curving corridor of industry. Steel mills, chemical and aluminum plants, coke ovens, brick works, oil refineries and electric power plants stain the sky at Steubenville, Wheeling, Moundsville, Ironton, Portsmouth, Cincinnati, Louisville, Evansville, and scores of lesser places.

Above Portsmouth the Scioto River leads past the old town of Waverly. Here is a hillside cave with a stone door inscribed:

WILLIAM HEWITT
THE HERMIT
occupied this cave 14 years, while all
was wilderness around him. He died
in 1834, aged 70 years.

Now the cave is overshadowed by a mammoth plant where thousands of electronic instruments refine uranium for the production of atomic energy. A four-lane high-speed highway passes the hermit's door.

Above Cincinnati, along the Great Miami, a rural landscape is invaded by the steel, machinery, appliance and paper plants of Hamilton, Middletown and Dayton. At Miamisburg, crouched under the country's largest Indian mound, is the big Mound Laboratory of the Atomic Energy Commission. The old and the new jostle each other in the heartland.

Fifty miles above the hill-framed Ohio the land levels out, and there begins the rich farm country of central Ohio, Indiana and Illinois. You can travel for five hundred miles, from Zanesville on the Muskingum River to Quincy on the Mississippi with no more dip and rise than an occasional bottomland along a creek or river. This central belt of the region contains the state capitals, Columbus, Indianapolis, Springfield, on a virtually direct line, close to the fortieth parallel, to the west. It has a surprising number of small industrial cities, each with its special products—glass at Lancaster, Ohio, electrical equipment at Mansfield, oil refineries at Newark, motor trucks at Springfield, locomotives at Lima; farm implements at Richmond, Indiana, glass products at Muncie, storage batteries at Anderson, brick and tile at Terre Haute; heating equipment at Bloomington, Illinois, corn products at Decatur, whisky and tractors at Peoria, steel plows at Moline. But all these cities are surrounded by leagues of farmland, and the greater production of this central belt is its huge crops of corn, wheat, soybeans, poultry, hogs and cattle. The richness of the region is evident in the green seas of corn and wheat and the deep shade of the bottom timber. On warm nights it finds a voice in the chorused insect sounds, the buzzing, chirping, shrilling that fills the summer land. Ironed out ages ago by the great glacier, the earth lies deep and rich, and a dependable forty-inch rainfall keeps it watered. The many farm implement factories of the region have a market all around them. No farming country in the world uses as much machinery as the thousands of gang plows, cultivators, hay-balers, corn-pickers and combines that plant, plow and harvest the Midwest crops. Every year they overflow the granaries and warehouses of this prodigal land.

Two generations ago this farming country was dotted with centers of local trade and culture. Hitching racks lined the small-town Main Street, the church corners, the shady square with its roofed bandstand, the Chautauqua grove and the race track. The towns are still there but their vitality is gone; automobiles carried it away. With "hard roads" and motorcars rural people drove straight through Main Street to the county seat beyond. Small-town America is dying, even in the Midwest. The younger generation will not stay there, and the older cannot. A recent poll in Shelbyville, Illinois, showed that half the high-school students did not expect to remain there when their schooling was done. People complain of congestion while they crowd in to the ever-growing centers. This is happening in other regions and other countries. The hill towns of Kentucky dwindle while Louisville expands; island Corsica steadily loses population to Marseilles and Paris. Everywhere a complex civilization draws people together in a tightening, strangling web. In the heartland the little towns wither while restless cities push out into the countryside.

Along the northern edge of the region stretches another band of industry. Steel at Youngstown, Canton, Cleveland, Lorain, Toledo, Gary, South Chicago, rubber factories at Akron, glass at Toledo, motors and aircraft at South Bend. For a century heavy industry has spread westward on a line just above the forty-first parallel, where the trade routes of the Great Lakes bring iron ore and limestone and long trains of gondolas bring coal from the Ohio Valley.

Railroads using the "water-level route" follow the long Lake Erie shore on their way to Chicago. They pass through the lake ports of Conneaut and Ashtabula and over the deep basin of the Cuyahoga, where the long freighters bring iron ore to the mills in Cleveland. After a rural interval comes industrial Lorain, and then the old fish wharves and the new coal docks of Sandusky. Beside the murky Maumee rise the blast furnaces and oil refineries of Toledo. Beyond South Bend, once famous for its wagon-works and now for automobile factories, begin the lonely sand hills of northern Indiana, rough eroded ridges with clumps of scrubby timber. Little creeks wind between green willows toward Lake Michigan's long shoreline. There are miles without a road, without a fence, without farms or houses or any sign of life. Father Marquette, a frail and chivalrous man with an iron will, came this way three hundred years ago; it must have looked like this to him. Then, abruptly, the twentieth century rises up in the smoke and gleam of Gary, the long gray mills with the spaced fires glinting, the farm-big parking lots with the cars ranked across them, the docks where the long Lakes ships stand under ridges of red iron ore and the gray water reaches into distance. Then emptiness and the wide wastes of sand. The heartland is massed with power and purpose; the heartland gapes with vacancy. Again the smoke and glitter, the black hills of coal, the red ridges of iron ore, the gray hills of limestone, the yellow mounds of sulphur; and the long mill sheds, the web of railroad tracks and ships lying in the docks of Michigan Harbor. More emptiness; but soon the blast furnaces of Whiting and Calumet pour angry gases at the prairie sky. There Chicago begins—with gas tanks, maltworks, coke ovens, the shudder of grade crossings, abrupt blocks of yellow brick dwellings with zigzag wooden stairways clinging to littered porches. Long streets wheel by with lines of cars waiting for the traffic light, a square of park under its sooty trees, vacant corner lots rank with ragweed. Beyond miles of rooftops the towers of Chicago catch the sun.

The new tollways carry a race of traffic over a machine-made landscape of their own, a route without towns, farms or crossroads, or any feature of the local life. But turn off onto a county road and immediately the land comes back, the long dip and swell of the midland country with its little towns marked by a water tower above the trees and white clouds drifting over. There is a feeling here of being deep in America. The towns have no landmarks—no citadel, no ruined castle, no ancient church or traditional town hall—only a grain elevator lifting blank walls above the railroad siding, a brick business block ending in a box-shaped church, and then the frame houses under the maple trees. The trees end suddenly and the cornfields shimmer with light. The unfenced road seems newly laid upon the land, like a trail, and there is no sign of any past. Yet it promises to lead, in the next county, over the next long prairie swell, to the heart of America. The promise remains, just over the horizon, while the wooden towns fall past—Pawpaw, Triumph, Utica, Peru—towns with weedy borders and exotic names, like islands in the open land.

So you go on, deeper into central Illinois, through Groveland and Greenview to Athens. Turn west there, five country miles to Petersburg, where you cross a tree-fringed stream and the road acquires a number—Illinois 97. Two more miles brings you, suddenly, to the vanished past. Straddling a wooded ridge above the Sangamon, New Salem stands now precisely as it was in 1833, when Postmaster Abe Lincoln lounged in the Lincoln-Berry store. It is a village of twenty buildings, all wood, all ax- and adz-work. Everything is hand-made—the mill, the shops, the houses, fences, implements, vehicles. From under the hill comes the steady voice of water through the millrace and the wind rustles the maple branches, as it did before the first ax thudded in the grove.

Here is something close to the heart of America. In the 1830's New Salem was a hopeful frontier settlement, with farmers bringing grain to the Rutledge mill and an occasional flatboat carrying pork and whisky down the Sangamon and the Illinois. Then Springfield grew and New Salem dwindled. It was almost empty by 1860, its buildings falling down and its people departed. But for six years Abraham Lincoln had lived there. He had been a surveyor, storekeeper, postmaster; had marched off to the Black Hawk War and back again. Then he had studied English grammar, geometry, and the common law, and his neighbors had sent him to the State legislature. New Salem was gone but not forgotten.

A hundred years after Lincoln lived there, New Salem was rebuilt, with the greatest pains and patience, exactly as it had been in the 1830's. Then it had a hundred people; now it receives a million visitors a year. They come from every state in America, from every country of Europe, from all parts of the world. For a sample summer month the register shows twenty-six visitors from South America, twenty-eight from Asia, nine from Africa, and fifty-two from "other" places like Iceland, New Zealand and Australia. More than the memory of Lincoln, it is a tradition that draws them here, the rude frontier life out of which Lincoln came, which nurtured him and his nation.

Ten miles from New Salem on Illinois 97 one first sees, over the endless cornfields, the dome of the Illinois State House—"a speck, a hive, a football, a captive balloon," Vachel Lindsay described it—growing on the prairie sky. New Salem is a reverie, but Springfield is restive. Politics and industry keep it growing and changing. Now the monumental Centennial Building occupies the site of the Edwards house where Lincoln was married, business pushes toward the Lincoln home on the once leafy corner of Eighth and Jackson, one-way streets wheel their traffic around the century-old Governor's Mansion, and new state buildings wall the green capitol grounds. With business and blight the old Springfield elms are gone.

This is the city that Vachel Lindsay loved and despaired of. He saw the ghost of Lincoln walking the streets at midnight, he heard the rhythms of the Congo in the African Baptist Church and the singing of a Chinese nightingale in the back room of Chin Lee's laundry near the Illinois Central depot. He spoke of all the midland capitals and all the heartland towns when he made his bittersweet song:

> In this the city of my Discontent,
> Sometimes there comes a whisper from the grass:—
> "*Romance, romance* is here."

2. Prairie Gibraltar

Seventy years ago at Starved Rock on the Illinois River some workmen unearthed a rusted piece of sword blade and a battered metal hook. For three generations Ottawa County farmers had been plowing up relics of French and Indian times—crosses, beads, flints, arrowheads, rude implements of stone and iron. But this discovery in 1892 sent a ripple of excitement through the valley. The first white man to stand on the Rock, bold and clear against the prairie sky, was Henri de Tonty. From Montreal to the Mississippi he was known as *Bras-de-fer* and *Bras-coupé*, the man with the iron hand. Now, with these rusted fragments, a newspaper at La Salle, Illinois, reported the recovery of the most famous hand in frontier history.

Of course the newspaper was mistaken. These artifacts were not the remains of Tonty, who died of yellow fever at Mobile and was buried beside the Gulf of Mexico. But with the up-turned iron a name had grown nearer. A living figure seemed to emerge from legend.

A slight man Tonty appears to have been, with far-seeing

eyes and a determined mouth. A bas-relief on the Marquette building in Chicago, where he passed many times in canoes heaped with trade goods and peltry, shows him with a curling mustache and a feathered hat. More likely he wore the *voyageur's* wool cap and a collard—brass-buttoned tunic; probably he went wholly unshaven. He had come from the cities of Italy and France to the savage wilderness. In the dawn of Illinois history he raised Fort St. Louis on Starved Rock and gathered a great Indian town in the valley. The son of an international banker, he built up a pioneer commerce on the prairies, only to see it strangled by jealous and petty men in Montreal and Paris.

Sicily is so unlike Illinois—a volcanic sea-washed land against a rolling prairie—that only a far-ranging man could span them. Henri de Tonty, aged eighteen, entered the French army as a cadet in 1668, serving for two years in seven campaigns and rising in command. On a battlefield at Messina, with prodigious Etna shouldering the sky, young Captain de Tonty repulsed a charge of the Spaniards. When a grenade exploded in his throwing hand, he hacked off the mangled flesh at his wrist. The metal hand that replaced it—iron, brass, silver, copper, bronze: historians have agreed only that he wore it gloved—became an instrument of authority in Illinois. It could carry a burden, rake up a fire, or subdue a surly Indian. The hand he left in Sicily could never have become such great medicine as the hand that felt neither fire nor frost, that could deflect a knife blade, that tirelessly drove a canoe paddle from the St. Lawrence to the Gulf of Mexico, that hauled up water on a rope windlass to the ledge of Starved Rock.

Illinois is a level land, stretching away like an ocean under a vast down-curving sky. In that country a modest height becomes a landmark. Starved Rock rises a hundred and twenty feet from the river current. It would be lost in a thousand other places, but it is commanding on the prairie. Its sandstone cliffs, tufted with shrubs and stained with lichen, have a craggy boldness. Its airy acre of table-top supported Fort St. Louis, the first outpost of civilization in the American heartland.

Now the Rock looks over a green and fertile country. At its base, in the bottom timber, sunlight glints on rows of motor cars in the big parking lot. Across a deep ravine stands Starved Rock Lodge, with its flag above the lookout point. Beyond, in all directions, rolls the prairie. It fades into distance, this land of mile-long cornfields, leafy farmyards and provincial towns with names from far places: Peru, La Salle, Utica, Marseilles, Hennepin, Norway. There is a heady sense of height, a vastness of view, as though from the Rock you could see beyond the circle of prairie. The long valley of the Illinois gathers its slow rivers, from the lower Spoon and Sangamon to the upper Fox, Du Page and Kankakee. Beyond these headwaters, over an indiscernible divide, other streams wind toward Lake Michigan. Follow a serpentine river beyond the old Des Plaines portage and see the heights that dwarf Starved Rock, the cliffs and towers of Chicago. They were not there when the portage paths gashed the prairie.

The heartland is an inland country bordered by two great lakes and two majestic rivers. From the Rock the prairie rolls westward to the Mississippi. A twentieth-century poet who grew up at St. Louis has reflected:

> . . . I think that the river
> Is a strong brown god—sullen, untamed and intractable.
> Patient to some degree, at first recognized as a frontier;
> Useful, untrustworthy, as a conveyor of commerce;
> Then only a problem confronting the builder of bridges.

But that was far in the future when Tonty gazed westward from the Rock. Eastward the prairie stretches to the Wabash. It is all level land to the north and east. Southward toward the Ohio River, the land grows hilly, lifting into knobs and ridges once dense with hardwood forest.

Before the coming of civilization the Wabash was more of a boundary than it is today. In Indian times it marked the end of the great forest and the beginning of the prairie. Now the prairie is tamed and the forest is gone. The land goes on without change or barrier. It is crossed by other rivers, the two Miamis which at their mouths frame modern Cincinnati, the Maumee (another version of the same Shawnee name) and the Cuyahoga flowing into Lake Erie, the Scioto, the Hockhocking and the Muskingum,which swell the Ohio. Then the lifting Allegheny ridges make a borderland.

When Tonty stood upon Starved Rock, the eye could go to the horizon but the mind could not go on. It was unknown country then. The Mississippi, which Marquette and Jolliet had descended to the Arkansas, was a river of dread and doubt. Illinois tribesmen had told La Salle that its waters were infested with serpents, alligators and unnamed monsters; its shores were held by fearsome tribes; and the river, swirling past rocks and reefs, plunged at last into an unknown gulf. What Tonty knew by toil and travail was only a hard path in a wilderness. He had measured the Kankakee marshes, the Chicago portage, the windy leagues of Lake Michigan. In 1680 the American interior was a country without features and almost without habitation. Fifty thousand savages froze and starved in the heartland that now supports twenty million people.

Everywhere in America there are two pictures, the vanished past beneath the living present. At Starved Rock the contrast is surprising. The present scene is rural and sylvan, a land of repose. But Tonty looked upon the camps and lodges of twenty thousand Indians, the largest settlement in seventeenth-century America.

On the left Bank in Paris, in the quiet rue de l'Université, above a gray stone courtyard, stands the old Ministry of the Marine; the Depot des Cartes occupies a balconied room on the second floor. Under two hanging lights and a sunless window is a tall cabinet crammed with folio maps of New France. There is the great *Carte de l'Amérique Septentrionnelle*, drawn by Jean Baptiste Louis Franquelin, "Hydrographer du Roy," in 1684. The ivory parchment, big as a tablecloth, has red and blue border decorations, a flowered scroll and a colored vignette of Quebec City as seen from the east. It shows a broad green waterway leading straight west to "Missilimackinac," and the lower Mississippi making a big bow through the present state of Texas. Framed in lakes and rivers, the interior country stretches wild and empty, waiting for its future. One bold name dominates this heartland, "Fort St. Louis" on the Rivière des Illinois. Around that landmark the map shows a complex of settlements, the savage camps and villages that Tonty saw.

On the north side of the river, opposite the Rock, spread the town of the Illinois, with twelve hundred warriors. Below it were the lodges of the Weas and the Piankeshaw village lining the river shore. On the south side, behind the jutting Rock, lay the big town of the Miamis and lesser settlements of the Shawanoes and Kilaticas. For miles the river was lined with lodges of bark and rushes. A close look through Tonty's telescope would show warriors stretched in the sun, old women tending the fires and carrying river water in buffalo skulls, young women bending in the corn rows where yellowing squash and pumpkins lay amid the vines, children splashing in the sandy shallows, dogs sniffing at scraps of hide and beaver bones.

This was a native city but a French accomplishment, the gathering of the prairie tribes for trade and protection in the shadow of the Rock. French cannon on the height held off the hostile Iroquois; French hatchets, knives, traps, kettles and blankets in the warehouse drew the prairie trade of buffalo and beaver skins. Fort St. Louis was the capital of an inland empire conceived by René Robert Cavelier, Sieur de La Salle, and erected by his lieutenant with the iron hand.

La Salle was the proprietor. A French aristocrat with lonely, lordly ambition, he had come to Canada in 1666 at the age of twenty-three and taken a seigniory on the St. Lawrence. But his mind went on inland; he was drawn to the wilderness. In 1669 he made a thrust into unknown country; he was the first white man to pass down the Ohio into the green heart of the continent.

When Marquette and Jolliet returned from their historic exploration of 1673, reporting the southward flow of the Mississippi and the rich land of the Illinois, La Salle began to dream of an inland empire. In 1678 he went to France, seeking royal authority to build a chain of trading posts in the Mississippi valley. In Paris he met young Henri de Tonty, who wanted to try his fortunes in New France. So began the only close friendship in La Salle's lonely life. They sailed in July from New Rochelle, arriving at Quebec in September. In America their names would be as closely linked as Romulus and Remus of infant Rome.

To Canada had come an adventure-seeking friar who wore a coarse gray capote, a peaked hood, and the cord of St. Francis about his waist. A rosary and crucifix swung at his side as he strode the waterfront of Quebec's lower town. A missionary lured by distance and danger, Father Louis Hennepin got himself assigned as historian to La Salle's expedition. Meanwhile, in the wilderness where the Niagara River plunged over its horseshoe ledge, Tonty was supervising the building of La Salle's ship *Griffin*, the first commercial vessel on the Great Lakes. To the awestruck Indians it was "the house that walked on water." In August they sailed west.

That was in 1679. Since then hardship and toil had left new lines in their weathered faces; fortune had lifted them up and cast them down. The first blow was the loss of the *Griffin*. Laden with peltry the ship cast off from Green Bay on the western shore of Lake Michigan—and was never seen again. It was late in the season, autumn gales were blowing, the pilot was ignorant and irresponsible. Somewhere the heaving Lakes closed over their first cargo.

Meanwhile La Salle, Tonty and Hennepin were on the way, in canoes with a crew of *voyageurs*, to the country of the Illinois. "It is nearly all so beautiful and so fertile," La Salle had written of the interior after his exploration of the Ohio valley, ". . . that one can find there in plenty and with little trouble all that is needful for the support of flourishing colonies." Now he was seeing it in the gray December, trudging between the St. Joseph River and the marshy sources of the Kankakee. It was a hungry country then. La Salle, never averse to solitude, struck off alone in search of the portage path. A thickening curtain of snow dimmed the prairie, and soon night obscured it. On a reedy hummock Tonty and Hennepin made a fire and discharged muskets to guide the leader back. It was near dusk the next day when he appeared, hollow-eyed and mud-stained, with two opossums swinging from his belt. La Salle was scornful of suffering, but the body required food. They consumed the rodents and pushed on. That night La Salle and Hennepin, sharing a lean-to of dried reeds, scrambled out when their shelter caught fire. Thin, worn, hungry, they passed a blackened prairie, fired by the Indians for their autumn hunt. Buffalo skulls strewed the snow-patched ground, but there was no game until they came upon an old bull mired in a slough. They killed him, hauled the carcass out with a ship's cable, and filled their hollow stomachs.

They traveled faster then, aided by the current of the widening Illinois which flowed past wooded shores within a frame of hills. Under a bold rock, which would later become their capital in the wilderness, they passed an impressive Indian town; Hennepin counted four hundred and sixty lodges on the riverbank. But there were no people. The place was silent, eerie, lifeless. Beaching their canoes the travelers looked at the empty lodges and the charred fire-circles on the ground. La Salle supposed the tribe had gone on their winter hunt; he did not speak of the grimmer likelihood that they had fled from invading Iroquois.

There were many warfares in the wilderness—Indians against Indians, Indians against white men, the French against the English in many combinations with the aborigines. Spurred by Dutch and British traders on the Hudson, the powerful Iroquois nations had depleted the game in their country south of Lake Ontario. Then the Iroquois turned westward, trapping the interior rivers and raiding Indian camps as far as the Mississippi. In Tonty's time there were no tribes in the forest south of Lake Erie. Iroquois warriors had annihilated the native Erie nation and driven the Miami peoples north to present Michigan and west to the Illinois country. The present Indiana and Ohio were nearly unpopulated then, the rivers winding empty under the wooded hills and only deer paths leading to the pool in the forest. There was a great lake tossing under the stars, the waves loud on the long Ohio shore and no one hearing. An early French map of Lake Ontario shows a lake-shore trail: "Route by which the Senecas go to make war against the Illinois." Soon the French would complicate that savage warfare.

In the lifeless Illinois town the hungry Frenchmen found grain pits filled with corn. (Now in the prairie towns long rows of steel granaries, sealed by the government, line the railroad sidings.) La Salle could tighten his belt and go hungry, but his men were less austere. They took thirty measures of corn, for which La Salle would make recompense, and pushed on down the river.

Beyond the widening of the Illinois that is now Lake Peoria they found an Indian village of eighty lodges. After a tense and wary meeting, the chiefs proffered a friendly calumet and a taste of the smoke of peace. The Frenchmen were fed from the tribal kettle, food being thrust into their mouths by the savage hosts, and their feet were rubbed with bear's grease. La Salle told of his purpose to build a great canoe in which he would descend the Mississippi, eventually to return with trade goods for the tribesmen's peltries. It was a satisfying session.

But that night a visiting warrior told the chiefs that La Salle was spying for the Iroquois, and the next day the temper of the Illini was changed. The Mississippi, they said, was a perilous river, with hostile tribes on its shores, monsters in the waters and rocks, whirlpools and cataracts in its course. This warning did not dim La Salle's purpose, but it frightened his men. Half of them deserted, heading across country for Canada, and the remaining *voyageurs* muttered of mutiny.

La Salle took his sullen party a few miles farther downstream and began construction of Fort Crèvecoeur. That somber name,

"Fort Heartbreak," prophetic of La Salle's fortunes in the wilderness, was chosen apparently by Tonty, not in low spirits but in memory of a victorious battle a few years earlier in the Netherlands. The fort contained barracks for the men, a house for the friars, a magazine and a forge. Hennepin held vespers for the party each evening and Father Zenobe Membré patiently visited the Indian camp, seeking converts to instruct and infants to baptize. It was a discouraging task, but the missionary would have been gratified by a long look forward. Now, three centuries later, at the busy Peoria corner of Madison and Fulton streets, the Sacred Heart Church of the Franciscan friars holds a perpetual novena to St. Anthony of Padua, patron of the explorer priests. Inside, the voices of the twentieth century retreat. It is dim and quiet where votive candles flicker before the saint.

At Fort Crèvecoeur La Salle waited with growing anxiousness for news of his *Griffin*. On its return voyage from Niagara the ship was to bring materials for construction of the bateau that would take him down the Mississippi. Weeks passed and no messenger came. Slowly he gave up hope, concluding that the *Griffin* was lost. He would have to plan anew.

At the end of February the leader sent Hennepin with two companions on an exploration; after descending the Illinois, they were to paddle up the Mississippi toward its source. Though at first he sought excuses, this was the great opportunity of Hennepin's life. When he was persuaded to the undertaking, he wrote: "Anybody but me would have been very much frightened at the dangers of such a journey." In the months that followed he was captured by a roving band of Sioux, who took him up the great river; he saw and named the Falls of St. Anthony at the site of future Minneapolis; he was finally ransomed from the Sioux by his countryman Duluth, whom the friar had met a few years earlier on a battlefield in Belgium where he was confessing the dying. Back at last in Montreal Hennepin had tales to tell, and in Paris he wrote his vainglorious but fascinating book which first made interior America known to the world.

In that bleak winter on the frozen prairie La Salle girded himself for a journey. With his faithful Indian hunter, two friars, and three *voyageurs*, he set out over the iron land for Fort Frontenac on the Niagara to obtain materials and supplies. Tonty was left in charge of fifteen men at Fort Crèvecoeur; he was directed to build a fort on the height (Starved Rock) which overhung the town on the Illinois. Accordingly he took some of his men to the new site, leaving the rest to finish the hull of a bateau. These were the notorious deserters who sacked Fort Crèvecoeur, looted its stores, and left on the keel timber a message for La Salle's desolate return: *Nous sommes tous savages.* It was the first European inscription in the American interior.

Here was a contest lost by men to the wilderness. The French brought to wild country a sense of order and tradition. They measured its distances in leagues and arpents and counted time by their religious calendar. Losing that order, men from an old and splendid civilization succumbed to the savage world. Retaining it, though they might die of violence, they kept their own culture in the wilds.

Tonty was a wilderness man who remained civilized; he was equally at home with Indians, squaw-men, and half-breeds, with governors and priests. In the pagan wilds he dated events, journeys and arrivals by the calendar of the church. "Having sailed on this lake till All Souls' Day we were wrecked, twenty leagues from the village of the Pontonatomis. . . . Our provisions failing us, I left a man to take care of our things and went off by land, but as I had a fever constantly on me and my legs were swollen, we did not arrive at the village of the Pontonatomis till St. Martin's Day." Again, "I departed thence with thirty Frenchmen and five [Indians] for the sea, which I reached in Holy Week." And, in a sentence colored with savage and Christian names, "We reached Missilimackinac about Corpus Christi."

Even a psalm could be a Frenchman's measure of time. Tonty's cousin Desliette, who made a hunting trip with the Illini, described the Indians' skill at making flame by rubbing sticks together. "In less than half a Miséréré they had a fire." Deep in the wilderness they clung to memories of France. Unmapped rivers were compared to the Seine and the Marne. A great buffalo path on the prairie was "as wide as the Cours de la Reine." These men called the Mississippi the Rivière Conception; they left Christian names on a wild land all the way from Sault Sainte Marie to the Trinity River in Texas.

In the wilderness the French were *voyageurs*—mere travelers —but they gave a new dimension to that word, a dimension that never got carried back to France. Look from a train window in the French provinces and see the "Café des Voyageurs" across the street from the town *gare*. Or on the Paris Métro, rumbling under the Place de la Concorde and the Madeleine, look up at the designation of the car's capacity—"148 vogageurs." In France the word is as commonplace as daily work and daily bread, but in America it has a heroic sound. After three centuries it still carries an aura of hazard and venture in the continental wilderness. The New World changed even the words that came to it from the Old.

When La Salle returned from Fort Frontenac, the season was late autumn. The tawny Illinois plain was thronged with buffalo, shaggy herds drinking at the river and dark lines of them crossing the prairie swells. Overhead passed airy wedges of geese and swans. The Frenchmen hunted and feasted and pushed down the Illinois with renewed spirit. As they neared the great Rock, La Salle's eyes searched upward; no sign of life showed on the height. His gaze fell to a scene of death and devastation. On the wooded shore the Illinois lodges were charred ruins; impaled on blackened stakes were human skulls stripped by buzzards. Then he saw movement, a pack of wolves around a mass of mangled bodies. The Iroquois had come, and this was the aftermath.

That night, bivouacked on the charred shore, La Salle lay sleepless, wondering about the fate of Tonty and his men. A sickening search next day turned up some shreds of French clothing, but only Indian skulls and corpses. He pushed on down the river, past Peoria Lake, and found another ruin, the demolished Fort Crèvecoeur. On the planks of his half-built vessel he read the desolate inscription: "We are all savages." Still hoping to find Tonty, he descended the Illinois to its mouth, where he left a message for his lieutenant in the fork of a tree leaning above the stream. Then he retraced his course up the Illinois. On those December nights a strange brightness grew in the sky, a comet casting an eerie light over the winter wilderness. It was the Great Comet of 1680 that caused dread and wonder in the Old World, that led Newton to a new astronomical principle, that for the Reverend Increase Mather in Boston portended doom to the nations of men. La Salle had found doom already. Briefly he noted this phenomenon among the winter constellations and traveled on toward Lake Michigan.

Near the Chicago portage the party found a bark lean-to, and in it a piece of wood cleanly cut by a saw. At that mute sign of civilization hope leaped up again. But it was weeks later, on the St. Joseph River near Lake Michigan, that some roving Indians from Wisconsin told him that Tonty was living among the Potawatomis and that the gray-robed Hennepin had passed through their country on his way to Canada. At that time La Salle was suffering from snow blindness; he sent word to Tonty to await him at Michilimackinac. The two met there at the end of May.

Tonty had a grim story to tell. When a big war party of Iroquois had arrived at Starved Rock, he vainly tried to dissuade them from attacking the Illini. Badly wounded, he fled toward Lake Michigan. On the way seventy-year-old Father Gabriel Ribourde was murdered. Tonty reported: "While we were repairing our canoe, Father Gabriel told me he was going aside to pray. . . . He went about a thousand paces off and was taken by forty savages . . . who carried him away and broke his head." Perhaps Tonty felt what an Illinois poet put into words ten generations later:

It is strange to sleep under the bare stars and to die
On an open land where few bury before us . . .

Years afterward Father Gabriel's breviary was found among the Kickapoos in Wisconsin, and it became known that a roving Indian, coming upon him at prayer, crushed his skull with a club and threw his body into a hole. The rest of Tonty's party paddled north in a leaking canoe and were wrecked on the Lake Michigan shore. Shuddering with chills and fever, Tonty struggled overland, alone, living on frozen squash and wild onions which he grubbed from the snow. At last he reached the friendly Potawatomis on Green Bay.

Now, in fine June weather, La Salle and Tonty paddled a thousand miles to the St. Lawrence, where they recruited men and supplies for their projected exploration of the lower Mississippi. The return journey brought them to the Des Plaines Portage in mid-winter. The Illinois was icebound. They dragged their canoes on sledges past the leafless forests and the lifeless Rock, and found open water at Lake Peoria. The worst was over, for that season. Down the Illinois they paddled and down the Mississippi, into spring and summer weather, until the vast slow river stained the blue waters of the Gulf. Here, with military and religious ceremony, La Salle claimed in the name of an indifferent king four thousand miles away possession of "the seas, harbors, ports, bays . . . the nations, peoples, provinces, cities, towns . . . and the river Mississippi and all the rivers which discharge themselves thereinto." Francis Parkman, the great chronicler of this and of all the French adventure in the wilderness, ends the account with one of his most eloquent and ironic passages. Describing this stupendous accession, from the ice-locked northern springs to the tropic gulf, from the Allegheny ridges to the Rocky Mountains, he says it all passed beneath the scepter of the French sovereign "by virtue of a feeble human voice, inaudible at half a mile."

The richest region in all that domain, according to Tonty, was the valley of the Illinois. "As for the country of the Illinois . . .

it may be said to contain the finest lands ever seen." The next year, 1683, brought the beginning of the French enterprise there. The exploration had convinced La Salle that he could open a commerce to the south, importing trade goods and sending Illinois peltry to France by way of the Gulf of Mexico. He would begin by establishing a French and Indian colony under the great rock on the river. Later he would build another post at the mouth of the Mississippi.

While Fort St. Louis was rising on the Rock, Tonty ranged for hundreds of miles over the prairie, making gifts to scattered chiefs and persuading their people to gather under the protection of France on the Illinois. The tribes came, the great Indian town grew. Before the year was over La Salle reported to the Minister of the Marine that twenty thousand Indians were living in the shadow of the Rock.

Among the tribesmen was a scattering of French settlers to whom La Salle, by authority of Louis the Great, King of France and of Navarre, had assigned land in generous tracts. The first land title in interior America reads:

> We have given and granted, do give and grant to Jacques Bourdan, Sieur d'Autray, . . . in recognition of his service which he had performed as well in the discovery of Louisiana and in the construction of Fort St. Louis where he has served well and has done his duty . . . a tract 126 arpents in length, commencing at the brook beside which we wintered and ascending the length of the river of the Illinois on the south bank, together with the island which is in the middle of the aforesaid river of the Illinois above the beginning of the great rock which the river bathes on the north side about one league above the aforesaid brook, with 42 arpents of depth going from the northwest to the southeast . . . with rights of hunting and fishing on the extent of the aforesaid land. . . .

This comprised nearly five thousand acres, and it is difficult to see what one *voyageur* could do with such a tract. Later grants were confined to some three hundred acres. All included rights to press wine, to keep pigeons, to build a protective palisade, and to trade for furs with the Indians provided the trading was done at the fort. So the first land in the American interior became private property.

To the Rock the Indians brought their furs. Peltry was sorted and baled in the warehouse. On the river *voyageurs* loaded canoes to make the long journey, by way of the Straits of Mackinac and Georgian Bay, to the St. Lawrence. A path of many waters led from the Rock on the Illinois to the great rock of Quebec.

The founding of empires seems an enterprise beyond accounting, but these explorers were launching a commercial venture, and they were deep in debt. La Salle had borrowed from many creditors in Paris and Montreal under the appointment of the king. Tonty had a nominal wage which was never paid; from his own funds he had supplied trade goods to bring the chiefs to Fort St. Louis and to make peace between rival factions among the Illinois. Now the enterprise looked bright. The tribes were at peace in their great town under the Rock and the canoes were coming and going on the waters.

Then came a new blow—political this time. In the citadel of Quebec, Frontenac, a friend of the Illinois venture, was replaced by Governor La Barre. Immediately La Salle's supplies were cut off and in Montreal the Illinois canoes were seized by his creditors. It was a contest of Frenchmen and Frenchmen. Fearing an overproduction of peltry, the Montreal merchants meant to protect their northern trade and to starve off the new commerce from Illinois.

La Salle had already seen the economic advantage of a trade route to the south. His men had canoed through drift ice, lost cargoes in the northern rapids, wintered on the ice-locked St. Lawrence. In his *Memoir* Tonty described the Mississippi as "a river that runs not less than 800 leagues to the sea without rapids." This was a heartland route, without hindrance or barrier, a warm-weather way to a tropic sea. Now, with opposition on the St. Lawrence, the Mississippi trade became a necessity. To accomplish it, La Salle must go to France again to get the king's approval and support.

On an end-of-summer day in 1683 the two leaders parted on the Rock. La Salle went down the zigzag path, stepped into the lead canoe and gave the signal. The little flotilla paddled north-ward. From the height Tonty watched them disappear around the bend of the river. He would never see La Salle again.

Henri de Tonty, commander now of Fort St. Louis and all the interior country, was a young man still—just thirty-two. For ten years, between long and dangerous journeys, the Rock would be his home. There he counseled with the chiefs, sent agents to outlying tribes, conducted the trade with Montreal. (The Mississippi commerce never materialized.) From the Rock he directed exploration, commerce and diplomacy.

Despite a popular impression, the early fur trade was not the work of lawless, free-booting, independent men. Hardy and elemental the *voyageurs* were; they married a new Indian woman every day in the week, Desliette stated, and they were more at home in a Piankeshaw camp than at the other end of the line in Montreal. But they were employees in a legal and systematic commerce. A *voyageur* was hired by written agreement for a stated term—one, two or three years. The standard contract gave him his equipment and subsistence, plus wages of 350 livres—about $70—a year; the payment was made in beaver skins to be added to the contract cargo. For this the *voyageur* agreed to take a canoe from Montreal to Illinois loaded with trade goods: blankets, knives, hatchets, tobacco, salt, linen, hard bread, dried prunes, quills, shirts, kettles, mirrors, muskets, powder, lead. At Fort St. Louis he would make himself useful as a trader and hunter and would "come back in a canoe loaded with twenty-five packets of peltries to the weight of 57 pounds from the Illinois to this city." On the return journey he could trade his gun, capote and blanket at Michilimackinac for his own interest. The *voyageur* got paid only for the furs he brought through safely: an upset canoe could cost him all his wages. This was the first employment contract in a region where a great trade-union movement would develop two centuries later.

The names of Illinois voyageurs appear in the Engagement drawn up by the lawyers-scrivener in Montreal: "Before Antoine Adhémar, royal notary etc., were present Bertrand Viau, called L'Espérance, voyageur, residing at Langueuil. . . ." Outside the notary's office the canoemen used legal names less often than nicknames. "Hope" (*L'Epérance*) is understandable, but it is surprising to find a gnarled "The Tulip," "The Violet," "The Prettyheart" signed for small advances from Montreal moneylenders before a new season in the wilderness. These men crossed themselves while passing an Indian graveyard, they strung bears' claws on their rosary chains, they went from one Indian woman to another singing old Norman songs of a sweetheart's Sunday ribbons and gay roses in May. They lived two lives, their own and that of the wilderness.

From his height above the valley Tonty watched the season change. Indian summer. . . . He saw the cornfields fade and the forest brighten: the scarlet of maples, the gold of hickories, the wine-dark color of the oaks. Days were warm and golden, but the dusk brought an edge of chill. Out of the prairie darkness rose the autumn constellations, long-striding Orion with his gleaming sword belt, linked Castor and Pollux and the radiant Pleiades. The same stars that circled over France and Sicily, but they seemed closer to this Rock in Illinois.

Ten generations later an Illinois poet, Archibald MacLeish, put down some thoughts that could come to a man on Starved Rock.

> It is a strange thing to be an American.
> It is strange to live on the high world in the stare
> Of the naked sun and the stars as our bones live.
> Men in the old lands housed by their rivers.
> They built their towns in the vales in the earth's shelter.
> We first inhabit the world. We dwell
> On the half earth, on the open curve of a continent.

All its history came to the heartland from the East, but its winds blow from the Southwest, and they smell of unfenced space and distance.

Every fall the Indians set fire to the brown prairie, driving the game into the river bottoms. For days the wind brought the sharp sweet tang of burning grass. From thickets and swales soft columns of smoke went up to the high October sky. At night campfires gleamed under the rock and flickering lines of fire ran over the horizon.

The days shortened and the wind grew sharp. Under gray skies the men went on the long hunt. They straggled back, laden with meat and hides. They lay in the lodges, eating and sleeping while the fire smoldered and the snow swirled down. Outside the women broke shore ice to dip their kettles in the river.

When the land turned green again and the river rose under the Rock, furs were counted and baled in the warehouse. A new load of trade goods arrived and the tribesmen carried off knives, hatchets, salt, tobacco, even iron arrowheads. Iron tips, listed at Montreal at two sols each, were a ready-made weapon to replace slowly chipped flints brought from the flint ridges hundreds of miles away. So quickly civilized trade could corrupt the savage arts.

Tonty was by turns an Indian fighter, a diplomat, a businessman, operating with frail lines of communication in a country bigger than all of France. In the spring of 1684 a band of Iroquois came down the Illinois, attacking the Illinois town and Fort St. Louis. After three days of siege Tonty sent a messenger, scrambling down the Rock in the dead of night, to Michilimackinac, six hundred miles away. That was the nearest help, and Tonty measured the corn in his small granary. But the Iroquois soon tired of the siege. They started home, with a pack of Illini yapping after them. Two months later the Michilimackinac commander arrived with sixty Frenchmen, and what he brought for Tonty was a governor's order to surrender Fort St. Louis to a rival trader and report to Quebec. In May Tonty packed his canoe and started north. He was in Quebec in August, 1684, and the Illinois venture seemed lost to political and financial rivals. Then a ship arrived from France bringing word from La Salle. Tonty, with a captain's commission, was instructed to return to

Illinois as governor of Fort St. Louis. With four vessels and the king's support, La Salle was sailing for the mouth of the Mississippi.

Ice blocked Tonty's return that season. He spent the winter in Montreal, and there he wrote, with a spattering quill in his jabbing left hand, his account of the explorations since 1678. He composed the *Memoir* from memory, having lost his diaries. Next June he arrived at the Rock. His first task was to end a quarrel between an Illinois tribe and their "allies," the Miamis, at a cost of $1000 in trade goods.

Now Tonty was a royally commissioned captain with a company, and he received but one year's pay (90 livres a month; $216 for the year). As the months went by, he waited restlessly, wanting to go to meet La Salle but held in Illinois by new Indian wars. At last, in February, 1686, he headed south, reaching the Gulf in April. He sent men east and west, but they found no trace of the leader. Tonty erected a trading post in Arkansas before returning to Illinois, where more warfare was brewing. It was not until 1689, when the factor from the Arkansas post arrived at the Rock, that Tonty knew La Salle's fate. Two years before (in March, 1687) the leader had been killed by one of his own rebellious men, and his bones were picked by the wolves in Texas. Tonty went south to search for the settlement La Salle had made there, but the journey was a failure. Worn with toil and wasted with fever, he came back to the Rock in September 1690.

For ten more years Tonty conducted his Illinois trading houses. By 1691 a decade of trading had depleted game near Fort St. Louis, and Tonty moved his headquarters to the southern end of Lake Peoria. Trade was brisk at the new post, but a steep rise in the cost of trade goods wiped out profits. The summer of 1692 brought a plague of caterpillars on the St. Lawrence, "the earth quite covered with them and the grain crop destroyed." That shortage of foodstuffs drove prices still higher, and with a new urgency Tonty turned toward the lower Mississippi. He was ready to build a vessel to descend the river and carry a cargo of furs to France, but authority was denied him.

Meanwhile the Montreal traders were sniping at Tonty, complaining that inferior Illinois furs were ruining the market. Tonty sent his boats up the Missouri to the country of the Sioux and went himself to the far northern land of the Assiniboines. He came to Montreal with two hundred canoes, a caravan that stretched far up the river; in the square before the Cathedral and the Seminary the furs were counted and the Indians stalked through the cobbled streets. Tonty got along with Indians and *voyageurs*, even with rival fur merchants. La Salle had lacked "popular manners," he was a De Gaulle–like man; but Tonty was easy. Now, however, he faced political opposition. Accused of trading in a northern country where he had no license, he was told to confine his activities to Illinois—where he would be limited to two cargoes of trade goods a year. This was insufficient even to arm and provision his fort; the Illinois enterprise was ended.

Turning again to the south, Tonty sought to ally himself with Iberville's attempt to establish a French post at the mouth of the Mississippi. In 1702 he canoed down the great river for the sixth and final time. In 1704 the ship *Pelican* arrived at Mobile with a cargo of provisions, a complement of priests and soldiers, and twenty-three giggling French girls. Within a month all the girls were married and some were dead, and half the ship's crew were buried in Mobile harbor. Aboard the *Pelican* had come an unseen epidemic; soon yellow fever was raging through the cottages of Mobile. Tonty died of the disease September 6, 1704. He was buried beside the tropic Gulf, far from the boisterous spring, the rustling russet autumn and the whirling snow of the heartland, where he would forever be remembered.

In the Illinois country quiet settled on the Rock. The Montreal traders had won; the western colony was finished. A few French *engagés* remained among the Indians, keeping up a trickle of trade until 1718. Then they moved down the Mississippi to

Kaskaskia, near present St. Louis, and Indians burned Fort St. Louis in 1721. Then nothing was left on the Rock but memory. Eventually Edgar Lee Masters would see Starved Rock as a "sphinx," timeless and enigmatic, whose

> . . . sleepless eyes look over
> Fenced fields of corn and wheat,
> Barley and clover.

and who remembers the echoes of old wars and vanished nations.

What was left of the French empire in the heartland? Some water- and mud-stained records in Paris, Quebec and Montreal in the precise hand of La Salle and the jagged hand of Tonty. A few artifacts in the prairie earth, some rusted fragments. And a lasting legend. Tonty was remembered as a man who belonged to the wild and vanished country. The Indians said he returned to Starved Rock to die, a white-haired old man with a staff in his live left hand, groping up the zigzag trail and emerging on the height. It is a local belief that the spirit of Tonty still haunts the Rock on nights when the moon gilds the river and silvers the wide prairie.

In southern Illinois the French habitants of Kaskaskia, Cahokia and Prairie du Rocher forgot the great dreams of French explorers. In time these villagers would pass under a nominal British rule, and it would make no difference in their remote and indolent life. They sang and fiddled, danced with Indian girls and dozed on the doorstep in the autumn sun. They would still be there in 1778 when George Rogers Clark led his lean men into the heartland—when another wave of history washed over the wild prairie and possession passed to a nation that had no existence in Tonty's time.

The Rock remained, no longer a prairie Gibraltar, but a place of legend in a prosaic land. In 1912 the State of Illinois created Starved Rock State Park, a nine-hundred-acre preserve of river, meadow and woodland, of caves, canyons and sandstone bluffs. The park is webbed with eighteen miles of trail, each one leading to the haunted past.

3. The Smoldering Fires

At the edge of Chanute Field, with its miles of offices, barracks, hangars and landing strips, little Okaw Creek gathers in the Illinois prairie and begins its wandering toward the Mississippi. It winds past the state university at Champaign, past the white frame Cartwright Chapel where the rugged circuit rider prayed and thundered, and through the old capital town of Vandalia. Four hundred miles from its beginning it joins the Mississippi, under whose wide slow waters lies the site of a famous town. In its meandering course the stream has become the Kaskaskia River, named for a vanished tribe of the Illinois nation. But for the first two hundred miles it is the Okaw. I learned to swim in one of its "holes" where the water rose waist deep.

Okaw is an echo left by the French in a land that has almost forgot them. "Rivière Aux Kaskaskia" was a prominent feature on the French maps. The vanished town of Kaskaskia—Notre Dame de Kaskaskia the Jesuits called it—was a landmark of the heartland for almost a century. In the 1890's the Mississippi broke through a protecting cape and swallowed the town entirely.

Below modern St. Louis for seventy miles along the Mississippi lie the American Bottoms, a shelf of land between the river and the limestone bluffs which border the eastward-rolling prairies. There is no more fertile district on the continent. This rich land had cradled the highest Indian culture in prehistoric America, a culture which has left lasting monuments in the great Cahokia mounds. Cahokia is a little-known name in the twentieth century, except to a small fraternity of scientists. Archaeologists around the world are as familiar with the mounds of the Cahokia Group as with the pyramids of Egypt. There is some resemblance—the Cahokia mounds command the level bottom as the pyramids dominate the Nubian desert sands. In fact the American Bottoms, periodically flooded like the valley of the Nile, were called Egypt by the American settlers who formed the towns of Thebes, Karnak and Cairo (*Kāro* in local usage) at the tip of the inverted Illinois arrowhead. Dominating eighty-five smaller mounds in the Bottoms is the huge Monk's Mound, a flat-topped pyramid covering sixteen acres, the largest earthwork in the world. Its name comes not from the aborigines but from the French order of Trappists who in 1809 built a monastery at its base. These monks remained but briefly before the ravages of malarial fever sent them back to France in 1813 with desolate memories of the New World.

> No vesper hymn consoled their troubled thoughts.
> Far o'er the plain the wolf's lugubrious howl,
> The cricket's chirp, and the nocturnal cry
> Of hooting owls was their sad evening song.

Today the scene is more cheerful. A paved pathway leads to a picnic site on the summit of Monk's Mound, where prehistoric tribesmen held their ceremonials.

Spread in a fan around this central height were three hundred lesser mounds, of which just eighty-five remain. Temple Mound, Round Top Mound, Red Mound are the largest of them. The vanished mounds have yielded thousands of artifacts which are now displayed in the Cahokia Museum. Archaeologists date the mounds' construction between the twelfth and fifteenth centuries. The region was lifeless when La Salle and Tonty passed down the Mississippi in 1682, but it became a center of French settlement a generation later.

The French colonists of the Illinois valley moved to the rich alluvial Bottoms in the early 1700's, forming the villages of Cahokia, Kaskaskia and Prairie du Rocher, pleasant Arcadian towns between the wide river and the wild prairie. The new location was safer than their scattered posts on the Illinois and it was closer to the French settlements on the lower Mississippi. Kaskaskia became the largest of the villages. Its houses were of stone and timber, quarried from the river bluffs and cut from their fringe of forest. Thatched roofs shadowed the deep galleries where the *habitants* took their ease in the long summer afternoons; in winter they sat by the fire in the broad chimney mouth. Picket fences ringed their gardens, orchards and trampled barnyards. Beyond each cottage stretched a plowed field a mile long and a few rods across; this pattern of ribbon fields came from the St. Lawrence, where every householder wanted a river frontage. On the far side of the village lay the Commons, dotted with the community's horses, cattle, chickens and geese. The swine ranged farther, foraging in the brushwoods, and the shaggy French ponies ran wild. The present Horse Prairie, beyond Prairie du Rocher, was named for French ponies that roved the wide tableland. Years later American settlers hitched them, or their descendants, to the plow.

Indian camps gathered near each of the French villages. Their dogs were a nuisance in the streets and Indian cattle strayed into the neat ribbon fields. But the *habitants*, indolent and philosophical, smoking their pipes on the gallery and playing card games by the fire, lived at peace with the tribesmen. There was no segregation in their towns. The priests gave daily instruction, mostly religious, to French and Indian children. The savages were regular attendants in the mission chapel, crossing themselves at Mass, chanting alternately with the *habitants* at vespers

—a couplet of a psalm in Latin followed by the guttural couplet in Piankeshaw. The ritual-loving Indians were always ready for confession, acknowledging endless sins of the flesh and the spirit. It took a patient priest to serve this hybrid parish.

After the Sunday Mass the *habitants* gathered in the street to hear the sexton read the public notices. Farmers unloaded carts and set up their weekly market. Young men raced ponies over the Common, and old women gossiped on the galleries. Like the morning Mass, the evening vespers were attended by all—Indians and whites, old and young, officials in broadcloth and *coureurs du bois* in buckskins. In the early years of the settlements many young French farmers married Indian women. But half-breed children were unruly; it seemed that the wild blood choked the disciplined inheritance and the depraved half-breed strain had neither the French nor the Indian virtues. After 1730 the French government prohibited the priests from performing mixed marriages. Still the two races mated. After a season in the wilds, *voyageurs* were given a festive welcome in the Indian camps. Half-caste children swarmed in all the settlements.

Living was easy for the *habitants*. With little labor their rich lands produced corn for the livestock, grapes for wine, potatoes, fruit, tobacco, and enough wheat to send down the river to New Orleans in exchange for goods to support a fur trade with the Indians. Merchandise came to Illinois in birch-bark canoes, hollowed pirogues and sturdy bateaux. It was a twelve-day trip downstream, carried by the river current, and a toilsome two-month journey in return. As furs soon spoiled in the hot and humid South, most of the fur traffic still went to the St. Lawrence.

In 1712, when the French treasury was drained by European wars, aging King Louis XIV shrugged off the huge domain of Louisiana, which had not enriched him as he had hoped. With one scrawled signature above the royal seal he gave the whole Mississippi valley enterprise to a rich and sanguine Paris merchant, Antoine Crozat, reserving for himself one-fifth of the gold and silver it might yield. The recently appointed Governor Cadillac, formerly commandant at Detroit, told Crozat of rich mines in the Illinois and Mississippi valleys. Quickly Crozat built up great expectations, which slowly vanished. Cadillac spent most of the year 1715 looking for precious metals in the Illinois country (the rather vague dividing line between Louisiana and Canada crossed the Wabash near the site of present Terre Haute), and Crozat poured money into a trading enterprise on the Gulf of Mexico. Nothing came of either undertaking, and in 1717 Crozat turned back his monopoly on a realm several times the size of France.

A few months later the colony was given to the Mississippi Company, a venture organized almost overnight by John Law, a Scotch financial adventurer in Paris. Law's proposals to develop a production of gold, silver, copper and silk fascinated European speculators. Newly engraved maps of the Mississippi showed the location of mines and quarries. Ingots of "Mississippi gold" were displayed in Paris shop windows. Broadsides told of savage tribes eager to trade gold and silver for French ribbons and kitchen-ware. The Mississippi was described as lined with native towns and villages where Indian women wove silk and Indian hunters staggered under loads of peltry.

In Paris, the Illinois country was spoken of as "the Peru of France . . . the most beautiful country in the world, full of lead, copper and silver." Stated a letter from Illinois printed in Paris in 1719: "We are not among treasures but above them; and we can say without exaggeration that we trample them underfoot since there are so many rich silver mines over which we walk. . . . Along the upper Mississippi the mountains are full of gold and silver, copper, lead, and quick-silver mines."

While the price of its shares swirled upward amid feverish speculation, the company built Fort de Chartres, "the Gibraltar of the West," between the drowsing towns of Cahokia and Kaskaskia on the Mississippi. Three hundred makeshift troops and servants from the slums of Paris were quartered there under a few aristocratic French officers. In 1720 a director of mining operations brought boatloads of Negro laborers up the river from the Gulf. They scratched for copper and silver along the Illinois, and found nothing but coal. Then the chimera of riches moved on to the immense country drained by the Missouri; rumors told of gold and rubies in the West. The Mississippi bubble burst in 1720, and John Law fled, penniless, from Paris, escaping the fury of thousands of ruined investors. Again the vast colony reverted to the king, a new monarch now, Louis XV, who would see the whole of Louisiana lost to Spain.

The Mississippi Company had impressed colonists in France —sullen boatloads of prisoners, vagabonds and orphans. They came unwillingly to the fabled land, but they willingly stayed after John Law's company had collapsed. Some settled in the parishes near the mouth of the Mississippi, while others joined the French communities in the American Bottoms, attracted not by gold and silver but by easy living in a pleasant land.

Occasionally the drowsing Illinois settlements heard reports of trading rivalries at Detroit and on the upper Ohio. Two enterprises were colliding there: the British pushing a pack-horse trade among the Ohio Indians and the French loading canoes with peltry for the Montreal merchants. England and France were two old adversaries. Now in the New World forests they met again. A struggle for the heartland was beginning.

While the *habitants* lived easily in Illinois, almost oblivious to the world, British traders had come over the mountains into the Ohio country. Pack trains laden with blankets, stockings, garters, paint, ribbons, kettles, razors, scissors, mirrors, jew's-harps and hawk bells returned to Harrisburg and Philadelphia with baled peltry. As the business grew, they penetrated farther, carrying trade to the Shawnees, Wyandots and Miamis, with whom the French had been trafficking from bases at Detroit and on the upper Wabash.

Already the English had made inroads; a Miami tribe had moved eastward from the Wabash in order to be closer to the British merchants. In 1747 a chief whom the French called La

Damoiselle (he was Old Britain to the English) established the Miami town of Pickawillany on the Great Miami River; the present Piqua, Ohio, occupies the site. British traders set up a warehouse there. Deep in the heartland, which the French had pre-empted, the British were contesting for trade with the tribes. Over the Kaskaskia prairie came invitations to the Illinois tribes to bring their trade to Old Britain's town of Pickawillany.

The most aggressive of the English traders were George Croghan, an Irishman, and Conrad Weiser, a German. They carried Pennsylvania goods over the mountains to Logstown, a Shawnee camp on the Ohio River highway. Here they met tribesmen of other nations and laid the groundwork of a growing British commerce.

George Croghan had come to Philadelphia from Ireland as a long-striding youth of seventeen. In the bustle of that new city (founded in 1682, when Tonty was building Fort St. Louis on Starved Rock) some instinct turned his mind to the West. On the Pennsylvania frontier he learned the Delaware and Iroquois tongues. He journeyed down the Ohio River and found the bones of mammoths, tusks six feet long and rib bones as big as a ridge pole. Hearty, eloquent and profane, a shrewd trader and a suave diplomat with ceremony-loving Indians, he established posts at strategic points near the sites of present Cleveland and Toledo. On his estate in Pennsylvania Croghan dressed richly, lived lavishly and at last died penniless, though he had claimed millions of acres of rich land. On the trail he carried a personal supply of snuff and whisky which he shared with the village chiefs. The Indians called him "Old Buck." In 1747, early in his wilderness career, Croghan reported to the governor of Pennsylvania: "I am just returned from the woods and have brought a letter, a French scalp, & some wampam for the Governor from a part of the Six Nations Ingans that has there dwelling on the borders of Lake Arey. Those Ingans were always in the French interest till now, butt this spring allmost all the Ingans in the woods have declared against the French."

By 1749 Croghan and his colleagues had thrust a British wedge into the French trading empire, between Canada and Louisiana. With shorter trade routes open the year round, the British could sell goods cheaper than the French—though one English trader sold needles at a dollar each, telling his Indian customers that the man who made needles had died and this was the last of his stock. English rum was less than half the price of French brandy, and it had the same effect; an Indian trading with the British could get drunk for a muskrat skin, with the French it required a beaver. The Ohio tribes complained that French traders gave but a pint of powder for a buckskin, while the English gave a quart.

To the French governor in Canada came reports that Indians at the French posts were growing surly and restless. When a trader on the Wabash offered a Wyandot one bullet and one charge of powder for a beaver skin, the Indian buried his hatchet in the trader's head. In February, 1748, a Frenchman was killed at the gate of the Miami fort (present Fort Wayne) on the Maumee, and his scalp was carried to the Hurons on Sandusky Bay. Later that year the commander at Detroit wrote the governor of Canada that the Miamis and Ouitenons were seizing Frenchmen and their property. From Kaskaskia came word of a roving Huron who said that Shawnees and Miamis were forming a league to destroy the French posts in the upper country.

In this uneasy time there was an able governor of New France, the Marquis de la Galissonière. To encourage French settlement in the West he offered a farm and all equipment—implements, tools, chickens, a brood sow, powder and lead—to any family that would settle in Detroit. But the French were not drawn to frontier life and there were few takers; the governor's plan recruited just forty-six families. In another effort to affirm French proprietorship in the West, Galissonière sent an impressive expedition into the Ohio Valley under command of Captain Céloron de Blainville. He was to win back the Indians to a French alliance and to reassert the claim of France in the Ohio country.

Céloron, a Canadian by birth, had a record of great success on the frontier. As commandant at Michilimackinac and Detroit he had governed with fairness and firmness. He was respected by the French traders and liked by the Indians. He had seen the clash of French and British commerce at Detroit, where for years English agents had been nibbling at the trade. For this touchy mission no better man could have been chosen.

In the summer of 1749, with two hundred French troops and thirty-five Indians in a fleet of canoes, Céloron left Montreal. By way of the St. Lawrence, Lake Ontario, the Niagara, Lake Erie and Chautauqua Creek, they came to the headwaters of the Ohio. At the portages the men staggered under loads of Indian gifts. Ahead of them Céloron sent a half-breed agent, Chaubert de Joncaire, to tell the tribes that a French ambassador was coming. When Céloron arrived, the chiefs were willing to accept his gifts but unwilling to make promises. (Indians did not give their word lightly.) In some villages he found British traders, whom he asked to withdraw from the country, "making them feel that they have no right of commerce or anything else on the Belle Rivière." He had been instructed to seize British stores and caches of peltry, but he found the British too well established to permit that. The French captain could only make his speeches and move on.

But at six strategic places he solemnly performed an empty ceremony. At the mouths of rivers entering the Ohio, out of sight and sound of the British and the Indians, he drew up his men on the shore and buried a lead plate in the ground. The six inscribed plates declared French possession of all territory drained by the Ohio and its tributaries.

At the mouth of the Scioto, the site of present Portsmouth, Céloron stayed in the Shawnee "lower town" for five days, but the plate intended for burial there was stolen by a Seneca hunter; it was taken to New York and eventually given to Governor George Clinton. Two of the buried plates, at the mouths of the Muskingum and the Kanawha, were found, generations later, by boys playing on the riverbank.

The pay-off of Céloron's tour was to come at Pickawillany on the Ohio River, where, according to instructions, he was to disrupt the British trade and disperse the traders. The expedition arrived at the town on the 12th of September and found that the British agents, after a busy summer, had gone back to Pennsylvania with laden pack trains. The only satisfaction left to the French was the smoking of calumets. "They carried the calumets to . . . all the officers and to the Canadians, who, famished for a smoke, wished that the ceremony had lasted a long time." Céloron stayed at Pickawillany five days, but except for one uneasy interview, he had no negotiations with leathery La Damoiselle. The chief refused the proffered French presents: four half-barrels of powder, four bags of bullets, four bags of paint, a box of assorted needles and thread.

The Indians got the plunder anyway. In the dry September season, without enough water to float his canoes, Céloron had to leave his gifts behind. Marching his men overland to the Maumee River, he built new canoes and headed for Lake Erie. In November they were back in wintry Montreal with a report of failure. Céloron had neatly traced the bounds of present Ohio and found it already lost to the French. His expedition ended not with a bang but a whimper. "All I can say is that the nations of these localities are very badly disposed toward the French and are entirely devoted to the English. I do not know in what way they could be brought back."

In the next year, 1750, woodsman Christopher Gist went landlooking in the Ohio country in the interests of a company of Virginia merchants and speculators. He started out from Maryland in November, and by Christmas he was in the Indian village at the forks of the Muskingum, site of the present Coshocton, Ohio, where Croghan had a trading house. In January two notable men rode in on shaggy ponies, George Croghan and his bizarre colleague Andrew Montour.

Through the dark border country the name Montour echoed like a legend. Madame Montour, a far-ranging woman of far-reaching influence among the tribes, was said by one writer to be a daughter of the Count of Frontenac, by a Huron woman; her name appears in an old document which charges Frontenac with propagating more than sixty half-breeds. After being captured by the Iroquois, Madame Montour lived with them for many years and helped to align the powerful Five Nations on the side of the British against the French. She married a war captain of the Oneidas and bore him a son, the notorious Andrew Montour. In 1752 she was blind, but she traveled on horseback through a hundred miles of dense wilderness from Logstown to Venango, where she died. According to one account her son led her horse all the way.

Except for this incident Andrew Montour appears an impudent, arrogant, headstrong man who was frequently wildly drunk; one morning at the start of a trip with Conrad Weiser he consumed two quarts of rum. This preposterous half-breed had two four-syllable Indian names, but he preferred his European name and European dress. He wore a brown broadcloth coat caked with mud, grease and ashes, a scarlet-lapel waistcoat, red breeches, and a black neckerchief weighted with silver bangles. From his ears hung pendants of brass and wire, "like the handle of a basket," a Moravian missionary said. He lived a roving life, going from tribe to tribe in the border country. The British put up with his drunkenness and impudence because they needed his services as interpreter and informer. He knew which traders had been killed by which Indians, what messages had passed between one chief and another, and where the next violence might come. All the Indians regarded him as one of their chiefs. To the British, if he could be kept sober at crucial times, he was very useful. He served as interpreter for young George Washington, for Colonel Fairfax, General Braddock, General Forbes, and Sir William Johnson. He could write messages to the Pennsylvania officials in urbane and formal English: "I once more take upon me the liberty of informing you that our Indians at Ohio are expecting every day the armed forces of this Province [Pennsylvania] to

their assistance against the French, who by their late encroach-
ments are like to prevent their planting [corn] and thereby
render them incapable of supporting their families; and you may
depend upon it as a certainty that our Indians will not strike the
French unless this Province or New York engage with them."
He also shared in the wildest drunken frolics of the Indians.

In February, 1751, Gist, Croghan and Montour left the Muskingum village for the West. Gist's journal describes a rich,
beautiful country with good grass even in that season for the
horses and herds of buffalo feeding in the meadows. The streams
were full of water. "The Miamee River being high, We were
obliged to make a Raft of old Loggs to transport our Goods and
Saddles, and swim our Horses over." At strategic Pickawillany,
with its crossing of important trails, they were given a ceremonial
welcome and the British flag was raised on top of Old Britain's
house. In the village they found a newly raised stockade, built by
the traders with the tribe's permission, enclosing a trading house,
several dwellings, and a cache of arms and ammunition. It was,
Gist declared, "one of the strongest towns on this continent." The
English meant to stay there.

On the evening of their arrival Montour made a speech in the
Long House, to which the Indians replied, Yo! Ho! In the following days presents were given and ceremonial dances were
held for the visitors. When they left, a tribal escort guided them
to the crossing of the Hockhocking.

To Illinois came word of the new trading house, with English
rum and cheaper trade goods, and the Illinois tribesmen forgot
their traditional loyalty to the French. In 1751 a party of
Piankeshaw warriors at Kaskaskia begged arms to fight the invading Cherokees; then they turned on the French, murdering a
soldier and attacking *habitants* outside the village. They meant to
massacre the Kaskaskians on a Sunday morning as they came out
of church, but the French commander learned of the plot and
drove the savages away. In this uneasy time French sentries
guarded the chapel and the *habitants* carried guns to Mass.

Elsewhere the Indians were showing hostility toward the French. From Canada in the spring of 1752 Governor Langueuil sent to Paris a gloomy report of French prospects in the interior. After reviewing the failure of Céloron's expedition, he added some somber items.

"On the 19th of October the Piankeshaws killed two more Frenchmen who were constructing pirogues lower down than the post of Vincennes."

"'The English have paid the Miamis for the scalps of two soldiers belonging to M. de Villier's garrison [at Fort Miamis on the Maumee]."

Smallpox had erupted in Indian villages friendly to the French: "Cold Foot and his son had died of it, as well as a large portion of our most trusty Indians." The governor had a gruesome wish about that pestilence: " 'Twere desirable that it should break out and spread generally through the localities occupied by our rebels. It would be fully as good as an army."

Even religion was aligned in this commercial warfare. Some English traders reported that the French missionaries told the Indians that the Saviour was of the French nation, and that those who crucified him were of the English nation.

Then came word of a meeting of the tribes at La Damoiselle's Pickawillany, where some fifty English traders had loaded pack trains during the summer of 1752. Pickawillany looked like the spearhead of English penetration, and the French determined to destroy it.

On the morning of June 21, 1752, Pickawillany was a quiet town. Breakfast was over and the Indian women were hoeing the corn rows north of the village. Some old men sat against the shady side of the lodges. In their huts outside the stockade were eight English traders. La Damoiselle, Old Britain, the Piankeshaw king, was there, smoking a clay pipe in his doorway, but the warriors were away on a summer hunt. Only the children were active, pelting the dogs with corncobs and splashing each other from a water kettle in the street. From the trees turtledoves sang their monotonous, languid song: *Curry coo, coo, coo.*

Sudden cries broke out and women came running from the cornfield. Gunfire slammed into the town. Dogs and children scattered. A band of painted Chippewas and Ottawas came whooping in. Five of the English traders and twenty Indian men and boys got into the fort and closed the timber gate. As the attackers came through the street, three English' traders surrendered. From nearby huts the invaders fired musket balls into the stockade.

There were two hundred and fifty northern Indians in the raiding party, led by Charles Langlade, a twenty-three-year-old half-breed from Wisconsin. From boyhood Langlade, the son of a French trader and an Indian woman, had lived a roving life. At the age of ten he accompanied his Indian uncles on a long war mission down the Mississippi. Now he was a war captain himself. Gathering Chippewa and Ottawa braves at Sault Ste. Marie and Michilimackinac, he had guided a great canoe brigade down Lake Huron. Though he was acting without orders, he was serving French aims. He meant to destroy Pickawillany.

After six hours of seige the invaders had killed fourteen Indians, including Old Britain himself. In mid-afternoon the firing ceased and Langlade offered to leave the town if the Piankeshaws would deliver the English traders. The leaderless Piankeshaws were willing. They had no water inside the fort and the hot June sun beat down. Two of the traders, Thomas Burney and Andrew McBryer, were hidden in the fort; the other three surrendered. One of them had been wounded. He was now stabbed to death by Langlade's men, who peeled off his scalp.

Before they left the town, the raiders feasted. Old Britain was boiled and eaten, and they dismembered the dead trader and ate his heart. They sacked the fort, burned some lodges, and stripped the trading post of all its goods. Then, loaded with plunder, they headed northward. While most of the party paddled back to Michilimackinac, Langlade took the two captive traders to Governor Duquesne. It was a gratifying present to the new commander. He rewarded Langlade with a pension of 200 francs and sent him back to Wisconsin in a new French uniform. Three years later he would lead a troop of Indians against General Braddock's army in Pennsylvania; then he would shift to the British side, serve the British in Pontiac's War, establish a trading post at Green Bay and die there in honored old age, "the Father of Wisconsin." It was a mixed-up seesaw war, and Langlade had shifted sides at the right time.

Langlade's raid on that June day in 1752 was the end of Pickawillany and the beginning of a long warfare which would end a decade later with the ceding of all New France to the British. From the ashes of Old Britain's town came the fire that consumed the French empire in America.

Governor Duquesne meant to preserve French control of the interior. He ordered construction of a line of forts from Lake Erie to the Forks of the Ohio, the present Pittsburgh; the forts were built in 1753. At the same time Governor Robert Dinwiddie of Virginia, maintaining Virginia's claim to that country, sent young Major George Washington to warn the French away. The French officers received Washington civilly, but told him they meant to take control of the Ohio River. Now the Forks of the Ohio, the junction of the Allegheny and Monongahela rivers, became a crucial point. Washington was ordered to seize the location and put up a fort. The French intercepted him at Great Meadows, where for years the English traders had made camp and pastured their ponies, and captured his expedition on July 4, 1754. They then built Fort Duquesne on the site of present Pittsburgh, and the French and Indian War began.

An old warfare had come to the New World. This was another chapter in the long conflict between France and England, a part of the Seven Years' War that was fought on four continents. The taste for luxury in Europe, for ladies' fur pieces and gentlemen's felt hats, sent armies against each other in the American wilderness and filled the Indian camps with destruction and death. One of the Delaware chiefs wondered why the English and French must fight on the tribal lands. Another, having drunk some of the English rum, exclaimed: "Damn you! Why do not you and the French fight on the sea?" They were fighting on the sea, as well as on the continents. Thomas B. Macaulay, looking at it nearly a hundred years later, blamed the war on Prussia's Frederick the Great. "In order that he might rob a neighbor whom he had promised to defend, black men fought on the coast of Coromandel and red men scalped each other by the Great Lakes of North America." Armies marched in Europe, Africa and India, as well as in the American wilderness.

The French and Indian War was fought outside the heartland —along Lake Champlain, in western Pennsylvania and on the St. Lawrence. But hundreds of western Indians were in the French service, and other hundreds of Iroquois fought for the British; and the whole American interior was at stake. Under Montcalm the French won early victories. Then came to power the great British imperialist, Sir William Pitt, who saw a chance to win the New World heartland. In 1758 Pitt sent three resourceful and determined generals to America. Soon General John Forbes captured Fort Duquesne, Lord Jeffrey Amherst took Ticonderoga, and Sir William Johnson won Fort Niagara. The taking of Fort Duquesne was a victory without a battle, accomplished by a Pennsylvania missionary, Christian Frederick Post, who in peril of his life went into the Ohio country and persuaded the Indians to refuse to fight the white man's war. Short of supplies and without Indian defenders, Fort Duquesne fell to the British, who rebuilt the stronghold as Fort Pitt. Meanwhile the British fleet had cut off French supply lines, English troops swarmed over the great rock of Quebec, and Montreal was surrendered to General Amherst. Then Amherst sent Major Robert Rogers and his Royal Rangers to take over the French post at Detroit.

At the Treaty of Paris in 1763 Britain came into nominal possession of the French West Indies rather than the continental territory of New France; the commissioners reasoned that the sugar trade of Guadeloupe was worth more than all the North American fur trade. At that time the American heartland, which had been strenuously fought for, seemed a doubtful asset. But Pitt, with his vision of colonial expansion, chose the continental wilderness, and British sovereignty was extended to the Mississippi. The Indians were asked to understand that the king of France had decided to give their lands to the king of England.

In taking over the key station of Detroit, the British dealt stiffly with the Indians. Though Croghan and Sir William Johnson knew how to treat the tribes, Indian policy was decided by Amherst, the commander in chief. Amherst thought that Croghan had been "too bountiful" with tribesmen at Fort Pitt; now in Detroit the commander offered no gifts and a strictly business trade. If they were kept in need, he argued, the tribes would be more industrious at gathering peltry. If they were kept short of powder and bullets, they would be submissive. The French had treated the Indians as allies; the British regarded them as subjects.

One Indian could not accept the idea that a king three thousand miles away had given the American interior to another king. He was Pontiac, war chief of the Ottawas. A proud, bold and commanding man, he emerged from the tribal discontents as the leader of resistance; he meant to drive out the English and resume the Indian alliance with the French. Encouraged by the French in Illinois, he plotted an uprising at Detroit. It failed because someone warned the British commander, but Pontiac's warriors besieged the post for five long months. Pontiac's Conspiracy is partly legend, a romantic story of a plot to overthrow in a single day all the British power in the West. But the legend dramatizes a widespread Indian resentment and resistance. During Pontiac's siege of Detroit violence spread throughout the interior. Fort Sandusky, Fort St. Joseph, Fort Miami (at present Fort Wayne) and Ouiatenon (near present Lafayette) on the Wabash all fell within the second half of May, 1763. And on June 2, during a game of lacrosse, the Chippewas seized old Fort Mackinac (Michilimackinac) and massacred its British garrison.

Each of these posts was the scene of sudden violence. At Fort

Sandusky, while warriors surrounded the stockade, a group of Wyandots were passed through the gate to deliver a message to Ensign Pauli. While the delegation sat smoking, the painted warriors stormed in. They killed the sentry, seized Pauli, and murdered and scalped a dozen troops and several traders. The stockade was burned and Pauli taken captive to Pontiac's camp at Detroit. At Fort Miami an Indian girl led her sweetheart, Ensign Robert Holmes, outside the fort to see her ailing mother in her lodge. As Holmes crossed the meadow, the Indian camp was serene as the summer sky, but when he stepped to the door of the hut, two warriors sprang up with leveled muskets. At the sound of gunfire a sergeant ran to the officer's aid. Another musket roared, and the sergeant fell. Whooping savages cut off Holmes's head and carried it back to the fort. Nine men inside were taken captive. At Fort Ouiatenon the commanding officer, decoyed outside the palisade, found himself surrounded by a circle of painted warriors. With his small garrison he was made prisoner, and the fort was burned. All the troops were killed except one young recruit who was adopted by an Indian woman. Her son had been killed by white men.

When his hungry warriors drifted away for the autumn hunt, Pontiac abandoned the siege of Detroit. Fort Pitt withstood repeated attack; the British flag still fluttered above the Forks of the Ohio. The Indians had neither organization nor supplies for sustained war, and the rebellion was ebbing. In 1764, Colonel John Bradstreet led an expedition along the shore of Lake Erie and Colonel Henry Bouquet marched fifteen hundred men west from Fort Pitt. The presence of this strong force ended the rebellion. The Ohio tribes came into Bouquet's camp, on the site of present Coshocton, and smoked the pipes of peace.

Still the Illinois tribes were hostile, and in March, 1764, Pontiac went to the Illinois country, canoeing down the Maumee and the Wabash and walking over the spring prairie to Fort de Chartres on the Mississippi. The French commander, reconciled to British occupation and anxious to get home to France, had no welcome for the still-smoldering war chief. But with Illinois tribesmen the name of Pontiac had a lingering power. He soon whipped up resistance to the prospective British occupation, which was expected to come upriver from New Orleans.

No British commander was disposed to march so deep into the interior, but diplomacy might win what war could not. The tribes were dependent upon trade—if not with the French, then with the English—and gifts could influence the most hostile chiefs. To open the Wabash and Illinois countries, the veteran George Croghan was sent west in 1765. He left Fort Pitt in mid-May with several Englishmen and a party of Shawnees in two big canoes. Beyond the Scioto he was in hostile country, and near the mouth of the Wabash he was attacked by a band of Kickapoos. Two white men were killed and Croghan "got the stroke of a hatchet" on his head. The Kickapoos divided the plunder and took the captive invaders through dry country in fierce June heat to Vincennes. Croghan described Vincennes as a village of ninety families "in one of the finest situations that can be found." The shrewd *habitants* immediately began trading with the Kickapoos for the booty they had seized from Croghan.

From Vincennes the prisoners were taken, on horseback now, two hundred and ten miles farther up the Wabash. Here Croghan's status changed from captive to visiting diplomat. The chiefs came to talk with him, and Croghan, always eloquent in Indian tongues, removed their suspicions of the British and won consent for British occupation of the former French posts. After much smoking of pipes and presenting of wampums, Croghan was escorted into Illinois. On the way to the Mississippi he met Pontiac himself, who was on his way to see Croghan. They returned together to Ouiatenon. There Croghan won a promise, "confirmed by pipes and belts," that the British would be received in the Illinois country "with open arms."

In Edgar County, Illinois, a commemorative boulder now marks the place where Croghan and Pontiac met. A few miles across the prairie is another boulder, marking the site of a treaty in 1809, when General William Henry Harrison obtained two million acres from the Indians for $4,000. By that time both Pontiac and Croghan were dead, but their agreement had pointed straight as an arrow to the purchase treaty and the dispossessing of the tribes.

From the council at Ouiatenon Pontiac returned to the Mississippi, and a swaggering Croghan went on to Detroit. Late that summer he presided over a conference with all the western Indians who had been summoned to Detroit by Colonel Bradstreet. The chiefs were wheedling; they hoped their English fathers would give them clothing and a little rum to drink on the road, since they had come a long way to this council. The prayer was granted. With one for the road, the tribes scattered over the prairie. Croghan then set out for Niagara, paddling a birch canoe along the north shore of Lake Erie. It was the last week of September, clear cool days and starry nights, and for a time the heartland was at peace, with British authority extending to the Mississippi. Croghan and Pontiac had smoked the calumet.

Neither the warrior nor the wilderness diplomat shared in the riches of the disputed country. Croghan died penniless when the American Revolution shattered his project of a great colony in the West. And Pontiac came to an ignominious and violent end. He was an alien in Illinois with Indian enemies enough to account for his murder, though the circumstances are vague. According to a persistent tradition, his death came on a June night in 1769. After a drinking spree in Cahokia, Pontiac stumbled toward his canoe on the riverbank. An Illinois warrior of the Peoria tribe (bribed by an Englishman, the legend says) split his head with a hatchet. So ended the trail for a proud and bitter red man.

Another legend describes an ensuing tribal war, in which the Ottawas and Potawatomis attacked the dwindling Illinois to avenge the death of Pontiac. A party of Illinois scrambled up the historic rock that had once supported Tonty's Fort St. Louis. On the height they were safe from their pursuers, but not from thirst and hunger. They died on Starved Rock, and so a hungry name came to a land of plenty.

4. A Priest and a Commander

More enduring than French commerce in America was the unworldly enterprise of evangelism. After the traders were gone, the priests remained, and when the flag of France came down, the cross still stood above the mission chapels. French churches remain today, though the original buildings have crumbled, in Cahokia and Vincennes; and memory has cherished the names of Father Marquette, Father Meurin and Father Gibault after the commandants have been forgotten.

Cahokia, beside the Mississippi in the American Bottom, was a summer camp of the Tamaroa tribe when Tonty guided three missionaries there in 1698. The simple, warm-hearted Father St. Cósme built a Cahokia chapel in 1699, the first church in the Illinois country and the first in the heartland. Around the mission grew a French village, whose trading houses immediately attracted a permanent Indian settlement. Sixty-five years later, when English authority had replaced the French in Illinois, the old Cahokia mission property was earning a rental of 333 livres ($66.60) a year. The money went to the Theological Seminary in Quebec, and during the 1760's it supported a young student who was destined for a part in the heartland's history.

Pierre Gibault was thirty-one when he was ordained at Quebec in 1768. A Canadian by birth, he had roamed the western wilds before beginning his theological studies; every family in Canada (there were no more than a thousand of them) was said to have a member in the bush. Upon ordination he chose to return to the wilderness, in a black robe rather than a *voyageur's* capote; he would be an expert hunter and fisherman all his life. There was then just one priest in the Mississippi valley, the aging Father Meurin, residing at Ste. Genevieve, a few miles below St. Louis on the west side of the Mississippi. When Father Meurin asked for a priest to serve the French villages in the American Bottom, the Bishop of Quebec assigned Pierre Gibault to the Illinois country.

In the spring of 1768 the young priest packed his theological library along with some clothing and provisions in a bark canoe and left the hushed chapels of Quebec for his distant parish. He reached Michilimackinac in July. There was no priest at that station, and Father Gibault spent a strenuous week confessing Indians and *voyageurs* (who were equally willing to confess themselves or to split a skull) and baptizing Indian and half-breed children. In the long days of midsummer he paddled down the wild shores of Lake Michigan, made the Chicago portage and descended the Illinois to the vast slow Mississippi. It was his intention to locate at Cahokia, but finding that Kaskaskia had become the chief settlement of the region, he made his residence there. His ministry would extend to all the Illinois villages, and even across the prairie to the Wabash. While getting settled in Kaskaskia, he was stricken with ague. Between fits of chills and fever he conducted services in the parish church; with trembling hands he gave the people his benediction. Like his congregation, he was to suffer year after year with that recurrent malady of the river country.

Kaskaskia was an Algonquin word whose hard consonants must have offended a French ear. Kaskaskia, Keokuk, and Kankakee are peculiarly Illinois names—only that dialect of the Algonquin tongue, some etymologist has said, contains words with three sounded *k*'s. The town of Kaskaskia was a somnolent, half-savage place. Early French missionaries had named it "The Village of Immaculate Conception," and a later priest referred to it as "Notre Dame de Kaskaskias." But sacred names were soon forgotten and the savage word survived.

French *habitants*, wandering *voyageurs*, half-breed and Indian families —all were the young priest's charges. After he had restored the church services at Kaskaskia, he set out on his wider mission. On a hardy French pony he rode to Cahokia and Prairie du Rocher in the American Bottom, to Indian camps as far as Lake Peoria up the Illinois, to Ouiatenon and Vincennes on the Wabash, and across the Mississippi to the Missouri settlements. For weeks at a time he was away from his books and his garden; he lived among primitive people in the remote places. In 1769 the Bishop of Quebec made him vicar-general of the Illinois country.

In bleak winter weather in 1770 Father Gibault made his first visit to Vincennes, riding his shaggy pony across two hundred miles of frozen prairie. It was a benighted place; a generation earlier Madame Vincennes, whose husband commanded the post and whose father was the richest man in the western settlements, signed her name with an X. George Croghan, seeing the French settlement with English eyes, had described "an idle, lazy people, a parcel of renegadoes from Canada, . . . much worse than the Indians." A generation later, in 1796, the philosophical French visitor Volney got the same impression: "In ignorance and idleness they beat the Indians." But on the winter day when Father Gibault arrived, the citizens crowded around him with smiles and tears of welcome. They had not seen a priest since 1763.

For two months the vicar stayed in the village, reviving the faith with such effect that a new wooden chapel was built beside the Wabash. (In this church, nine years later, George Rogers Clark would meet the British general and accept his surrender.) On his return to Kaskaskia in the spring, twenty men from Post Vincennes escorted the priest across the flowering prairie.

In his huge parish, waving with long-stemmed grass, washed in sunlight, swept with wind and snow, Pierre Gibault took his place in a notable tradition. To the Wabash Indian camp named Chippe Coke, or "Brushwood," before it became Post Vincennes, the Jesuit Father Jean Mermet had made a visit about the year 1715. While he was there, a malady broke out, and the Indians gathered round the primitive fort to make an offering to their manitou. They killed forty dogs, hoisted them on poles, and danced day and night around the sacrifice. When the epidemic grew in the camp, they appealed to the missionary. All he could do was to bless the dead and dying. Half the village perished in that season, and with a heavy heart Father Mermet journeyed over the prairie to Kaskaskia.

In 1742 Father Sebastien Louis Meurin, just a year away from France, came to the Illinois country. After two decades' missionary service he was removed, despite the pleas of the French and the Indians, when the French authority was surrendered in 1763. He was sent to New Orleans, and there he asked the privilege of returning to the scene of his life's work, though he should have no official subsistence. When his request was granted, he took charge of parishes on both the English and the Spanish sides of the Mississippi—a French priest under two alien regimes, taking his ministry to Indian camps and boatmen's barracks. By nature a gentle man, he inured himself to hardships which broke his health though they did not quench his spirit. One of his last letters describes his itinerant life:

> Sometimes in England, sometimes in Spain, a trip by canoe, one on foot, one or several on horseback; sometimes living well, sometimes fasting several days; sometimes passing several nights without sleeping, at other times not being able to sleep on account of gnats and more malignant creatures, such as lice, fleas, bedbugs, etc.; sometimes too tired to be able to eat or sleep . . . sometimes with the rain

on my body, sometimes hiding in the trunk of a tree; in the morning freezing with cold and at noon scorched by the heat of the sun; sometimes full of sorrow and at other times filled with comfort. . . . Such is my life in Illinois.

This was the veteran whom young Pierre Gibault succeeded, and whose life he embraced.

A slight man with a lean ascetic face and a scholar's deep-set eyes, the new vicar became the friend of Indians and woodsmen. He helped the illiterate villagers with letters and accounts; he advised them on trade and agriculture as well as on the will of God; he instructed their children, consoled their sick and buried their dead. In his pastoral rounds he swam rivers, slept on the ground, went hungry on long journeys, and tried to keep himself clean amid the flies, fleas, dogs and dust of Indian camps. Each summer he endured the onset of ague, keeping up his duties while his body shook with chill and burned with fever. Saying matins and vespers in bark chapels, he must have missed the gleaming altars of Quebec.

In the spring of 1775 Father Gibault paddled the long waterways to the St. Lawrence. It was like returning home—to walk the busy waterfront streets, to kneel in the cathedral with colored saints in the windows, to see old friends in the Seminary, to hear news of the world. In the cafés and market places there was excited talk of the American Revolution. From Boston British troops had marched to Lexington and Concord, on Lake Champlain American farmers had taken Fort Ticonderoga, the colonists had raised a Continental Army, and in a costly battle at Charlestown the British had stormed Bunker Hill. Pierre Gibault was a British subject, but from Quebec his eyes went over the river toward the distant places where men were fighting for freedom.

There were rumors that Ethan Allen was leading a ragged army toward Canada when Father Gibault set out again for the West. He paddled up the Ottawa River and through North Bay, reaching Michilimackinac in September. For a month he stayed there, waiting restlessly for a party bound for Illinois. Then in stormy autumn weather he paddled down tossing Lake Huron. Winter closed in on him at Detroit. There he remained, helping the two old priests with their offices, until early spring. He jogged into Kaskaskia on horseback when the prairie was turning green.

This was the momentous year 1776, but the Illinois settlements seemed as far from events in the New World as in the Old. Cherry blossoms came and went, in June the cottonwoods snowed faintly on the grass, wheat turned golden in the ribbon fields and the Indian corn withered in September. Indian summer brought bright days and star-filled nights. The tawny autumn pastures were rimed with frost, children gathered walnuts and hickory nuts in the prairie groves. Then winter drove the farmers to the chimney corner, while boatmen in buffalo coats dodged drift ice in the Mississippi.

Another cycle of seasons passed and the year was 1778. The prairie spring deepened into summer. On a June day a solar eclipse turned noon to night. In the startled Indian camps old men thumped ceremonial drums and raised a wailing chant to Manitou; then the shadow paled on the prairie, the summer sky brightened and the sun blazed down again. On that day Father Gibault must have quieted the superstitious fears—it was a natural thing and no disaster. A week later, as suddenly and silently as the eclipse, Revolution came to drowsing Kaskaskia.

The British government in that remote place was represented by a Frenchman, Philippe François Rastel, Sieur de Rocheblave, who had chosen to stay in the West after the French surrender in 1763. He had served in the French army, helping to defeat Braddock's expedition in Pennsylvania, and had commanded a French post, Fort Massac, on the Ohio. But now he had taken a British command, under appointment by the English king. His small pay was in arrears and the stingy British government in Canada had disregarded his request for military goods. He had asked to be relieved of his command, but no successor came.

On July 4, 1778, Rocheblave crossed the Mississippi to dine with the Spanish commander at New Madrid. He returned to Kaskaskia that evening, passing through the warm village streets —fiddle music and the sounds of dancing came from an open door—and into his quarters in the riverside stockade. He wrote a letter to Lieutenant Governor Hamilton in Canada before he and Madame Rocheblave retired.

A few hours later, awakened from sound sleep, he stared at two half-savage figures, a flickering lantern throwing their huge shadows on the wall. George Rogers Clark and Simon Kenton took the commander downstairs in his nightdress and informed him that his town was now under the control of Virginia. Outside, one of Clark's captains gave the signal and an uproar began. Through the streets roamed a hundred and seventy-five invaders, whooping, roaring, shouting. When lights showed in the windows, Clark's sentries proclaimed the capture of Kaskaskia and warned the citizens to stay within doors until daybreak. Kaskaskia had fallen to the Americans without a gunshot.

For two days, while marching overland from the Ohio River, Clark's men had subsisted on wild berries. That morning, in fear and curiosity, the French housewives provided pork, mush, hominy, beans, potatoes, and the soldiers feasted. Clark then marched them to the edge of town and posted them there. Back in the village, Clark and his captains walked through streets as silent as a ghost town, with the banner of Virginia floating over the fort and the frightened *habitants* peering from their windows. Clark intended no violence to these people, but he was in hostile country and greatly outnumbered. He must keep the villagers frightened and guessing. Evicting a family in the center of town, he made their cottage his headquarters.

As the fearful citizens stepped into the streets, they saw their town encircled by men with long rifles on their shoulders and hunting blades in their belts. Mitchi Malsa, Big Knives, the Indians called them. It was a forbidding name. (With the Indian vocabulary printed in his *Travels*, Volney noted that most words implying beauty and goodness began with *p*, and most *m* words were fearsome.) The Kaskaskians knew that British-armed Indians had harried the Kentucky settlements. Was this a retaliation?

The villagers looked to Father Gibault for guidance. He had told of the uprising of the colonies and their war with the British. Now, leading a committee of six nervous citizens, the priest went to the door of Clark's headquarters. So began Pierre Gibault's familiar role in frontier history.

Inside the room, Clark and his captains sat around a bare table. In the warm summer morning they had stripped off their buckskin shirts. Dirty, sweating, scratched with brambles in the river thickets, they looked up at the priest and his delegation. When Father Gibault asked for the commander, a powerful half-naked man with sandy red hair and a stubble of smoke-stained beard pointed to a chair. Clark asked what the committee wanted. Facing the red-haired colonel, Father Gibault made his request: The citizens of Kaskaskia, British subjects as they were, expected to be separated and carried off as captives, perhaps never to meet again. Might they, before their exile, gather in the church to seek God's blessing?

Clark answered brusquely. They could go to their church if they wanted. He had no objection. But no person was to leave the town. With no other word he dismissed them.

In the chapel the whole village gathered while certain older citizens recalled how the Acadian French had been driven from their homes in Nova Scotia. The priest tried to quiet these fears; he offered God's blessing, but he could not predict the will of the Big Knives. After an hour they emerged into the silent sunlit streets. Father Gibault went again to the commander. He found a more civil-looking man; Clark was freshly bathed and in a clean hunting shirt. This time the priest expressed a hope that the French families might not be separated and that the women and children could be allowed to take with them some clothing and provisions. The citizens, he added, knew little about the American Revolution, and they had never felt like British partisans.

Clark was trying a strategy, and this was the moment he had waited for. After filling the town with fear, he could fill it with rejoicing, and so win the gratitude of the French citizens. Now his manner changed. This mission, he said, was not to cause suffering but to end it. He had come to Illinois not to plunder but to prevent violence. The citizens could remain in their village, in peace and harmony, without fear of danger. Then he added that France had come to the aid of the American colonies; at this moment French ships were bringing men and materials to support the Revolution.

As his words went through the town, joy replaced desolation. Men laughed in the streets and women carried fresh food to the Virginia troops. When Clark offered them an oath of allegiance, the citizens cheered and sang. In the chapel Father Gibault gave thanks for deliverance and mercy. After less than a day of captivity these British subjects were American citizens. A new future had come to Kaskaskia, which in time would become the capital of the State of Illinois.

That evening Clark sent a troop of men, mounted on French ponies, over the old Fort Chartres Road to Cahokia, sixty miles north. Some young citizens of Kaskaskia galloped with them into the golden sunset. All night they traveled under the summer stars. At dawn the villagers of Cahokia heard a clatter of hooves and looked out at a line of dusty horsemen. The Kaskaskians explained the invasion and urged their neighbors to join the American future. Cahokia, like Kaskaskia, was won without a bullet.

With the American Bottom in his control, Clark turned his thoughts across the prairie to Vincennes on the Wabash. From that base the British had armed scores of Indian war parties for raids on the Kentucky settlements. The Illinois country would not be won until he had control of Post Vincennes.

The day after the capture of Kaskaskia Clark sent three scouts, Simon Kenton, Shadrach Bond and Elisha Beatty, to explore the military strength of Vincennes. The three men traveled warily over two hundred miles of prairie. Near Vincennes they hid in a thicket, waiting for darkness. By starlight they crept over the wide grazing common, leaving their rifles and their wide-brimmed Kentucky hats in the rank grass. Wrapped in blankets they strode like Indians through the town. They saw a peaceful place, with no British garrison and no alarm of American invasion north of the Ohio. One visit was probably enough, but spying was an exhilarating mission. The scouts hid outside of town and came back a second night, and a third. Then they turned back to Kaskaskia with their reassuring intelligence.

In Kaskaskia, waiting for the spies' report, Clark used a psychological strategy. He let the citizens know that he was thinking of ordering an army from Kentucky to attack Vincennes. That town was in Father Gibault's parish, and the priest came to Clark with the suggestion that force would not be required. He knew that the British governor was absent, on business in Detroit. He felt that the citizens of Vincennes could be peaceably won to the American side. He offered to go there to explain the American cause.

The priest set out with a small party of horsemen, including Dr. Jean Laffont, a native of the French West Indies, who carried his medical practice over the huge country of Father Gibault's ministry. Like the priest, the physician had the confidence of the French people. Clark could be assured that it was a persuasive delegation that clattered over the prairie.

In two weeks they were back, with good news. The Vincennes *habitants* were ready to pledge allegiance to America; even the Indian chiefs on the Wabash wanted to smoke the calumet with the Big Knife commander. Clark promptly sent trusted, weathered Captain Leonard Helm to treat with the Indians and command the fort at Vincennes. As the summer ended and the prairies withered to autumn, Clark controlled the Illinois country.

But the Indians were an uncertain quantity; they feared the advance of the Americans and they had British encouragement and support. With his single regiment Clark could not fight a dozen tribes, though perhaps he could lure them away from the British. He knew the Indian curiosity and love of council, and he waited for the chiefs to approach him. The overture came at the end of summer; an Indian messenger rode in to Kaskaskia telling of a gathering of tribesmen at Cahokia. They wanted to see the chief of the Big Knives and to receive American presents. Clark was ready.

When he rode in to Cahokia, an impressive sight appeared. For miles around the town the prairie was circled with Indian camps. Here were warriors of many nations—Chippewas from the northern forests, blanketed Ottawas from the shores of Lake Huron, Sauks and Foxes from Wisconsin, Miamis and Wyandots from beyond the Wabash, and all the prairie tribes of the Illinois people. At night the ringed horizon gleamed with campfires.

Now the young commander drew upon all that he had learned of Indian diplomacy. He listened to the speeches and smoked the feathered pipes. For three days he waited, silent; during that time a party of Puan warriors tried to take his life, but were driven off at midnight by Clark's sentries. When their chiefs came to make amends, the colonel stood at full height outside the doorway of his cottage. "I am a man and a warrior," he said. "I do not care who are my foes or my friends." The chiefs went away, humbled. In a later time Clark recalled with wry satisfaction that he "gave Harsh language to supply the want of Men."

The next day he stood above a symbolic fire, holding up two belts of wampum. "I carry in my right hand war"—a blood-red belt—"and peace in my left"—a belt of white. It was for the chiefs to choose. Then, still holding up the belts, he gave a compact history of America, drawing a parallel between the colonists and the native tribes:

> They don't know well how to make blankets, powder, and cloth. They live chiefly by making corn, by hunting, and trade, as you do. But the "Big Knives" are daily growing more numerous, like the trees in the woods, so that the land got poor and the hunting scarce. Then the men learned to make guns and powder so that they did not

have to buy so much from the British. They, the English, got mad
and put a strong garrison through all the country (as you see they
have done among you, on the lakes, and among the French) and
would not let our women spin, nor the men make powder, nor let
us trade with anybody else, but said we should buy all from them—
and since we have got saucy, they would make us give them two
bucks for a blanket that we used to get for one—and that we should
do as they please, and killed some of us to make the rest fear. This
is the truth and the cause of the war between us.

He told this history in human terms, making pictures that
every Indian could understand. "Our women and children were
cold and hungry. The young men were lost and had no coun-
cillor to put them in the right path. The whole land was dark,
and the old men hung their heads for shame, and they could not
see the sun; and there was mourning for many years."

When Clark paused, he seemed to stand taller above the ceremonial circle of the chiefs. "At last the Great Spirit took pity on
us and kindled a great council fire that never gave out, at a place
called Philadelphia, stuck down a post, left a tomahawk by it,
and went away. The sun immediately broke out and the sky was
blue. The old men held up their heads and assembled at the fire,
took up the hatchet, sharpened it, and put it into the hands of the
young men, and told them to strike the English as long as they
could find one on this side of the 'Great Water.' "

Slowly Clark swept his eyes over his listeners. "Thus the war
began, and the English were driven from one place to another
until they got weak and hired you red people to fight for them
and help them. The Great Spirit, getting angry at this, he caused
your father the French king to join the 'Big Knives' and fight
with them all their enemies so that the English is become like a
deer in the woods." Again his eyes moved over the tribesmen.
"You can judge who is in the right. I have already told you who
I am. Here is a bloody belt and a white one. Take which you
please."

All night there was dancing round the tribal fires and the
chiefs counciled together about the words of the Big Knife.

Next day they formed a ring and lighted the ceremonial fire. A feathered chief advanced, holding the white belt of peace. Another approached with a calumet of white pipestone from the Minnesota quarries. A third brought fire to kindle the pipe. The calumet of peace went to Clark and his captains around the circle of sachems.

That night campfires winked far out on the prairie; the tribes were going home. It was October, Indian summer, and Clark rode back to Kaskaskia through the golden haze of the American Bottom.

Meanwhile word of the capture of the Illinois towns had reached General Henry Hamilton in Detroit. Not knowing that tribal chiefs were on the way to Cahokia for council, he called warriors from the scattered camps and sent his British captains to dance with them around the war post. In mid-October he embarked an army of one hundred and seventy-five British troops and three hundred and fifty Indians to Vincennes. They paddled down the Detroit River and crossed the western end of Lake Erie in a curtain of snow. They ascended the Maumee, past the site of present Toledo, and reached the nine-mile portage at the end of October. With ninety-seven thousand pounds of stores and ammunition the army staggered over the muddy path to the Wabash. On the way they were joined by two hundred additional warriors. It was a strong frontier army that moved on to Vincennes.

In the Vincennes fort Captain Leonard Helm commanded some twenty French militiamen who had come over to the American side. As the British force approached he wheeled cannon into the gate, but there was no alternative to surrender. With Helm as his prisoner, Hamilton took over the fort and quartered his men in the town. As winter came, his scouts brought word that Clark had but eighty troops in Kaskaskia. It would be easy to crush him when the weather was right.

To Kaskaskia a messenger brought the desolate news. Clark stared across the winter prairie, brooding on the loss of Vincennes. Half his troops had gone back to Kentucky as their terms of enlistment expired. He had no money to pay the men who remained; he could feed them only through the generosity of Kaskaskia merchants who accepted his doubtful Virginia scrip and the faith of Father Gibault, who borrowed from the church tithes to supply the Americans. When Clark thought of Hamilton's army entrenched in Vincennes, the American cause in the West seemed as desolate as the bleak winter sky. General Hamilton might now be launching an attack upon Kaskaskia. Clark could not resist that army, but he did instruct the French-Americans how to act if they were captured. Then he set out for Cahokia, to instruct the citizens there. His party, rocking over a frozen road in two-wheeled carts, stopped for the night at the halfway village of Prairie du Rocher. There the hospitable villagers entertained with a ball. Clark could not have felt like dancing, but he talked with French farmers around a smoking punch bowl. Then the door burst open and a wind-bitten horseman brought a stunning message: General Hamilton was nearing Kaskaskia with eight hundred troops and warriors.

Clark ordered horses with a blanket roll behind each saddle. He might have thought of flight to Spanish ground across the Mississippi, but he was thinking only of Kaskaskia. While the men waited he coached them in a border stratagem; if they found the fort under attack, they would blanket themselves like Indians and infiltrate the enemy. At the gate of the fort they would make themselves known to the defenders and join the battle.

While they galloped over the iron road, Clark listened for sounds of battle. There was only the clatter of hoofs and the creak of saddle leather. When they reached Kaskaskia, the town was sleeping. The timbered gate swung open; the fort was secure. Clark had got there ahead of the enemy.

Before daybreak he set fire to houses adjoining the fort; he would leave no cover for attackers. Aroused citizens roamed the street while soldiers crouched beside cannon at the portholes. Dawn broke over the silent snow-patched prairie. Then a file of men rode in from the Fort Chartres Road. Major Bowman leapt down with word that the alarm was over. What had been mistaken for Hamilton's army was merely a scouting force; it had lost its way and was now returning to Vincennes.

Day and night Clark kept sentries patrolling the approaches to Kaskaskia. Late in January they accosted a single horseman who wanted to see the American commander. The visitor was Colonel Francis Vigo, a rich merchant who traded throughout the Illinois country. He had come from Vincennes, and he gave Clark a report of the situation there. General Hamilton was making himself comfortable in the fort with a well-provisioned commissary and a strong garrison. He had sent Indian parties on raids to Kentucky, and some of his regulars had gone back to Detroit. In the spring he would gather his forces and march on Kaskaskia.

In the spring. . . . Clark had a bold mind, now made restless by the false alarm of Hamilton's attack. He peered out at the winter prairie. He looked at a map, studying the curve of the Wabash and the lowland approaches to Vincennes. At this moment, he wrote later, he would have bound himself to seven years' imprisonment or slavery to have five hundred troops for a fortnight's service. In fact, even with the Kaskaskia volunteers, he had barely a hundred and fifty men. Still, he had won the Illinois town not by strength or logic but by audacity. *A desperate situation*, he thought, *needs a desperate resolution. The season being so hostile, no enemy would suppose an attack would come over impassable country. Surprise can outweigh numbers. . . .* That night he called his captains in and told them.

Clark's resolve went through the town like a contagion. New French volunteers joined his depleted regiment. To the fort citizens lugged bundles of food and clothing. With funds borrowed from Merchant Vigo Clark bought a flatboat and mounted six small cannon on its deck. The improvised gunboat, in charge of Captain John Rogers, the commander's cousin, pushed off into the gray current of the Kaskaskia. It would go down the

Mississippi, up the Ohio and up the Wabash, to hide in the Vincennes thickets until the arrival of Clark's regiment. Then it would bombard the fort while the troops attacked.

That night Clark wrote a letter to Governor Patrick Henry of Virginia. ". . . I know that the case is desperate; but, Sir, we must either quit the country or attack. . . . Great things have been effected by a few men well conducted. Perhaps we may be fortunate."

On the next day, February 5, 1779, the regiment drew into formation inside the stockade. When the drums were silent, Father Gibault raised his hand in blessing. Clark's men marched out of the gate in a thin chill rain. The watching townspeople called farewell. In five minutes the little army was on the sodden prairie. It was a smaller force than Clark had counted on—some of his troops had been assigned to the gunboat. There were just a hundred and thirty men facing an exhausting march and a superior enemy in a timbered fort.

A week out of Kaskaskia they reached the Little Wabash. That minor stream was now a mile-wide flood. Beyond it lay the drowned bottoms of the Embarrass River and then the swollen Wabash. They were sixty nightmare miles from Vincennes, and over all that desolation a cold rain was falling.

Their march seems incredible now. A third of the men were sick with chills and fever. All were wet, gaunt, cold and wretched. They had no sense of history to nerve them. Not even Clark with his dramatics dreamed that this campaign would be ranked with the military feats of nations, that his gaunt regiment would be immortal. They were merely miserable men slogging through mud and water, wading waist-deep rivers, building rafts to ferry their sick and their baggage, making cold camps in enemy country.

When they reached the Wabash, nine miles below Vincennes, their rations were exhausted. Here they were to meet the gunboat from Kaskaskia, but the swollen gray river, pitted with rain, was empty. They made "Camp Hunger," and in the gray daybreak they heard the boom of cannon—the morning gun from Fort Sackville at Vincennes. Chewing the bark of slippery elm to forget their stomach pangs, the men chopped logs and laced them together with vines. Next day they ferried the Wabash and floundered toward Vincennes. Through mud and misery they struggled on, arms around each other's shoulders. Late in the day the rain gave up and a thin sunlight slanted through bare trees. From a ridge they saw the houses of Vincennes, the timbered church, the heavy-walled fort with five square blockhouses pierced with portholes.

They captured a stray duckhunter, a Frenchman from the town. Clark opened his baggage, rubbed his stiffened fingers, and wrote a letter:

To the Inhabitants of Vincennes, Gentlemen:
Being within two miles of your village with my army, . . . I take this step to request such of you as are true citizens and willing to enjoy the liberty I bring you, to remain still in your houses, and that those (if any there be) that are friends to the King of England will instantly repair to the fort and join his troops and fight like men. . . . Those that are true friends of Liberty may expect to be well treated as such. I once more request that they may keep out of the streets, for every person found under arms on my arrival will be treated as an enemy.

G. R. Clark

While the Frenchman returned to town with that message, Clark had his men chop twenty saplings and raise flags sewed by the women of Kaskaskia. With every seventh man a flag-bearer, he started a zigzag march that gave the appearance of twenty companies. In the winter dusk they entered the town. At the log church they broke lines and crept under the bastion towers of the fort. The British cannon could swivel but they could not tilt. When Clark gave the order, his men fired through gaping palisades. From the fort came the shrilling of a bugle, the thud of boots, the rumble of cannon.

All night the fighting flowed and ebbed and flowed again. Clark's strategy was confusion and bewilderment; he kept his men moving, firing from various quarters, whooping like savages.

The French citizens came out with bread, meat and cheese. With food in their stomachs the men yelled like demons. But they cooly poured their rifle fire into the gun ports. One by one the British cannon were silenced.

Firing slackened at dawn, and Clark sent a message under a white flag to the bastion gate. It was addressed to General Hamilton.

> SIR:
>
> In order to save yourself from the impending storm that threatens you I order you to immediately surrender yourself up with all your Garrison, Stores, etc., for if I am obliged to storm, you may depend upon such treatment justly due to a Murderer. Beware of destroying Stores of any kind, or any papers or letters in your possession, or burning one house in the town, for by heaven if you do there shall be no mercy shown you.
>
> G. R. CLARK

When the messenger brought an answer Clark read it with narrowed eyes.

> Gov' Hamilton wishes to acquaint Col. Clark that he and his Garrison are not disposed to be awed into any action unworthy of British subjects.
>
> H. HAMILTON

Clark gave the word and firing was resumed. Crouching in ditches and under makeshift barricades, the men fired through gaping timbers. The sun broke through at noon, and a British messenger came out. A curt exchange led to a meeting in the log church—General Hamilton agreeing to surrender the fort at ten o'clock the next morning.

That day, February 25, was clear. At midmorning a company of Clark's mud-stained men drew up at the timbered gate. The British ranks marched out and Clark's gaunt regiment moved in. They fired the cannon thirteen times, for thirteen colonies that had become the American nation which now was master of the entire Ohio Valley.

Colonel George Rogers Clark, twenty-five years old, was at the peak of his career. The rest of his life was downhill—quarrels with officialdom, controversies with jealous and grasping rivals. He was wholly defeated in that warfare.

Three years after the capture of Vincennes the West was quiet and the Revolution was over. When Clark rode home to Kentucky from a campaign against the Ohio tribesmen, peace talks had begun in Paris. To Kentucky came an official Board of Commissioners, sent from Richmond to make a settlement of Clark's accounts. Clark had received no pay for five years; neither had the men under his command. The commissioners had an impossible task—reviewing piecemeal payrolls and ledgers, sorting fragmentary account books and countless scraps of paper noting goods, supplies and services received by one officer or another. There were claims for lost horses and butchered cattle, for buffalo beef, flour, Indian meal, tallow, lead, iron chains, stave pickets, harness, horseshoes, flints, powder, "rum for the troops" and "rum for a treaty"—the items seemed endless. Father Gibault had asked compensation for the loss of a colt whose mare was taken in the public service, for four bushels of corn supplied to hungry troops; he had parted with his cattle and his tithes of corn and flour until he was all but destitute.

The commission worked through a mountain of papers and made its report. But nothing was paid. Virginia passed the debt to the federal government, where it rested. Clark then urged that land be granted to members of the Illinois Regiment. They had won millions of acres of new territory for America; of this the Virginia Assembly promised a bounty tract of 150,000 acres on the northwest side of the Ohio.

A few years later, by an Act of Congress in 1791, four hundred acres were given to "each of those persons who, in 1783, were heads of families at Vincennes, or in the Illinois country on the Mississippi," in compensation for their losses during the Revolution. In addition to these "Donation Tracts," the Act granted one hundred acres to each man who had not obtained such a tract and who had served in the militia of the Illinois country.

Father Gibault had no military claim, but he had served the American cause as devotedly as any soldier. In fact the British recognized the importance of his actions more clearly than did any American official. From Vincennes in 1778 General Hamilton described Pierre Gibault as "this wretch . . . who absolved the French inhabitants from their allegiance to the King of Great Britain. To enumerate the vices of the inhabitants," he continued with increasing rancor, "would be to give a long catalogue . . . still the most eminently vicious and scandalous was the Reverend Monsieur Gibault."

In his alliance with the American invaders, the priest had risked everything. Now, when military compensations were being settled, he asked for the old Cahokia mission property (its rent had paid for his theological education in the Seminary at Quebec), which had had no claimants since the American regime. It was a small tract, about five acres, half of it in swamp. On its solid ground he hoped to have a cottage, with garden and orchard, as a dwelling place in his declining years. The ground was granted to him after long deliberation and delay, and so the aging priest came into possession of a little piece of the heartland whose future he had helped to shape.

5. The Big Land of Little Turtle

In 1797 Little Turtle, the great chief of the Miami nation, had his portrait painted in Philadelphia. He dressed up for the sittings: a headpiece of ten eagle feathers and three rattlesnake tails, bone earrings dangling to his shoulders, silver arm bands and a necklace of bears' claws; around his neck he wore a silver pendant, presented at the Treaty of Greene Ville, showing President Washington handing a long-stemmed pipe to an Indian who had dropped his hatchet. The portrait, hung in the Capitol rotunda in Washington, was destroyed when the British burned the government buildings in 1814. But Little Turtle is still remembered. He was a bold enemy of the United States who became a warm friend.

Indian chiefs had raised the Fleur-de-Lis over their villages for French visitors and the Union Jack for British agents. The tribes had no flag of their own, but they were willing to indulge the sentiments of the traders. Then, in 1783, Britain surrendered the interior country to the United States, and over the spacious Indian realm crept the shadow of a new nation.

In 1788 the first American settlements were established in the Northwest Territory—forty-eight Yankee emigrants arriving at Marietta on the Ohio and sixty men from New Jersey landing on the site of present Cincinnati. In that same year came Governor Arthur St. Clair, in a twelve-oared barge flying the American flag, to set up a Territorial regime. The next year five hundred French *émigrés* created their wilderness town of Gallipolis, and new families swelled the settlements at Marietta and Cincinnati.

Marietta lay at the mouth of the Muskingum, directly across from Fort Harmar, an army post erected for the protection of surveyors who were running boundary lines in the first Seven Ranges west of the up-curving Ohio. At Marietta, while the forty-eight men were building their picketed town, a band of Delaware Indians gathered, looking for presents from the white men. They were given a feast on a long table under the trees— barbecued venison, turkey, bear meat, and a huge broiled pike, as long as a man, that had been speared in the Muskingum River. Already the settlers were choosing land, each householder receiving an in-lot for his dwelling and an out-lot for farming. One of the first buildings in the town was the Land Office, where the survey of the Seven Ranges was recorded and the land allotted. The curious red men could not understand that building, with no blankets on the floor and no kettles in the fireplace. But they could understand the clearings in the forest, the new mill wheels splashing in the creeks and new settlements on the river. These were not trading posts for tribal traffic; they were white men's towns in Indian country.

The first resistance was furtive and stealthy, a moment of violence in the forest. Weeks later the surveyors might come upon a scalpéd body gnawed by wolves or a blood-smeared canoe caught in the willows. Then, on a winter night in 1791, a roving band of Indians slaughtered a dozen careless young men at Big Bottom on the Muskingum and burned their half-built blockhouse. Governor St. Clair called a tribal conference at Fort Harmar; he gave gifts and made a treaty, but the stubborn

Shawnees and Miamis stayed away. In the Miami country, above Cincinnati, war parties stole horses, ambushed surveyors and hunters and set fire to outlying farms. Fort Washington had been built at Cincinnati, with St. Clair making his headquarters there. In 1790 the makeshift frontier militia came down the Ohio in a fleet of flatboats. They mustered at Cincinnati for a wilderness campaign. The heart of Indian resistance was in the Maumee Valley, in northwestern Ohio, where British agents, still holding onto the fur trade, allied themselves with the tribes against American settlement.

General Josiah Harmar had a bright record in the Revolution. At Fort Washington, in September, 1790, he took command of an army of gangling boys and slouching men, riffraff collected from the streets and prisons of the Pennsylvania cities. They had poor equipment, little organization and no discipline at all. With this scarecrow outfit Harmar was ordered to punish the warriors of the Maumee Valley.

With a plodding pack train they trudged north in fine October weather, past the present locations of Xenia and Springfield and the site of the vanished Pickawillany on the Great Miami. They followed the old portage to the St. Marys River and found some Indian villages burned and abandoned on the Maumee. The army was in good spirits; it looked as though the tribes feared their presence and would not fight. Then, on a moonless night a hundred of Harmar's horses were stolen. Still the expedition could find no Indians, though that was soon to change.

As they were nearing Little Turtle's town, a few miles from present Fort Wayne, a storm of fire burst from the woods. The militia dropped their guns and ran. Little Turtle, with a hundred and fifty warriors, had routed Harmar's army. All that night one of the American officers, mired in a swamp, heard the cries of savages dancing around the bodies of dismembered soldiers.

Next day Harmar rallied his troops. He sent them back, across the fording place of the Maumee, to surround the Indian camp. Little Turtle was waiting in the woods. As the troops splashed into the water, they were struck with a rain of bullets. Men and horses piled up in the sluggish river. The rest fled, and the campaign was over. Harmar got his battered force together and headed back to Fort Washington, leaving the dead behind.

Bold with success, the Indians determined to hold off American settlement north of the Ohio. An intertribal resistance was organized by Little Turtle, along with the Shawnee Blue Jacket and the Delaware war chief Buckongahelas. They knew that another test was coming.

A year after Harmar's fiasco Governor St. Clair gathered a new expedition at Fort Washington. He had hoped to launch his campaign in August, but it was late September before his three thousand troops were assembled. This was a real invasion—scouts, soldiers, pack trains, wagon trains, even women camp-followers moving into Indian country. Under St. Clair's own leadership the force marched north. They built Fort Hamilton on the Great Miami (where young William Dean Howells fished and swam forty-five years later), and fifty miles farther north they built Fort Jefferson. St. Clair's troops were almost as undisciplined as Harmar's—one regiment deserted en masse, turning back toward the Ohio, and the commander had to send a company to the rear to protect his supply wagons from the defectors.

By the beginning of November St. Clair had advanced a hundred miles into savage country, though he was still fifty miles short of the Indian towns on the Maumee. November 3 was a chill gray day. A thin snow whitened the ground when they made a desolate camp on a headwater creek on the Wabash. That night they cooked supper over guttering fires and toasted their numb feet. The scouts saw no Indian sign; the army was cold and tired. As they rolled up in their blankets, no one knew that Little Turtle was throwing his warriors around them in the bare November woods.

In the gray daybreak the troops poked up their fires. They were rubbing stiff hands and getting out breakfast rations when a chorus of war whoops sounded. From all sides came the slam of rifle fire. St. Clair's army broke into hopeless confusion. Its only successful movement was a retreat to the newly hacked-out road. There, stung by Indian bullets, the troops threw down their arms and ran. Soon the road was strewn with guns, swords, haversacks, powder bags and ammunition pouches. For four miles the Indians chased them, with continuing slaughter. Then they dropped back to plunder the abandoned camp and round up its hundreds of oxen and horses. The Indians had lost sixty-six warriors while killing seven hundred of St. Clair's men. It was the worst disaster in U.S. military history until Custer's ambush on the Little Big Horn three generations later.

St. Clair's defeat became a dark legend on the border. For years men recalled how Little Turtle kept his warriors hidden till he was ready to give the stunning blow. How the gout-ridden old general had four horses shot at his side while an orderly was helping him into the saddle; eight rifle balls passed through St. Clair's clothing, they said, before he got onto a sway-backed old pack horse. How Jake Fowler saw an Indian squatting down to screen himself while reloading his musket: "I drew right at his butt and shot him through." How the fleeing men stumbled over dropped bayonets. How the captured white women, camp followers and wives of the militiamen, who hoped to live in the wilderness when the Indians were routed, had stakes driven through their bodies. How Red Head Nance outran six warriors who wanted her streaming hair. How another woman threw her baby into the snow and the Indians carried it to the Sandusky towns and raised it. How in the morning frost the scalped heads looked like "pumpkins in a cornfield in December." How young William Kennan leaped over a blowdown "to the height of eight or nine feet" in his flight from whooping pursuers. How William Wells, a white man who had been reared by Indians, tomahawked the wounded soldiers until he could no longer raise his arm. How an Indian trying to scalp the dying General Butler was shot by a surgeon who died soon after. For years frontiersmen sang the bloody ballad of "Sainclaire's Defeat":

Such a dreadful carnage may I never see again
As happened near St. Mary's, upon the river plain.

Back in Cincinnati with the remnant of his army, Governor St. Clair wrote an account of his defeat and submitted his resignation as military commander in the West, though retaining the office of territorial governor. That winter he went to Philadelphia to report to the committee assigned to investigate the failure of his campaign. Meanwhile the Indians kept up a pressure on the chain of posts he had left in the Miami Valley, attacking cattle guards and parties of militiamen and intercepting supply lines of pack-horse and wagon trains.

To General Anthony Wayne, whose name shone with luster from his victories in the Revolution, were entrusted the defenses of the frontier. In June, 1792, he arrived at Fort Pitt and took command of the riffraff gathered there. To escape the distractions of the rowdy settlement, he moved them twenty miles downriver to "Legionville," where the men were set to felling timber and building their own barracks. It was a foretaste of life in the wilds. Here he molded the motley troops into a disciplined army of four divisions. In April, with a substantial commissary department of draft animals, wagons, stores and ammunition, he took his force down the Ohio in a great fleet of flatboats. They debarked at Cincinnati when Wayne's junior officers, including young William Henry Harrison, polished off their training—the handling of arms, taking of cover, shooting of targets through the tangled woods. At evening quarts of whisky were awarded the best marksmen of the day. Meanwhile an armed force was cutting a road, Wayne's Trace, which has become U.S. 127, seventy-five miles north to the site of present Greenville. There in October they built Fort Greene Ville, spacious and strong in a big clearing on Greenville Creek. It was a halfway point between Cincinnati and the Indian towns on the Maumee.

All winter Wayne drilled his army here in the disputed land. He spared neither men nor ammunition, loading and firing, loading and firing. Every trooper must be a marksman who could charge his muzzle-loader on a dead run through tangled country.

"Old Hoss" Wayne had gout and rheumatism, but he also had determination. He meant to end the border warfare.

In December Wayne sent a company twenty-three miles north to the site of St. Clair's defeat two years earlier. They arrived on Christmas Day and found the ground littered with skeletons and skulls. They buried the remains and built on the site of St. Clair's disaster a stronghold called Fort Recovery. When a war party attempted to storm the fort a few months later, they were beaten off with heavy Indian losses.

To his army Wayne added a corps of scouts, men who had lived among the Indians, who knew the savage tongues and stratagems, who could spy out the tribal moods and movements. The chief of these woodsmen was Williams Wells, the white "Indian" who had tomahawked St. Clair's wounded until his arm was limp and who was said to have commanded three hundred warriors in the battle. Now Wells was changing sides; he had come to Wayne's headquarters, offering his services as scout and interpreter. To his shrewd mind came the surmise that the Indians had won their last victory; he did not choose to be a loser.

Wells was one of those border men—like the notorious white renegades Antoine Lasselle, Simon Girty, Alexander McKee and Matthew Elliott—who lived two lives. He knew all the disputed country and could see it as both a savage and a white man. At the age of eleven he had been stolen, with two brothers, from his home near Louisville by a band of raiding warriors. He had been reared by the Miamis, in their chief town on the Maumee. As a boy he had been used to decoy settlers' boats ashore, calling out that he was lost in the woods, and then joining in the Indian murder and plunder. Little Turtle liked the sturdy white youth and adopted him. Since then Wells had grown to manhood and had married Little Turtle's pretty daughter, Sweet Breeze. He became a valuable interpreter in frontier councils and a savage fighter of white men in the wars. He was with Little Turtle in the defeats of both Harmar and St. Clair.

After his butchering of St. Clair's wounded, Wells is said to have had pangs of remorse which led to a change of partisanship. He told Little Turtle that he wanted to fight on the white man's side, pointing skyward and saying he would leave the Indians for the whites when the sun passed the topmost bough of a tree overhead. According to tradition his foster-father and father-in-law wished him well in his new allegiance. It was still a mixed-up warfare.

Amid the massive movement of Wayne's army against the tribes there occurred odd personal dramas, stranger than any fiction. In June, 1794, Wayne sent his spies into Indian country to bring back a tribesman for questioning. Three scouts, Wells, Robert McClellan and Henry Miller trekked together to the Auglaize River. These were three storied men. McClellan was a Pennsylvanian who had taken to the wilderness. He amazed the Indians with his swiftness of foot and his ability to leap over any barrier, even a canvas-covered wagon, in his way. His later fortunes took him to Oregon; he figures in some dramatic episodes in Washington Irving's *Astoria*. Henry Miller, like William Wells, had been captured by Indians in his youth, along with his younger brother Christopher. The two grew up as Indian boys, and when in his early twenties Henry Miller determined to go back to his own people in Kentucky, his brother chose to stay among the tribesmen. Henry Miller had changed over; now he was a white man scouting for General Wayne.

On the Auglaize River, going softly in Indian country, the three scouts came upon a small camp above a creek bed. Screened by the leaves of a fallen tree, they crept near and saw three Indians feasting on fresh venison. While they watched, two of the Indians got up to replenish their fire. In an exchange of signs the scouts agreed that Wells and Miller would shoot the standing Indians and the swift McClellan would race in and catch the seated man. At the bang of rifles the two Indians fell and the third one bounded toward the river. Hearing McClellan behind him, the savage leaped into the creek bed, where he sank to his waist.

McClellan sprang after him, and the two were struggling in the water when Wells and Miller arrived. They dragged the two men out and made the Indian a captive. He refused to speak. When they washed the war paint from him they found they had a white prisoner—who still would make no sound. On the way back to headquarters Henry Miller, on a sudden impulse, spoke to the captive by his brother's Indian name. Startled, the man responded, and Henry and Christopher Miller went in to Fort Greene Ville side by side. Wayne questioned the prisoner about Indian intentions and then released him, at the request of the scouts who had brought him in. When they persuaded Christopher Miller to remain at the fort, Wayne had another scout in his corps.

That summer, 1794, two companies of horsemen arrived from Kentucky under Colonel William Clark, a younger brother of George Rogers Clark, the conqueror of Illinois. He joined Wayne's staff, and so became a colleague of a young ensign, Meriwether Lewis, from Virginia. Theirs would be a long and famous friendship.

Late in July Wayne moved his main army north on a zigzag course into the Maumee country. Ten days later they camped at the junction of three rivers, the Auglaize, the Tiffin and the Maumee, on the site of present Defiance, Ohio. They found the Indian towns abandoned. While Wayne was raising the big walls of Fort Defiance, scouts brought word that painted warriors were gathering farther down the Maumee, where a recent windstorm had left a swath of fallen timber which would hamper Wayne's cavalry.

On the 20th of August Wayne sent his troops against the enemy. The morning was overcast and rainy. Through wet woods rose the whoops of warriors and the bang of musket fire. Wayne hurled his men, wave after wave, into the broken timber, charging the crouching tribesmen with bullet and bayonet. It was a brief, furious and decisive contest. After a year of preparation came one hour of combat before the Indians broke into flight.

The Battle of Fallen Timbers was won, and with it the heartland of America.

In November Wayne brought his army back to Fort Greene Ville. They wintered there, and received the humbled chiefs who asked for terms of peace. Wayne announced a general treaty council to be held that summer. At the appointed time the tribesmen came in, over the deer trails and the hunting paths and the newly slashed army traces, from the Wabash, the Maumee and the shores of the Great Lakes, pitching their camps on the stumpland around Fort Greene Ville. Eleven hundred of them had assembled when the council fire was kindled on the 16th of June.

For seven weeks the chiefs and the American officers negotiated in the log council-house. Outside, the warriors feasted on army beans, bread and molasses, with a frequent ration of whisky. (It cost the United States ten cents a day to feed an Indian at a congress.) They danced in the firelight, gambled with locust seeds, held running and jumping contests with the troops, raced ponies over the stumpland. In the council house the logs smoldered night and day, but for the tribes it was a dying fire.

Around the council ring there were long preliminary speeches, smoking, the giving of presents. Said Wayne: "I have this day kindled the council fire of the United States; we will now cover it up and keep it alive until the remainder of the tribes assemble. . . . In the meantime we will have a little refreshment to wash the dust from our throats. We will on this occasion be merry, but without passing the bounds of temperance and sobriety." That night the fires leaped up in the camps and dancers stamped to the beat of savage drums.

Each day in the fine June weather new chiefs arrived: Buckongahelas with his Delaware warriors, Tarhe the Crane, Keeper of the Calumet of the Wyandots; Bad Bird, with his party of Chippewas; Blue Jacket, the white man who had become a chief of the Shawnees; New Corn, with his feathered braves from Lake Michigan; and Little Turtle, at the head of ninety-five warriors representing the Miami tribes from the Eel River to

Kaskaskia. The Fourth of July Wayne observed with a thunder of fifteen cannon, the raising of flags and the delivery of a lengthy sermon by a Welsh chaplain, the Reverend Morgan Rhys. Interpreters passed it on to the assembled tribesmen.

Then negotiations began. Day after day the white men presented their position, recounting past treaties and payments for Indian lands. The chiefs made long oratorical replies, with the interpreter repeating sentence by sentence; William Wells was the chief translator there. Some days were allotted for Indian discussion among themselves, and there were days of "no council" for sports and feasting.

The most eloquent address was heard July 22, when Little Turtle stood above the smoldering council ring. In paint, beads and feathers, with sunlight slanting on his tattooed body, he recalled the spacious lands of his fathers and—scooping up a handful of earth—the shrunken tribal grounds. Once they had been a populous nation; shaking the seeds in a locust pod he indicated how their numbers had dwindled. Yet there had been no legal surrender of their country.

The chiefs brought no maps of forest and plain, of lakes and rivers to the council, but they carried the whole heartland in their minds. Little Turtle swept an arm from north to south. "It is well known by all my brothers present that my forefather kindled the first fire at Detroit; from thence he extended his lines to the headwaters of the Scioto; from thence to its mouth; from thence down the Ohio to the mouth of the Wabash; and from thence to Lake Michigan. . . . I have now informed you of the boundaries of the Miami nation where the Great Spirit placed my forefathers a long time ago, and charged him not to sell or part with his lands, but to preserve them for his posterity."

It was a fine speech but a futile one; it changed nothing. The Americans were bound to get what they wanted; and what they did not want in 1795, they would want, and acquire, later.

On August 3 the treaty was ready. Covering two sheets of parchment as big as a cabin door, it was signed by eighty Indian chiefs and agents (each chief made his mark) and by Anthony Wayne and twenty-five members of his staff. In the council house the fire died to ashes and the chiefs went home to their diminished lands. The treaty had transferred to the United States twenty-five thousand square miles of territory—the southern two-thirds of present Ohio—and along with it sixteen separate tracts "in order to provide for that convenient intercourse which will be beneficial to both parties" at strategic points on the interior lakes and rivers. In return the Indians were given $20,000 in goods (one-sixth of a cent an acre) and an annuity of $9,500 in articles of trade to be divided among the twelve tribes. Eight months after the council fire went out, settlers were chopping clearings along Greenville Creek. They burned the empty fort to get iron nails and hinges for their cabins.

While settlement poured into the Ohio Valley, Little Turtle lived with his two wives—one, weathered and wrinkled, the other, a comely Miami girl—at his home near present Fort Wayne in a frame house which the U.S. Government built for him. He had other official gifts: a fine horse and a Negro slave from Kentucky. He had resisted strenuously; now he accepted the facts of history and became the white man's friend. Nearby lived his son-in-law and recent adversary, William Wells, who served as Indian Agent at Fort Wayne. It was a pleasant country, with seasonal flocks of pigeons and wild turkeys and rich soil for pumpkins and Indian corn. The old chief was fond of good eating and before 1800 he was suffering from gout, a white man's disease. This and a personal annuity from the United States Government kept him from working, though he urged his tribesmen to take up agriculture. He could sit on his porch at sunset and think kindly of the white men.

One of Little Turtle's good friends was an erect, firmly handsome man with a weathered face and iron-gray hair—Colonel John Johnston, Indian factor at Fort Wayne. Born in Ballyshannon, Ireland, of Scotch-Irish Huguenot people, Johnston had first come to Ohio as a seventeen-year-old wagon driver for

Wayne's army. After the Battle of Fallen Timbers he returned to Philadelphia, but in 1802 he was back in the West, having ridden horseback over the mountains with his young Quaker bride. At Fort Wayne he built up the frontier's largest fur post, buying great quantities of deer, fox and muskrat skins from Indians on the upper Wabash. As the game decreased, Johnston hoped to turn the tribes to farming. When the Pennsylvania Quakers sent "farming missionaries" to teach the Indians agriculture, he distributed seeds, hoes, plows, hogs, horses and cattle, and provided land for demonstration farms. One of the missionaries, zealous young Philip Dennis, cleared and fenced a field on the Wabash and proceeded to demonstrate. A row of young braves took seats on the fence and watched with close interest while the white man toiled and sweated. But when they got down, it was only to lie in the shade. For centuries Indian men had refused to work in the fields, and they were not ready to begin now. Missionary Dennis left the Wabash before his crops were visible.

Little Turtle blamed the Indian laziness on whisky, which he occasionally enjoyed himself. He asked President Jefferson to curb the liquor trade and to send a blacksmith who could mend axes, hoes and guns. Chief Black Hoof, speaking for the Shawnees, proposed some agricultural advantages for his people. Telling the President that they lived in a bad place for farming, he asked for "a good piece of land where we may raise good grain and cut hay for our cattle." He had a tract in mind and he described it—running from Logan County, Ohio, to the mouth of the Wabash; it comprised some millions of acres. This request was denied, but the Pennsylvania Society of Friends furnished the Shawnees with a gristmill and sawmill and some cattle and farm tools. The yearly meeting of Friends in Ireland sent £150 to provide the tribe with farming equipment, and an elderly lady in Cork sent a personal gift of £100 for plows, hoes and hayrakes. Still the Indians could not get interested in tilling the soil.

In 1797, dressed in white man's clothes, Little Turtle made a visit to the President in Philadelphia, accompanied by his son-in-law Captain William Wells. There he enjoyed some good meals, was inoculated for smallpox and met the visiting French philosopher Volney, who made a vocabulary of the Miami language and published it in his *Travels*. Little Turtle also had an interview with the Polish-American patriot Thaddeus Kosciusko, who gave him a pair of pistols and some belated advice: "Shoot dead the first man who comes to subjugate you or to despoil you of your country."

A year later Little Turtle visited President John Adams and urged control of liquor traffic among the Indians, and in 1807 he made a final trip to the capital to ask the President for a flour mill at Fort Wayne.

Old and crippled and disregarded by his tribe, which was swayed by the war talk of Tecumseh, the chief of the Miamis died in the home of his daughter, Mrs. William Wells, in 1812. One of his grandsons, Wayne Wells, was graduated from West Point in 1821.

The chief's son-in-law, William Wells, who had gone over to the white man's side at the right time, amassed a small fortune. In addition to his salary as Indian Agent, he received a lifetime pension and generous land grants. Among other lands, he came into possession of 1,160 acres along the Miami River, including the site of Fort Pickawillany, where Old Britain was butchered by the French Indians half a century before. Wells was dismissed as Indian Agent in 1809, when the $350 annuity for the Eel River tribe stuck to his hands. Still he died a hero, in the massacre at Fort Dearborn, during the frontier's dark summer of 1812.

6. Eschicagau—The Lonely Station

Of the sixteen "isolated tracts" which the tribes surrendered in the Treaty of Greene Ville, number 14 was "one piece six miles square at the mouth of the Chickago River on Lake Michigan." It was a lonely place, alternately swept by wind and snow and seared by the long summer sunlight. Occasionally some Indians came down the lake, their canoes tossing, and paddled up the sluggish river between its fields of marsh grass and wild onion. Gulls cried overhead and the lake made its timeless lamentation on the shore. James Monroe had taken a dim look at the country before the forming of the Northwest Territory, and he wrote to Thomas Jefferson: "A great part of the territory is miserably poor, especially that near Lakes Erie and Michigan, and that upon the Mississippi and the Illinois consists of extensive plains which have not had from appearances, and will not have, a single bush on them for ages." Now Monroe's name marks a street in the heart of the Chicago Loop.

After the Greene Ville treaty nothing was done with the cession at the mouth of the Chicago River. The lake surged upon the sand under the high June skies and the April fogs and the knife-edge of the January wind, with one man there to watch the seasons pass. This first proprietor of Chicago has become one of the region's legends. He was a handsome Negro named Baptiste Point du Sable, a native of sunny San Domingo who according to tradition had wandered up the Mississippi and built a trading post where the Indians passed into the Onion River from Lake Michigan. A less romantic account says he was a runaway slave from Lexington, Kentucky—the first of the multitude to escape to Chicago from the color-bondage of the South.

Du Sable lived with an Indian woman and kept a stock of trade goods, a few traps and blankets and ten big barrels of rum. If one accepts Jefferson's view that "virtue has her seat in thinly populated places," this solitary man should have been a paragon. Actually he was his own best customer, as were many traders who kept a stock of rum; he caroused with all the Indians who passed up the Onion River, which they called Eschicagau. It is said that he wanted to become chief of the Potawatomis.

Transfer of the river mouth to the United States made no difference to Du Sable; he was unaware of it. But he was a restless man, and about the year 1800 he wandered away from Chicago and never came back. The next season a half-breed trader found his empty house and moved in. Within a few seasons four other men settled nearby. One was the famous John Kinzie, a native of Quebec who grew up in Detroit, where he had learned the Indian trade. Another was Antoine Ouilmette, a scrawny, illiterate French Canadian who made a living by carrying baggage over the portage. The third and fourth were footloose farmers, named Burns and Lee. These were the proprietors of lonely Eschicagau.

In the summer of 1803, while Lewis and Clark were organizing their great expedition to Oregon, the sloop *Tracey*, ninety tons, loaded a cargo of supplies and building materials at Detroit and sailed for the West. A month later, after passing the Straits of Mackinac, the vessel anchored off the sand-barred Chicago River. At the same time a company of forty men marched overland from Detroit to the Lake Michigan shore. Their mission was to build a fort at the Chicago river mouth. Work began, under Captain John Whistler, on the fourth day of July.

Captain Whistler had come a long way to this lonely place. Born in Ireland of English parents, he had run away from home to join the British army; soon he was en route to America with Burgoyne's troops. He served in the force that was defeated and captured at Saratoga. That sorry campaign might have soured him on America, but after return to England and discharge from the army, he eloped with a high-spirited girl and brought her to the new United States. In 1791 he joined the American army, serving with Wayne in the Indian campaign that preceded the Treaty of Greene Ville. Now, in the summer of 1803, he was directing construction of Fort Dearborn.

Axes thudded in the woods on the north fork of the Chicago and logs were floated in the sluggish current to the river mouth. The *Tracey*, anchored off the shallow shore, discharged cargo by boats, men heaping boxes, bales, barrels, along with piles of brick and three light cannon, on the sand. This activity drew a crowd of Potawatomis, who watched while the troops raised a row of tents along the shore and the huge "canoe with wings" sailed over the horizon, bound back to Detroit.

By September the fort was taking shape—a palisade of pointed logs, with two blockhouses at diagonal corners, enclosing a parade ground, officers' quarters, barracks and a brick fire-resistant magazine. Captain Whistler had prepared a scale plan of the fort, a drawing with an artist's shading and design. (Sixty years later a portrait by his grandson, James McNeill Whistler, who had left West Point for the studios of Paris and London, was delivered in an armored wagon to the Chicago Art Institute on the lake front.) They built a palisade and got a blockhouse up that first fall. They dragged one of their cannon up the ramp and lashed it at a porthole under the peaked roof. The flag fluttered over the parade where the troops mustered at bugle call. A timbered gate opened in the south wall of the stockade; from the north side an underground passage led to the riverbank. The fort stood on a slight mound near the present Rush Street bridge; at that time the river channel turned sharply southward, paralleling the lake shore, and emptied into the lake where Grant Park has been formed. Just west of the fort was built a log Agency House for Indian trade goods.

Directly across the river was the house of Baptiste Point du Sable, occupied in 1803 by a half-breed trader named Le Mai. In the spring of 1804 came trader John Kinzie with his family. He bought the house, enlarged it, and set out a row of poplar trees on the riverbank. This was the "Kinzie Mansion" whose doors were open to all travelers. A rope ferry crossed the river from the fort to Kinzie's landing. John Kinzie was already a veteran trader, known to most of the Indians between Lake Huron and the Mississippi. He made the Chicago post the center of his business, which included trading stations on the Illinois and Kankakee rivers.

Behind Kinzie's place were the scattered cabins of half-breed Ouilmette and farmers Burns and Lee. Antoine Ouilmette had some small trade with the Indians, and he hired out, with his strapping Potawatomi wife, to other traders, hauling their cargoes over the portage from the Chicago River to the Des Plaines. In a treaty twenty years later Mrs. Ouilmette was allotted a tract of land fourteen miles north of the river. It became the Wilmette Reservation, and eventually the site of suburban Wilmette. Farmers Burns and Lee sold some grain and vegetables to the quartermaster at the fort.

Life at Fort Dearborn was pure monotony. Out of the lake rose the sun; it set over the prairie. The soldiers had some close-order drill; then they were detailed to work in the fields and gardens. For diversion they shot ducks and muskrats in the marshes. The flag came down at sunset. Tattoo in the starlight was followed by taps. The last bugle note faded, the candles went dark and there was only the wash of water on the shore.

Somewhere beyond the empty horizon, things happened, there

were new voices and new faces, men talked about events and the changing times. Here the talk was about the trader's whisky, the rank Kickapoo women, mosquitoes and the Des Plaines swamps, the mud at the portage. Sometimes a band of Indians passed up or down the river. Occasionally there were visits from Little Turtle or his son-in-law William Wells, Indian Agent at Fort Wayne, the nearest military station. When the visitors were gone, Fort Dearborn seemed outside the world.

Once a year a schooner came from Detroit with pork, flour, beans, soap, salt, vinegar, candles and army-issue clothing, and with news of the world. For weeks men stared across the water. In that lonely place they had an obsession; they could not keep their gaze from the empty lake and sky where someday a sail would grow up on the horizon, or some night a glimmer of lights, like the Pleiades, would swim in the darkness. They checked off days on their hand-made calendars, waiting for the schooner. At last a speck appeared on the spring-blue water. It grew, took a vessel's shape and substance, and men lining the shore could hear the clank of anchor chain and the halloo of voices. Boats put out and boats pulled ashore, bringing newspapers, mail, word of the world outside. For a week the beautiful schooner lay offshore, boats shuttling back and forth discharging commissary goods and loading the season's peltry. Then she was gone, fading to a fly-speck on the skyline or a wink of light in the darkness.

In the early 1800's the U.S. Army totaled some six thousand men, and these were less American than English, Irish and German. Most recruits were penniless immigrants, fugitives and drifters who for five dollars a month took up the harsh, monotonous life of the frontier garrisons. After a study of fifty-five men in one company an army surgeon reported: "Nine tenths enlisted on account of some female difficulty, 13 of them had changed their names, and 43 were either drunk or partially so at the time of their enlistment." They dressed in blue regimentals, soon faded, and wore their hair in pigtails tied with a greasy thong. More than half were illiterate. Some had enlisted for free transportation to the West, planning to desert at the first chance. Drunkenness was frequent, though it was punished by fifty lashes on the bare back. Recovered deserters were given six months of hard labor with ball and chain.

Winter was the bleak time at Fort Dearborn. Ice far out on the lake, a raw wind, a gray scud of clouds over the prairie. From November to April the post was isolated. No traders, no messengers on the trail, no migrant Indians. The night wind brought the howling of wolves and the grumble of drift ice on the shore. Yet in this desolation twenty-two-year-old Surgeon Isaac Van Voorhis walked the prairie with long thoughts and dreams. "In my solitary walks I contemplate what a great and powerful republic will yet arise in this new world. Here, I say, will be the seat of millions yet unborn; here the asylum of oppressed millions yet to come"—as though he looked beyond the huddled shacks and blackened Indian camp sites and saw the towers of Michigan Avenue against the prairie sky.

In 1810 Captain Whistler was transferred to Detroit, and Captain Nathan Heald arrived from Fort Wayne to take command of Fort Dearborn. On furlough he had spent the winter in New England, and the next spring he stopped in Kentucky to marry Rebekah Wells, the niece of Captain William Wells, with whom Heald had served at Fort Wayne. They were married in May, and their wedding journey was a brisk horseback trip over the spring prairies to Chicago. They traveled by compass over the grasslands and made good time, six days on the way. Rebekah Heald was a sturdy, spirited girl who, like her "Indian uncle," took naturally to the wilderness. She liked the wild and lonely post of Fort Dearborn.

Even to remote Chicago came a sense of Indian unrest in 1811. Reports drifted in of two Shawnee brothers, Tecumseh and the Prophet, who had set up a camp at Greene Ville. The Prophet, a gaunt one-eyed man of religious eloquence, exhorted hundreds of visiting tribesmen, urging them to renounce the white man's ways, his guns, traps, clothing and whisky, and resume their

primitive dress, hunting and warfare; this return to tribal past
was the "open door" to a recovery of their lost power and
possessions. Meanwhile his brother Tecumseh, "Shooting Star,"
was calling for a military alliance of the tribes to throw off the
bondage of the whites and drive them out of the country. Symbolic of their purpose, the brothers had built their village at
Greene Ville, on the white man's side of the Treaty Line. Day
and night drums throbbed on the Mud Creek prairie as the fanati-
cal Prophet passed among the Shawnees, Miamis, Ottawas,
Wyandots, Chippewas, Potawatomis. The brothers shared an
effective collaboration, Tecumseh rousing patriotism and the
Prophet stirring savage superstitions.

After repeated warnings from the government they moved
their noisy camp a hundred miles west, to the mouth of Tippecanoe Creek, halfway up the Wabash. For them it was a good
location, midway between the American post of Vincennes and
British Fort Amherstburg on the Detroit River, and within fifty
miles of the chief Miami, Potawatomi and Ottawa towns. Tippecanoe had been successively the site of Miami, Shawnee and
Potawatomi villages. It was a nice illustration of Tecumseh's
concept that the Indians shared their ancestral lands, which therefore could not be sold or surrendered except by all the tribes in
concert. Now the new town of Tippecanoe became the center of
Indian unrest.

Every season since the Treaty of Greene Ville settlement was
growing in the Ohio valley, and each year Territorial Governor
William Henry Harrison was negotiating new surrenders of
forest and prairie.

The winning of the West was a heartless business—to be accomplished by peace and war, by treaty and trade, by keeping
a constant pressure on the tribes. Even the high-minded Jefferson
was an imperialist as he looked toward the western country. His
confidential instructions to Governor Harrison are realistic to a
point of cynicism. "Live in perpetual peace with the Indians. . . .
We shall push our trading houses and be glad to see the good

and influential individuals among them run into debt. . . . When these goods get beyond what the individuals can pay, they will be willing to lop them off . . . by a cession of lands."

America was impatient. The new nation coveted, without waiting, all the Indian lands east of the Mississippi. Harrison had his orders and he executed them, fifteen great land cessions in a term of twelve years. In 1803 he summoned the Illinois tribesmen, now reduced by whisky and disease, and for an amount of $400 the United States acquired a sweep of land from the Ohio River to Lake Michigan. The next year he bought off the Delaware and the Piankeshaw chiefs, giving an amount of $300 and some farm animals for a tract from the Falls of the Ohio to the mouth of the Wabash. A few months later he was in St. Louis, bargaining for the huge country between the Illinois, Wisconsin and Mississippi rivers. In Vincennes in the dog days of August, 1805, he met some old friends, Chief Little Turtle, Indian Agent Wells, chiefs Buckongahelas and Winamac, and bought the land from the Ohio boundary to the Falls (Louisville). Special gifts of silk shawls, felt hats and a tooled leather saddle accompanied their deal for the last Indian lands on the Ohio. During his first five years in office young William Henry Harrison acquired from the bewildered and divided chiefs the southern half of Indiana, southern Wisconsin and all of Illinois. Further cessions, after the War of 1812, would complete the American claim to Indiana. The intertribal movement, with its capital at Tippecanoe, had come too late. By 1811 the Indians were demoralized and white invasion was massive and irresistible. Yet it was an inevitable, instinctive struggle of a doomed people.

All along the frontier acts of violence began. White men's horses were stolen, surveyors were ambushed, outlying farms went up in smoke. In April, 1811, a surly band of Winnebagos appeared at a farm on the south branch of the Chicago River. They killed and mutilated two white men who had been growing garden crops for the garrison at Fort Dearborn. The marauders got away, and at Chicago the Kinzie family moved into Fort

Dearborn for protection. The twelve civilian men in the settlement formed a militia. It was an uneasy season. From across the Detroit River British agents were providing the Indians with arms and ammunition. To hold the West, America had six frontier forts, each garrisoned with less than a hundred men. Against these isolated posts the Indians could throw several thousand warriors; if the tribes were joined by British troops, the forts could not stand.

Then, in the fall of 1811, came news of Tippecanoe. William Henry Harrison with a thousand troops had moved against the tribes on the upper Wabash. He had engaged the Indians in a brief, decisive battle. The savages withdrew from the battleground, and after salvaging six wagonloads of corn, Harrison burned their town. Then, while the best of his troops were ordered to Detroit, Harrison returned down the Wabash to Vincennes. The frontier was still defenseless.

Pioneer settlers in the West appealed to the government for action. They wanted to crush the Indians and to curb the British power. Though the East was reluctant, war was declared on June 18, 1812. The news reached remote Chicago three weeks later. It was brought not by a military messenger but by a roving half-breed.

General William Hull, governor of Michigan Territory, was given command of the Army of the Northwest to launch an invasion of Canada. He remained inactive, believing that Detroit was imperiled by British control of the Lakes. His fears seemed confirmed when two Chippewas came with stunning news from the north: the British had captured Fort Mackinac. Fort Dearborn was doomed; there were no wagon roads west of Detroit, and at Mackinac the British were astride the water route to the West. Hull sent an Indian runner to Fort Dearborn with orders for Captain Heald to abandon the post and retire to Fort Wayne. Then Hull looked fearfully at his own position. He was threatened from the north by British Indians and from the south by Tecumseh's warriors. A British army under bold General

Isaac Brock was pushing west from Niagara. At their threat of attack General Hull surrendered his troops, his fortified post of Detroit and the entire Michigan Territory.

It was the 16th day of August, 1812, when the American flag came down at Detroit. That same day saw the burning of abandoned Fort Dearborn.

Hull's orders to Captain Heald instructed him to destroy all arms and ammunition and to give the supplies in the Agency House to friendly Indians who would escort the Americans to Fort Wayne. The Potawatomi chiefs were glad to receive the trade goods and to provide the escort. Captain Heald began the loading of baggage wagons and the dumping of guns, powder and rum in the shallow river. With these acts of helplessness he must have felt the vastness and hostility of the country.

When Hull's orders reached Fort Wayne, Captain William Wells started for Fort Dearborn with thirty Miami tribesmen to assist Heald in his evacuation and help him get his people through a hundred and fifty miles of Indian country. He arrived at Chicago on August 13. The next morning Commandant Heald delivered to the local Potawatomis food and trade goods—chiefly blankets, broadcloth, calicoes and strouding—which he could not transport. The Indian demands for ammunition and liquor were refused. An old Potawatomi chief warned Heald that he had heard ominous bird song, and that his young warriors were out of control. But Heald could only go on with his evacuation.

On the morning of August 15 the wagons were loaded, and soldiers, traders, farmers and their families were packing personal belongings. It was a hot clear summer day. The gates opened and the wagon train rolled out. Wells and his mounted Miamis led the procession, then came the garrison troops pacing beside the baggage wagons, then the walking women and children and the dozen civilian militia. They followed the sand beach (on the course of present Michigan Avenue). Near them on the sand and along the dunes moved the escort of seemingly friendly Potawatomis. Trader John Kinzie was pacing beside the baggage wagons, though he had sent his wife and children to St. Joseph by boat. He had been warned of Indian treachery.

The motley file splashed over the sand bar at the river mouth and crunched onto the smooth beach beyond. Here for several miles the shore was treeless; the Grand Prairie met the great lake. However, the sea of grass was separated from the sea of water by a long ridge of sand. One by one the escorting Potawatomis slipped over the ridge. Behind the creaking train Indians were already plundering the fort and shooting the garrison cattle. The procession kept near the western edge, where the sand was hard enough to carry the wagons. The file had lengthened now, straggling over the beach.

After a mile's progress Wells with his advance warriors saw a knot of Potawatomis crouched behind a hummock ragged with dune grass. As he was warning Captain Heald, a row of heads showed along the ridge. From the dunes came a chorus of rifle fire, and whooping Indians rushed upon the baggage wagons. The massacre was swift and violent—gunfire, war whoops, the thud of tomahawks and bayonets. In a few minutes the farmers and traders were dead—Trader Kinzie was the only surviving civilian—and the Indians were clubbing women and children. One of them was Mrs. Heald's colored servant Cicely; she saw her infant son (either half white or half Indian) tomahawked by a frenzied young Potawatomi who had climbed onto a wagonload of children, where he slaughtered all but one.

Captain Wells's Miami warriors were already galloping toward Fort Wayne; they did not stay to fight. But Wells was in the eye of the battle. After a few fierce minutes at the head of the line he turned back toward the women and children. He was already wounded when a bullet struck his horse. The animal fell, pinning Wells to the sand. There he loaded his musket and felled an approaching Indian. But there were others coming. The next shot ended the life of a man who fought both for and against his own people. Now his name marks one of the streets which form the Chicago Loop.

In fifteen minutes the trampled beach was strewn with dead and dying. Captain Heald with his regulars now stood on high ground where the Potawatomis could not surprise him. Satisfied for the time, they sent word by a half-breed interpreter, offering to spare the survivors if the troops would surrender. Heald had no choice, and he and his men were led as captives past the gruesome wagons. At the fort he found his young wife sobbing amid a circle of Indian women. That night the Americans lay in the Indian camp beside the river while the savages, men and women, held an orgy of plunder and torture. Next morning the fort was set on fire. As smoke streamed up to the summer sky the Potawatomis scattered over the prairie. They left fifty-three mutilated bodies, twelve of them children, on the gashed and trampled shore.

One of the surviving women was the seventeen-year-old wife of young Lieutenant Helm; another was Mrs. Heald. In later years both gave accounts of the tragedy. Mrs. Helm told the story to Juliette Kinzie, who included it in her famous book *Waubun;* Mrs. Heald gave it to her son Darius Heald, who recorded it in a vivid narrative.

Some of the survivors were taken to Indian camps on the Kankakee and Illinois rivers; others were delivered to the British at Detroit as prisoners of war. At Chicago remained Antoine Ouilmette and his Indian wife. He was considered more Potawatomi than white man and he had never been in danger. Now he was sole proprietor of the place—the charred walls of the fort, the empty pasture, the blackened circles of the Indian camp.

In sun and rain and snow the bones of the slaughtered lay on the shore while the unmarked seasons passed. It seemed that Chicago had had its brief and violent history. Meanwhile, in a slow reversal of fortunes, General Harrison made his toilsome march from the Ohio to the Maumee, Oliver H. Perry at last swept the British from Lake Erie, the American army established a beachhead across the Detroit River and Tecumseh, wearing the uniform of a British general, was killed in the Battle of the

Thames. That ended Indian resistance.

Four years after the Chicago massacre, when peace had been concluded and American authority again embraced the heartland, a company of United States troops came to rebuild Fort Dearborn. They gathered some remains and buried them beside the river. Among them were the bones of Ike Van Voorhis, the young surgeon from New York who had watched the sunrise over the empty prairie of Eschicagau and had dreamed of its future.

II

THE COMING
OF THE
PEOPLE

*Let them come by thousands and tens of thousands.
They will find rich lands and good water.*

—ILLINOIS CENTRAL RAILROAD PAMPHLET

7.
Simon Kenton's Prisoner

It was spring in the Miami country, the creeks brim full of water and dogwoods white in the underforest, when the big battered man came home, sitting easy in the saddle while his shrewd gray eyes gathered it all in—the new cabins and the new clearings, the new mill hunched beside the creek, the new roofs of Urbana showing through the unleafed trees. In the shadow of the cabin he pulled off the saddle and his old blanket and some gear, and turned Cap into the snake-fenced pasture. Then he looked again, sharply, toward the growing town.

He had been a long way off from Ohio—the Seminole camps, perhaps, or out in the Osage country beyond the big slow river, or down in the Cherokee hills of Tennessee. But he walked in the cabin door like a man just back from the neighbors' or the mill.

"Well-with-thee, Betsy," he said in his soft voice, over his shoulder, and if his young wife was surprised in any way, it did not show. He was a coming-and-going man.

"You're in good time for supper, Simon," and she poured

101

another gourd of cracked corn into the blackened kettle.

He leaned a bundle of switches in the corner, and his long rifle beside them. Pear whips, they appeared to Elizabeth Kenton, watching from the fireplace, and so he had been somewhere south, to Kentuck, or farther, over the Big Stone Gap and the Blue Wall to Carolina. She would get those whips into the ground, and by the time the buds were swelling, he might talk a little—about lands he had studied and places he had seen and people who had shared their fire with him on winter nights. But now the children came tumbling in, Matilda lugging little Mary and Lizbeth rocking to her mother.

He fumbled in his plunder, finding a piece of ribbon for Matilda and a feather, green as April, for the baby, and while small Lizbeth watched from her mother's skirts, he took something from his sagging powder bag. A bright beaded bracelet with a tinkling bell, it made a tiny music as he held it to the child.

"A pretty!" cried her mother. "A pretty for Lizbeth!" and the child crept out.

There stood in the middle of the room a big round maple stump, still rooted, solid as an anvil and hollowed by the pounding of hominy. When he laid the bracelet on that worn table, the child put out a hand. A minute later she was shaking the little bell and reaching for his tangled hair, while he rumbled, "Well-with-thee! Well-with-thee, wee one!"

Then, suddenly remembering, she cried, "High up!" and he swung her to his shoulder. Her hand, jingling now, held to his craggy head, finding a hollow he had carried from a Shawnee tomahawk in a time before she, or even her mother, had been born.

A scarred and dented man with a craggy face and a gentle far-off smile had come home, this spring of 1810, to the budding woods and green barrens of Champaign County. Word went through the town, to Colonel Ward and Joseph Vance at their surveyors' table, to Will Fyffe in his dusty saddler's shop, to

Mark Norman in his smithy, to Major Moore, Ezekiel Arrowsmith and George Fithian in the dusky tavern room. *Simon Kenton is back.* It went across the fields to the Indian camps, pitched on Kenton's land, or what had been his land before the surveys and the sorry Symmes Purchase, where squat old Bo-nah and lean Captain Johnny watched their women dropping corn in the dark gashed ground. *Cutta-ho-tha is back.* It went over the road to Springfield and the third brigade of the first division of the Ohio militia. *General Kenton has come back.*

There, in the busy town of Springfield, a lawyer from Kentucky hired a horse and buckboard from Abel McElwain and rattled over the thirteen miles to Urbana. That evening the sheriff stood in Kenton's door, shifting a paper in his hands. He was uneasy, shuffling his feet and looking back to the road where the buckboard stood, but finally he said, "In the name of the court of Champaign County I serve you, Simon Kenton, with this writ of capias."

He dropped his eyes then—he was a sergeant in the third brigade, summoning his general.

Simon Kenton could write his name, as he could draw the course of a remembered river, but he could not read a syllable. Still he looked awhile at the paper, his eyes thoughtful under the rough brows, and then he looked over the sheriff's shoulder and saw the lawyer standing there.

"What is it for?" Elizabeth Kenton asked, her dark eyes darting at the sheriff and the stranger. She was the daughter of a Frenchman, Stephen Jarboe; she spoke sharp and high and her hands kept working. "Whatever is it for?"

"It's for a debt that is owing to my claimant in Kentucky," the lawyer said, tapping the pocket of his black buttoned coat. "The debt bears the name of Simon Kenton as surety, and it's long overdue."

"They've taken his land," the woman said, "his lands and houses in Kentucky, his land in the Territory, his lands along Mad River and the Miami, his farms and mills and trading post in this county. How can he pay more?"

"Then," said the lawyer, pointing to the sheriff's writ, "the law will have his body."

"Where?" she demanded.

"In jail," the lawyer said.

"Whenever we get a jailor," the sheriff added. "Since you went away, Gen'ral, we've raised a jailhouse. There's been horse-thieving in the next county. But we haven't named a jailor. They mean to do that now."

That night the township officers gathered in the tavern—trustees, treasurer, fence viewers, and supervisors—and when George Fithian pounded on his dinner iron, the citizens straggled in. Right away the room was full of voices. Simon Kenton had signed his name to another man's obligation and now was charged under the debtor's law. But who was not in debt to Simon Kenton? He had defended the Kentucky settlements in the time of the Revolution and the year of the bloody sevens. He had spied for Clark at Vincennes, stalking like a hunter through the enemy town, counting the British and the British Indians. He had scouted the Shawnee and Miami camps for Wayne. He had been captured, tortured and imprisoned—eight times he ran the gantlet, three times bound to the burning stake. Since then he had made his own peace with Tecumseh and the Prophet and had piloted the first party to the upper Miami country. He had cut Kenton's Trace, eight days' wagon journey to the Ohio, and had brought millstones all the way from Pennsylvania. The settlers used his mill and trading post before they had anything to trade, and the Indians wore paths to his corncribs and his fodder house.

But, said Colonel Ward from Greenbriar, his gold watch chain glinting in the candlelight, law had come to the western country. Kenton had signed his name to another man's debt, and if he could not pay it, the court could have his body for a twelvemonth. They must elect a jailor.

When the votes were counted, little Rob McRoth stood on the plank table where the candles made him an eight-foot shadow on the wall. "Election is declared," he stated. "By legal vote and lawful ballot this township has named Simon Kenton for its jailor."

So Kenton moved his family into the jailor's lodgings and took possession of the body of his prisoner, Simon Kenton, debtor. The jailhouse stood at the corner of Locust and Market streets, in the shade of a big sycamore. It was a dark log building, four rooms upstairs and four down, with a recessed gallery on the side away from Market Street. The family spread out in more room than they had ever had, upstairs for sleeping, downstairs for cooking and eating, and a couple of cell rooms at the lightless end for Kenton to put his prisoner in. He looked into those dim rooms—each one had a high narrow opening that only showed a slit of sky—and then went out and pounded hominy to feed his prisoner.

But he was not required to shut himself in a cell room. That first day three of his "boys," whom he had piloted to the county seven years before, came on legal business, explaining to the jailor how he could allow his prisoner town bounds if that fellow had proper bondsmen. Then they produced the bondsmen's paper, signed with their names—Will Fyffe, George Fithian and Zephaniah Luce. After that the prisoner walked town bounds, from High Street to the alley on Scioto, from Ward to Reynolds Street, measuring the blocks with his long loose stride, out and back, out and back, as a patient man might pace a cell. He carried a hickory staff, rifle high, grasping it near the top, like a shepherd in an ancient land.

When the neighbors stopped, the jailor sat with them on a bench in the shaded gallery. They told how Colonel Ward, with Joe Vance to run the lines, was laying off quarter sections along King's Creek. They told of settlers' wagons rocking into Union County and spreading out on the barrens there. Word was, they said, Tecumseh had met with William Henry Harrison in a grove beside the Wabash and had thrown the Governor's peace pipe on the ground, and the British were doling out rations and rifle bullets to Indian parties near Detroit.

If Kenton was restless, hearing these things, it didn't show in his guarded eyes. He was a prisoner, bound to the limits of the town.

That summer little Lizbeth romped on the gallery and built corncob houses in the empty cell rooms. Sometimes she walked beside the shambling man to town limits, tugging at his big paw when he stoppped to talk with a teamster on a load of wood or hay. One September day she ran down Locust Street to meet him, her face flushed bright as she rattled the bell on her wrist. "High up!" she cried, and he carried her home on his shoulder.

That night Kenton woke out of a dead sleep. He woke sharply, as he had done in canebrakes in Kentucky and thickets on the Wabash, to a sense of danger. Before his eyes were open his hand went to his side. There was no cold rifle barrel, only the rough bedpole frame; and then the cornhusk mat was rustling and he was back in town again, in the dark jailhouse with his prisoner. But the danger was there. The doorway showed a flickering light and he heard a whimpering, like a fox kitten in a leaf-lined den.

On bare feet he crossed the other room and stood above his wife, bending at the bedside. As if it was his own throat, he felt the quick hard breathing, and even the pale candle showed the dark struggle in the child's face and the glassy eyes. When he touched her, a hand flung out, hot and tight, and the little bell rang from her wrist. The woman brushed damp hair from the fevered face.

Kenton went downstairs, groping in the dark, and came back with a dripping gourd of water. The child could not swallow, but the woman put a wet cloth to her open lips. Downstairs again, sitting on the gallery, Kenton counted, over and over, the seven stars that had guided him in hostile country. At last a rooster began crowing somewhere, and a green and yellow light spread up from Ruffin's Ridge.

When he went upstairs his wife was kneeling at the bed and the darkness was gone from the child's face. For the first part of a minute he thought she was smiling at him. Then he saw the blue eyes empty and the woman's shoulders shaking.

At the funeral reading people overflowed the jailhouse, standing on the gallery and in the street while Mark Norman spoke from a worn Bible and a hymnbook. Then Simon Kenton raised the new box to his shoulder and they all followed him out Locust Street—even the Indians and the Indian children. At Ward Street, the town limit, the big man stopped. The box came down from his shoulder and the Arrowsmith brothers took it from him. He watched the procession move on, across the sloping meadow to the new fenced cemetery under the ridge.

Once in his youth, before he gave up trapping, he found a bear that had dragged his trap and the oak anchor log till it caught in a locust thicket. A shaggy beast with bloodshot eyes and a vise-held foot, he had no fierceness left when Kenton raised his rifle. Now, standing in the autumn sunlight, looking over a brown prairie where the people halted in the withered grass, something went out of Simon Kenton. He saw them shoveling the brown earth back again, and while he watched, a part of him was buried there.

All his life he had been free—though in seasons a captive— free as his townsmen had never known freedom and could never find it. Now he realized, entirely, his imprisonment. Around him was a changed time and a changed country, and he could not stand at the grave of his small daughter. That desolate knowledge made the whole world darken.

He looked northward, where the Wyandot camps were dwindling along the Sandusky and beside the English Sea. He looked west, where he had made his way into new green silent kingdoms —before axes thudded in the valleys and the sky hazed up with smoke from the clearings. He looked south toward Kentuck, a country he had known mysterious and empty, now shingled over, three, four, and five deep, with conflicting land claims. He looked east, where he had been a lean and tireless youth ranging out of Fort Pitt in a border country now fenced and farmed and every acre platted in the land offices. North, east, south, west, he had known it all, and all of it different, no two tracts alike, all of it dangerous and beautiful. Now he had reached the end.

He had been a prisoner before—bound hand and foot by the Shawnees and the Miamis, double-guarded by the British at Detroit—and always scheming, plotting, waiting. When a man has waited, he can wait again. But now there was nothing to wait for. In his youth in Virginia an old farm wife, reading the moles on his neck, had foretold imprisonment and death. The Indians still called him *Cutta-ho-tha*, the Condemned One. He had escaped many times, but he could not escape now. Something had gone out of him, like the flame in a lanthorn. Before the burial party came, he took himself, alone, to the jailhouse.

Winter brought a straggle of Indians from the northern camps. They found Cutta-ho-tha in the jailhouse, staring at the fire. He sent to his old storehouse on Lagonda Creek for the remnants there—a few blankets, kettles, files and awlblades, some spools of thread and twists of tobacco—and traded for what the Indians had brought: bear's oil in coonskin sacks, smoky maple sugar, honey, and cranberries. Molly Kiser in her greasy buckskins was with them, interpreting. A white woman, captured in childhood in Kentucky, she had never gone back to her own people. In other seasons Kenton had talked with her till the fire burned out. Now he was not interested in what she tried to tell him about British gunboats on Lake Erie and Tecumseh and the Prophet gathering the woods and prairie tribes at Tippecanoe Creek.

When Colonel Ward came back from visiting Kentucky, he went straight to the jailhouse. It was a wet cold evening and the fire felt good. He rubbed his hands and warmed his backside before sitting down beside the jailor. From the doorway Elizabeth Kenton watched them, two different men—one in

buckskin, one in broadcloth; one carrying the country in his
head, the other in a record book; one a finder and the other a
keeper.

The colonel had a paper folded in his wallet. He brought it
out deliberately.

"Your freedom, General," he said.

Kenton looked at the paper like a man who could read that
close small writing. He studied it while Colonel Ward told how
he had met a man in Lexington who had paid the debt that
Simon Kenton's name was signed to. So the debtor's law was
lifted. Kenton was a free man now, as the paper proved.

Then the colonel rubbed his hands again and talked about
the land business. He had hired Joe Vance to lay off quarter
sections all the way to the Union County line. Times were
changing, changing fast. The Miami country would be full of
people in a few more seasons.

When Colonel Ward went out the room was silent. Rain
dripped from the roof. Kenton leaned over and dropped the
paper in the fire. It blazed up quickly and was gone.

Elizabeth Kenton came in. "Now we can leave this jailhouse,
Simon."

"Leave?" he said.

"You're not a prisoner now the debt is paid."

"Yet a jailor still," he said.

It was true, he had been named jailor for a twelvemonth, but
it was not that that brought the trouble to her face. As the fire
burned down, she saw him sinking into the shadows. At first,
when the law possessed his body, he was not an altered man,
merely a man restricted, waiting for the freedom which would
come. But now his spirit was imprisoned. All the signed papers in
Kentucky could not set it free.

In April he moved out on the gallery, but his eyes did not
catch the restless light. His twelvemonth was nearly over, and
he did not think of that. He was not waiting. When the ground
dried, he went to the garden, a thing he had never done, hoeing

up corn rows for his wife to drop the kernels in. Woman's work, squaw work, but he had no desires beyond it. He had become his own prisoner, like any disheartened man.

The first word of a horse thief in the county came from Colonel Ward: one May morning his Kentucky saddle mare was missing. Then other animals were gone, from farms on Dugan's Prairie and along King's Creek, and even from stables in the town. The sheriff blamed Indians, but Kenton shook his head. The Indians had changed, too. When that horse thief was brought to jail, he would be a white man.

"How can you know that, Gen'ral?" the sheriff asked. "And who can catch him?"

Kenton knew who could—old Boh-nah and Captain Johnny in their shacks on Lagonda Creek. Give them a pair of horses . . .

"And two more critters gone," said the sheriff.

But he took Kenton's word and sent the Indians out, and two days later the jailhouse had a new prisoner.

He was a runty-looking man with a weathered face, wandering blue eyes, and a strawlike stubble glinting on his chin. He shook hands with his jailor in the friendliest way.

"I b'lieve you once stole some horseflesh yourself, General Kenton. Shawnee horses, I b'lieve."

"Kentuck horses," Kenton said. "Stole them back." He looked down at his prisoner, a smiling, harmless-seeming man. "But that's long gone."

The stranger brought a strong rich smell of horses into the jailhouse, and when hoofs sounded in Market Street, his eyes went after them. Horse crazy. Kenton was half sorry to shut the cell door on him.

Out at the oak stump, cracking corn, or hoeing in the garden, Kenton heard his prisoner singing.

> Come jump up behind me and away we will ride
> To yonder fair city; I'll make you my bride.

He had a far-carrying voice that wouldn't stay in those dark walls.

For a small man the horse thief had a surprising appetite, and Kenton pounded a lot of hominy. When he took the plate at mealtime, dropping the wooden bar from the heavy door, the little man stood smiling in the dusky room.

"I been picturing the Twin Creek country, Gen'ral. You know where the fork swings north—fine land up that valley, good farms and good horses. And the German flats on the Mahoning —big Pennsylvania horses there. I don't know though but I like Scioto horses better. Good stock from Virginia and Kentucky— I guess you know those horses, Gen'ral."

At his own dinner Kenton's wife was silent, strange for her, till the meal was over and the children went outside. Her dark eyes looked up then.

"A year will soon be ended, Simon. A slow hard year."

"The cricks froze tight in Janooary," he said absently, "but the sun grew warm in Aprile."

"Not hard that way, but other ways." Her eyes strayed off. "You know what day it is, Simon?"

"I couldn't tell that, Betsy."

"The last day of your twelvemonth. The last day here. To-morrow they can get a new jailor, and we can go."

"Go? Is it that troubles thee?"

"No, Simon," she said sharply. "What troubles me is you. You have made yourself a prisoner. The law took your body, but it was you shut up your spirit. This is not your place, Simon. Not this dark jailhouse."

"Where else?"

"Oh, Simon. . . . Once you took me on a journey, the first year we were wed, by pack horse through the forest and rafts across the rivers. We looked at woods and meadows where the world was new."

"That's long gone, Betsy."

Outside little Mary fell on the doorstep and lay there crying.

Elizabeth went to pick her up, and Simon wandered back to the garden.

Once he heard distant voices, and he looked off where Joe Vance and his chain-men were laying out the lines on Ruffin's Ridge. He bent to the rows again. From the jailhouse came another voice.

> I'll sing you a song and it won't take long,
> Concerning a man who wouldn't hoe corn.

When he opened the cell door, the room was still. It was a minute in that dimness before he saw the prisoner—face against the wall and hands outspread, one eye squeezed shut and the other pressed to a crack in the logs' chinking.

To Simon Kenton that tense, oblivious figure brought back something buried, something almost gone. In the dim room, dark as the huts of the Indians or a stockade's lightless cell, he knew what his prisoner was seeing—May wind running in the grass, sunlight washing the creek bank, the hazy, far, half-shadowed hills and the white clouds drifting. He saw it all, clear and bright and calling, as though his own eye were pressed to the prison wall.

While he stood there, the door blew shut. The prisoner whirled around and saw his jailor watching.

"Well-with-thee, horse thief."

The little man's smile came back slowly. "It's a soft day, Gen'ral. A soft bright living day. I felt it through these black walls. I wondered . . ."

"The sun lies warm," said the jailor, "and the cricks are full."

"You've been captured, Gen'ral. The British and the Indians. You know what it is."

Kenton sat on the prison bench. "Tell me, horse thief, how you fared with the animals you stole. Before the sheriff fetched you here, all those horses had got back to their stalls and stables."

"Sure," said the prisoner with his widest smile. "I turned those horses loose."

"Why, then, did you take them in the dead of night?"

The little man's face drew near. "Humans are 'bout alike, Gen'ral. But horses—they're all differ'nt. Barbs, roans, cobs, galloways; pack horse, cart horse, post horse. Carolina hackneys, Kentucky pacers, big Pennsylvania draft animals and little French ponies on the Wabash—I hear they have Spanish horses over the big river, fast enough to run down a buff'lo."

"Aye, horse thief."

The little man drew a breath and shook his head. "All those horses, Gen'ral, I like the feeling they are mine. Not to sell or not to put in harness. Not to keep, but just to have a little while and then be on my way. At night"—his blue eyes were lighted now—"in a barnyard or a pasture, it's like *finding* them. Can't you see how it would be?"

"Horse thief," said Kenton, "you must be touched a little. Yet you talk like a deserving man."

Next morning the prisoner was gone. No one knew how he had forced the heavy door in the dead of night, and taken Will Fyffe's best horse—that came trotting back up the road, stirrups swinging, just at breakfast time.

"He was a small man," Elizabeth Kenton said, "but not so small he could pass through that slit in the wall—if he could get up there."

"Not that small, I'd think," said Kenton.

He was different today, making ready for something. She watched him pack his powder horn and fill his bullet pouch, and still she didn't know.

"Before winter," she said, "there will be another baby. Should it be a girl, we could name her Lizbeth—not to take the place, but to . . ."

"Aye, woman," he said gently.

Even when he threw the old blanket across the pommel and slipped his rifle in the holster, she wasn't sure. She stood beside him, putting a bait of cornbread in his game bag.

"Simon," she asked, "do you aim to catch that horse thief? To bring him back to jail?"

He shook his head. "No, Betsy. I wouldn't prison any man."

He looked far off then, with the deep light in his eyes, and she had her answer.

She watched him ride away in the long morning shadows, never looking back. He was a coming-and-going man, and the fading hoofbeats were like music to her.

So Simon Kenton lit out for Missouri—where he claimed new land in an unmarked country, and lost it lightly when the New Madrid earthquake sent the Old Big Deep Strong River right through his location. But that was another season, and he was nobody's prisoner then.

8. *The Forest of the West*

The first page of the best novel ever written about the Ohio wilderness shows a Pennsylvania family on their way into the deepening forest. Conrad Richter began their story in *The Trees*, continued it in *The Fields* and concluded it in *The Town*. In one lifetime the forest vanished and roads crisscrossed the open land. But when young Sayward Luckett walked into the Ohio gloom with a bundle on her shoulder, the trees seemed everlasting.

After the Luckett family had poled a raft across the big river under the Alleghenies, they were in a different country. Now the mud on their feet was black and overhead arched a green roof, spattered with sunlight. From a ridge they looked upon a green and heaving ocean, a forest sea rolling westward without end.

It did end, after four hundred miles, in a sea of grassland. There were two landscapes in the interior, forest and prairie, and both were like the ocean. Both were wild wastes, swelling to the horizon in moods of vast tumult or serenity. Storms more violent than Europe ever knew lashed the wilderness, and the New World languor lulled it. After the crashing of thunder and the rivers of lightning the frenzy rolled away. For days and nights a profound stillness filled earth and sky. In that spell of silence nothing moved, not a leaf in all the forest, not a grass blade on the ground. Morning brought a soundless flood of light, noon was a blazing trance, in the hush of dusk the wilderness seemed changeless and everlasting. It could swallow men without a trace of their intrusion.

This unfenced, unmarked country was open to all. Hence the squatters, who went ahead of survey and legal settlement, finding a bench of land above a creek or building a lean-to at the edge of a prairie grove. In that wild country squatter's law became as binding as legal entry. A man slashed corner trees or piled up chunks of prairie sod, and by that act proclaimed possession. In his burlesque on western emigration Major Walter Wilkey pictured the arrival in Illinois of Yankee newcomers, "squatting very composedly on their hams, in a circle around a blazing fire." The major had no time to lose; he must drive the squatters off immediately, he declared, "as two hours' peaceful possession would entitle them to an indisputable right to the land."

For centuries the Indians had lived in the wilderness like deer and foxes, leaving the land unchanged. But white men in a few years would change it beyond recognition. They settled the forest first, opening their clearings to the sun and hacking at the margins of their fields. When they, or their children, pushed on westward to the prairie, they had to learn new skills, new crafts, new folkways. Then they remembered the woods as another country. Some men learned the demands of both landscapes; after a boyhood in the Indiana forest Abraham Lincoln became a prairie surveyor and a circuit lawyer in Illinois.

Conrad Richter pictures the Luckett family, on foot in a forest trace, carrying their plunder into the deepening wilderness; they followed the woods as some families follow the sea. They had only the vaguest idea of the country that had swallowed them in green immensity. Having crossed the Ohio River, they were in the interior; somewhere north lay the English Seas—the Great Lakes—with tribes other than the Shawnees and Delawares of the upper Ohio. Somewhere unknown rivers laced the forest, and Indian paths led to trading posts at a junction of waters. It was a new country and it was old . . . old. The great trees had grown for centuries, huge sycamores, elms and walnuts that were there when Columbus sailed for the Indies and Cortez landed in Mexico. On the trail settlers marveled at hollow trees big enough for a man to live in, at vines as thick as a roof pole, at mysterious earth mounds covered with forest.

As they pushed on, the huge interior took possession of home-seekers' minds. This strange, dark, timeless land was theirs to contend with and subdue. Sometimes that thought was exhilarating; they saw sunlight shafting through the canopy to a mossy glade where their cabin would grow. More often, it was a somber, fearsome realization; the woods were ancient, dark and mighty, and against them a man raised his tiny ax. But the ax would destroy the forest, first in one small clearing, then in enlarging fields. The settler learned to girdle trees, cutting through the living bark, and to plant corn and potatoes in the leafless forest. Then he felled the deadened trees and burned them, soft columns of smoke ascending to the sky. Soon the wind brought the tang of another burning and the faint thudding of another ax. There were neighbors in the forest.

In the twilit country superstitions flourished. Prairie people would never have as many dreads and omens as those of forest settlers. A dog crossing a hunter's path meant an aimless hunt and an empty-handed return to the clearing—unless a man hooked his little fingers together and pulled till the dog disappeared. Hogs must be slaughtered in the waxing of the moon or the bacon would shrivel. A bird alighting on a window ledge, a new moon seen over the shoulder, a dog baying at an old diminished moon, a cough of a horse, the sight of a sloughed snakeskin or a dead snake—these common things were freighted with good and evil. Signs of the moon governed all planting. There were strong forces in the wild land; by signs and gestures people hoped to enlist or appease them.

Every man in the new country had an eye for soil. Soldiers in the expeditions of St. Clair and Wayne talked about sloughs, bogs, bottoms, about clay, loam, marl and deep black earth. Even in dense woods they judged the make-up of the forest floor. White oak, walnut, hickory, sugar maple meant good soil; locust and swamp oak were signs of heavy, undrained earth. The timber told what poverty or fertility lay out of sight. White oak and chestnut lands were good for corn; soft maple and sycamore land was wet and cold. Sassafras, gum, persimmon and small-leafed oaks told a story of thin and stubborn earth; beech and hard maple were a badge of warm, rich, loamy ground, easy to plow and ready to yield.

A land-looker wanted good soil and running water; he sought a location beside a river or a creek. He would avoid lowlands and hillsides. If he could find a natural meadow ringed in forest with a steady trickle from a spring, he had his heart's desire. The ideal farm site was "rich as a barnyard, level as a house floor, and no stones in the way."

All things in the West were big. At salt licks hunters marveled at rib bones big as a ridge pole, the remains of extinct mammoths that had once fed in the deep canebrakes. A wild vine on Paint Creek in Ohio was sixteen feet around at the base; it divided into three branches, each one as big as a tree trunk. When cut down, the vine yielded eight cords of firewood. Old sycamores were frequently hollow; farmers used them for hogpens and granaries. Settlers talked of the big woods, the deep forest, the lost timber. "Oh you had to be a stout body to be a woman way back here," thought Sayward Luckett in *The Trees*, "for this was way up West in the Ohio wilderness. The trace ran through the deep woods. . . . Harvests of old leaves covered the black ground. Overhead the trees were thick as always. Branches and vines fought and locked up there. At the other end you could just see the promise of light. That light was George Roebuck's clearing."

Man was a small presence in the old, deep, shaggy forest, with bigness all around him. *Big* was a recurrent word in the settler's language. In *The New Purchase* Baynard Rush Hall referred to the Big Bear Settlement in Indiana, and remarked: "All things out here are big; if two things of the same name are to be distinguished, one is called big, the other powerful big."

The ax is the oldest implement in the world, but the stone ax of the savage could not fell a tree. The Indians, like the Mound Builders before them, planted maize and squash in the natural meadows. If only God could make a tree, only a white man with his wedge of steel on a wooden handle could make a clearing. Swinging his ax in the Ohio forest, a settler was in the act of "making land." One man seemed powerless there. When wind stirred the branches, the thudding of his ax was drowned in that green and murmuring ocean. But soon tens of thousands of axmen were hacking at the forest. In half a century they made twenty million acres of land. Their first clearings looked something like a battlefield, gashed and charred and trampled, but they had let the sunlight in. The wilderness was becoming cropland.

English travelers in the West were startled and astonished at "farms" where smoke seeped up from piles of logs and branches, and where seed was sown in fields of oak stumps. William Cobbett, remembering the parklike countryside of Surrey, said that American farmers knew nothing about hedging, ditching, banking and other refinements of field care. "They have no idea of the use of a *billhook*," he wrote, "which is so adroitly used in the coppices of Hampshire and Sussex. An *axe* is their tool, and with that tool, at *cutting down* trees or *cutting them up*, they will do *ten times* as much in a day as any other man I ever saw. Set one of these men upon a wood of timber trees, and his slaughter would astonish you."

On the frontier trees were an enemy, to be killed, felled, uprooted, burned. The settler chopped down every tree in his way and hacked out every bush. Sooner than he could realize the clearing would be too bare, the townsite too denuded. Sons of pioneer farmers planted trees above the well and beside the farmhouse. On frontier college grounds trees were laboriously replaced on the site of a destroyed forest. In raw streets and courthouse squares villagers planted trees where their fathers had felled them.

In Indianapolis, where a forest was cleared to make room for the new capital in 1820, some foresighted citizens preserved a grove of maples in the center of the town; on that leafy site the community's first church meetings were held. A generation later an old settler told young Henry Ward Beecher, recently installed as pastor of the Second Presbyterian Church, how the maples had disappeared. Early one morning the old resident heard a thudding in the grove and found one of Indiana's leading lawyers exercising himself before breakfast by felling one of the largest trees. His example brought other vigorous citizens with their axes, and one by one the great trees came down. "Now," said the old settler, "we have a huge yellow brick building in the center of this [barren] circle."

Beecher went on to tell how a few years later the county commissioners set out a number of locust trees to shade the courthouse square. But the jailor's cow, being pastured there, proceeded patiently to bark the young trees or break them down until the square was as barren as before.

Thus in all our towns [the young minister concluded] comes first extermination; then came scorching summer suns and too late the wish that the trees had been spared; and at last planting begins, and we who live amid the immense forests of a new country—on whose town plat not fifteen years ago grew immense oaks, maples, sycamores, beeches, tulip trees and elms—are planting the short lived locusts (*Robinia pseudo-acacia*) to obtain a speedy shade! I can think of but three forest trees now standing in this town within a space of one mile square—two elms and one buckeye. The same scenes are enacting in every town which springs up at the West. We are gaining meadows, and corn bottoms, and green hillsides, and town plats, by an utter extermination of the forest. Here and there an Indian may be found lingering around the old possessions of his nation, as if to mourn their loss, and to remind us of his ancestors; but of the forest, it is almost true that not a single tree is left to recall to our minds the glory of its fellows. Indeed, I have thought that those who were obliged to clear farms or timber land, imbibe the same feelings toward trees which the pioneers have toward the Indians—as things to be destroyed, of course. This devastation of our forests the political economist regards as a blunder, and says it is an unthrifty practice; but one who looks upon trees almost as if they had souls, witnesses this needless extermination with some feelings which cannot be expressed in the pound and penny language of the mere economist. I think it is Michaux who pronounces the full-grown elm to be the most magnificent production of the vegetable kingdom. Is not an old, and tall, and broad, and healthy tree nobler to the eye than any temple or cathedral? The wonder of a century's growth ends in an hour by some man who never for one single moment thinks of the majesty or beauty of his victim—who only thinks how soonest to get it down, and burned up, and out of the way of the plough.

To the forest farmer trees were not the only enemy. Into newly cleared fields came the forest predators. Armies of squirrels rushed out of the woods when corn was ready for husking. Green carpets of caterpillars crept over the clearing, stripping it of every leaf and blade. Deer came by starlight to feed on growing crops. Wolves took a toll of colts and calves; foxes preyed on the poultry. Every spring clouds of migrant pigeons settled in sprouting fields. Desperate farmers waded among them, hacking at the blue-gray bodies that covered the earth like a shadow. When they flew up, the denuded field was harrowed by a million tiny claws. In 1803 a pigeon roost on the Muskingum was said to have covered a thousand acres. Forest trees broke under their weight and their flight obscured the sun for half a day. On summer days children were stationed in the fields to drive the squirrels away and scarecrows were set up in the kitchen garden. But foxes, raccoons, skunks, weasels and opossums came at night, raiding the chicken roosts, and forest wolves preyed on sheep and cattle.

Fencing was a necessity on cleared land, and the forest provided rails that made an angular border around the clearings. Winter was the time for rail-splitting. Zero temperature made the wood brittle, ready to cleave open with the grain. A big tree, preferably walnut, cedar or hickory, felled near the fence line, would produce two hundred rails; it was a day's work for a pair of tireless men. Six to ten rails high, the fence was interlaced in a zig-zag line. Some thirty thousand rails were required to enclose a section of land. Fencing was more costly, in labor or wages, than the land's purchase price.

Year by year the fenced clearings grew. By 1850 Ohio was the nation's leading wheat state, with a belt of golden grain extending for a hundred miles through the central counties. In that tamed land the wild predators were diminished, but the livestock ran free. Cattle were not fenced in but "fenced out" of the cropland. At the end of the nineteenth century it was said that Illinois had ten times more fencing than all Germany.

The first settlers could only burn the timber from their clearings, but when towns began to grow, there was an unending need for lumber, and the thud of the ax was followed by the scream of the saw blade. Mill sites on the smaller streams were the eagerly sought locations in the early years. The county histories of Ohio and Indiana list hundreds of crude sawmills. Logs were delivered to the mill for a dollar each. Sawed lumber—poplar, cherry, walnut, ash, oak—was exchanged for flour, hides and tallow. To the wagon factories went loads of hickory and elm logs; nonsplitting elm was used for wagon frames and ladders. All over the growing West there was need for native lumber. Quickly the settlers learned to use various woods for various purposes, for houses, barns, sheds, for wagons, rakes, fences, for barrels, tubs and hogsheads; they even used wooden pipes in pioneer water systems.

Thousands of logs went to the mills, but millions were burned in the trampled clearings. The ashes, reduced to potash and pearlash (for use in making soap and glass), were a first commercial product of the hard-won fields. From perpetually smoking "asheries" barreled potash went to the cities.

The growing Midwest was a land of wooden barns and houses, of wooden schools and churches, wooden sidewalks in the towns and plank or wood-block streets in the cities. European travelers, puzzled at the frontier's frame houses, were astonished to see wooden factories, hotels, and even wooden courthouses with oak or ash columns painted like clouded marble. For a few years before the coming of railroads, plank roads carried the overland commerce of the West. In 1840 the National Road across the state of Indiana was leased to a private company which laid a plank roadbed and collected tolls until the planks wore out. Chicago in its marshy land became a center of plank highways in the late 1840's. Local contractors described a system of three hundred miles of smooth plank paving that would cover every street and alley and radiate over the surrounding prairie. In 1848 the Southwestern Plank Road was extended for sixteen miles from the Chicago River—horse-drawn scrapers leveling the roadbed and fresh-cut planks laid across; the tollhouse at the southern end of the road still stands at Hinsdale on U.S. 34. The Northwestern Plank Road reached eighteen miles toward Milwaukee; it had a branch leading to the Des Plaines River. The Western Plank Road ran straight across Du Page County, and the Southern struck south from Madison Street. For a few seasons farm wagons rumbled over these miles of planking. In 1851 a traveler on the Illinois River found plank roads at every town and landing, with plank roads projected between towns on the inland prairie. Even after the railroads were begun, some men believed that plank roads were better suited to frontier commerce. There were thirteen plank-road bills before the Illinois legislature in 1851. At the same time "railroad conventions" were meeting in Ohio, Indiana and Illinois.

Plank roads were the frontier's poorest investment and its briefest improvement. They warped in sun and rain, froze brittle in the icy winter, and at last sank in the prairie mud. Railroads replaced them in the country and wooden-block pavements were laid in city streets. At the time of the Chicago fire, in 1871, the city had 56 miles of wood-block paving and 651 miles of wooden sidewalk.

When railroads spread over the interior, the vanishing forest supplied crossties, passenger and freight cars, bridge trestles, freight warehouses and station depots. Until late in the century wood fueled the locomotives, as it had fired the boilers of the river steamboats. When news was first carried "by lightning," whole forests went into the telegraph lines that paralleled the railroads. From early times the western commerce had moved in barrels. At first flour, pork, cheese, fish, whisky traveled in barrels. After 1860 kerosene and crude oil required more barrels. Every town and city had its cooperages, binding sapling hickory hoops around white oak staves. In 1814 one packer in Cincinnati bought fifteen thousand hoop poles for one cent each. In the middle years of the century the white oak forests of southern Indiana fed the insatiable barrel trade.

As the forest dwindled, lumber yards grew in Portsmouth, Cincinnati and Evansville on the Ohio and in Cleveland, Sandusky and Toledo on Lake Erie. The heartland furnished hardwoods; from lake ports in Michigan and Wisconsin came rafts of pine logs and cargoes of sawed lumber. Wide-spreading Chicago, the greatest consumer, became also the greatest lumber market in the world. For miles cliffs of lumber framed the Chicago River like palisades. In 1872, the year after the Chicago fire, the city handled enough lumber to cover a thousand acres to a depth of sixty feet.

While Chicago was spreading over the prairie, hundreds of towns were growing along canals and riverbanks where the great woods had been cleared. Only the street names—Vine, Walnut, Race (Millrace), Chestnut, Locust—were left from the vanished forest.

Such a town was the fictitious Americus in Conrad Richter's trilogy. In *The Trees* Sayward Luckett came into the Ohio forest as a wondering girl; in *The Fields* she had her own brood of children; in *The Town* she was a grandmother, and all her world had changed. Her only reminder of the early years was the old sugar maple rustling in the town square of Americus. Then, one October night, a windstorm brought it down. That was to be expected, and yet the loss of the last tree troubled the old woman. She remembered that all her life she had hated the trees like a mortal enemy. Long ago her little sister Sulie had wandered off in the big woods and was never seen again. For years they had wondered: did she die of hunger and privation, or did the Indians carry her away? Even Worth Luckett, their father, had been swallowed in the forest. The woods called him, as the sea calls a sailor; he left his family in their twilit clearing and went on toward the far French settlements in the West.

"All your life you had to fight them," the old woman remembered, "chop, split, nigger them off till nothing was left." But that October morning, after the stormy night, she climbed to the third floor of the big house and looked over the town. What she saw was roofs and streets and church spires, a city of brick and wood like the city she had dreamed of in the gloom of the woods and the close little clearing. Now the dream was reality, and it troubled her.

When the ground had thawed at the end of March, she asked one of her sons to drive her to the country. Across the canal and up the hill and between fields still gray with winter, they stopped at last at a patch of second-growth timber. The farmer didn't mind their digging up a few whips; he was soon going to clear the ground for corn. The old woman picked out six saplings—three young maples, a buckeye, a basswood and a poplar. When they drove back to town, the whips waved from the back of the carriage; the roots were bound in burlap.

On the way home a dark picture came to Sayward Luckett out of the past. "Everywhere she went the trees stood around her like a herd of wild beasts. Up and up shot the heavy butts of the live ones. Down and down every which way on the forest floor lay the thick rotting butts of the dead ones. Alive or dead they were mostly grown over with moss. The light that came down here was dim and green. All day, even in the cabin, you lived in a green light." Now only a few people in the restless town of Americus could remember that.

Three of the saplings she set at the side of her house; the other three went in front. That evening she wondered about the vanished trees that she had fought and hated, and about these young trees that she had saved. In one lifetime the cycle was complete.

9. "This Upstart Village"— Chicago

Westward from Fort Dearborn ran the great Sac Trail, straight across the prairie to a bench of tableland between the Rock River and the Mississippi. Here the Sac Indians had their chief town, the center of their tribal life. Around the lodges of Chief Black Hawk and his people lay big fields of corn and pumpkins and above the Mississippi was the tribal cemetery. In 1830 it was a busy, orderly, peaceful place.

Twenty-eight years earlier, when Fort Dearborn was a lonely outpost in an empty country, the Sac and Fox tribes had accepted an annuity of $300 for the cession of their lands—which they should continue to enjoy as long as the land remained public domain. It looked like an annuity for nothing, and the chiefs were pleased. But time brought white settlers into the Sac country. Bands of squatters pushed ahead of the survey crews and found the *V* of fertile fields between the Rock and Mississippi rivers. Every autumn the Sacs crossed the Mississippi for their winter hunt. When they returned in 1831, they found their lodges in ruin, their cemetery plowed, and white families claiming their land.

So began the brief and tragic Black Hawk War, the last Indian contest east of the Mississippi. It ended four months later with the beaten remnant of the Sacs fleeing across the Mississippi and Chief Black Hawk a prisoner of war. He was delivered by Colonel Zachary Taylor to a young officer from Mississippi, Lieutenant Jefferson Davis, and taken down the river to Jefferson Barracks, below St. Louis. A few months later, dressed in a stand-up collar and a broadcloth coat, the old chief was brought to Washington, with throngs of people cheering him at every stop on the way.

The Sacs were assigned a reservation on the Des Moines River —until settlers should push on across the Mississippi—and there in 1838 the old chief died. Already he had become a legendary figure. Soon after its burial his body was stolen from its grave and exhibited in towns in Illinois. In time the Territorial governor of Iowa recovered the skeleton and stored it in a law office in Iowa City, the new capital. One winter night the building burned to the ground, and there was nothing left of Black Hawk but a memory. Now on the tableland above the Rock River stands Lorado Taft's heroic statue of the defeated chief. The fierce old Hawk could not have understood the complexities of American folklore.

The end of Black Hawk's "rebellion" was a signal for a land rush to northern Illinois. These were the yeasty years of Jacksonian democracy, with dramatic developments in the West. President Jackson proposed to open vast new public lands to settlement. He called for a congress of Indians, all those remaining in the border country of Michigan, Wisconsin and Illinois.

In these years the American frontier was the most magnetic place in the world. The Ohio fever had run its course, and now it was the Illinois country that inflamed the imagination. Twenty years earlier emigrants had sung:

> And so my boys I guess I'll go
> To the pleasant O-hi-o

Now a new generation moved west with another song.

> Way down upon the Wabash
> Such land was never known.
> If Adam had passed over it,
> The soil he'd surely own;
> He'd think it was the garden
> He'd played in when a boy,
> And straight pronounce it Eden
>   In the State of El-a-noy.
>
> She's bounded by the Wabash,
> The Ohio and the Lakes.
> She has crawfish in her swampy lands,
> The milksick and the shakes;
> But these are slight diversions
> And take not from the joy
> Of living in this garden land,
>   The State of El-a-noy.
>
> Then move your family westward;
> Good health you will enjoy,
> And rise to wealth and honor
>   In the State of El-a-noy.

To the "garden state" flocked land speculators, merchants, missionaries, adventurers, riding horseback, trudging on foot, jolting in carts, buckboards, wagons, stagecoaches, stepping ashore from steamboats, along with the great tide of home-seekers from all the older regions of the United States and half the countries of Europe.

In these years also came the "travelers," with notebooks in their baggage, ready to report the wonders of the West to readers on both sides of the Atlantic. Journalists, feature writers, scientists, gossipists, economists, reformers, adventurers and sportsmen, they were as various as the settlers themselves. Alexis de Tocqueville; Captain and Mrs. Basil Hall; the cultivated Kirklands from New York; the Trollopes; the one-legged reporter Charles Fenno Hoffman; far-ranging, sharp-tongued Captain Frederick Marryatt; Charles Lyell and George Featherstonhaugh, with their sacks of specimens; Harriet Martineau, raising her tin ear trumpet; starchy little Anne Royall in her balloon sleeves and sunbonnet. They were all after the same inexhaustible story—a new land, a new people. The valleys of the Ohio and the Mississippi, the dense forest and the windswept prairie, the long wild shoreline of the Lakes and their bustling harbors, settlements springing up like magic, towns emerging overnight, crossroads becoming cities. Never in history was there a country like this.

Besides the actual cities there were chimerical ones. "Ghost town" is an American phrase from the Rocky Mountain West, where mining camps were abandoned when the gold gave out. But there was another kind of ghost town in the heartland wilderness, an airy town that had no corporeal existence but was promoted and sold by land speculators. The best known was Dickens's "Eden," drawn from Cairo, Illinois, in *Martin Chuzzlewit*. It was preceded by Major Walter Wilkey's "Edensburgh" and James K. Paulding's "New Pekin"—fictitious towns that mirrored actual townsites, pictured on engraved plats and plans and located in swamps, thickets or roadless forest tracts.

In a frontier yarn James K. Paulding told of the arrival of journalist Zeno Paddock at a new settlement in the West.

> Truth obliges us to say that on his arrival at the city of New Pekin, as it was called, he found it covered with a forest of trees, each of which would take a man half a day to walk around; and that on discovering the public square on which all the public buildings were situated, he found to his no small astonishment on the very spot where the courthouse stood on the map a flock of wild turkeys gobbling like so many lawyers, and two or three white-headed owls sitting in the high trees listening with most commendable gravity. Zeno was marvelously disappointed, but the founder of New Pekin swore that it was destined to be the great mart of the West, to cut out St. Louis, Cincinnati and New Orleans, and to realize the most glorious speculation that was ever conceived by the sagacity or believed by the faith of man. Whereupon Zeno set himself down, began to print his paper in a great hollow sycamore, and to live on anticipation as many great speculators had done before him.

For each of these fictitious towns there were scores of actual speculations, from Ohio to the Mississippi. Maps printed in the late 1820's showed a chain of towns in the old Miami Indian country on the Maumee. "Manhattan" appeared at the mouth of the river, the site of present Toledo, with the towns of "Oregon," "Austerlitz," "Orleans," "Mendota" and "Marengo" a few miles above. Oregon was advertised as a vital center of the pork business; Marengo was described as a bustling port at the head of the river's navigation. Eleven phantom towns were mapped on the Maumee, and when purchasers arrived, they found only the charred site of old Indian camps on the shore.

The middle 1830's brought a frenzy of land and townsite speculation to Illinois. In three years more than five hundred "towns," most of them unpeopled, were laid out in the state. In 1835 the Plato Land Company advertised in Boston and New York a town "at the head of navigation on the Iroquois—one of the handsomest locations for a city in the world." Lots brought higher prices than lake-front property at Chicago, though there was no settlement on the Iroquois. Eventually the village of Bunkum was established there. In 1836 nine towns in Will County on the Des Plaines River were advertised in eastern papers while the wind blew over the empty Des Plaines prairie. The towns of Adamsburg, Caledonia, Montezuma, Moscow, Gloster and New Bedford never existed in Illinois, but were vigorously advertised in the East. A young Yankee settler in Illinois wrote back to Massachusetts: "If you accost even a farmer in these parts, before he returns your civilities he draws from his pocket a lithographic city and asks you to take a few building lots at half their value."

In 1836 the lithographer N. Currier, on Nassau Street in New York, published a handsome plat of Oquawka, Illinois. It shows the town extending fourteen blocks along the Mississippi, from Wayne Street on the north to Calhoun on the south; and containing two public landings, two markets and a town square. Oquawka had great expectations then, with the internal-improvement program projecting a railroad across the prairies to the town's steamboat landing. But the great transportation scheme collapsed in the panic of 1837, and when at last a railroad reached the Mississippi, its terminus was not Oquawka but Burlington. Tiny Oquawka drowsed beside the great river, and no one wanted N. Currier's colored lithograph.

Chicago in 1833 had not attracted the speculators; no one could see a future for the town at the weedy river mouth. Yet it had shown signs of growth. Log houses and shops lined Water Street, along the river, with a few cross streets jutting onto the prairie. It was a place of a hundred and fifty houses, with new buildings going up. The smell of stables, cattle yards, hogpens, tanyards mingled with the morning fog off the lake and the smoke of Indian campfires. Vessels were still compelled to anchor in the open lake, but work was beginning on a channel through the long sand bar that blocked the river mouth. That improvement was going on when bands of Indians arrived for the great tribal congress called by President Andrew Jackson.

On September 13, 1833, a party of eight travelers left Detroit in a four-horse stage for Chicago; they would arrive at Chicago at the height of the great Indian council. By chance two of the travelers were writing books, and so there are two accounts of that wagon trip to Chicago. One of them was an earthy Scot from East Lothian who signed himself Patrick Shirreff, Farmer; the other was the English scientist, alpinist, and essayist Charles Joseph Latrobe, a nephew of the architect who had designed the national Capitol.

Latrobe, accompanied by a nineteen-year-old Frenchman, the Count de Pourtales, had come to America a year before, on the ship *Havre*, along with Washington Irving. Irving took a liking to the cosmopolitan Latrobe, whom he called a man of a thousand occupations: botanist, geologist, hunter of butterflies and beetles, a musical amateur, a sketcher and a sportsman; and so Latrobe had accompanied Irving on a horseback tour of the trans-Mississippi prairies, a tour conducted by the Indian Commissioner Henry L. Ellsworth. Now Latrobe and young Pourtales, continuing their tour "of curiosity and information," were en route from Detroit to Chicago.

It was a six-day journey across country without a regular stagecoach service. The party included a stiff-backed U.S. Army major, and a profane old Revolutionary veteran and his wife, who were on the way from New York State to join a son who had settled in Illinois. The ride was too rough for conversation, but when they stopped at the spacious White Pigeon Prairie, golden now with sunflowers, the old soldier, echoing the "El-a-noy" song, remarked that this must have been the garden of Eden. At Niles, halfway to Chicago, the stage was exchanged for an open wagon with four plank seats. (This trip marked the inauguration of a post service to Chicago; the route was as new to the driver as to his passengers.) Here they were joined by a French-Canadian trader and a loquacious long-nosed farmer whom Latrobe, in his notebook, called Snipe. Snipe was going to Chicago to present a claim to the Indian council. When he had recently rounded up his pigs from the woods, twenty were missing. The Indians were not above shooting pigs, and Snipe expected the government agent to compensate him out of Indian funds. He allowed that wolves might have eaten his pigs, but wolves couldn't be made to pay.

The fifth day out of Detroit brought them to the high sand hills bordering Lake Michigan. Here the passengers went on foot, slipping and sliding down the dunes to the broad beach, the horses floundering behind them. The beach was soft, and to spare the tired team, the passengers kept on walking. The driver thought it was twenty-eight miles to the nearest house.

The day ended in a magnificent sunset, towering clouds of gold above the golden lake. Slowly the color faded. Then came a rumble of thunder and stabs of lightning in a purple cloud bank. Ripples wrinkled the darkening water. A wind sprang up. With a nearer crashing, the deluge came.

It was an Illinois cloudburst which ended as suddenly as it had begun. The drenched travelers plodded on at the edge of the lake. Then, with another cannonade, another storm was on them.

For an hour they were pelted with rain, shaken by thunder, blinded with lightning. It was a night of alternating storm and calm. During three hours the travelers huddled on the beach. In the intervals they trudged on toward Chicago.

Seventy years later this sandy waste would be one of the world's centers of oil refining and the manufacture of steel. At the end of the century hills of sand were leveled, suction pumps drained the marshes, breakwaters framed man-made harbors where huge freighters delivered coal, limestone and iron ore. Railroads webbed in to the industrial plants of Hammond, Gary, South Chicago, and over the Calumet marshes spread miles of gas and oil tanks, refineries, generators, coke ovens, blast furnaces, steel mills. At night over the long lake shore hung the glare of the furnaces and the gleam and glitter of the mills.

It was a dark and lifeless shore in 1833, but at last the storm-soaked travelers saw a feeble light. It guided them to a hovel where they found a family of half-breeds. After washing down some dry bread with a mug of whisky—the only refreshment the place could provide—they fell asleep on the dirt floor. Farmer Shirreff, drying his clothes by the fire, reflected on the elegant Mr. Latrobe rolled up in the half-breed's blanket in a sleeping place "inferior to the bed of many an East Lothian pig."

At daybreak the wagon arrived. After another ration of bread and whisky, the haggard, disheveled travelers took their seats for the final miles to Chicago. The old soldier, having downed a double portion of whisky, took to denouncing the pomposity of the British (this was aimed at Latrobe) and praising republicanism and Andrew Jackson. Five miles out from Chicago they passed a ragged cluster of wigwams and a herd of hobbled ponies; a pack of snarling dogs startled the tired horses into a run. This was the first of hundreds of Indian camps scattered over the prairie. "Five thousand Indians," wrote Latrobe, "were said to be collected round this little upstart village for the prosecution of the treaty by which they were to cede their lands in Michigan and Illinois."

The tribes were feasting at government expense while the

treaty terms were pondered in the council house. Warriors roamed through the town, whooping and shouting, looking for whisky pedlars. One drunken Potawatomi with a painted torso and muddy cotton trousers repeatedly staggered to the doorway of a shop, asking for whisky. When the proprietor shoved him back, he fell flat in a pool of mud. This was repeated, time after time, to the amusement of a guffawing circle of Indian men and women.

From Fort Dearborn a signal cannon called the chiefs to council. They assembled, some of them staggering and tipsy, in an open-sided pavilion, across the river from the fort. The assemblage had feasted for a week, and now the commissioners urged the chiefs to discuss the treaty. But the Indians could conduct business only in clear weather, and the sky looked cloudy to the chiefs. It was, however, a good day for horse racing. Leaving the smoldering council fire, the delegates began to bet on their ponies. Between the clustered wigwams riders, naked except for a blue breechclout, whooped and shouted above the flying hooves. There was a race of double riders, their bodies painted blue, black, white, vermilion, yellow, pounding their ponies and yelling like fiends. Hundreds of Indians swarmed around a makeshift corral milling with horses. Through the bedlam rose a jangle of harness bells. Big freight wagons were arriving every hour with loads of trinkets and whisky.

To Latrobe Chicago seemed a chaos of mud, rubbish and racket. His hotel, the famous pioneer Sauganash House, was overrun with French-Canadian traders, farmers, land agents, pedlars, half-breeds; he could find no place to read and write. But the officers of Fort Dearborn took him grouse-shooting on the prairie, and the Indian Commissioners invited him to attend the treaty sessions in the council house. At sunset, which was ration time, he walked through the turmoil of the encampments where tribesmen were restlessly awaiting the commissary wagons. He learned to distinguish the Sacs and Foxes, with shaved heads and greasy eagle feathers; the lithe Chippewas, with colored hatchets in their belts; the blanket-wrapped Ottawas; the Menominees, with painted shirts and beaded moccasins; the Winnebagos, with bells jingling on their leggings.

When the wagons arrived, the Indians swarmed like dogs; and like dogs, they carried their rations off to their separate places. As the prairie sunset paled, the scene was both picturesque and repellent. For miles the supper fires twinkled over the plain and the air was spiced with sizzling pork and bacon. But a closer look, past tent poles hung with meat and moldy moccasins, showed drunken Indians lying on piles of baggage. As the stars came out, drums throbbed near and far, and the young men went whooping through the camps. In one encampment two young braves, before a crowd of red and white men, fought for an Indian girl. They dashed at each other on horseback, stabbing with hunting knives. Amid a frenzy of cries both fell to the ground and died.

The government had not supplied the Indians with liquor, but traders dispensed it from open casks in blanket tents and wagons. Indian men and women, daubed with paint, went reeling through the village streets, from one pedlar to another. This was the last great Indian congress in the heartland, the last chance to prey upon the tribesmen.

After repeated speeches, discussions and deliberations in the council house, the treaty was concluded. The Indians were to receive immediately a large quantity of goods, and in exchange for their ceded lands they would be assigned five million acres beyond the Mississippi. They agreed to move within three years. The government would transport them to the reservation lands and provide houses, schools, mills, blacksmith shops, farming implements and farm animals. In addition to tribal annuities of $16,000, a sum of $175,000 was provided to pay the Indians' debts to traders and other claims against them. To influential chiefs went personal gifts and annuities. Old Antoine Ouilmette was given $800, with an additional $1,600 to his three daughters. Certain American traders and interpreters who signed the treaty got as much as $5,000, and the far-flung American Fur Company collected nearly $20,000 on account of claims against the Indians. The Kinzie family was granted $20,000 for claims that went back to the war of 1812.

After the final puffing of the calumet and x-ing of the treaty, the Indians lined up for their trade goods and their cash annuity. The money was paid in silver half dollars to the heads of families. From the paymaster's window the coins were thrown—two hundred, three hundred, four hundred of them—into the Indians' dirty blankets, and the braves ran off with their jingling burdens. The whisky pedlars were waiting to be paid for past purchases and new ones.

Day after day the payment went on, and every night mud-smeared Indians rode through the village, ringing bells, shrilling whistles, whooping and roaring. A schooner laden with whisky had arrived offshore, but a southwest wind kept it too far from the river mouth to bring the cargo in. With Chicago temporarily drunk dry, the Indians rolled up their tents and blankets, lashed their baggage onto the ponies and started home.

The two British travelers, Shirreff and Latrobe, had already departed. Latrobe found a place in a light carriage that rolled over the tawny autumn prairie, past groves of golden maples and hickories. From a rise of ground he looked back at the raw village whose people regarded it as the germ of an immense city. Eventually he would become a provincial governor in Australia, but nothing in that new realm would impress him so vividly as the "upstart village" of Chicago. Farmer Shirreff left Chicago on foot with his knapsack rustling (he collected seeds from wild and tame plants on the prairie) on his shoulders. He was bound for Springfield and St. Louis. For three days he passed Indians traveling in various directions. Then he was alone, and in good spirits, on the golden grassland under the high October sky. He gathered seeds of Indian grass and tested the soil with vinegar. It was good soil, but in all the low places the ground was wet and soft. He concluded that the prairie would never be farmed because it lacked drainage.

Two years later, in August, 1835, the Potawatomis returned to Chicago for the last treaty payment before their removal to the West. Outside the council house they held a final dance. With tufted heads and painted bodies they stamped over the wooden bridge and went whooping down Lake Street to the gate of Fort Dearborn. There, in a final frenzy, shouting and whooping, waving knives and hatchets, leaping and writhing and wailing, they bade farewell to the land of their fathers. That night their empty camps smoldered on the shore.

By that time Chicago was in a frenzy of its own, a fever of land speculation. With a breakwater pier and a lighthouse guiding shipping into the deepened river, Chicago had become a port of entry, and soon work would begin on the Illinois and Michigan Canal, linking the Chicago River with the Mississippi. When in 1837 it was incorporated as a city, Chicago had four thousand people and a seemingly boundless future. Then came the panic, and land values collapsed. Yet Chicago went on building wharves, warehouses, grain elevators, brick yards, wagonworks, tanneries, breweries, and packing houses. From the newly plowed prairie came long lines of farm wagons laden with corn, wheat, oats, barley, beef, pork, lard, potatoes, wool, hides and tallow.

In 1843 Chicago's first census counted 7,580 residents. As yet the shops and dwellings had no street numbers (an employment agency was on "Clark Street, opposite the Saloon, over Russell's Land Office"), but in 1844 a directory "regarded as an experiment" listed every householder and every shop and business. By that time Chicago was polyglot, its population "derived from almost every nation under heaven." The *Directory* shows a city of artisans—stone quarrier, lumberman, drayman, sailor, waggoner, blacksmith, carpenter, machinist, printer, mason, hostler, tinsmith and coppersmith, cooper, brick maker, millwright, shingle-maker, house-mover. From the pages rises the clamor of the prairie city, with the future all before it.

10. The Grand Prairie

A few steps more and a beautiful prairie suddenly opened to our view. At first we only received the impression of its general beauty. With longer gaze all its distinctive features were revealed, lying in profound repose under the warm light of an afternoon's summer sun.

—George Flower

> *These are the gardens of the Desert, these*
> *The unshorn fields, boundless and beautiful,*
> *For which the speech of England has no name—*
> *The Prairies.*
> —William Cullen Bryant

In the midst of the heartland there lay a natural border where the wilderness of forest met the open prairie. An irregular line, like a broken seacoast, marked the end of the woods and the beginning of the great grasslands. Generally the Wabash River was a dividing line, though tongues of forest pushed into the prairie like capes and promontories, and estuaries of meadowland penetrated the woods. From the Wabash to the Mississippi the land lay open to the sun, with island "groves" scattered on the

sea of prairie. One long estuary in the grasslands border was Door
Prairie (the French had called it La Porte) in northern Indiana.
It was a corridor of grass fifteen miles long, framed in walls of
forest, leading to the West. In the winter of 1834 the one-legged
journalist Charles Fenno Hoffman came on horseback to that
forest opening. "It formed a door," he wrote, "opening upon an
arm of the Grand Prairie, which runs through the states of Indiana and Illinois and extends afterward, if I mistake not, to the
base of the Rocky Mountains."

The French, having come into the heartland by Lake Michigan
and the Mississippi, discovered the forest-prairie border from the
West. Tonty's nephew, Sieur Desliette, observed that the Illinois
grassland "is the most beautiful country in the world as regards
soil." When he reached the Wabash, the landscape changed. "We
begin to see here those reeds . . . which shoot up to a height of
fifteen feet. On the other side there are no more prairies."

But most travelers came upon the prairie after weeks of groping through the forest gloom. It was a dramatic emergence into
a new world of grass and sky, of space and freedom, of light and
distance. Over it lay a vast stillness, and travelers drew an instinctive breath before wading in. One could soon be lost in
those great wastes. The philosopher Volney told of three men
who wandered seventeen days on the bushy plain between Vincennes and Kaskaskia. He named the landmarks in this two-
hundred-mile crossing: Ombra Creek, the Elm in the Meadow,
the Cat River, Yellow Bark, Walnut Point, the Three-horned
Acacia, the Meadow of the Hole, and the Great Rib. A young
Quaker from Carolina said that the "Wild West" began at the
Wabash. Volney's landmarks, listed in 1796, recalled past periods
on this southern Illinois prairie. His "Ombra Creek" was the
French explorers' "Embarrass," and his "Great Rib" was left
from another time. The prairie mastodons and mammoths were
prehistoric, but some huge bones remained. Henry Rowe Schoolcraft observed that the buffalo was generally called the "Illinois
cow"—a name which Pierre de Charlevoix reported commonly

used among the French *habitants*. In 1821 Schoolcraft found
bones of buffalo and elk bleaching on the prairie, though the
animals were then extinct in Illinois. They had been driven
across the Mississippi by hunters and, said Volney, by the bells
of tame cattle. The eagle, wolf and panther, once common in
Illinois, had moved west with the bison.

This was an ancient land as well as a new one. Burial mounds
were heaped in its groves and on its riverbanks. A web of Indian
trails gathered at the prairie portages where slow creeks flowed
north toward Lake Michigan and south toward the Illinois and
the Wabash. Though they had no compasses and no measurement
except a day's travel, the tribesmen knew the vast prairie like a
map. Juliette Kinzie saw a Potawatomi trace in the ashes of his
campfire the outlines of the whole country, its lake and river
borders, its wandering creeks and wooded bottomlands, and the
thin threads of its trading and hunting trails.

The first names on the prairie, before the pioneer settlements
dotted the map of Illinois, were given to creeks and groves in
the encircling grassland. *Creek*, the Anglo-Saxon word for a
tidal inlet, a small arm of the sea, found a new designation here,
as the French *prairie* took on a new spaciousness and wildness.
Kickapoo Creek, Sugar Creek, Beaver Creek, Rice Creek, Rock
Creek, Hay Creek, Horse Creek, Cow Creek, Paint Creek, Smallpox Creek, Salt Creek, Vermilion Creek, Potato Creek, corrupted
from Petite Creek—they were frozen fast in winter, alive and
overflowing in spring, and all but dried up by the end of summer.
The islands of forest—Buffalo Grove, Sugar Grove, Keg
Grove, Troy Grove, Dutch Grove, Deer Grove, Fox Grove,
Downer's Grove, Table Grove—were the first sites of settlement
in the country; they offered wood and water at the edge of farmland. Within the Great Prairie were lesser prairies, bounded by
marshy bottoms or timbered ridges, and their names were all
inviting: Cloud Prairie, Marine Prairie, Pretty Prairie, Garden
Prairie, Looking Glass Prairie, Blooming Prairie, Blowing
Prairie, Rolling Prairie, Fountain Prairie, Flower Prairie.

Before the breaking plows sliced into the matted sod, the prairie was a realm of rich, rank grass as various as the forest trees. In 1824 three land-lookers from Ohio joined a band of Potawatomis and crossed the big prairies of Benton County, Indiana. When one of them turned his horse off the trail and rode a few paces into the bluestem, the rest of the party passed him unseen. In the giant bluestem cattle were hidden and a man on foot was swallowed without a trace. On the ridges grew the spiky Indian grass, and the swales were rank with slough grass, sedges, joint-grass and wiry, stubborn switch grass. In the spring, before the tall grasses took over, the land was starred with scarlet lily, shooting star, sweet William, yellow rosinweed, ox-eye, and Indian dye flower. Prairies of little bluestem made a velvety vari-colored terrain; the hollows glowed with golden cowslips and the ridges were glossy with pasqueflowers. In May, bird's-foot violets colored the sunward swells as blue as the bending sky. A pioneer folklore attached to the compass plant, whose leaves indicated "with a mathematical certainty" the northern and southern points of the compass. When Caleb Atwater went to Illinois in 1830, he took direction from this plant while noting another species. "We saw the *mineral plant* with its blue leaves and most beautiful flowers, growing in clusters, bunches and rows, indicating where beds and veins of lead ore existed beneath the surface." The dandelion that now spatters the prairie pastures was not native; it came with Yankee settlers from New England. And corn, the Indian maize, that would become the heartland's and the nation's largest food crop, never grew wild on the prairie. It was a grass, the giant grass, kept alive for ages by the Indians and brought west in improved strains by Virginia and Kentucky pioneers.

Prairie land-lookers in the 1830's gazed upon empires of blue-stem and Indian grass. Fifty years later these wild grasses were replaced by corn, wheat, oats, barley and by the tame timothy, clover and bluegrass—alien species brought in by prairie farmers. Plants that evolved in thousands of years of primeval prairie now lurk in the fence rows and on the railroad shoulders and in remote corners where the plow has not disturbed them. In recent years botanists have studied this native flora, tracing the succession of grasses through growth and decay and replacement by other species. Every prairie had lowland "sloughs" where the evolution began. First were the bulrushes, which gave way to sedges and slough grass, marsh species developed in long ages of wind, sun and solitude. In patient sequence, as the sloughs filled up with the decay of older species, came blue joint grass, tall panic grass and finally the giant bluestem, the fulfillment of the prairie evolution.

Prairie plants were never found in the woods. Species that belonged to sun and wind did not penetrate the forest shadow. In cool, wet, cloudy years forest plants crept tentatively onto the prairie, but they retreated with the return of normal seasons. The line of forest and prairie was as strict a border as a shore line. For ages the Indians had burned off the autumn grassland to keep it open for hunting. Without that burning the forest would have extended to the Mississippi.

This was the land that Farmer Shirreff from Scotland considered worthless because it wanted drainage. In 1821 John Tipton, surveying the Indiana-Illinois boundary, sank nearly out of sight. "After wading in this swamp for four & a half hours, many times to our waist and having almost killed our horses and Drowned ourselves we made good our way Back to the place where we first entered the swamp." At another try they crossed the swamp "having waided about 5 miles in Travling 8," and so escaped "the merciless attack of the muscheeter who almost darken the air with their numbers."

The French had learned a century before that travel west of Detroit was nearly impossible until winter hardened the endless swamps and marshes. Even in winter the Kankakee valley was hard to negotiate without canoes. A land-looker in January, 1829, examining country that had been ceded a year before by the Potawatomis, made a dismal report: "We soon found ourselves in the vicinity of the celebrated Kankikee ponds. The river rises near central Indiana and flows west through a low valley four to eleven miles wide. In spring it is covered with water. In summer there remains a marsh or swamp 60 miles long and impossible for man or horse to pass."

In 1831 Juliette Kinzie was making her first journey with her husband from the Rock River to Chicago. "There is no difficulty," they were told, "if you keep to the north and strike the Great Sauk Trail. If you get too far to the south you will come upon the Winnebago Swamp, and once in that there is no telling when you will get out again."

Immigrants traveling down the Ohio settled the southern counties, while the marshy lands in northwestern Ohio and across Indiana and Illinois remained empty. Another stream of immigrants boarded lake steamers at Buffalo and came ashore at Chicago, having by-passed the swamp districts of the Maumee, the upper Wabash and the Kankakee. Early lake steamers, in the 1820's, had run from Buffalo to Cleveland and Detroit, with an occasional trip to Green Bay and Chicago. On return from the upper lakes these vessels were decked in evergreens, tied to the masthead, flagstaff and bowsprit, as an indication of the far-off regions they had visited. All this was changed in the 1830's, when vessels called regularly at Milwaukee and Chicago and settlers streamed onto the western lands.

Still settlement lagged in northern Indiana; it was the last province in the heartland to be taken up. People in the East had luring ideas of Ohio and Illinois but only a vague notion of a never-never land of Indiana. With appropriate sentiment but mistaken geography, Longfellow urged a Chippewa chief who was visiting Boston: "Back, then, back to thy woods in the regions west of the Wabash." Some New Englanders thought that Indiana must be a great deal farther distant than Illinois and were not sure it had been settled at all; it sounded like Indian country. Others had heard of the Indiana marshlands, infested with toads, frogs, snakes and miasma. Travelers had given the region a black account. Only in a later and more comfortable time were the swamplands romantically treated in Hoosier literature. Thirty miles southwest of Fort Wayne lay the Big Loblolly Swamp which, when a hunter named Limber Jim was lost in its green waters, became the Limberlost. Gene Stratton Porter built a house at the edge of the great swamp and made it known to the world as a realm of mystery and beauty. She lived there for twenty years, writing her romantic novels, until the Limberlost was drained in 1913. Another mysterious marshland is in the heart of the more recent *Raintree County*, where Johnny Shawnessy searched the great swamp for the Tree of Golden Rain.

In 1820 Illinois had fifty-five thousand people, nearly all of them in the wooded southern counties. The great prairie seemed too immense and lonely to subdue. Despite the toil and gloom of forest clearings, early settlers preferred the wooded country. In the 1830's farmers on the forest edge thought they had reached the western limit of habitation. Treeless land, they believed, would not produce crops. Neither would it provide logs for a cabin, fuel for a fire, rails for fences, mast for hogs. The early homesteads in central and northern Illinois were located in the prairie groves or on timber-bordered creeks. In 1826, making one of the first attempts to plow the grassland, General Thomas A. Smith of Virginia called his prairie farm "Experiment." The experiment was a startling success, and soon other settlers were breaking the deep rich prairie soil. Word of this Garden of America quickly spread to New York and New England, to New Jersey and Virginia, to the British Isles and the countries of Europe. Spacious, sunwashed, open, free, the Grand Prairie was suddenly the most magnetic symbol of the West—a land waiting for the people who would give it a future.

During the 1830's more than 300,000 settled on the prairies. They came from New England, from New York and Pennsylvania, from Kentucky and Ohio, and from half the countries of Europe. Some came alone and some came in colonies—like the

Galesburg colony from New York, the Albion colony from the English midlands, Cleng Peerson's Fox River colony from Norway and Eric Janssen's Bishop Hill colony from Sweden. By 1840 the old Potawatomi Trail leading west from the Wabash had become a rutted road. At every hour in the day farmers looking up from their fields around Parish Grove could see wagons moving westward.

Speaking their various languages, working alone or in communities, the prairie settlers shared the same toil and promise. They hitched four teams of oxen to the breaking plow and turned the first furrows. In ax cuts in the broken sod they dropped seed corn for their first planting. Even that crude culture yielded twenty bushels an acre. Europeans were astonished at the soil's fertility. A German traveler wrote that no fertilizer would be needed for the first century and the soil was too rich for wheat during the first decade of cultivation.

In two years the turf had rotted; after three winters the fields were mellow. Still the stiff soil stuck to the plowshare. While a man held the handles a boy tramped beside him scraping off the earth with a wooden paddle. Seeing that cast-iron plows would not scour in prairie soil, a blacksmith named John Lane began reshaping an old saw blade. In his forge where the Central Station now stands on the lake shore in Chicago, he made the first steel plow. From that blade the earth curled away in rich dark folds. Five years later John Deere at Grand Detour made a steel plow as big as a shield and bolted it to a wooden frame. He produced ten more plows that year, and forty in 1840. By 1846 John Deere had moved his works to Moline on the Mississippi and was manufacturing plows by the thousand. With steel plows the farmers broke new sections of prairie, first the dry prairie ridges and then the lower land where joint grass and slough grass waved in the wind.

The Scotch farmer Shirreff had said that, lacking drainage, the prairie was worthless. As the ax-man "made land" in the Ohio forest, the ditchdigger made land from the prairie sloughs and marshes. The first drainage was done with spade, shovel and horse-drawn ditching plow. A county historian in Indiana observed that "the Irishman with his shovel was a necessity . . . an angel of mercy." At intervals of sixty yards cuts four feet deep led into a central drain as wide as a wagon bed. These "dredge ditches" were the only water courses for miles around. Countless prairie boys learned to swim in the waist-deep mud-bottom dredge ditch, with its ragged fringe of cattails where the red-winged blackbirds sang.

Underground drainage began after the Civil War. In many prairie towns the first industry was the tileworks, and the first co-operative enterprise was the crisscross tiling of wet land. In 1880 an Indianapolis man established the Drainage *Journal*, which every month reproached the proprietors of soggy land. By the end of the century hundreds of thousands of acres had subsurface drainage, the water running secretly under miles of corn, oats, wheat and barley. Where stagnant water had stood in the hollows and joint-grass had tangled in the sloughs, the land yielded richly. After drainage the notorious Kankakee valley was described as an Eden, "the real scene of Adam and Eve's paradise." In 1930 Illinois had 10,317 miles of drainage ditches, enough to reach from Chicago to Outer Mongolia. Underground were 150,000 miles of tile, enough to girdle the earth six times.

The waving bluestem was gone by 1860, and long fences framed the prairie fields. The first sod fence, turned up by a breaking plow, was followed by a thorn hedge, and that gave way to the hedge of Osage orange, which had been brought to the prairie from the hills of Arkansas. In 1870 hundreds of miles of border were provided by these stubborn shrubby trees which dropped their big green useless fruit in the September grass. Then came an invention by Joseph Glidden of De Kalb, Illinois. Soon De Kalb was "the barbed wire capital of the world" and millions of miles of "bob wire" enclosed prairie fields and pastures.

The long prairie horizons gave men large thoughts and spacious undertakings. In the 1850's Michael L. Sullivant, a son of the founder of Columbus, Ohio, went to Illinois and bought from the Illinois Central Railroad Company an immense tract of prairie in Champaign County. There he developed his famous "Broadlands" farm, employing 200 men, 2,000 horses, mules and oxen, fleets of breaking plows, ditching plows, gang harrows, cultivators and hayrakes. On wild prairie he pastured 5,000 cattle and 4,000 worn-out government horses. In one year he harvested half a million bushels of corn. After the Civil War Sullivant sold Broadlands and established in Ford and Livingston counties, a hundred miles southwest of Chicago, his huge Burr Oak Farm. Soon he had 16,000 acres in crops, 150 miles of seven-foot ditching, and 300 miles of Osage orange hedge girdling his fields and pastures. In his green oceans of grain he kept 250 German and Swedish farm hands working, and every fall he hired a hundred gunners to drive away wild fowl from his cornfields. In 1871 an artist and a reporter from *Harper's Weekly* visited this farm, "probably without a rival in the world." In one field they found 123 men at work with two-mule cultivators and they watched a 68-ox team dragging a ditching plow with a blade eleven feet tall. In a double-page spread the *Harper's* artist pictured an eight-ox team breaking prairie, a farm gang as big as a cavalry company taking their teams to work, and other crews plowing fields, ditching wet lands, and harvesting wheat and corn.

Still the prairie kept its long undulation and its radiant light. In spring it was swept with a southwest wind, a high wind hurrying starch-white clouds over the land, rattling the withered cornstalks where gang plows were marching. Summer brought a fecund heat and stillness, a humid somnolence broken by crashing thunderstorms that drenched the earth and gave a sheen to ribboned corn leaves when the hot sun shone in the returning stillness. Fall brought the tawny color of Indian times, the brown pastures and the tattered cornfields, a haze on the horizon and the golden moon of harvest. Winter was a time of gray skies and an iron earth, often transformed overnight to a polar whiteness. "Climate exceedingly mild," said the railroad pamphlets. "Winters short, cattle thrive on the prairies for nine or ten months of the year." But the wind could swing suddenly into the northwest, bringing icy sleet and a blinding curtain of snow. In other land-scapes snow might be "four feet deep on the level," but it drifted on the prairie; one farm might be blown bare and the next one buried house deep. In later years snow fences kept the drifts away from roads and railroads.

Its people changed the wild prairie into a huge, prolific garden, a green landscape turning to gold as the harvest ripened. At every village grain elevators shouldered the sky, corncribs lined the railroad siding, cattle bawled in the loading pens. And the prairie changed its people. Said Stephen A. Douglas, who had come West from the stony valleys of Vermont: "I have found my mind liberalized and my opinions enlarged when I get out on those broad prairies, with only the heavens to bound my vision, instead of having them circumscribed by the narrow ridges that surround the valley where I was born." Picturing the prairie pioneer, a Whitmanesque editor at Keokuk on the Mississippi saw "his mind expand, his eye light up with the fire of a new energy, and his whole nature grow to the liberal standards of Nature's doings in the West." In the contagious expansive temper of Chicago, New York journalist Charles A. Dana declared: "About this great West there is a broad, vigorous, muscular and marrowy humanity, genial, generous, radiant, warmly courteous, that somehow conquers more than all ironbound puritan strict-ness."

In 1830 the prairie was wild, free and timeless, with the seasons coloring the land and the stars circling over. By 1880 it was all possessed and occupied, measured with roads, hemmed in fences, weighted with towns and cities. It was vastly productive, sending long trains of grain and cattle to the insatiable market of Chicago. But something also was lost. The men who first plowed the prairie must have halted at the furrow's end, looking at black broken earth in the blowing grassland. Perhaps some of them returned their hands to the plow reluctantly, knowing the coun-try's wildness and beauty which they were altering forever.

11. *Hoosier, Yankee and the Western Man*

Stand at Cumberland Gap, said Frederick Jackson Turner in one of the famous statements of the American past, and see the procession of pioneers, with ox teams and covered wagons, on horseback and afoot, bound from the Southern uplands to the long horizons of the West. The early movement to the frontier was northward as well as westward. The Wilderness Road turned north at Cumberland Gap, threading the forests and meadows of Kentucky and leading to Louisville at the Falls of the Ohio. The first important road in Indiana was the Vincennes Trace, running north and west from Louisville. Virtually a continuation of the long road from Cumberland Gap, it became the overland route to the Wabash prairies. After 1815 the great migration deepened the trace and settled the Ohio Valley while the Indians held on to the northern sections of Indiana and Illinois. In 1818, the year of statehood, Illinois had thirty-five thousand people. Two-thirds of them were from the Southern states; the rest were European and Yankee in about equal numbers.

After the War of 1812 Congress created a vast Military Reserve, a cornucopia-shaped tract between the Illinois and Mississippi rivers, extending almost to the Rock River in the north. Veterans of the war were granted a land bounty of a hundred and sixty acres in the Reserve. Most soldiers sold their land warrants, so that some millions of acres fell into the hands of speculators. To serve as land agent for some Boston speculators who had bought up thousands of warrants, John Tillson left Massachusetts for Illinois. He was just married, and his young wife went with him.

Sixty years later in Amherst, Massachusetts, an old lady recalled her years in Illinois as life in another country. "In 1819," wrote Christina Holmes Tillson, beginning a reminiscence for her children and grandchildren, "going to Illinois was more of an event than a trip now would be to the most remote part of the habitable globe."

The route was by sea from Boston to Baltimore, across the mountains in a jolting coach on the new Cumberland Pike, a flatboat from Wheeling to Shawneetown, and on horseback over the barrens to the valley of the Illinois. Settled near the Mississippi, Christina Tillson found herself an object of mingled curiosity and suspicion. One of her Southern neighbors, the wife of a mud-stained farmer named Buzom, frequently stopped in the road to inspect the Tillson house. One day Mrs. Tillson called her to the door and offered her a piece of fresh-baked "Yankee pie." Said Lizzie Buzom: "I don't think you should say the like of that; I allus knowed youens were all Yankees, but Billy said 'Don't let out that we know it, kase it'll jest make them mad.' "

Throughout the Ohio Valley Southerners were dominant in the early years. The first generation Buckeye and Hoosier were Southern types, who returned the condescension of educated New Englanders in double measure.

The migration over Cumberland Gap had opened clearings in the Ohio forest and had planted farms on the prairie. But a larger migration was coming. Stand on the wharves of Buffalo in the 1830's and see the procession of Yankees and Europeans streaming off the canal barges and boarding steamers for Cleveland, Detroit, Milwaukee and Chicago. The lake vessels were crammed with horses, cattle, sheep, pigs, poultry, wagons, plows, cradles, chests of food and clothing. In the spring of 1832 a thousand emigrants passed through Buffalo every day. A rush of settlement came to the interior. Ten years earlier regular lake transportation had ended at Detroit; on rare trips to Lake Michigan vessels returned with evergreen on their rigging, a token of a voyage to the remote wilderness. But in the 1830's steamships were a familiar sight to the Indians at Mackinac and settlers thronged the western lake ports.

In this decade appeared the successive editions of J. M. Peck's *New Guide for Emigrants to the West,* published in Boston chiefly for the New England trade. It declared: "The desire to emigrate to the West has increased, and everybody in the Atlantic states . . . inquires about the Great Valley." Observing that the Erie Canal had brought the West closer to New England, Peck wrote from Illinois in 1836: "If Distance is measured by time and facility of intercourse, we are now several hundred miles nearer the Atlantic coast than twenty years since. Ten years more and [the railroads will] place the Mississippi within seven days' travel of Boston." But even now the rush was on, and the gazetteer exclaimed: "Such an extent of forest was never before cleared—such a vast field of prairie was never before subdued and cultivated by the hand of man in the same short period of time. Cities and towns and villages and counties and states never before rushed into existence and made such giant strides, as upon this field." Peck dismissed reports of frontier crudeness and violence in a single statement: "Some parts of the West have obtained this character from the Fearons, the Basil Halls, the Trollopes, and other ignorant and insolent travelers from England." To the West, he declared, industrious and God-fearing people were coming in endless numbers.

The lure of the West was indeed powerful, and it drew upon all the older American regions. Along with the two great streams

of Southerners and Yankees came an admixture of settlers from
the central seaboard. (In the West New Yorkers were "blue-
bellied Yankees.") To the frontier came an all-American society.
Both Southern and Yankee types appear, for example, in the
richly regional *Spoon River Anthology*. The two towns from
which Edgar Lee Masters derived most of his portraits were distinct and representative. Said the poet:

> Both Petersburg and Lewistown are full of quaint and picturesque
> types of character, but of a dissimilar sort. Petersburg and its
> environs are noted for their high-bred Virginians, their buoyant,
> zestful, rollicking Kentuckians, given to story-telling, to fiddling,
> dancing and horse-racing. . . . There are some of this class of people
> around Lewistown, but they lived on a less joyous level, while the
> town itself took a more serious tone and even an intellectual one
> from the New Englanders who divided the control of affairs with
> the Liberals and threw each other into a clear relief unknown to
> Petersburg.

Hoosier was a term drenched in Southern connotations. "Pages
of pioneer history in the Hoosier state," wrote Meredith Nicholson, "might have been lifted bodily from Kentucky chronicles,
so similar is their flavor." All Northern settlers on the frontier
were Yankees ("York Yankees is the meanest"), and their neighbors from the Southern states were Hoosiers; the term was as
current in early Illinois as in Indiana. Western Yankees regarded
Hoosiers as ignorant and shiftless, while Hoosiers considered the
Yankees sly and grasping. Southern settlers first met the New
Englander in the person of the pedlar, a sharp trader ready to sell
wooden nutmegs along with his tinware, needles, thread and
household remedies. In Illinois the early legislature, dominated by
Southerners, showed its distrust of Yankee merchants by charging fifty dollars for a license to sell clocks, while a liquor-
dealer's license cost but two.

The Southern settlers came lightly laden and with little sense
of distinction. They settled where fancy led, with only the
vaguest notion of their whereabouts; some never learned the
name of their township and county. Moving was natural to them;

if a family was not moving this season, they had neighbors who were. Dr. Samuel Hay of Salem, Indiana, whose son, John Hay, would move farther than any Hoosier could imagine, complained of the transient community, saying that the word *moving* grew as tedious to him as *revolution* to a Frenchman. The Lincolns, moving from Kentucky to Indiana to Illinois, were typical. "We lived the same as the Indians," said Dennis Hanks, Abe Lincoln's cousin, " 'ceptin' we took an interest in politics and religion."

Meanwhile the Yankee emigrants were settling in permanent colonies. Their transplanted New England towns took root first in the woods of Ohio and then in the western grasslands. In 1805 two hundred people loaded their household goods and creaked out of East Granville, Massachusetts, leaving an empty village and lifeless farms behind them. They built a new Granville in the hills of Licking County, Ohio. In 1815 a line of wagons rocked out of Chatham, Connecticut, bound for the Western Reserve on the shores of Lake Erie. Already the Western Reserve was becoming a New Connecticut. White church spires lifted above its village greens in Jefferson, Chardon, Painesville, Ravenna, Warren, Hudson, Ellsworth, Cleveland and Wooster. Colonies from Plymouth, Norwalk and Greenwich established Plymouth, Norwalk and Greenwich, Ohio.

A generation later this migration had moved on to Indiana and Illinois. Compact New England settlements were rare in Indiana, but Yankees helped to develop Crawfordsville, Richmond, Bennington, South Bend, La Porte, Orland, Bloomington and Lowell. Montpelier was a community transplanted from Vermont, and Wolcottville was founded by George Wolcott of Torrington, Connecticut. Solon Robinson, an orphan boy from Tolland, Connecticut, went west as a pedlar at age eighteen. He opened a store in the Indiana backwoods, trading with new settlers and old Potawatomis. To preserve his Lake County holdings in Robinson's Prairie, he organized a Squatters' Union. Later he founded an agricultural society which led to the establishing of the U.S. Department of Agriculture.

Thirty-two New England colonies have been counted in Illinois. The church was at the center of this movement; frequently a pastor and his congregation formed the nucleus of a migration. Wethersfield, Illinois, was founded by a congregation from Wethersfield, Connecticut. People from hill-framed Pittsfield, Massachusetts, settled the prairie town of Pittsfield, Illinois. In Henry County there were four New England communities: Andover, Wethersfield, Morristown and La Grange, and the town of Geneseo was founded by people from Geneseo, New York. Both Mount Hope and Delevan were planted by Rhode Islanders. Maine township in Madison County was a settlement of ex-sea captains from New England, and Rockton was founded by emigrants from Maine. Rockford was laid out by Yankees, though it filled up with Swedish immigrants after the Civil War. New Rutland was settled by two hundred families of the Vermont Emigration Association. Other New England communities were Wheaton, Geneva, Fremont, Stonington, Freeport and Bloomington. In Princeton, laid out by devout colonists from Northampton, Massachusetts, one of the early settlers was John Howard Bryant of Cummington, Massachusetts. John Bryant wrote some verses, along with editing a paper and organizing a high school and an agricultural society. In 1832 his brother William Cullen Bryant came West for a visit. Under the spell of light and distance he wrote a sunwashed poem on the prairies.

Southern settlers took life easy in their small clearings and plowings. They let their cattle forage and the weeds take their fields. In all Williamson County in southern Illinois no individual in 1830 had property worth a thousand dollars. As late as 1859 a New England missionary reported that no family in his southern Illinois congregation had a lantern to light the way home from church in mud and darkness. While Yankee farmers planted grass seed, mowed hay and rotated grain, their Southern neighbors were content with a sequence of "corn, weeds, hogs, mud and corn." In one of the first satiric writings on this frontier, Thomas Chandler Halliburton sent his itinerant Yankee clockmaker, Sam Slick, over the Western roads. Sam Slick described the man of Illinois: "unlettered, ignorant, uncivilized, self-dependent, free, lawless, unpolished, resolute, confident, tobacco-chewing, whisky-drinking, suspicious of good clothes or good manners, and finally, to use his own expression, 'don't care shucks for law, gospel, or the devil.'" This, of course, was the Southern settler who had come cheerful and unburdened to the West.

Yankees used straight board fences while the Hoosiers split rails and laid worm fences, as their fathers had done in Kentucky, Virginia and the Carolinas. "Cow-milking" Yankees built barns for their cattle and made butter and cheese. They planted fruit trees—Johnny Appleseed himself had come West from Massachusetts. The methodical Yankees wrote out notes for loans and mortgages; they scythed their fence rows; they even cut firewood into regular lengths and stored it under a roof. These things were stranger to a Hoosier than seeing them eat hominy with molasses. Southern farm wives who dried their wash on weeds and bushes were endlessly amused at Yankee clotheslines and clothespins—"them little boys ridin' a rope." Beyond these folkways was the deeper, sharper difference regarding slavery, an issue which sent thousands of Southern settlers across the big river to Missouri. Even poor Hoosiers, with no slaves to justify, clung to the principle. Said a ragged farmer crossing Illinois: "Well, sir, your *sile* is mighty *fertil*, but a man can't own niggers here, God-durn ye."

"My grammar I have forgot," wrote a Yankee settler, "as I have no one to talke it to"; and another one apologized for his unpracticed hand: "Excuse my scrawl. I am so long out of practice writing." Nearly every Yankee colony brought some books—at least a Bible and a "blue-backed" Webster speller— among their tools and implements. Many of the frontier schoolmasters were Connecticut and Massachusetts men, and most often it was Yankee settlers who organized local school boards. Scores of Midwest colleges owe their existence to New England men.

Rufus Putnam of Massachusetts and Manasseh Cutler of Connecticut founded Ohio University in the year of Ohio's statehood. Oberlin College was begun by two Congregational ministers, once schoolmasters at Powlet, Vermont, who went west for the Connecticut Missionary Society. Benjamin Shurtleff of Boston used some of the profits from his large Illinois land speculation to establish Shurtleff College at Alton, above the river from St. Louis. In 1817 five Collins brothers from Litchfield, Connecticut, laid out Collinsville, Illinois. They set up a waterpowered sawmill and gristmill and opened a distillery, a tanyard and a general store. A few years later, having repented of the distillery, they closed it and built a steamboat, the *Cold Water*, for the Mississippi trade. They gave their profits to establish Illinois College at Jacksonville, and Edward Beecher left a famous Boston pulpit to become its first president. The colony brought west from New York State by the Reverend George Washington Gale founded Knox College at Galesburg. That historic college brought their town its only fame, until a Galesburg farmer developed popcorn, taking it to England and a command demonstration before Queen Victoria.

Even more successful than Yankee educators were the Yankee businessmen. In 1856 a Massachusetts farm boy arrived in Chicago and started work for a dry-goods firm. He slept in the store and saved half his $35-a-month salary. Twenty years later he was one of the richest men in America and his Marshall Field Emporium was a national institution. John Wentworth of Sandwich, New Hampshire, Walter L. Newberry of Windsor, Connecticut, John S. Wright of Sheffield, Massachusetts, Orrington Hunt of Bowdoinham, Maine, Philip D. Armour from Stockbridge, New York, and Gustavus Swift from Sandwich on Cape Cod all rode the crest of Chicago's prodigious growth. They became merchant and manufacturing lords, and founders of the feudal families of Chicago.

With early settlement concentrated in districts bordering the Ohio River, the first capitals of the heartland states were located in southern counties. Chillicothe, lying between Paint Creek and the Scioto River, was founded by a Virginia surveyor and speculator, Nathaniel Massie. In the spring of 1796, on a natural meadow waving with fox grass and orange lilies, he plotted the town and gave it its Shawnee name. Two years later Zane's Trace was opened from Wheeling on the upper Ohio, and wagons rolled into Chillicothe. In 1800 the town became the capital of the Northwest Territory. On hills outside the town rose fine Virginia mansions, and matched teams of Virginia horses drew carriages through the muddy streets. Flatboats carried trade up and down the Scioto. In 1803, when Ohio became a state, Chillicothe was its capital.

A hundred miles up the Scioto at the junction of the Whetstone (later the Olentangy) River lay the village of Franklinton, founded by another Virginia surveyor, Lucas Sullivant. Franklinton had grown into a busy trading town by 1812, when Ohio needed a centrally located capital. A group of citizens offered the state two ten-acre tracts for a state house and a penitentiary— equal sites for the lawmakers and the lawbreakers—on the high east bank of the Scioto across from Franklinton's flatboat landing. After wrangling over other sites, the Ohio Assembly accepted this offer and named the projected town Columbus. The first public sale of lots was held on a June day in 1812 when Congress was declaring war with Great Britain.

Columbus was laid out in dense forest, through which ran the old Indian trail "Athiamoiwee," linking Kentucky's hunting grounds with the fishing camps on Lake Erie. In 1816 the village raised $200 to dig stumps from High Street and the Ohio Assembly moved into a new brick State House; the brick was made from clay in an Indian mound on the present Mound Street. Six years later, when squirrels threatened the crops, a community hunt on the last day of August yielded twenty thousand squirrel scalps. In 1833 the National Road, reaching all the way from Baltimore, passed the State House door. Every spring clouds of passenger pigeons filled the sky. Travelers on the swaying stagecoach shot them for sport and farmers fed them by the bushel to the hogs. In 1842 Columbus had a balloon ascension and was regarded by one of its own people as "a place with metropolitan curiosity and tastes."

On a hillside in Harrison County in the deep south of Indiana, drowses the old town of Corydon, named by William Henry Harrison for the young shepherd in his favorite song, "The Pastoral Elegy." Harrison was the first owner of the land between Big Indian and Little Indian creeks, where the town was laid out in 1808. The old state capitol stands on Market Street, between Beaver and Walnut, a solid building of rough blue limestone with a bell tower on its roof. Near it, under a sandstone pergola, is the dead trunk of the Constitution Elm, under whose shade the Hoosier delegates drew up the state constitution during the hot weeks of June in 1816.

At this time the northern two-thirds of Indiana was Indian land, with settlement nibbling at its borders. In 1818 in a treaty at St. Mary's, Ohio, three commissioners bought from a group of Indian chiefs the whole central section of the state. This "New Purchase" was opened to settlement in 1820, and a squatter village on the west fork of the White River was chosen as the site of a future capital. Indianapolis was laid out by an English engineer, Elias Pym Fordham, who had come to the New World with Robert Owen. In 1824, in four farm wagons, the Indiana government was moved from Corydon to the new town of huts and cabins in the stumpland. There were a few frame houses, a church or two, some stores and taverns with lawyers' offices above. Here a legislature of mud-stained, sunburned men projected a government over the half-wild land.

From Indianapolis the National Road ran westward, spanning the Wabash at Terre Haute and pushing on to the brush and grass lands of southern Illinois. In 1850 it reached its terminus, the old capital of Vandalia. When the Illinois delegates had first convened there in 1818, there were no surveyed roads into the town and no sidewalks on its muddy streets. The original log statehouse, burned in 1823, was replaced by a structure of Southern design, with a two-story galleried porch and a cupola above the gabled roof.

For twenty years this town on the Kaskaskia River was the political center of Illinois, though most of the legislators made long journeys to get there. Springfield had not existed when Illinois became a state; no one then dreamed that the central prairies would be occupied except as rangeland for cattle. In 1821 a legislative act created Sangamon County, a vast green solitude inhabited by a few far-scattered families. The three first county commissioners met in John Kelly's cabin on Spring Creek, near its junction with the winding Sangamon River.

John Kelly was a roving young hunter from North Carolina who lived beside a deer run between the open prairie and the wooded bottoms. He had found truth in the Indian name Sangamo, "place where there is plenty to eat," and he sent word to his brothers in Carolina: deer were plentiful as squirrels and wild turkeys roosted in every tree, there was endless grazing for cattle and rich mast in the bottoms land for hogs. Though he was no town-site promoter, Kelly attracted a settlement to Spring Creek, and the commissioners made it the seat of justice, agreeing "that the said county-seat be called and known by the name of Springfield." They then hired John Kelly to build them a log court-house for $24.50. The site chosen, on the edge of a prairie swale, is now the busy corner of Second and Jefferson streets.

A few years later a committee from Vandalia came to choose between Springfield and neighboring Sangamo Town as a permanent location for the county government. Sangamo Town, seven miles northeast of Springfield, had been laid out by W. S. Hamilton, a son of Alexander Hamilton, who owned a tract of river-bordered land. (A few years later Abe Lincoln would swing an ax in this timber, building Denton Offutt's flatboat.) When the committee arrived in Springfield, one of John Kelly's neighbors offered to guide them to the rival settlement. He took them through sloughs, brush and brambles until the exhausted inspectors gave up on Sangamo Town and agreed that Springfield should remain the county seat. So history began on the Sangamon.

In the 1830's, when settlement poured into northern Illinois, there was an irresistible demand for a capital near the center of the state. Peoria, Decatur, Jacksonville and the crossroads hamlet of Illiopolis all sought it. But the Long Nine legislators from Sangamon County—laid end to end they would measure sixty-some feet—swung the vote for Springfield. Their home-coming at the end of the session set off a celebration, with ungainly Abe Lincoln getting the chief praise. In 1837 the legislature convened in the straggling town of fifteen hundred people.

To the frontier capitals came lawmakers speaking with Southern drawl and New England twang. In the bare legislative halls there was a clash of temperaments and talents, men of diverse character and background whetting each other's minds and tempering their convictions. Gradually, as New England and European settlement increased, there came a yielding of Southern dominance to the newer Yankee faction and the emergence of a viewpoint that was natively Western. Picturing the positive young lawmakers in 1835, William H. Herndon wrote: "The vigor and enterprise of New England fusing with the illusory prestige of Kentucky and Virginia were fast forming a new civilization to spread over the prairie." It was a naturally democratic civilization, with land available to all and another chance for those who failed. There was no elite in the heartland. Its leaders would emerge from its common life.

Throughout the new commonwealths the lean, lank, close-mouthed Yankees and the volatile, quick-tempered Southerners drew together. After a generation the terms Yankee and Hoosier lost their opprobrium, and Western settlers were more aware of what they had in common than of how they differed. The heartland was not to fulfill the dream of the Boston merchant who envisioned a New England village every six miles in the West, nor was it to be a tobacco and cotton land of galleried houses and field-hands' quarters. In time the Southern drawl and the Yankee twang blended into what has been called the "general American speech," and the heartland towns had a vigorous and friendly character of their own.

By mid-century the two strains had all but disappeared—they could no more remain Yankee and Southerner in that setting than their ancestors in Massachusetts and Virginia could remain Englishmen—and a new strain, the Western man, emerged from their molding. In 1858 no one could think of Kentucky-born Abraham Lincoln as a Southerner, or of Vermont-born Stephen A. Douglas as a Yankee. Two Western men were contesting for the office of Senator from Illinois. They debated the crucial questions of the time, while the whole nation listened.

12. Men of Many Nations

On a midsummer day in 1832 a young Maine Yankee traveling down the Ohio reflected on the fortuitous invention of the steamboat at the precise point in history when millions of people were migrating to new lands. Then he made a sharper observation. As he stood at the rail watching the Ohio hills swing past, he heard the mingled tongues of his fellow travelers. Every vessel is a little world, but this pulsing paddle-box was a microcosm. He counted the nations represented there: English, Scotch, Irish, Welsh, French, Dutch, German, Swiss, and off to one side a group of seven black-robed priests from Austria.

On a windy autumn night in 1833 a one-legged journalist, Charles Fenno Hoffman, writing frontier feature stories for the *New York American*, limped aboard the steamer *New York* at Cleveland, amid the cries of stevedores and the clamor of immigrants "in half as many languages as were spoken at Babel." He saw an English mother nursing a child, a bearded German puffing a meerschaum pipe, a gnarled Irishman with a stubby clay pipe, a Swiss family perched on a painted chest. Around them were boxes, bales, trunks, portmanteaus and wagons jutting with plows, shovels, axes, clocks, chairs, candlesticks, and hung along the sideboards with pots, kettles, tubs, tongs and ladles.

In 1837 an American sailor in Liverpool, with thoughts too deep for his eighteen years, watched the people boarding immigrant ships—bent old men and infants in arms, girls in bright bodices and women with wrinkled faces. At evening they gathered on the forecastle to sing and pray, in German, Welsh and Irish, their voices echoing from the walls of the dock. Wrote young Herman Melville: "Settled by the people of all nations, all nations may claim [America] for their own. You cannot spill a drop of American blood without spilling the blood of the whole world."

From the beginning the interior was a land of mingled voices. A frontier traveler might hear Elizabethan ballads on an Ohio River flatboat, French minuets in the woods at Gallipolis, Welsh lullabies in covered wagons, Irish jigs in canal shanties, Scotch airs beside the Wabash, Swedish and German hymns in log churches in Illinois. For half a century the heartland was a frontier of Europe as well as of the United States.

Along with the Hoosiers and Yankees came the rich ferment of immigration, men of many nations clinging to their Old World memories while they searched the wilderness for a future. Some came in colonies which have left memorials—a steepled church at Bishop Hill, a symbolic garden at Zoar, a stone granary at New Harmony—while their blood stream flowed into the frontier population like prairie creeks into the Mississippi.

In 1815 the Rappites, in steeple hats and peasant blouses, floated down the Ohio, singing old hymns from Württemberg. They turned up the Wabash, and on a blowing prairie built their sturdy town of Harmonie. In 1817 two hundred German Separatists came up the Tuscarawas River in Ohio. Doffing their hats to no one, they took up five thousand acres and paid for it by working on the Ohio Canal which bisected their land. In the same year two liberal-minded Englishmen, Morris Birkbeck and George Flower, led a train of English colonists to the Boltenhouse Prairie on the Illinois side of the Wabash. They called their community Albion, and Birkbeck's *Letters from Illinois* drew new streams of settlers to the West. One of the newcomers was Robert Owen, millowner from Lanark, Scotland, who bought the Rappite "Harmonie" and arrived on the Wabash in 1825 with a dream of Utopia on the prairie.

In 1823 a Norwegian sailor who had left his ship in New York to wander over America walked west to Illinois. At the end of a summer day he boiled his kettle of tea and lay down to sleep on a grassy knoll above a curving river. That night he dreamed of orchards, fields and gardens, and of bright houses gathered about a steep-roofed church from which came the strains of an old hymn of Norway. The next day Cleng Peerson started back to the seacoast, walking past the huddle of huts at the mouth of the Chicago River. Four months later he was in Norway, stopping people on the mountain roads to tell of the broad rich lands of America. The next summer he led a colony of Norwegians to the Illinois prairie. For thirty years Cleng Peerson roamed the country and sailed back to Norway to tell of lands he had found for his people. He planted more than thirty settlements before he died in 1865. He never owned a rod of land himself, but he guided others to farms and townsites all the way from Texas to Minnesota. A hundred years after his dream the State of Illinois erected a bronze memorial where he had slept one summer night on the starlit prairie.

In July of 1846 four hundred Swedish immigrants crossed the great grasslands to Henry County near the Mississippi. They were religious dissenters, led by slight, tireless Eric Janssen. They moved across the prairie like an Old Testament tribe seeking the promised land. The journey ended on a hill above Edwards Creek, overlooking miles of grassland. Here they built sod dugouts and raised a cruciform tabernacle large enough for a thousand worshipers. They broke three hundred and fifty acres of wild land, planted corn and wheat, and milled flour and lumber while Janssen met new bands of Swedes at Chicago and guided them to Bishop Hill. By 1850, with fourteen hundred acres farmed by eleven hundred people, Bishop Hill was the largest settlement between the Illinois and Mississippi rivers. Then came John Root, a young Swedish adventurer who fell in love with Janssen's niece. When the leader tried to separate them Root turned from pistol practice and shot him dead.

Rule of the colony passed to Janssen's handsome widow. The loss of a husband was not new to her; she had outlived a drowned seaman, a Swedish schoolmaster, a Bishop Hill farmer, and now Eric Janssen himself. She knew the affairs of the colony better than any man. But for these people the Bible was binding, and Saint Paul had said: "Let the women keep silence in the churches, and let them be in subjection." To govern in silence was not easy, and authority passed to seven trustees. Janssenite teachers went out to spread the socioreligious doctrines. On Shaker Prairie, near Vincennes, one missionary met another sect which flourished in the fertile West. He came back to Bishop Hill preaching the Shaker doctrine of celibacy. When two dogmas collided at Bishop Hill, the community began to shatter, and in 1861 the property was divided among the heads of families. Like all communal societies on the frontier, Janssen's colony ended in dissension. But the town remained, with an oddly Old World flavor in the spacious New World landscape. The old Swedish church now serves as a meeting hall, and from the eight-sided cupola of the Steeple Building the colony clock tolls the hours over the prairie town.

The first great wave of Europeans surged into the heartland following the cold European winter of 1830. These were the people Herman Melville saw on the ship *Highlander*, gaunt with seasickness, twisted with rheumatism, burning with fever. Bad weather drove them below decks, where they lay in the tiered bunks or huddled around a table under the dim light of swinging lanterns. For weeks they heard the creaking of keel timbers, the banging of the anchor chain, the smash and thud of seas against the hull. When the weather changed they crowded on deck, searching for the shores of America. The lorn gray seascape cheated them, but their minds held a picture of broad fair lands washed with wind and sunlight.

Hundreds of ships brought them across the sea in the 1830's, when the western states were launching "public improvements" on a prodigious scale. At the seaports labor contractors hired workmen and sent them on to canal towns, road camps and railroad barracks. The immigrants had no money to buy land, even at $1.25 an acre on the installment plan. It cost $12 to cross the ocean, and $7 more to get to Cleveland, $8 to Detroit, $14.50 to get to Chicago. They came without money or tools, with only their coarse wool blouses, knee breeches, woolen stockings and battered brogans, and their rough bare hands. Thousands of them had to "work off the dead horse"—the cost of transportation. They were paid $10 a month in the barracks, tents and shanty towns. For this they attacked America with pick and shovel, with hammers, spikes and crowbars, with wheelbarrow and dumpcart, opening up routes of travel in the deep interior.

Ohio farmers looked up from the furrow and saw a brigade of Irishmen advancing with mules and scrapers and blasting powder. They graded the roadbed and pounded rock for the long straight National Road, now U.S. 40, through Zanesville, Columbus, Springfield and to the West. Villagers along the Cuyahoga, the Scioto, the Wabash and the Des Plaines heard a clatter of hammers and saw the shanties going up to house canal crews. With shovels and wheelbarrows, mules and manpower, they dug the long ditches, toiling from daylight till dark, in clouds of dust or knee deep in mud and water. At nightfall they devoured their supper in the mess hall and gulped the ration of whisky to dull the ache in their bones. The air was thick in the barracks, but outside the night was sharp and fresh. There were the pale lights in the shanties and the foreman's shop, a lantern swinging past the long dark stable and overhead the high white stars. They must have thought of Ireland then. For a ditch-digging job in a wilderness they had left a land full of legends and inscriptions, of holy wells and holy mountains, of stone circles, round towers and engraved crosses on the hills. "The poor Irishman," wrote Ralph Waldo Emerson after a visit to the West, "the wheelbarrow is his country."

On Saturday night the Irish danced to jig tunes, "The Keel Row" and "The Rakes of Mallow," and fought each other if there were no Swedes or Germans in the camp. An Irish war followed the canal and railroad lines, "Corkians," "Fardowns" and Connaught men bringing their old feuds to the new country. But in larger ways they were all alike. Noisy, gregarious, care-less, mercurial, gifted with eloquence and laughter, they loved the land that gave them long hours at low wages, drafty quarters and coarse food. To Cork, Dublin and Belfast they sent passage money for friends and relatives. So the movement grew.

During the 1830's more than a thousand miles of canal was under construction in a frontier country without resources of men and money. Early sections of the Ohio Canal were dug by prisoners from the state penitentiary, working with fifty-six-pound iron balls chained to their ankles, while Boston investors bought the first canal bonds. But more labor and more capital were needed, and the Old World could furnish both. To carry on the huge public improvements capital came from the great banks of Threadneedle Street and manpower came from the hungry counties of Ireland.

At Fort Wayne on a chill February day in 1832 a group of Indiana commissioners ceremoniously dug the first shovel of earth for the Indiana canal system. Contracts were let and shanty towns sprang up at a dozen points along the Wabash and Mau-mee rivers. Soon sledge hammers were driving iron drills into solid rock and blasting powder boomed across the fields. Behind the brigade of sweating men stretched the excavation, 19 feet across at the bottom, 27 feet at the top, with a wall of hewn stone holding a 6-foot horseway. Men white with dust and black with powder burns timbered the basins, built the big lock gates and graded the towpath. Down the line sounded the rattle of cranes, the shriek of dry pulley sheaves, the creak of the windlass, and cursing in English and Gaelic while mules heaved at the dumpcarts. So the long ditch lengthened.

A generation later employers would advertise, "No Irish need apply," but in frontier Indiana, with less population than present Indianapolis, the brawling red-faced buckos were welcome. They did a job that no Hoosier or Yankee settler would do, laboring in heat and cold, cutting through swamps, swales and forests, amid swarms of mosquitoes and stinging snow. Every six feet of canal, it was said, cost a life. Quinine, calomel and blue mass, aided by three daily rounds of whisky and six on Sunday, did not check the fever or the accidents. Men died of "canal chills," mule kicks, powder blasts and cave-ins. Grave-digging was a constant job. When a thousand dead were buried, a cemetery was covered up and a new one was opened two miles farther on.

In Ireland the summer of 1845 was cold, wet, sunless, and the potato crop rotted in the ground. This was the first of three dark years when hunger and disease hung over the island. Gaunt cattle lay down with foot-rot and potatoes never blossomed. In cold hovels people boiled seaweed for soup and tried to eat straw on which the grain had blighted. Wrote a heartsick landowner: "I have this day, returning to my home, witnessed more than one person dying by the roadside . . . and I am at this time giving food to a girl of 12 years old, the only remnant of a family consisting of eight persons, her mother and father included, all of whom were alive one fortnight ago."

In 1846 Captain Asa Waters of Marietta, Ohio, came back from Philadelphia with word of the famine in Ireland. Forty years earlier Marietta shipbuilders had built tall-masted vessels and Marietta men had sailed them down river to the Gulf and across the Atlantic. Now Captain William Knox built a barque and Washington County farmers filled it with ten thousand bushels of grain. On high water in February, 1847, the *John Farnum* sailed down the Ohio. In March she passed out the Mississippi delta. Two months later her cargo was unloaded at Queenstown and the ship returned to Ohio with a load of Irish immigrants.

But relief cargoes could not feed a nation. Irish peasants were found dead in the fields, others dropped by the roadside. Typhus and dysentery swept through the weakened population. In four fearful years nearly one-fourth of Ireland's people died of starvation and disease. Holy Ireland had become hungry Ireland.

In these years Irish emigration reached its crest. Roads to the seaports were thronged with desperate people. On the wharves they fought for passage to Liverpool, where ships sailed to America.

One of the Irish buckos who threw his bundle on his shoulder and sailed across the sea was John Sheridan. He came to Perry County, Ohio, to work on the National Road. There little Phil Sheridan, one of his six children, grew up beside the great road where the stagecoaches rattled by and the freight wagons rumbled. In Somerset on Muster Day the Irish had a free fight, with scrappy Phil Sheridan always in the middle. When the historian Henry Howe, with a knapsack on his back and notebooks in his pocket, sat down in front of a Somerset harness shop to sketch the one-story courthouse, he saw across the road a pink-faced boy lugging goods into a general store. It was Phil Sheridan. A generation later he would be called the greatest field general in the history of warfare.

A few miles over the Perry County hills lived another Irish boy who was destined for fame. Januarius Aloysius MacGahan was the son of an immigrant farmer from County Derry who died when MacGahan was six. Hungry for books, the boy worked on farms until harvest and then attended the Pigeon Roost school. At sixteen he was teaching in a country schoolhouse. Two years later he was a newspaper writer in St. Louis, and from there he went to Europe to study languages. Soon he was covering the Franco-Prussian war for New York and London papers. For ten years he ranged the Continent, from Paris to Asiatic Khiva, reporting on the stormy 1870's. When his account of Turkish atrocities in Bulgaria led to the Russian campaign against the Turks, MacGahan was called "Bulgaria's deliverer." A favorite of the Russian court, he rode and shot like a Cossack, and it was said that he spoke nine languages. He was preparing to cover the International Congress at Berlin when he died of a fever in Constantinople—age thirty-three. This Irish farm boy from Ohio, declared an English historian, had changed the face of eastern Europe. Six years after his death his bones were brought home to Perry County, where eight thousand people thronged the village of New Lexington for his belated funeral. It is said that his birthday is still remembered in Bulgaria.

Generally the Irish did not take to pioneer farm life, with its loneliness and isolation. In Indiana workmen on the Wabash and Erie Canal were offered land, from 40 to 160 acres, as part of their wages. A few Irish settlements sprang up on the canal lands, the "black Irish" sent home for wives and sweethearts, they shaved their beards and exchanged the sledge hammer for the plow handle. In Illinois canal workmen were paid in land scrip when the Illinois and Michigan Canal Company ran out of cash. But farm life was too lonely for most Irishmen, and most of them sold their scrip for a few dollars. At one time there was a project to create an Irish colony in Illinois where sons of Erin could work together in the land of plenty, and in the 1850's an Irish Emigrant Aid Convention conceived of a vague Irish state somewhere on the frontier. Their plans pictured Irish villages, like those of County Kerry, with people living close together and working the surrounding fields. To support this notion an Irish journalist in New York urged his countrymen to leave the city slums and find independence and security in the West. He appealed to them in verse:

The Irish homes of Illinois,
The happy homes of Illinois,
No landlord there
Can cause despair,
Nor blight our fields in Illinois.

But the spacious American landscape did not encourage the tight village system, and the gregarious Irish felt a magnetic pull in the growing cities.

The nearest thing to an Irish colony in the West was the domain of "Lord Scully," who exploited both Irish workmen and the frontier soil. Not a hungry peasant but an aggressive Irish landlord, William Scully came to the United States about 1850 to buy up Mexican War land scrip. He acquired more than 200,000 acres, and at one time was said to be the largest land-owner in America. Much of his land was in Illinois; he had 30,000 acres in Logan County alone. Scully's agents brought hundreds of Irish peasants to labor on his huge farms. While they plowed the cornfields and harvested the wheat, he lived lavishly in England, where he was known as "the greatest American farmer."

The Irish could be homesick on a farm, but not in a raucous city. With ten dollars in his pocket, said a frontier journalist, the Irishman is abashed by nothing in heaven, earth or Chicago. There they became labor bosses and contractors, and soon ward captains as well. Their sons would be police chiefs, aldermen and mayors.

If one wanted an example of what an Irishman could come to in the new country, there was James Shields—soldier, jurist, statesman, the only man ever to represent three states in the U. S. Senate. Like many an Irish lad before him, young James Shields had tramped the streets of New York vainly looking for gold. Then on to the West, where the work gangs were pounding stone and pushing wheelbarrows. But James Shields did not work on the roadbed; he stood up in the Senate chamber to enact a land grant for a Central Railroad in Illinois. Some called him "General" (he was a brigadier-general in two wars), some called him "Senator," but the Irish called him "Paddy"—though never to his face. His life became a legend to his people.

Born in 1806 in the village of Altmore in the rugged northern county of Tyrone, Jamie Shields attended a "hedge school," where the village priest met his scholars at the roadside. At sixteen he went to Liverpool and took passage on a ship for Quebec. Two days out of the Mersey they ran into a storm which hurled the ship onto the rocky coast. Three survivors dragged themselves ashore and were taken in by a Scotch fisherman. Penniless and empty-handed, James Shields became a tutor in a Presbyterian manse. After a year he went to sea, fell from a yardarm and broke both legs. For six months he lay in a Scottish hospital, and then he shipped again. The third time was successful; he landed in New York in 1826.

On the road in America he fell in with a German youth, John Krum, and the two tramped West together. At Kaskaskia, Illinois, the villagers were looking for a schoolteacher who could speak French. Shields had learned French in Ireland from a veteran of the Napoleonic Wars; he stopped at Kaskaskia and Krum trekked on to St. Louis. Forty years later the two men met and recalled their youthful wanderings. John M. Krum was then mayor of St. Louis, and James Shields was a member of the U. S. Senate.

In Kaskaskia Shields taught school and read all the law books in the office of a scholarly German solicitor in nearby Belleville. They became law partners—Koerner and Shields. After a season of marching in the Black Hawk War, Shields was elected by the Democratic party to the state legislature. In Springfield, with his dark hair and mustache, his flashing black eyes and fiery language, he was an arresting figure with an evident career before him.

A few years later as State Auditor, he faced the aftermath of Illinois' spending and speculation in the years of the canal boom. As a legislator in 1837 he had voted for the grandiose Public Improvement Program, and in the celebration following its passage he had mounted a table to sing Irish lilts and market songs to the cheers of his colleagues. Now in 1842 he was compelled to rule that depreciated paper money was not acceptable for state taxes. On this account he became the target of the Whig press, and one of the attacks led to his "duel" with Abraham Lincoln.

In the Sangamo *Journal* at Springfield there appeared a criticism of Shields's financial policy and also—he was a dressy bachelor of thirty-two—of his social vanity. The article asked whether Shields's $2,400 salary would be paid in paper or silver, it ridiculed his cockscomb manners, and finally observed: "With him truth is out of the question; and as for getting a good bright passable lie out of him you might as well try to strike fire out of a cake of tallow."

This lampoon, signed "Rebecca," was written by two vivacious young women of Springfield, one of whom would soon become the wife of Abraham Lincoln. The joint authors asked Lincoln to get their screed printed in the Sangamo *Journal*. It was followed by a further caricature making fun of Shields as a fire-eater "who might seek personal satisfaction for the attack."

That was the case. Shields asked the editor for the identity of "Rebecca," and was told that the articles had been brought in by Lincoln. When Shields wrote a challenging letter, Lincoln's seconds replied that since Illinois had outlawed dueling, Lincoln would meet Shields with broadswords across the river in Missouri. Arrived at the dueling place on a warm September day, Lincoln took off his coat and made some practice swings, while the militant Shields took the classic attitudes of swordplay. It was both a comic and a somber scene, the lanky Lincoln towering above his fiery opponent while the seconds stood in earnest discussion on the weedy riverbank. Lincoln stretched his long arms and slashed a twig from a branch overhead. Then, glancing at Shields, he sighed and sank down on a log. When the seconds had further conferred with the principals, the two men put down their weapons. Lincoln signed a statement that the "Rebecca" article "was written solely for political effect and not to gratify any personal pique against Mr. Shields, for he had none and knew of no cause for any."

With honor satisfied, the two shook hands, and talking pleasantly, boarded the horse ferry for the return to Illinois. A crowd watching on the landing went home disappointed. From that day Lincoln and Shields remained political opponents but good friends.

For two years Shields served on the Supreme Court of Illinois, ending his term when President Polk appointed him Commissioner General of the United States Land Office. The war with Mexico interrupted that; he volunteered for military duty and was named Brigadier-General of Illinois Volunteers. Wounded in the Battle of Cerro Gordo—he was reported dead by General Winfield Scott—he recovered in time to lead his brigade through the Belin Gate of Mexico City, though with a fresh bullet wound in his shoulder.

Shields was now a national hero, and President Polk appointed him Governor of Oregon Territory, an office which Lincoln had considered and declined. While Shields was packing for Oregon, the people of Illinois elected him to the United States Senate, the colleague of Stephen A. Douglas. He served for six years and then went to Minnesota to distribute "halfreed" land scrip. There he established the Irish colony of Shieldsville and attracted Irish settlement to the newly organized townships of Erin, Kilkenny, Montgomery and Faribault in southern Minnesota. In 1857 he was elected one of Minnesota's first two senators.

Three years later Shields went to California, where at last he found time to marry—his wife was the daughter of a friend of his youth in Ireland—while becoming interested in a mining venture in Mexico. He was in Mazatlán at the outbreak of the Civil War. Immediately he offered his services to President Lincoln, who made him a brigadier general. In the Battle of Winchester, pitted against Stonewall Jackson, Shields was badly wounded. But the luck of the Irish had not left him. He recovered and went to live on a farm in Missouri, where he was soon elected to the U. S. Senate. He died while on a lecture tour in Iowa, in 1879. A few years later his monument was erected in the rotunda of the Capitol in Washington.

In 1848 the first railroad trains were carrying wheat from Indianapolis to Madison on the Ohio, Cyrus McCormick began turning out harvesting machines in Chicago, an Illinois and Michigan Canal barge had delivered a cargo of New Orleans sugar for transshipment on the lakes to Buffalo. On the Cincinnati levee—where Stephen Foster was singing a new song, "O Susannah, don't you cry for me"—$3,000,000 worth of pork was loaded onto river boats, and from New York Horace Greeley was about to predict that in fifty years Cincinnati would be the greatest city on earth.

In London in 1848 Karl Marx and Friedrich Engels issued the *Communist Manifesto* and in Paris Alexis de Tocqueville cried: "We are sleeping on a volcano. . . . Do you not see that the earth trembles anew? A wind of revolution blows, the storm is on the horizon." All over Europe people were waiting for the execution of King Louis Philippe, which would set off uprisings from Spain to Hungary. Louis Philippe was in his seventy-sixth year, an old, vain, uneasy king who must have forgotten a lesson in democracy in his youth. After the execution of his father, the Duke of Orléans, young Louis had come to the United States.

At the forks of the Muskingum, sixty miles north of pioneer Marietta, the first settler was shrewd, genial, profane "King Charley" Williams, who had come west from Maryland. Originally a hunter, trapper and trader, he had established a ferry and a tavern at the river forks, a place of "accommodation for man and beast," with a plentiful stock of whisky. Among the motley travelers who stopped at his tavern, there was, according to a stubborn Coshocton County legend, a young man who would become the king of France. After a noisy night Louis Philippe complained to the landlord about the rude conditions of the

Forks Tavern, too rude for a Duke of Orléans. The proprietor shrugged. Since he had opened his hostelry, he said, he had entertained hundreds of sovereigns.

"Who were they?" asked the Duke.

"All are kings here," declared King Charley, adding that if Louis Philippe did not find the place to his liking, he could leave. The visitor gathered his baggage and departed, helped through the door by the toe of Charley's boot. Louis Philippe trekked on to Gallipolis on the Ohio River, where the French settlers entertained him in a manner befitting his rank. From there he went down the rivers to New Orleans and back to France. He was crowned in 1830, and the loafers at Coshocton began telling the story of how Charley Williams had kicked a king out of his tavern.

In 1848 King Philippe did not die; he fled to England as "Mr. Smith," and died there in bed two years later. But the revolution came, the volcano rumbled, the storm broke over Europe. It sent a new wave of emigrants across the sea to Coshocton and hundreds of other places in the hospitable West. "King Charley," however, was not so hospitable; he even objected to Yankees. In his autobiographical sketch he recalled, "Wee was the hapest pepel in the world ontill our Countery was filled with ireash and yankes and other spakendavels."

As the tide of Irish migration ebbed in the 1850's, a tide of German migration rose. Ohio had been a familiar name in Germany for a generation. Since the early 1800's Cincinnati had been a German-American city, with a German press, German churches, German gymnastic and singing societies. By mid-century there were large German communities in Cleveland, Columbus and Dayton. Hundreds of German families had settled in northern Indiana, in the vicinity of Fort Wayne. Illinois had German colonies in Galena, Chicago, Peoria, Quincy, Alton and elsewhere.

From the early nineteenth century there had been German

proposals to create a German state in the American West. One plan was to purchase a tract in the Mississippi Valley and parcel it out to association members in fifty-acre lots; houses were to be built by the association and later purchased by the landowner. The Geisenger Company set out in two ships in 1834, one bound for New York and the other for Baltimore. The first group was decimated by smallpox, yellow fever and cholera; its survivors settled individually in Henry County, Illinois. In mid-Atlantic the second group decided to withdraw from the company and to locate independently in Illinois. Most of them went to St. Clair County, where they found the community of Dutch Hollow on the edge of Looking Glass Prairie. In nearby Teutopolis a colony of North Germans established a Catholic community. Sturdy, stolid, with the Teutonic love of order and industry, they broke several thousand acres of wild land, raised a church and a four-armed windmill, and filled the prairie pastures with herds of sheep and cattle. On market days their wagons rocked in to Vandalia, loaded with tubs of fine cheese and butter. The early German religious communities at Harmony, Indiana, and Zoar, Ohio, were tight bands of people held together by their primitive Christianity and a communistic economy. They were in decline by the mid-nineteenth century.

In the 1830's a notable group of German liberals had made the village of Belleville in southern Illinois a place of cosmopolitan culture. Their town of eight hundred had a courthouse, jail, post office, two inns, a flour mill, four doctors, three lawyers and a bilingual newspaper in English and German. Here fiery James Shields became a law partner of scholarly Gustavus Koerner. The "Latin farmers" in the district came in from their half-tilled fields along the Kaskaskia to read Virgil and Horace and to write letters to schoolmen, scientists, poets and philosophers on the Rhine and the Danube.

All the German communities in the heartland had been founded or enlarged by refugees from the abortive revolution of 1830. A fresh wave of liberalism came with the Forty-

eighters, refugees from a later struggle for freedom and opportunity. Beginning in Paris on February 22 with a surging celebration of Washington's birthday, the Revolution of 1848
quickly spread to Belgium, Austria, Italy and Hungary. After
the February outbreak in Paris came the March uprisings in
Boden, Berlin and Vienna. All were suppressed, and the por-
tentous year of 1848 ended in frustration and defeat. Germany,
the land of philosophers and poets, had failed to establish a
republic, and while the country sank back into reaction, the
beaten revolutionists took refuge in America. University students, young lawyers, journalists and teachers, they were a
resource which no country could afford to lose and which would
enrich the land of their adoption. Some five thousand of them
came to the United States between 1848 and 1851.

The Forty-eighters, setting out from the port of Bremen, had
a pent-up hunger for freedom like the Irish hunger for food.
They were not farmers but city men, and they quickly made
their presence felt. In Cincinnati, Indianapolis, Cleveland, Columbus and Chicago they gave new impetus to German-American institutions—newspapers, orchestras, choruses, churches
and colleges. When Louis Kossuth, hero of the ill-starred
revolution in Hungary, made his triumphal tour of America
in 1852, he observed that "The West is the place where
the great bulk of European immigration hastens." In Cleveland
Kossuth's party was welcomed by a torchlight procession and
a German serenade. In Columbus he was escorted to the State
House by a company of Germany artillery, a German marching
band, the Turner society in gymnastic suits, and a column of
German butchers mounted on their dray horses; at midnight he
was serenaded by a German male chorus in front of the Neil
House on High Street. Here and at Cincinnati and Indianapolis
Kossuth was impressed by the German-American zeal for
political participation.

These were years of ferment in America, with abolition, free
soil and states' rights debated throughout the land. The wind of

revolution was still blowing from abroad, but Europe was a long way from America in the 1850's and the German liberals found new causes in the struggles of their adopted country. Because of its antislavery stand, they rallied to the new Republican party; all the Western states had organizations of German Republicans in the late 1850's. The German vote was important to any candidate, as Abraham Lincoln saw so clearly that he became the owner of a German newspaper.

Theodore Canisius, a native of Prussia, had settled in Illinois. In 1859 he became editor of the *Staatz-Anzeiger* in Springfield, and he published a letter from Lincoln on the equal citizenship of native- and foreign-born citizens. Canisius was soon in debt for rent on his printing shop. The owner took over the paper and sold it to Lincoln, who turned it back to Canisius with the understanding that he would run a Republican paper in the German language with some articles in English. Lincoln had paid $400 for this political asset, which would serve him well; it was commonly said that he owed his election to the support of the German-Americans in the Western states. On December 6, 1860, one month after the election, he conveyed the type, the rolls of newsprint and all the intangibles of the *Staatz-Anzeiger* to Canisius. No one knew that the President-elect had owned a German newspaper. A few months later tall, handsome, auburn-bearded Theodore Canisius was appointed U. S. Consul at Vienna. In Austria he wrote a biography of Lincoln which was read all over Europe. In later years he served in consular posts in Germany, England and the languorous Samoa Islands.

Many of the Forty-eighters had public careers in America approaching that of Carl Schurz, soldier, Senator, editor and diplomat. Young Gustavus Koerner, the first schoolmaster at Belleville, Illinois, carried scars from the Frankfurt barricades. Across the street from the Belleville schoolhouse was his law office, where James Shields came to study torts and contracts. In 1860, while serving as lieutenant governor of Illinois, Koerner had a strong hand in shaping the Republican platform and in the nomination of Lincoln. Five years later he was a pallbearer at Lincoln's funeral. In the 1870's he served as an American minister in Spain and France, representing his new country in the Old World which he had fled.

There were many kinds among the Germans—scholars and farmers, statesmen and churchmen, men of action and men of thought—and America was broad enough to give them all a future. Though he was a relative of Prince Bismarck, Henry C. Brockmeyer rebelled at Prussian militarism and set out for America as a youth of sixteen. He landed in New York in 1844 with one schilling and three words of English. For a season he worked as a bootblack and a cobbler. Then he went west, tramping through Ohio, Indiana and Illinois. He crossed the Mississippi and for two years lived alone, like an immigrant Thoreau, in the Missouri woods. Emerging from solitude, he taught philosophy in St. Louis, translated Hegel, and roamed through the Midwest—a tall, long-striding man with restless eyes and a hawklike disputatious nose, lecturing on German idealism. Indifferent to the world he was given food and lodging by his students. In 1876-1877 he served as Acting Governor of Missouri, but his heart was in philosophy. During his last years he wandered in the Western Territories, hunting and fishing with the Creek Indians and camping alone on the Arkansas.

Koerner had one kind of success, Brockmeyer another, but there were many German-Americans who knew nothing but failure. One was John Peter Altgeld, a slow-minded peasant who came to the United States in stormy 1848 with no more motive than to earn a living. He had been a farmer and wagonmaker in the village of Nieder Selters (whose chief product was "seltzer" water). The crop failure of 1847 ruined both his trades. When some German-Americans sent passage money Altgeld came to Ohio and rented a farm near Newville in Richland County. Already this was a land of legends—of the wandering Johnny Appleseed and of strange Eleazer Williams, who was thought to be the lost dauphin, the rightful king of France. Here a hundred years later Louis Bromfield developed his Malabar Farm. In 1848 Richland County was half wilderness, and a man of more purpose than peasant Altgeld would not have rented another's land.

The oldest Altgeld child, brought to Ohio as an infant, was a serious, clumsy boy with a harelip and a brushy mat of hair that would not part. Young John P. Altgeld worked in the fields, peddled cabbages, potatoes and turnips in the town of Mansfield, and hired out to neighboring farmers when he could be spared at home. In winter he sat in a district school, an awkward friendless boy in homespun clothing, listening with strained concentration. When he was twelve, he could read and write English, and then his schooling ended. But his education went on. Home from soldiering in the Civil War, he set out for himself. In the Old World a young man belonged to his native village, but America was a land for roaming. He tramped south to Cincinnati and then went across Indiana and Illinois. For five years he drifted over the frontier, working as a farm hand and railroad laborer, occasionally teaching school and reading law books. In Chicago in 1875 he began a law practice, invested his small savings in real estate and was occasionally troubled by the realization that in that powerful city, rising like a phoenix from the ashes of the great fire, the rich were growing richer and the poor were growing poorer year by year. From the Superior Court of Chicago he was elected Governor of Illinois in 1892, and soon he had pardoned the surviving "conspirators" of the Haymarket Riot. For that act of courage and conscience he was maligned from New York to San Francisco.

Despite bitter opposition Altgeld was renominated for the governorship in 1896. Though defeated he scored an impressive vote, running ahead of the Democratic presidential candidate. Had he not been of alien birth he was the logical man for the presidential nomination. He gave his support to young William Jennings Bryan, and in Springfield youthful Vachel Lindsay watched an event that went into a poem twenty-five years later:

When Bryan came to Springfield and Altgeld gave him greeting,
Rochester was deserted, Divernon was deserted,
Mechanicsburg, Riverton, Chickenbristle, Cotton Hill
Empty: all Sangamon came to the meeting . . .

Not only Sangamon County but all the nation listened to the eloquent Nebraskan and the son of an illiterate German wagon-maker.

Despite Bryan's defeat Altgeld, as leader of the party, insisted that the Democratic platform of 1896 must be upheld again in 1900. Though in failing health, he fired the party with crusading zeal. Upon Bryan's second nomination Altgeld made a speaking tour through New England. Back in Chicago he resumed his law practice and spoke on urgent public issues. On March 12, 1902, after a speech at Joliet, Illinois, he collapsed and died. His body was taken to Chicago and laid in a flower-banked bier in the north corridor of the public library. It was a raw March day with a wet wind gusting in from the lake, but on Michigan Avenue, a never-ending line of Altgeld's fellow citizens stood in the rain. Fifty thousand filed past his coffin. He had been hated and reviled during his stormy life, but death brought his vindication. There was an air of eternity about him, said his young friend Edgar Lee Masters, like the cold clear light that rests at dawn on the hills.

13. The Iron Road

Five dollars was the fare from Buffalo to Chicago in 1850, and as he left the canal barge for a lake steamer, the traveler had a choice of routes. One way was by water, over Lake Erie to Detroit, up Lake Huron and through the Straits of Mackinac and down the long reach of Lake Michigan to Milwaukee or Chicago. It was a thousand-mile journey, and the fare included bed and board for five full days. This bargain was available because of steamship competition with another route—a lake voyage to Detroit and a clattering railroad ride through woods and marshes. Track's end was at New Buffalo on the lake shore at the extreme southwestern corner of Michigan. This was as far as the railroad could go on a Michigan charter, but a steamer was waiting to run the remaining fifty miles to Chicago. By land and water it was a 533-mile journey.

The first railroads in the West were, like the canals, a means of linking water routes of transportation. In 1850 no railroad came into Ohio, Indiana or Illinois from outside the state borders, though each state had "stub" lines leading to lake ports and river landings. The most ambitious rail line of the West crossed Ohio north to south, from Sandusky to Cincinnati. Cleveland had a railroad heading for Columbus which it had not yet reached; by a junction at Xenia this road would eventually join the line to Cincinnati. The pioneer Indiana line linked Indianapolis with the Ohio River; it was projected to Lake Michigan. On the bumpy run to the Hoosier capital passengers helped the firemen take on wood and water. Fuel was loaded from woodyards beside the track and water was bailed with buckets from a creek. The operation was called "jerking water," and so Indiana had the original jerkwater train. In Illinois fifty miles of railroad reached west across the prairie from Chicago toward the Mississippi and the busy river landing at Galena. Another fifty miles of iron road connected Springfield with the Illinois River at Naples. All the early locomotives and railroad cars were delivered to the tracks by water.

The railroad short cut across the state of Michigan led through dank forest and marshland, with a few straggling villages on the way. A British traveler in 1851 wondered how a railroad could be supported by that wilderness. When the train stopped at a station, he heard a burst of cackling and squawking from a carload of cooped chickens. The brakeman opened a door and a fox jumped out—it had come aboard at the previous station. On another run in a snowstorm the train stopped when the locomotive boiler went dry. The fireman filled the tank with snow, but by that time he had run out of wood. The engineer tramped through the forest, roused a settler from his bed and came back with a team of horses. They hauled the locomotive to town, where it took on wood and water. So the Michigan Racer got through. But Lake Michigan was frozen and the Chicago steamer was laid by till spring. Passengers were transferred to stages for the cold ride to Chicago.

The road was supported not by the wilderness but by the growing Chicago commerce, and it needed a rail entry into the city. To secure a right of way, the Michigan Central company bought stock in the New Albany and Salem Railroad of Indiana and in the newly projected Illinois Central. The Chicago city council had assigned the Illinois Central a route along the lake front provided the railroad men would build a breakwater to keep the lake from washing into the city streets. Now the construction crews had an amphibious project. They built pilings at the lake's edge and ran their iron above the restless water. So the first railroad train clanked into the city that would become the home of the "Zephyr," the "Rocket," the "Chief," the "Hiawatha," the "Twentieth Century Limited," the "Diplomat," the "Abraham Lincoln." Twenty years later, after Chicago's great fire, the track was walled on the lake side with rubble from the destroyed city.

In 1837, with the brashness of the West, Illinois had enacted its grandiose Internal Improvement Bill, calling for an outlay of $10,000,000 for canals, roads, railroads, bridges and river improvements. The state had just four hundred thousand people, the size of present Indianapolis, most of them living hand to mouth on half-tilled farms. In a flurry of great undertakings the state hired engineers and surveyors and bought hundreds of miles of railroad right of way. Six months later came the panic of 1837 and the state was penniless.

Indiana suffered the same excitement and the same collapse. After a year of reckless speculation, financial panic broke across the state. Instead of a rich trade with Eastern markets, Hoosier farmers sold oats at six cents a bushel, eggs at three cents a dozen and chickens at five cents each. At the great Cincinnati market cattle and hogs brought two and a half cents a pound. In 1836 the Indiana land offices had sold twenty million acres of public land. In 1838 business was one-tenth of that. By 1840 just 281 miles of the "Mammoth Internal Improvement Program" were completed.

As a result of this debacle the public-improvement projects passed from the control of the states into the hands of private companies. Like a farm boy on a hayrack, the Western economy could fall hard and recover quickly. Within a few years the great projects were under way again. If the capital came from Boston, New York, London and Amsterdam, it was still the promise of the heartland and the pressure of new populations that created the commerce of the West.

The longest railroad in America before the Civil War was the Illinois Central. Its construction, its land policies, its colonization program were new chapters in the surging saga of the railroad. It brought a new future to the windswept prairie, it poured population into a rich and empty country, it turned the grasslands into an enormous granary.

Illinois is a long state, shaped like an arrowhead, lying between three broad rivers and a great lake. In 1835 Galena at the northwestern corner was its chief city, and a railroad was planned from there to the southern tip of the state. Cairo at the junction of the Ohio and the Mississippi seemed a place with a future, though it lay on a muddy shelf threatened by both rivers. The original plan of a central railroad came from a group of Cairo promoters. Unfortunately Charles Dickens was an investor in the stock of the Cairo Company. When it failed to pay dividends, Dickens took a dismal view of Cairo; he gave the place an infamous and international publicity, portraying it as the desolate "Eden" in *Martin Chuzzlewit*. The Cairo Company, having found itself unequal to the building of a Central Railroad, was glad to let the state gather that item into the Internal Improvement Bill of 1837. After three years and an expenditure of a million dollars for surveys, rights of way, office buildings and stations, the state began to realize the magnitude of the project. This railroad could be built only with a subsidy of lands from the public domain. In Washington Senator Stephen A. Douglas began to work for a land-grant bill.

In 1850 the federal government gave to the state of Illinois a railroad right of way through the public lands. Along the Y-shaped route from Galena and Chicago to Cairo were granted the even-numbered sections on each side of the road. The total grant was 2,595,000 acres, nearly the size of Connecticut, a princely domain which should yield enough revenue to lay the iron road from Lake Michigan to the Ohio. In making the grant, Congress stipulated that in addition to the main line from Cairo to Dunlieth on the upper Mississippi the company should lay a "branch line" to Chicago; soon after its construction the branch became the trunk of the system. A railroad was a creator of values. The government, it was reasoned, could give the even-numbered sections to the Illinois Central Company at no loss of public revenue since the remaining odd-numbered sections would bring twice their original price. This was the origin of the policy which would build the great trans-Mississippi railroads in the next decades.

When the land grant was enacted, a group of Eastern bankers, railroad and steamship men descended on the sunburned lawmakers at Springfield, seeking the railroad charter. Organizing the Illinois Central Railroad Company, they brought Senator Robert Rantoul from Massachusetts to present their plans for marketing the land, constructing the long rail line and bringing settlement to empty counties. Rantoul was a reformer and abolitionist about whom John Greenleaf Whittier wrote a fervid poem. Like Cromwell and Milton, said the poet, Rantoul "felt the heat of freedom's march." He also felt the pressure of emigrants marching to the frontier. Rantoul died in 1858 while delivering a protest against slavery, but his name lives on in an Illinois Central town which has become known afar. As the site of Chanute Field, Rantoul vibrates to the roar of aircraft over the wide prairie.

From the start the Illinois Central was as much an Eastern as a Western venture. The promoters and officials were Eastern men, and the policies of the company were decided far from the prairie towns that would hear the locomotive whistle. After careful surveys it was estimated that construction of seven hundred miles of road—a stem coming up from Cairo to Centralia (which

is now the center of United States population) and two arms
leading to Chicago and Dunlieth—would cost $16,500,000. The
directors were rich men, but not that rich. They proposed to sell
bonds secured by a mortgage on two million acres of the granted
lands.

The most likely market was in England. A generation earlier
English investors had bought $7,000,000 worth of Erie Canal
bonds, to their own and America's profit. But despite its melliflu-
ous syllables, Illinois had a bad sound in the ears of British
bankers. The state had failed to pay interest on debts incurred
in its collapsed program of public improvements, and more investors than Charles Dickens had sunk money in the bankrupt
Cairo Company. This time, however, there were millions of
acres of land beneath the speculation and the directors issued
pamphlets in London describing the riches of the prairie and the
promise of Illinois. Other pamphlets in French and German,
describing this longest railroad in the world, were circulated on
the continent. When a British firm subscribed $5,000,000 con-
struction of this road began. Meanwhile the sale of securities
continued on both sides of the Atlantic. Stephen A. Douglas,
Harriet Beecher Stowe and Wendell Phillips were among the
American stockholders. But the chief flow of funds came from
the Old World, which was also sending workmen for the construction crews and immigrant farmers to settle the railroad lands.
By the time the last spike was driven, the railroad was largely
owned by foreign investors. Some British stockholders crossed
the ocean to travel on their railroad and examine the lands. One
of them, the free-trade statesman Richard Cobden, sent back
glowing reports of the Illinois country, declaring that the railroad
lands were "the noblest domain ever transferred in one convey-
ance."

In the mid-century a clamor of railroad building spread across
the heartland. In 1850 Ohio had 300 miles of railroad; in 1857
the state was webbed with 3,000 miles of iron track. Indiana's
first hundred miles of rails joined Madison to Indianapolis in

1847; in the next decade the state's railroads were multiplied ten times. Illinois had 15 miles of railroad in 1850 and 2,400 miles in 1857. Few of the pioneer roads were profitable: though the Chicago & Galena paid dividends of 16 per cent in the mid-1850's, many of the early railroads paid little or nothing. When the Steubenville and Indiana line was built through Coshocton County, Ohio, most of the stock was paid to contractors or holders of right-of-way. It was a hollow compensation, for no dividend was ever paid. But every district wanted a railroad in the 1850's, and the building went on.

The Illinois Central builders had a deadline to meet; the charter called for completion of the road in 1858. Work began on all twelve sections of the line in 1852, and labor contractors scoured the Eastern cities for workmen. In the summer of 1853 placards appeared in the immigrant halls and hotels of New York:

WANTED!
3000 LABORERS
on the 12th Division of the
ILLINOIS CENTRAL RAILROAD
wages, 1.25 per day

Constant employment was promised for two years or more "in a healthy climate where land can be bought cheap and for fertility is not surpassed in any part of the Union."

The contractors hoped to keep ten thousand men and three thousand teams at work on the long roadbed staked out across the prairie. Horses and mules stayed on the job, but men came and went, so that recruiting was never ended. While New York agents hired Irish and German immigrants, other recruiters in Quebec and New Orleans provided free transportation to Illinois for railroad laborers. One contractor sent to Ireland for a thousand men. They were shuttled from ship to train (Chicago was connected to the Atlantic coast by rail in 1852), and their first lodging was a tent town on the prairie amid the uproar of digging, blasting and hauling. The men fought clouds of mosquitoes in the summer and felt the sting of snow in January. Cholera was epidemic in Illinois in the 1850's, and ague was as certain as the next season. Beside the hazards of accident and disease there were deadly rivalries among the work crews: North Irish against South Irish and Irish against German. It was said that "a murder a mile" marked the progress of the iron road in Illinois.

Over the prairie came the boom of dynamite and the clang of iron. Construction was done ahead of schedule. On September 21, 1856, the last rail was laid at Centralia, a sweating foreman swung his sledge on the final spike, and the longest railroad in the world was ready for traffic. Commerce would grow with settlement, and settlement was the railroad's business. The western railroads brought in the people who would produce a commerce for the rails to carry. In 1853, while Illinois Central track was being laid in Champaign and Coles counties, a land agent noted: "We rode for thirty miles on this division without seeing a tree, a house or any living thing save an occasional prairie dog." Four years later, with a regular schedule of trains going through, this wilderness had become crop-patterned farmland. In 1856 the railroad company was selling at $5 to $25 an acre land which for years the government had offered at $.62½ to $1.25.

Every ten miles in the empty country the railroad built a siding of track, set up a boxlike station and gave a name to a future town. For these prospective settlements a standard plat was prepared, complete with street names. A town staked out in the grasslands without a tree to the horizon began with Mulberry Street on the eastern border and Ash Street on the west, with Hickory, Walnut, Chestnut, Oak, Locust and Poplar between them. The streets running north and south were numbered. There was no wrong side of the tracks in these towns-to-be; the railroad ran directly through the center between Chestnut and Oak, and at the end of every street wild grass waved in the wind. Prairie towns would be monotonous by nature—without hill or bluff or curving stream to break the checkerboard—but the prefabricated town plat would make them indistinguishable.

Many Illinois towns became replicas of this pattern, the depot in the center with one or two business streets alongside, and strung on the track in the heart of town its grain elevators, corncribs, lumberyard and a trampled cattle pen with a cleated ramp pitched at the railroad siding.

The larger towns broke through that rigid pattern. A county seat had its courthouse for a focus, and the town could spread away from the track in one direction or another. Having outgrown its plotted grid, it could find new street names—Front, Grove, Park, Wood, Prairie, Empire. Along with Washington, Franklin, Jefferson and Jackson came such streets as Griswold, Gridley and Neal. Nowadays their residents never wonder about those lackluster names, but one might guess where they came from. David A. Neal and George Griswold were Eastern capitalists and early officials of the Illinois Central. Asahel Gridley was an Illinois speculator-politician who sold vast tracts of railroad land in McLean and Woodford counties and plotted his own townsites on the prairie.

In the 1850's Illinois was the fastest growing state in the Union. The population doubled in ten years, "an unparalleled growth," the Superintendent of the Eighth U.S. Census observed in 1860, "by the regular course of settlement and natural increase." But the course of settlement was hardly a natural process; it was the result of an unparalleled program of advertising and promotion. In these years the Eastern towns and cities were flooded with circulars picturing the beauty and fertility of Illinois lands, listing prices and credit terms and quoting Illinois residents on the healthfulness and prosperity of their state. Newspaper advertisements of Illinois railroad land appeared in New York, Boston and Philadelphia, addressed to newly arriving immigrants and to ambitious laborers and mechanics. Amid the clatter of Second, Third and Sixth avenues passengers in New York horsecars stared at placards picturing a prairie farmer standing in the shadow of corn fifteen feet tall and announcing:

ILLINOIS CENTRAL RAILROAD COMPANY
offers for sale
ONE MILLION ACRES OF SUPERIOR FARMING LANDS
in farms of
40, 80 and 160 acres and upwards at from $8 to $12 per acre.
These lands are
NOT SURPASSED BY ANY IN THE WORLD.

Agricultural magazines, emigrant gazettes, even *Godey's Lady's Book*, the *Phrenological Journal* and the *Water Cure Magazine* advertised "Homes for the Industrious in the Garden State of the West." At one time a hundred magazines and newspapers were carrying the message to almost every reader in America. Inquirers about Illinois land promptly received an illustrated pamphlet showing a farmhouse and a commodious barn, contented cattle in the shade of a timber grove and a train passing in the distance. Other pictures showed a plow breaking prairie sod and a reaping machine mowing golden wheat. "In their natural state," the reader learned, "these prairies provide the richest pasturage in the world. To prepare them for the most luxurious crops, no process is required but the simple turning over of the sod. Stable manure here is a nuisance. . . . Two, four or six feet of loam is not easily exhausted."

The appeal was pitched to speculators as well as to farmers. "In this country it is well known that nearly all the princely fortunes that have been accumulated, and perhaps all that have stood the test of time, have been the result of judicious investment in land. . . . Europe and the Atlantic States of North America may retain the business of administering to the artificial wants and luxuries of the world, but its granaries will be filled from the broad 'prairies' of our western country. All that has been wanting to produce this result is now being furnished—men and roads."

Farsighted investors had already seen the promise of the prairie lands. Solomon Sturgis, having bought sixty-five thousand acres in eastern Illinois, advertised in the *Chicago Democratic Press:* "Now as I hold in abhorrence all speculators, none such need apply. I wish to sell to actual settlers. . . . I hold that Congress should keep their lands as a sacred trust for this and succeeding generations. . . . I want to take care of my part for my six sons, and I don't know how many grandsons. I hope, reader, you will think this is right and acquit me of all motives but those of the most benevolent character." It was this same Solomon Sturgis who built the first big grain elevator in Chicago, erecting it on land leased from the Illinois Central.

Even a minister concerned with the salvation of souls could see this earthly promise. In the winter of 1857 a villager in Avon, Maine, wrote to his former neighbor Eben F. Day, who had migrated to Freedom, Illinois, in La Salle County, with fourteen children:

> Having the knowledge of Illinois that you now have, would you sell out and go there to live if you were in my condition as to family and poverty etc.? I could go out to Illinois and get there with $300 or $400. What can I do? Could I take a farm which would be of much profit, and do you know of any to let? . . . Tell me about it as to buildings, farming tools and water. How far are you from Middleport the county seat of Iroquois County? One Brother Dunn, a preacher who lives in New York state, has a few thousand acres of land in that vicinity for sale. He has written me about an 80-acre lot which is on a stage road and which is five miles from Middleport. His price is $13 per acre. He requires $100 in advance. . . . What kind of bargain would it be? There is no wood on it and not a stump or a stone.

The Illinois Central ran through Iroquois County and through the county seat, which was soon renamed for the Potawatomi wife of fur-trader Gurdon Hubbard, the first white man in the region. After two years Hubbard had tired of his swarthy mate and he gave her to his partner. But her name was remembered by later settlers, who called their town Watseka. Most of the country was marshland, and the railroad agents could not sell it for $5 an acre. If Brother Dunn got his asking price, he must have had some bitter purchasers.

There were better lands in other counties, and the railroad agents offered a wide choice. Along with sectional maps describ-

ing the terrain, their pamphlets traced, step by step, a bright
future for prairie farmers:

> Now what may the poor man or European immigrant do in
> Illinois to attain an independence? Assume that on arrival he is
> penniless. Labor here is always in demand. He will easily find em-
> ployment. One or two years so spent will give him a knowledge of
> the country, have seasoned him to the climate, and if he has been
> prudent left him with two or three hundred dollars to begin his
> operation. He purchases a quarter section and pays down two years'
> interest, say fifty dollars—he gets a yoke of oxen and a plough for
> say one hundred dollars, and lives on the balance of his means till
> he can raise a crop. In June he breaks up, with the assistance of his
> neighbors whom he pays in kind, say twenty acres of prairie, then
> purchases the right to cut rails from the neighboring timber, and
> hauls them on his ground. In September he harrows his twenty acres
> and plants it with wheat. He earns some money by assisting in
> harvesting, pays for his seed, and buys some necessary tools and
> perhaps half a dozen calves and pigs. During the year he fences in his
> twenty acres. In the spring he throws among his wheat some herds'
> grass and clover. In July he gets a crop of say three hundred bushels
> of wheat, which are worth $200. Having in June broken up another
> twenty acres and pursued the same process, he attains the same
> results. In the meantime his calves feed on his unbroken prairie and
> on the clover sown on his first wheat patch, which he plows up in
> April and plants with Indian corn, so that the second year he has,
> besides his 300 bushels of wheat, some 1000 bushels of Indian corn,
> worth $400. With this means thus afforded he may easily in the
> third year break up 40 instead of 20 acres and he will have, by pur-
> suing the same course in the fourth year, his 600 bushels of wheat
> and 2000 bushels of corn. His calves will now have become a herd
> of cattle. He will have a fenced farm of 80 acres and 80 of unbroken
> prairie for his future operations. He is independent.

This was but the beginning of the success story. The account
went on, charting the yeoman's progress to a farm property
worth $5,000 at a cost of $500.

Another example was cited for the benefit of land speculators,
that of a land investor who purchased nine sections, an area three
miles square, and rented it for half its produce. It would produce
crops worth $92,000, half of which reverts to the owner. This
was a good start, with more riches to come—for "cultivated lands

will quadruple in value. Illinois has yet to be studded with towns and villages. . . . Sixty acres laid out in lots would give back the whole outlay, and the remaining 5,700 acres, thus greatly improved, would be had for nothing."

The land pamphlet was issued in successive editions, each one larger and more alluring than the last. In the 1855 edition appeared a testimonial letter from a Methodist minister, the Reverend John S. Barger of Clinton, Illinois, who had made a good thing out of land investment while preaching the gospel. He bought 400 acres of Illinois Central land on which he counted in the first year a profit of $2,305.07. "I might have added considerably to the avails of the first year had I not been eighty miles distant, engaged in the labors of the Jacksonville District of the M.E. church." Then his voice rose, as though from a pulpit. "Let them come by thousands and tens of thousands. They will find rich lands and good water." He went on to tell of Mr. Jesse Funk, who began by making rails for his neighbors at twenty-five cents per hundred. With $200 he bought his first quarter section and purchased cattle. "Now he owns 7,000 acres, and his last year's sale of cattle and hogs at Chicago totaled over $44,000."

Another farmer on railroad land testified: "I have grown corn with stalks upwards of 9 feet in length, ears 13 inches in length and 9½ around. . . . Times have changed since I commenced in this state. Instead of 5 or 8 cents a bushel for our corn, we now get 25 to 40. Instead of 25 to 38 cents for wheat, we now have $1.25 to $1.60 per bushel. And in place of spending some four days getting to Chicago, we can go up on a morning, do our trading and get back the next day."

The long state of Illinois was pulled together by the Illinois Central. In 1850 Frink and Walker's stage made the trip from Springfield to Chicago in three days of hard travel; in 1856 the railroad train did it in twelve hours. With fireworks, band music and speech-making the downstate towns welcomed the first train on the prairie.

Said the railroad pamphlet of 1854, "Now all Europe is pouring in upon us," and to increase the flood the railroad company sent agents abroad. In England five thousand colored posters were tacked onto the walls of railway stations, parish halls and market buildings. An agent traveled through the Scandinavian countries distributing circulars printed in Swedish on one side and Norwegian on the other. In Germany a pamphlet stressed the rapidly growing German settlement in Illinois, and prairie lands were advertised in Hamburg, Bremen, Berlin and other cities. Thousands of pamphlets and maps were distributed in German seaports, and captains of immigrant ships were paid to issue Illinois land circulars to their passengers. In Chicago, the dispersal point for Western emigrants, Illinois Central men strove with agents of rival land companies for settlers on its prairie domain.

In the middle 1850's, month after month and season after season, long lines of applicants waited to buy railroad land. By October, 1857, half the railroad sections were sold. Then the panic came, like a numbing northwest wind, and the land offices were empty. The collapse was followed by bad seasons, with a double blight of scanty crops and falling prices. In June of 1860 a writer in the *Atlantic Monthly* described the Illinois Central as "a railroad which has not enough business to earn a dividend." The weather improved, but not the Western economy; bumper corn crops glutted the market and drove prices lower. Corn was taken for land payments, the railroad company loading it at Chicago into lake steamers for Buffalo and Oswego. Some of that prairie maize went across the sea to Liverpool. When the outbreak of war cut off traffic from the South, land sales almost ceased. But at the end of 1862 the sun came out. Land transfers climbed to 250,000 acres in each of the next two years, while war business swelled the railroad traffic.

In the 1860's Illinois led the nation in production of wheat, oats and corn; it was first in shipment of hogs and second (to Texas) in cattle. Over the iron road rolled trains of grain and cattle cars, and back came loads of Lake Michigan lumber to build the prairie towns. The first prefabricated houses in America were shipped from Chicago; ready-framed farm dwellings with a kitchen-living room and three bedrooms were set down anywhere along the Illinois Central for $150 plus transportation.

Meanwhile the speculators had been reaping their own harvest. The building of the Illinois Central set off a scramble for the alternate sections of government land along the railroad and the land immediately beyond. Hundreds of thousands of acres of public land were claimed by military warrants left over from the bounty acts of the Mexican War and the War of 1812, and other tracts were bought at auction. When the railroad route was announced, speculators rushed in to bid on blocks of land along the way. The minimum price for government land along the railroad was $2.50 per acre; six miles back the figure was $1.25. Speculators bought the land at a few cents above these prices, and held them for many times the cost. Thirteen million acres of public land in Illinois were sold between 1849 and 1857; then the land offices, scattered down the state from Chicago to Shawneetown, closed their books and their doors. Some of the public land was bought by farmers who wanted more acres than they could use, some was taken up by local businessmen for investment, some was acquired by public officials. Virtually all members of the state legislature and many members of the U.S. Congress owned Illinois land. Hundreds of thousands of acres were held by great speculators like Colonel Joseph Watson and the Berrian brothers of New York, and Romulus Riggs and John Grigg of Philadelphia.

"Egypt," the deep southern district of Illinois, was the last area to prosper. But in 1863 and 1864 land sales quickened in the southern counties. Wartime crops of cotton were bursting white along the railroad; tobacco striped the southward-facing slopes; from orchards and berry farms fruit-car specials hurried to Chicago.

Beneath the black prairie loam lay vast black beds of coal.

Fuel wood, the railroad company had advertised, could be delivered at any Illinois Central station at three to four dollars a cord. But in the pamphlet of 1857 that announcement was replaced by another: "Eastern men, on first coming to this state, sigh for more woodland; but they soon learn that there is coal enough below its surface to warm up the hearts and bodies of all of Uncle Sam's family, besides generating steam enough to drive all the engines in creation to all eternity." In 1855 an Illinois Central fireman heaved the first shovel of coal into his firebox. A dozen years later all the railroad woodyards were gone and locomotives puffed black coal smoke at the prairie sky. Then the coal-fueled engines hauled southern Illinois coal to the industrial plants of St. Louis and the spreading steel mills of South Chicago.

By 1870 four-fifths of the railroad lands were sold, and dividends were being mailed to shareholders in England, Holland, Belgium and France; until the twentieth century the Illinois Central was largely owned by European investors. Then the long whistle wavered over the prairie and long trains rolled through a land of plenty. The iron road was strung with towns, and every cross street led to the X-shaped warning, "LOOK OUT FOR THE CARS."

14. The Prairie Lawyer

We must be prepared to take him as he was.
—WILLIAM H. HERNDON

It cost a dollar and a half to ride the stagecoach, but walking was free. On that spring day in 1834 Abraham Lincoln tramped the twenty miles to New Salem, reading the big worn volume he had bought at an auction in Springfield. After each page he closed the book and recited to himself, while his long loose stride covered the miles. *The rights of persons considered in their natural capacities are also of two sorts, absolute and relative. Absolute, which are such as appertain and belong to particular men, merely as individuals or single persons: relative, which are incident to them as members of society, and standing in various relations with each other.*

At New Salem, a scatter of cabins on a wooded ridge of prairie, he went to the Berry & Lincoln store, took off his shoes and sat under a tree, still reading Blackstone's *Commentaries on the Common Law*, published in London in 1769. *For the principal aim of society is to protect individuals in the enjoyment of those absolute rights, which were vested in them by the immutable laws of nature; but which could not be preserved in peace with-*

out that mutual assistance and intercourse which is gained by the institution of friendly and social communities.

When he got tired, he lay on his back, propping his feet on the tree trunk. At dusk he moved inside the store and stretched out on the counter with a candle at his head. Sir William Blackstone in a powdered wig and poplin gown had first read his lectures to the students of Oxford University in 1753. Now they had found their way to the Illinois prairie. *Political therefore, or civil liberty, is no other than natural liberty so far restrained by human laws (and no farther) as is necessary and expedient for the general advantage of the public. Hence we may collect that the law which restrains a man from doing mischief to his fellow-citizens, though it diminishes the natural, increases the civil liberty of mankind.*

"Of course when I came of age," Lincoln wrote, years later, "I did not know much." Most of his education was obtained after his arrival in Illinois, aged twenty-one; much of it he acquired during his six years at New Salem. He came to that village an aimless, ignorant backwoods youth. Three years later he was a member of the Illinois legislature, elected by his neighbors for whom he had pitched hay and cradled wheat while campaigning. New Salem was a Southern community with a sprinkling of Yankees. With his Kentucky easiness and his Hoosier drawl, Lincoln fitted in. Now, in 1834, he was studying law in preparation for his first session of the legislature. It would meet in Vandalia in December.

Besides being an officeholder, Lincoln was half-owner of a store. His partner, Bill Berry, the son of a minister and strong temperance man, was the best customer of the Berry-Lincoln stock of whisky. While Berry tapped the barrel, Lincoln read books, and the store sank deeper into debt. Lincoln was also a part-time surveyor, ready to close up shop to run the lines on someone's half or quarter section. Being too poor to buy a chain, he used a grapevine for his measure. The pay for running a farm boundary was two dollars, but on one of his jobs Lincoln took two buckskins which a neighbor woman foxed onto his pants; then he could wade through brush and brambles. He was also the New Salem postmaster, keeping receipts in an old blue sock under the store counter. The office paid him $30 a year, and it went well with storekeeping and surveying. On a surveying tour he put in his hat any mail for people in the neighborhood and delivered it on the way. Mail came to New Salem on horseback once a week. It included a newspaper, the postmaster's perquisite, which Lincoln read aloud to himself, column by column and page by page. He was a good, obliging postmaster, except that he sometimes went off for the day, leaving the door open and the place untended. He took odd jobs, splitting rails, pitching hay, handling bags of grain at the Rutledge mill. Between times, in the summer of 1834, he studied Blackstone, lying on a woodpile or under a rustling tree, with the breeze bringing the low roar of the millrace on the Sangamon.

New Salem in 1834 was as big as Chicago, and it seemed to have more future. It had a mill, a ferry, three grocery stores and a tavern. It was a trading center for the central Sangamon valley; on fine days as many as forty horses waited at the Rutledge mill. But the town had a short history. By 1840 its people had moved to more eventful places—Petersburg, Jacksonville or Springfield. In 1866 just one empty hut remained, and soon that was gone. Fire and salvage and decay, winter snows and summer sun, the rooting of hogs and the rubbing of cattle erased the town as though it had never been. Recalling it now, one can feel that New Salem existed for Abraham Lincoln. It gave him employment, with time for books and daydreams. It elected him to office. And for him it assembled its diverse people—wise Mentor Graham; boastful Denton Offutt; steady James Rutledge; roistering Jack Armstrong; leathery Dr. John Allen, smelling of camphor pills and arguing against slavery and whisky; Jack Kelso, perched on a fence rail, reciting Shakespeare and Burns. All his life Lincoln remembered them all.

To New Salem Lincoln had come on a flatboat, floating down

the Sangamon. He was a backwoods youth carried on the currents of frontier life. There was not much behind him, only a rude boyhood in Indiana and some drifting on the frontier.

"My father taught me to work," he once recalled, "but not to love it." Tom Lincoln was a dull, heavy, shiftless man, a persistent failure in a country jostling with opportunity. He took up six land claims in his life and could not pay for one. He never learned to write, though in 1848 he sent a letter to Springfield asking his son for $20 to keep his last farm from going. By that time he was too old to move on when debt pressed him.

Tom Lincoln had followed the frontier. His log cabin at Hodgenville, Kentucky, was as rude as a cave, and the fields were barren. Indiana promised better; they moved to Spencer County when Abe was seven. Though trees were everywhere Tom Lincoln could provide nothing better for his family than a "half-faced camp," with one side open. The first winter they spent in that poor shelter, feeding a fire on the open side, crouching under the low roof in snow and rain. Nancy Hanks Lincoln lived to see her family in a four-walled cabin, and then she died. Nine-year-old Abe whittled pegs for her coffin. She was buried without prayer or praise; months later a roving preacher from Kentucky spoke some words over her snow-covered grave.

The next year Tom Lincoln went to Kentucky, married a widow and brought her, with her three children, to Indiana. Then Abe had a stepmother, strong, gentle, warm-hearted Sarah Bush Lincoln. She sent him to Azel Dorsey's dim little school with greased paper windows and a puncheon floor. There he had a few months' learning at age ten; four years later a few months at Andrew Crawford's, and still later some weeks at Swaney's school, walking four miles through the woods to get there. Altogether, by the time he was sixteen, he had one year's schooling. He was a towering youth then, lean, long-armed, with a deepening, drawling voice, and he worked for thirty-seven cents a day, running a ferry raft across the Ohio at the mouth of Anderson's Creek. Not far away was New Harmony, a town full of books, ideas, philosophers from England, France and Germany. Abe Lincoln would have liked that place, but he was hired by James Gentry to take a flatboat loaded with wheat and pork to New Orleans.

In Indiana 1829 was a hard year, a time of poor crops and sickness of men and animals. Illinois, it was said, had good, open, healthful land, and Tom Lincoln was ready to move again. They loaded their goods into a farm wagon, hitched up two yoke of oxen and headed west. It was the end of winter when they reached the Wabash, and the light of spring was on the grand prairie that opened beyond the river. A surge of green ran over the long swells, the spring wind smelled of grass and distance. It was a new, wild, spacious country with the future all before it, and Abraham Lincoln had just turned twenty-one.

After two weeks of jolting travel they came to Macon County and the raw village of Decatur on its rise of ground. They creaked through the town, a mud-stained wagon with its gawking Hoosiers, and asked the way to the Sangamon. Ten more miles brought them to the place. They built a cabin, four miles from the nearest neighbors, at the edge of the Sangamon timber.

That winter was a season the Illinois settlers never forgot. "The winter of the deep snow" showed the newcomers another mood of the prairie. In the last week of December the sky hung low over the frozen land. Then snow drove in on a northwest wind—all day and all night, another day and another night. When the storm passed, they were buried in three feet of snow, with drifts as high as a cabin chimney. Sun melted the snow and wind froze it, and a new blizzard brought two more feet of snow. Families were walled in their cabins, horses and cattle floundered and froze in the fields. A numb traveler rode in to Springfield and could not get down from his horse; his overcoat had frozen to the saddle. At the tavern door two men loosed the girth and carried the man and saddle to the fire to thaw him free. After that long winter the Lincolns moved again—fifty miles southeast to Goose Nest prairie.

In Coles County Abe Lincoln became known as a tireless ax-man and a good hand with a pitchfork or mattock. He worked here and there, splitting rails for zigzag fences, cutting cordwood to sell in the village of Charleston. He wandered back to the Sangamon valley, looking at the country and ready for an odd job there. So he met a man who made a difference in his life.

Denton Offutt was the kind of character Mark Twain pictured in *The Gilded Age;* he was an earlier Colonel Sellers, talkative, expansive, expectant, a drifting man with big ideas, a Western man full of hope and promise and buoyed up with whisky. He took an instant liking to Lincoln and hired him as one of a crew of three to take a flatboat cargo to New Orleans. Offutt had neither flatboat nor cargo, but he sent the crew—Lincoln, his cousin John Hanks and his stepbrother John Johnston—into government land to cut boat timbers while he looked around for a cargo. When the ark was ready, they loaded it with barreled pork and pushed off for Louisiana. They were barely started when the boat hung up on the mill dam at New Salem. Lincoln shifted the cargo, bored a hole in the bow to let the water out, and eased the lightened craft over the dam. Offutt was not sur-prised; he had already said that Abe Lincoln could make any-thing go.

On the way to New Orleans Offutt kept thinking of New Salem. It was a village now, but when steamboats came up the Sangamon, it would be a city. Returning from the long trip to market, Offutt had money in his pocket. He bought a stock of goods, fitted up a store in New Salem and put Lincoln in charge. While Lincoln kept store, sleeping on a cot in the back room among empty barrels and boxes, Offutt came and went between the settlements. In New Salem he drank the store's whisky, and sitting on the counter under the empty shelves, he talked with Lincoln about the town's future. The fact that their store was going downhill did not diminish Offutt's expectations, and when it failed, he moved on to look for something better. Lincoln took up a new partnership, the Berry & Lincoln store, with another whisky drinker. He seemed to belong to New Salem, though sometimes his thoughts were far away from the loafers gossiping about a shooting match, a horse race, or the price of a double harness.

But already New Salem was a dwindling town. There had been no improvements on the Sangamon and its commerce never came. In the spring of 1832 the steamboat *Talisman* had churned up the river to Portland Landing, near Springfield, with Lincoln steering it around the shoals. Then came word that the *Sylph* was loading Cincinnati cargo for the Sangamon, and the future of the valley glowed like sunrise. But the airy *Sylph* never appeared. In 1836 the *Utility* steamed up to New Salem and was moored to a tree below the dam. Then came a dry spell. The river shrank in its weedy channel and the *Utility* was grounded. When fall rains failed to float her, the vessel was abandoned. That is the whole story of steam navigation on the Sangamon.

By 1837 Springfield had become the market town of the Sangamon valley as well as the newly chosen capital of Illinois. It was the place for a new-fledged lawyer, and Lincoln had just been admitted to the bar. Under the windy sky of April, 1837, in debt and riding a borrowed horse with all his belongings in the saddlebags, he left the village that had been his home for six impressionable years. Now at the entrance of the New Salem State Park stands a nine-foot bronze figure of Lincoln as he was departing for Springfield. In his left hand is a frontiersman's ax which he is laying aside; in his right hand he carries Blackstone's *Commentaries*. Some years later he would write: "A nation may be said to consist of its territory, its people and its laws."

In Springfield he rode through muddy Fifth Street, tied his horse at the rack, and went in to the store of Joshua Speed to buy a bed. It would cost seventeen dollars, he found; but bachelor Speed offered to share his double bed in a bare room above the store. Lincoln carried his saddlebags upstairs. (Twenty-seven years later he appointed Joshua Speed's brother Attorney-General of the United States.) The next day he began the practice of law as a partner of John T. Stuart in an office on a muddy corner above a room where the county court was held. The office contained a battered couch covered by a buffalo robe—Lincoln's favorite place for study—a hacked wooden bench, a makeshift bookcase and a bare board table.

Four years later Lincoln was an established lawyer and the husband, after some anguished misgivings, of a vain, vivacious and cultivated woman who had been courted by Stephen A. Douglas and other ambitious bachelors of Springfield. They were married by the Reverend Charles Dresser in canonical robes— the first ceremonial Episcopalian wedding in frontier Springfield. Placing the ring on the bride's finger, Lincoln repeated the prescribed words: "With this ring I thee endow with all my goods and chattels, lands and tenements." Beside him stood burly Judge Thomas C. Browne, who was less struck with the irony of the poor husband endowing the rich wife than with its needlessness. "God Almighty, Lincoln," he muttered, "the statute fixes all that."

The Lincolns went to live in the Globe Tavern, formerly Spottswood's Rural Hotel, at Fourth and Adams streets, where they sat at table with Albert Taylor Bledsoe, a lawyer recently come to Springfield. Bledsoe was a brilliant and versatile man. After graduation from West Point he had taught mathematics at Miami University, where he was a colleague and close friend of William Homes McGuffey. Later he studied theology and became ordained in the Episcopal Church, then turned to law and was admitted to the Illinois bar in 1839. A Virginian with strong convictions on states' rights, he became a close friend of Lincoln despite their political differences. A keen-minded jurist and a tenacious logician, he helped to mold and to whet Lincoln's mind. In 1847 their paths parted. Bledsoe went south to join the faculty of the University of Virginia; eventually he served as Assistant Secretary of War in the Confederacy. Elected to Congress, Lincoln took his wife to Washington in 1847, where they lived in Mrs. Sprigg's boardinghouse on Capitol Hill, on the site of the Library of Congress.

When his Congressional term was over, Lincoln was offered by President Tyler the office of Territorial Governor of Oregon. A frontier country, a new and different place, a fresh beginning —all Lincoln's restless past prompted him to accept it. But Mary Todd Lincoln did not like the sound of Oregon. Illinois was frontier enough for her. So, back in Springfield, Lincoln began law practice with young William H. Herndon. Billy Herndon was an argumentative, humorless man who never saw any good in Lincoln's wife, and she returned his feeling fully. For years Lincoln lived between two animosities. Herndon was also a hard drinker, though he worked in the temperance movement. Called at midnight to bail out of the Springfield jail his drunk and disorderly partner, Lincoln must sometimes have sided with his wife. But he was loyal to his young colleague, and Herndon venerated Lincoln all the years of his life.

The office of Lincoln and Herndon, the back room of a brick building across from the courthouse, was a place of casual disorder, like a squatter's cabin. A young law student, wanting to be useful, once tried to clean up the place. On the littered table he found some packets of seeds which Lincoln had brought home from Washington to distribute among Sangamon County farmers. Starting to sweep the floor, he saw green blades springing from the cracks; the seeds had sprouted in that rich bed.

At nine in the morning Lincoln came in, stretched out on the battered sofa and read the newspaper, aloud. No protest could silence him; reading with both sight and hearing, he explained to Herndon, helped him to remember. When clients came in, Lincoln seemed uninterested until something reminded him of a man he had known in Coles County or Beardstown or New Salem. Then he put his feet on the table and launched into storytelling. On Sunday mornings, while his wife went to church, he brought his small sons, Willie and Tad, to the office. It was a treat for the boys. They romped over the room, pulled books from the shelves, scattered papers, put pencils in the spittoons, emptied inkstands on the floor—while Lincoln lay on the sway-backed sofa, playing with the kitten they had brought along.

Springfield in the 1840's was still a country town straggling around the public square. Between the courthouse and Lincoln's home on Eighth Street were cornfields and scraps of pasture. Morning and evening Lincoln milked his own cow, fed and curried his horse, sawed wood and split kindling. He tried to make a garden behind the house, but it went to weeds during his long absence on the district court.

The Eighth Judicial District extended from the Illinois River to the Indiana border. To the sparse frontier counties it brought the court—the circuit judge and the itinerant attorneys—twice a year. Lincoln and Herndon sometimes rode the circuit together, sharing a bed in drafty country inns; usually the room housed other lawyers and travelers as well. The beds were too short for Lincoln, his bare feet hung out in the air. While the others went noisily to sleep, he lay with a book in his hands and a candle on the chair beside him. In the night hours, to the rattle of rain on the roof and the rustle of wind in the trees, he read the dramas of Shakespeare and learned the propositions in Euclid's six books of geometry. He was the last to sleep and the first to rise. When the lawyers came down in the morning, they found Lincoln by the fire, looking up distantly from an open book.

These were Lincoln's happy seasons. He never tired of the rude life of the circuit, though it took half his time—three months every spring and fall—for nearly twenty years. He attended every court until 1858; occasionally, when Judge Davis's extensive business interests called him away, he presided. Most of the traveling lawyers managed to spend Sundays at home, but Lincoln rarely returned to Springfield until the term expired. Herndon, who could not keep a lump from his throat when writing about Lincoln, recalled striking out for home at the end of the week with "a mingled feeling of pity and sympathy" for

Lincoln, who was left with the local loungers in the tavern. Though it was never mentioned, all his colleagues knew about Lincoln's troubled home life. But Lincoln did not seem to regret those homeless Sundays. He sauntered through the village, nodding to people on the way to church, speaking gravely to dogs and children, listening to the creak of a windmill and the raucous crows in the treetops. After dinner the hitching rack was lined with wagons and townsmen gathered in the tavern, filling it to the walls and windows while the rawboned lawyer talked. Then the stories spilled out, droll, drawling, earthy stories, serious as law until the "nub" of the tale appeared. At that point Lincoln's gray eyes began to gleam, his lined face broke into laughter, and a roar of appreciation filled the room. He was a man both distant and near.

As it was organized in 1839, the Eighth Judicial District embraced fourteen counties in central and eastern Illinois. It was a long circuit, four hundred miles of prairie travel, on horseback in the worst seasons and by buggy when the roads were passable. To the itinerant lawyers the Eighth District was the "Mud Circuit"; it was all rich black prairie loam, prodigal of corn crops but bottomless after a night's rain. Sometimes Lincoln rode the circuit with huge Judge Davis in his buggy behind a matched team of grays. Sometimes he drove his own horse, "Old Buck," in his own rig, or he traveled in a surrey with four or five other lawyers. In the worst weather he rode horseback, with books, papers and a spare shirt in his saddlebags. He never tired of traveling through the prairie solitude. Often he rode after nightfall, over a country pale with moonlight or white with snow.

The route, now marked by tablets placed by the Lincoln Circuit-Marking Association, led from Springfield fifty miles north, with an overnight stop on the way, to Tremont in Tazewell County, where the new brick courthouse had a belfry to announce the arrival of the court. The next stop was Metamora, twenty miles farther north; and then the route swung back southeast, over thirty miles of high rolling prairie to Bloomington.

This was Judge Davis's home, and here Lincoln used the judge's office, which was shared by the sheriff and the clerk of court, as a waiting room between court sessions. With his feet on the judge's desk he talked, loafed, napped and sorted out the papers in his hat. Southeast again, thirty-five miles, to Mt. Pulaski, then twenty miles east to Clinton in De Witt County. Both the county and the seat were named for Governor De Witt Clinton of New York—whose broad determined face would later scowl from internal revenue stamps. Southeast again the route led to Monticello, and northeast to Urbana in lonely Champaign County. Settlement lagged in this county because the land was undrained, and travel was most arduous here. The creeks were unbridged and the road was but a wagon track in dust or mire. Still, when the court convened, the whole six thousand population of the county managed to come to town—"courting," as the Urbana *Clarion* said. From Urbana the route led to Danville, thirty miles straight east across the Grand Prairie, and then thirty-five miles south to sleepy little Paris, in Edgar County, where prairie and forest met. From Paris the route turned west, fifty-five long miles to Shelbyville, then north to Sullivan and Decatur. Most of the pioneer courthouses burned, but at Decatur the original Macon County Courthouse, a two-story log building with a "cat and clay" chimney, is preserved in Fairview Park. In the years of my own youth the Decatur Boy Scouts kindled fires in its chimney and cooked their rations on a stick; the old building survived that hazard, too. From Decatur the route led southwest to Taylorville and then northwest to Springfield, where the long zigzag L-shaped circuit was completed.

By 1850, as settlement increased and the dockets grew longer, the district was reduced to eight counties. Each county had a "court week," spring and fall, which might last two days or a fortnight. In the 1850's the first court on the schedule was in the village of Postville (now Lincoln), the seat of Logan County. Originally the court convened in Deskin's Tavern. After a frame courthouse was built nearby, the tavern continued to furnish meals and lodging for the court—judge, lawyers and prisoners all sharing the same fare and the same talk. The old courthouse is now in the Ford Museum at Dearborn, Michigan, and on its site, just off U.S. 66, stands a memorial tablet.

When the railroad was being laid through Logan County in 1853, Lincoln collected a fee for legal service: on a quarter section just west of straggling Postville he recorded a new townsite which the proprietors named Lincoln, despite their lawyer's warning that he never knew anything of that name that amounted to much. According to tradition he broke a watermelon over a wagon wheel for the town's christening. Though Lincoln was present at the first sale of town lots, he made no purchase. He never had an instinct for profit.

Now the trail-markers trace the circuit route through some of the richest farmlands in the world, through tree-shaded towns with grain elevators against the sky and long rows of storage bins glinting in the sun, over high-speed highways between huge fields of hybrid corn. In 1850 the roads were mere trails snaking through wild prairie, with an occasional farmhouse and infrequent fields of broken land. A web of wagon tracks led in to the primitive county-seat towns.

The circuit lawyers were rivals in the courtroom, but they were comrades on the road. They traveled together in the restless light of spring and the golden haze of fall, splashing through creeks, rocking over roots and stumps in a prairie grove, swishing through wild grassland. They knew each other like brothers— huge, handsome, theatrical Ward Hill Lamon, urbane Henry Clay Whitney, fiery Leonard Swett, massive Judge David Davis and gaunt Abe Lincoln. Led by "Hill" Lamon, they sang Negro spirituals while the team splashed through the mud and the April rain poured down. On the empty prairie they shared their memories and their hopes, their talk and their silence. Once, jolting across country, Lincoln talked for hours about his own people, his memories of Kentucky and Indiana and his first arrival in Illinois, when he never dreamed that he might become an attorney traveling the judicial circuit, bringing law and justice to the half-wild districts.

Court week was the big event in the sparse counties. From miles around people drove in for horse-trading and auction sales of hogs, cattle, wagons, implements and to hear the lawyers' news of affairs and politics. Everybody came—"camp outfits, musicians, parrots, pet dogs and all," reported Henry Clay Whitney. They tied their teams to the hitching racks, they ate and drank in the shade of the courthouse trees. When the bell rang and the judge called the court into session, they crowded in to hear the cases—disputes over the ownership of a litter of pigs, a wagon lost in a wager and sold before the winner could claim it, the dog that killed a brood sow, the loss of sheep by foot-rot and who was liable, wrangling over boundary lines and mortgages and many kinds of slander. At noon recess the entire court ate at a long table, like a diverse family, the judge at the head and then the lawyers, jurymen, witnesses and prisoners out on bail. Back in the courtroom, while the hot sun slanted in, they resumed the parade of scandal, rancor and dispute, with the law making its grave judgments.

At night the lawyers gathered in an upstairs tavern room with a pitcher of whisky and an endless flow of talk. Judge Davis, with a prematurely white fringe of beard making a half-circle around his massive face, settled his three hundred pounds into a creaking chair. Around him were his cronies—Lincoln, Lamon, Treat, Whitney, Swett and whatever local magistrates, editors, land commissioners and farmers he might care to include. Davis had a huge capacity for humor, politics and earthy wit and wisdom; his colleagues were ready to pick up any subject of opinion or speculation. Their talk went from horseplay to conviction and back again; it ranged through history, philosophy, politics, government, metaphysics and men. Judge Davis kept the conversation going, while Lincoln punctuated it with pithy anecdote and pungent comment.

Davis and Lincoln were wholly dissimilar men closely drawn

together. They had first met in the old Illinois State House at Vandalia in 1836, and their friendship endured until Lincoln's death. The son of an aristocratic slave-owning family in Maryland, Judge Davis was educated at Kenyon College in Ohio and the Yale Law School. He was at home in any society, but he never tired of the mud-stained people in the rural county seats. In court, which he conducted with brisk authority and earthy asides, he counted on Lincoln for the leaven of humor. Once, holding out a long document drawn up by a notoriously lazy lawyer, the judge remarked: "Astonishing, ain't it? Brother Snap did it. Wonderful, eh Lincoln?"

Though Lincoln often sat abstracted in the courtroom, he was always ready. "It's like the lazy preacher," he said, "that used to write long sermons. He'd get to writin' and was too lazy to stop."

Lincoln's friend Whitney reported this story as "rather feeble"; it was doubtless improvised, he said, and forgotten at once. But whatever question, serious or playful, the judge might ask, rolling his bulk in the groaning chair, Lincoln was prompt to answer.

At night in the smoky free-for-all the judge still leaned on Lincoln. Once they were discussing metempsychosis—the belief that when a person dies a new-born child inherits the departing soul—and from that the talk shifted to a disreputable local lawyer named Quirk. Lincoln had been silent, and at last the judge called him out of his distance. "Queer doctrine!" he said in his high husky voice. "Queer doctrine! ! Eh, Lincoln?"

Lincoln looked up with a reply that bracketed both metempsychosis and lawyer Quirk. "I rayther reckon that's good doctrine, and it's nothin' that when Quirk was born no one died."

All Lincoln's colleagues recalled his comments at times like this, though in reporting them, they add that the remarks are in less than Lincoln's best vein. His best stories did not circulate in print, and they lost something when another told them. It was more than his gifts of mimicry and drollery. Some quality of the man, the dimensions of his own enjoyment and his distance from it, was the essence of his storytelling.

Like the life at New Salem which crested during Lincoln's few years there, the itinerant county courts lasted only as long as Lincoln's life on the circuit. The Eighth Judicial District was organized in 1839. Twenty years later railroad trains were panting in the county seats and the long rides over the prairie trails were past. With the railroads came a rush of settlement. Towns sprang up, travel quickened, mail and newspapers came in daily, and the county courts became sedentary and routine. There were no circuit lawyers before Lincoln, nor after. It is a surprising realization now that the frontier period in the heartland was so brief; that it came and was gone in a single generation, so that a swamp village on the Chicago River in 1835 could become the seat of the Republican National Convention in 1860.

The circuit lawyers were in the midst of a social evolution that came but once in a region's history. They handled land claims, deeds of entry, partnerships, speculations, transfers, the recording of surveys, the incorporation of towns and cities. Many of Lincoln's colleagues grew rich. At auctions and tax sales Judge Davis acquired vast tracts of land in Illinois, Iowa, Missouri and Kansas. In a shady grove just east of Bloomington he built a stately brick and stone mansion (now a state memorial) like an English manor house. In the twentieth century, when Bloomington had spread across the Illinois Central railroad line, the Davis road became Jefferson Street, but the mansion was still aloof in its feudal park, with a white board fence stretching out of sight under the maple trees. I was one of the Bloomington boys who on summer afternoons walked the long fence in the dappled shade. We knew the Davis land went farther than that, but we could not know how far. As a young Illinois lawyer, long before our time and before the Bloomington mansion, Davis was retained by a New York client to collect a claim of $800. He failed to get the money, but accepted instead eighty acres of land on what was then the southern edge of Chicago. When his client refused this settlement, Davis paid the $800, taking the land for himself. He did not see his property for sixteen years, and when he looked at it in 1860, he found it overrun by a settlement of Irish squatters. Chicago was pushing onto his acres, which he ultimately sold for a million dollars.

Lincoln was never in the way of these opportunities, or at least he never seized them; by his own account he had no money sense. For service in the Black Hawk War he had come into possession of a quarter section of prairie in Crawford County in western Iowa and forty acres in Tama County. These lands never yielded him any profit, and except for his home in Springfield, they were his whole estate.

But Lincoln had other gains from his years on the prairie. It is strange, said one of his colleagues, that he should have puzzled his great mind over trivial and acrimonious disputes about a wood-stealing Irishman or a half-crazy horse thief; and Herndon, looking back on his professional practice, recalled fraud, deceit, slander, cruelty, broken promises and blasted homes. Yet from problems like these Lincoln learned the shrewdness, patience and humanity of his statesmanship. From his seasons on the circuit came his understanding of common men, his political sagacity and the long ground swell of his popular support. His Presidency grew out of his prairie years.

The first linking of Lincoln's name with high office came in 1856, a few days after his reverberating "Lost Speech" at the Bloomington convention which organized the Republican party in Illinois. It was mid-June, and an extra court session had been called in Champaign County to clear the docket for the term. In Urbana Judge Davis, Lincoln and Whitney shared a room in the comfortless American House kept by dour John Dunaway. Directly under their window hung a gong which the proprietor hammered long and loud before each meal. The weather was hot, the trial docket was tedious, and the lawyers grumbled over the landlord's mealtime clangor.

One sweltering day Whitney went to get the Chicago *Press,* which arrived on the noon train. Returning with the paper, he met proprietor Dunaway searching for his gong, which he said had been stolen. Whitney climbed upstairs, where he found

Lincoln tilted back in a chair with an amused and guilty look and Davis saying, "Now, Lincoln, that is a shame. Poor Dunaway is a most distressed being." (Half an hour earlier, when they came in from the courthouse, Lincoln had taken down the gong and hid it in the false bottom of the dining room table.)

"You must put it back," the judge concluded.

Lincoln got up sheepishly and peered down the stairs. With Whitney standing guard at the door, he retrieved the gong and hung it in place. Then he bounded up, three steps at a time, with Whitney following.

With Lincoln again tilted in his chair, his hands clasped and thumbs chasing each other, Whitney opened his newspaper and read aloud the report of the Republican convention in Philadelphia. "The convention then proceeded to an informal ballot for Vice-President, which resulted as follows: Dayton 259, Lincoln 110, Ford 7, King 9 . . ." At this point, Whitney recalled years later, "Davis and I were greatly excited, but Lincoln was phlegmatic, listless and indifferent. His only remark was: 'I reckon that ain't me, there's another great man in Massachusetts named Lincoln, and I reckon it's him.' "

Two days later the Urbana court was adjourned. Lincoln collected about forty dollars for the term's business and packed his old carpetbag for the long drive to Springfield. He said nothing more about the Republican convention. But with that vote for the vice-presidential nomination, his friends declared, the idea of national office first lodged in Lincoln's mind.

Four years later it was his colleagues of the Eighth Judicial Circuit—Davis, Swett, Logan, Lamon, Whitney—who led the Lincoln movement in the turbulent Wigwam convention in Chicago. There was no question then about the Lincoln who headed the ticket, for already a victorious song was swelling across the nation:

> "Old Abe Lincoln came out of the wilderness,
> Out of the wilderness, out of the wilderness,
> Old Abe Lincoln came out of the wilderness,
> Down in Illinois."

III

TRAMP, TRAMP, TRAMP, THE BOYS ARE MARCHING

Many are the hearts that are weary tonight,
Wishing for the war to cease;
Many are the hearts looking for the light,
To see the dawn of peace.

—WALTER KITTREDGE

15. Cap Grant's Mule

In 1885, when Grant was buried above the Hudson, people all over America were telling stories of him—the heavy man who spilled tobacco ashes in the White House, the rumpled man whose cigars drove Queen Victoria out of her own drawing room at Windsor Castle, the quiet man who wrote with a stub pen "Unconditional Surrender," and who said with no expression on his bearded face, "I propose to fight it out on this line if it takes all summer." But along the Mississippi they were telling other stories—how he came back to his family from California not General Grant but Cap Grant, a silent, shabby man with a liking for horses and an understanding of dogs.

You wouldn't think he could be easy in a granite tomb above the Hudson. Of course he wasn't an easy man. But there's such a thing as a man's belonging to a certain place so that his memory keeps alive there and becomes a part of that earth. In Georgetown, Ohio, they remember the lazy boy who hung around his father's livery stable, and at Galena on the Mississippi they have saved his house for a shrine. And down near St. Louis they remember Cap Grant of Hardscrabble Farm, a sad, slow man who was first cousin to poverty and a close acquaintance of debt.

Some people seem born for misfortune and failure: things don't turn out for them. Grant was such a man, until history found him stacking stinking cattle hides in the tanyard at Galena. Before that time, everything went wrong. It goes way back to sleepy Georgetown, where he grew up beside the Ohio River. Ulysses was a hard name to those people, but they still called him "Useless" when he went by his other name, Hiram. Even his initials —H.U.G.—were an embarrassment, until his mother's name, "Simpson," got into his appointment to the Military Academy. After Fort Donelson "U. S." Grant meant Unconditional Surrender; but that was a long way off in 1840 when he was bound for West Point. He had to pry the *H U G* off his tin trunk before he carried it up the hill to the Academy.

Ten years later, an army man in lonely barracks above the Pacific, things still went wrong for him. An investment in a potato farm in Oregon, just before the Columbia River overflowed and rotted the crop in the ground. A schooner loaded with ice for San Francisco, and the ice all running out of the scuppers before they could sell it. After he lost his commission, more things went wrong—chills and fever finished his sorry years of farming, and he tried St. Louis real estate in the panic year of 1858.

But that's ahead of the story, because he dickered for Henry Pellet's mule in the summer of 1855, his first year out of the army. He had come back to private life a tired-looking man, already stooped in the shoulders at thirty-three. He didn't look like a farmer, but he didn't look like an army man either. With that ragged brown beard and his strong somber face he looked like a mothy bear just come out of a cave. His eyes blinked a little in the strong light on the Mississippi. Silent and sad and slow, his own father up at Galena was calling him the family failure, and Colonel Dent grudgingly gave his returned son-in-law eighty rough acres on the margin of White Haven, the big Dent plantation. Even Julia Dent, who was busy bearing his children, couldn't manage to make that severe face of hers look as though she saw any prospect for an ex-army man who had lost his commission at thirty-three.

Maybe you can't blame them, though Hank Pellet always said afterward that he could have told anybody. And it is a fact that even then he had one thing to make up for all the rest—a slow and everlasting will, like a bear squatting down beside a honey tree. You could plainly see it in his hands, slow as time to take hold of a thing but slow as all eternity to let it go. Put that in a man and it makes some difference. So you get those other pictures to go with the homesick army captain at Fort Humboldt, lounging on the wooden steps of Ryan's store in the frontier backwash of Eureka, California. You can see him at Appomattox, with the four battered stars on his shoulders, or you can see him in a President's stovepipe hat, getting off the train at Central City, with Senator Jim Teller pointing out the wonders of that lofty Colorado town and escorting him to the Teller house over stepping-blocks of solid silver. You can see him in the gardens at Windsor, a blunt square man nodding to a squat little woman in a widow's black bonnet, and you remember that Cap Grant of Hardscrabble Farm was a world figure at the end.

Back in 1855, he was a sad man with a somber patience and a jaw like a bulldog's under the ragged brown beard. Henry Pellet thought he saw beneath that beard. Afterward he would talk about Cap Grant's mule, though he needn't to because everybody on both sides of the river—Missouri and Illinois—thought they had as much claim to the story as Hank himself. It was a question whether Hank Pellet told it any better than the rest, though he was a good deal more emphatic. "Right there Cap Grant stood in his pasture," and "I could see at the time he wasn't a common man." Funny how arrogant an old fellow can be about a story. He'd take you down and show you where he'd been plowing when the constable came, and point out where the mule was stabled and just where his harness hung. I guess he never had enough money to buy another mule, or he'd have passed it off for the one that Grant dickered for in 1855.

You'd think from Hank's pride that it was something he had done for Grant, when it was just the other way round. Henry Pellet was a poor man who lived over beyond Hardscrabble Farm at the edge of Lost Timber. He'd had sickness in his family all that winter and a grass fire that burned up his hay crop, and he had to borrow money to keep corn pone on the table and to get seed into the ground. But still he was a cheerful, friendly man, always ready to help a neighbor. He had built half of Cap Grant's log house for him, while the ex-captain was trying to get the hang of an ax and the grain in those oak and ash timbers.

Hank Pellet was chronically in debt. At this particular time he owed forty-some dollars to a Yankee storekeeper, Aaron Powers, and he hadn't a stick of property except for a big three-year-old mule that Hank had raised himself. When he was plowing his little blade rows of corn one June day, Constable Giles Kinney came walking across the field.

Hank pulled his mule up and pushed his straw hat back on his head. He wasn't an old man then, but his face was wrinkled and the ague had left him bleached out like a cornhusk. "Howdy, Constable," he said. "You looking for law-breakers?"

The constable shook his head and looked at Hank like a judge.

"Looking for horse thieves, or chicken thieves, or what?"

"Looking for a mule," the constable said, and his eyes fixed on Hank's big Jeeter, who was switching his tail like a black-snake and tossing his head for the flies.

"Well," said Hank, "Jeeter here is a law-abiding critter. But I expect there's some mean mules hereabouts. You might take a look at Samuels's."

Constable bent down and unhooked the tugs from the single tree. "This here mule is the mule I'm after."

"What do you want with Jeeter?"

"Lawyer's orders," and he tapped a paper in his pocket. "Aaron

Powers wants to collect his money and so I got to take your mule."

"Look here," Hank cried. "This is the only mule I've got. The only animal. I haven't got an ox. I haven't got a cow. My woman hasn't even got a pair of chickens."

"If she had," the constable said somberly, "I'd have to take them."

"How'm I ever going to get this corn raised without a mule?"

"Can't help it," the constable said. "I got to sell him."

He had Jeeter unhooked by this time, and started to lead him away. Hank caught hold of the other side of the mule's bit, arguing. "I got all this corn in. When I get the crop I can pay Aaron Powers that money. But if I haven't got a mule, I can't plow the corn and I won't even have Job's turkey."

Constable said, "It's the law."

"I borrowed that money to get seed corn, and now I can't raise a crop if I haven't got a mule to plow it. Aaron Powers said I could pay next winter."

"He's changed his mind."

By this time they were out in the road. Hank's wife looked out the window and saw them walking off with the mule between them, and Hank arguing every step he took. She tied the baby to the bedpost, pushed the johnnycake back on the stove, and took out after them.

Her voice traveled ahead of her.

"What's trouble, Henry? What's trouble?"

Hank looked over his shoulder. "They're taking my mule on the money I owe Aaron Powers."

"They're taking the mule," the woman repeated, and then she started to cry.

That was the way they came past Hardscrabble Farm, where Cap Grant was standing in the pasture, talking to a pretty chestnut colt in the shade of a sweet gum tree. Now he looked up and saw two men marching along at the head of a big black mule and a woman crying like a goose behind them.

When she saw Cap Grant, the woman ran right up to the pasture fence. "Help, Cap'n Grant! Help us 'fore they carry Jeeter clean away."

Cap Grant left the colt standing there on his four spindle legs and came over to the fence. "What's the trouble, Mrs. Pellet?" he asked in his slow voice.

"They're taking Jeeter and now there ain't any way in the kingdom we can get our corn raised. Stop him, Cap'n. Stop him," and she hung on the fence rail, crying.

Cap Grant was a kind-hearted man. It wasn't so many years later, at Cold Harbor, that the bonfires were blazing before the Confederate lines and word came back to Union headquarters that the rebels were celebrating the birth of General Pickett's son. "Can't we spare some wood for the little Pickett?" General Grant asked, and soon the fires leaped up all along the Union lines. General Pickett across that no-man's-land must have swallowed hard over the contour maps he was studying.

Now Grant called to the constable. He wasn't a man to move any more than was necessary, and so Constable Kinney and Hank Pellet and the mule all came over to the fence. The mule reached his long neck over and sniffed at Grant's brown beard and his old army jacket until Grant pulled a carrot out of his pocket.

"That's a pretty smart mule," he said, putting a hand on the animal's nose. "A big fellow, too."

"And gentle," Hank Pellet said eagerly. "I've gentled him like a rabbit."

"He ought to bring twenty, thirty dollars at a sale," the constable said.

"Why, he ain't but a young fellow," Cap Grant said, pushing the mule's mouth open to show the big yellow teeth.

"I've raised him myself," said Hank Pellet. "This here's the first year I've worked him."

"Might even bring forty dollars," said the constable.

Grant looked round slowly, "What do you want to sell him for?"

"Lawyer's orders"—and the constable tapped the folded papers inside his coat. "I'm told to seize Hank Pellet's property to satisfy Aaron Powers for what's owed him. I looked over the place and this mule is the only property I can find."

The woman had been standing there anxious as a hen, and now she started crying again. "We can't ever raise a crop without a mule. We'd pay Aaron Powers when we put the corn by."

The constable tugged at the mule. "Powers don't want to wait."

"Where you going to sell him?" Cap Grant asked.

"Three Corners, tomorrow. Public auction. That's what the law says." He hauled the papers out of his pocket.

Cap Grant squinted at the warrant. "Looks like it's according to law. I guess you'll have to let him go," he said to Hank Pellet.

The constable hauled the mule off and started down the road. The woman cried louder and Hank looked pretty sick himself. But Cap Grant said, "You come over in the morning and we'll go to Three Corners and buy the mule back. That's all we can do."

The woman stopped her crying long enough to say, "We ain't got a lead washer to buy him with, Cap'n."

And Hank said, "It's a fact, I ain't."

"You come over in the morning," Cap Grant repeated.

Next day they went to Three Corners and bought the mule for twenty dollars. Grant had managed to raise the money some way. "Take him home," he said, turning Jeeter over to Hank Pellet. "Now you can get your corn plowed."

Hank Pellet beamed at Grant and he beamed at the mule. He stroked Jeeter's nose and pumped Grant's hand, and in his excitement he turned to shake hands with the mule. "Thank you,

Cap Grant. I shorely thank you, when my crop is in I'll pay you."

So Hank Pellet led his mule home, proud as a winner with a race horse, and Grant went back to Hardscrabble Farm to cut timber. There wasn't much that farm would produce except pasture and poles. And it would take a lot of mine props to make up twenty dollars.

When Grant's wife found out about the mule, she was pretty sharp. "A man that can't pay his own debts," she said in a voice like a corn knife, "hasn't any business buying mules for his neighbors."

"Debts," Cap Grant said in his patient way. "How about my owing Henry Pellet? He worked half last spring with me putting up this house. Without him and the rest of the neighbors, we wouldn't have a roof to shelter us."

Then the baby cried, little Nellie Grant was the baby then, and Grant was left to pull the dog's ears in peace.

A week later he was sitting in the sunset with the dog beside him when his eyes sharpened on the road. Constable Kinney and Henry Pellet were walking at the head of a mule, each one with a hand on the halter. Grant got up to meet them.

"Good evening, Cap'n," the constable said.

"Good evening."

Hank Pellet lowered his eyes and looked miserable.

The dog sniffed at the constable's heels. He growled in his throat and his hair bristled. "Quiet, Rouser!" Cap Grant said. He looked up. "What are you doing with the mule?"

"Got to sell him again," the constable said.

Grant's heavy face clouded. "How's that?"

"Aaron Powers ain't paid up yet."

"You sold him once. Didn't Aaron Powers get the money?"

"Yes, he got it. But there's more owing him. So I got to take the mule again."

Cap Grant puzzled over that. "I can't figure it out," he said finally.

Hank Pellet spoke up for the first time. "I can't figure it either. He carried the mule off once and got the money. I don't see how the law can take him again."

"I got papers," Constable said, pulling out a warrant.

Cap Grant scowled over it. "No change of possession," he read. He turned the paper over. "Looks like it's according to the law. Still I can't figure it out. What does Aaron Powers want?"

"He wants his money," the constable said doggedly. "Come on, Jeeter," and he started down the road.

Hank Pellet stood there beside Cap Grant, the two of them watching the constable away. Hank was pretty down in the mouth, but Grant had a slow set look on his face. As Hank used to tell it afterward, he looked a whole lot like that mule himself. Finally Grant lifted up his voice. "When you going to sell him?"

The constable looked over his shoulder. "Tomorrow."

They watched silently till the constable and the mule were around the bend.

"You better stay home this time," Grant said, still looking down the empty road. "I'll see if I can buy him again."

The next morning Cap Grant went to Three Corners. Word had got around among the neighbors, and when Hank Pellet's mule was put up again, the bidding was slow. Cap Grant got him for five dollars. This time he led him away himself, walking down the road with Jeeter at his shoulder, his big ears flopping. He passed Hardscrabble Farm without looking in, the horses came down to the fence and whickered as he passed, and Jeeter cocked his ears and brayed in answer. He delivered the mule to Henry Pellet in the cornfield, where Hank was hand-hoeing his corn and making pretty slow business of it.

Hank put his arm around the mule as though it was his wife. "I shore do thank you, Cap, I shore do." His voice started to choke up and Grant went on back to Hardscrabble.

Young "Buck" Grant was three years old that summer. His grandfather, old Colonel Dent, called him Ulysses and his mother called him Junior, but Cap Grant called him "Buck," and he used to toddle around the farm with his hand in his father's big paw. Grant had been far off in Panama when the youngster was born—perhaps he was thinking of that the night in 1864 when Pickett's men were celebrating and he had the bonfires lighted along the Union lines. When he wasn't cutting wood or swinging a scythe in his sorghum or his haylot, Grant liked to wander about the farm with little Buck beside him. People would see them together down by the pigpen or in the calf yard, and the way the animals lifted their ears and the way young Buck kept looking up all wonder at his father, they could tell that Grant was talking away like a preacher. It was strange because he was a mute man generally.

Every animal on that farm was a pet. The chickens would follow Grant and little Buck—sometimes they would come right up on the porch and settle down in a circle in the shade where Cap Grant was lighting the stump of a cigar. The hogs would come and rub their backs on his boots and the horses would nose around his pockets for a green apple or a turnip. Grant would tell young Buck all about the animals and maybe tell the critters about young Buck, because the youngster would put his chubby hands on their big noses and they would smell of him gently and take the clover carefully out of his fingers.

One morning Grant was out in the cow yard tending to a calf that had been dropped in the night, and Buck was beside him. He was explaining gravely to the youngster that this was a mighty nice calf, with four white feet like he had stepped in his mother's milk pail, and a white gentle face. Yes, this was a mighty fine calf and would be nice to have growing up on the place, but they'd have to sell him. Not enough feed to keep all the animals they had already, and besides they needed the money. "A dollar is a dollar, Buck, though it seems a shame to say it."

Buck appeared to agree with that; he put out a chubby hand to touch the calf's soft nose. Grant picked up the calf in his arms and Buck's blue eyes grew big as plums as the thin white

legs kicked the air. They were halfway to the barn when Grant
saw something in the road.

It was Constable Kinney and Hank Pellet walking beside a
big black mule.

A set look came into Grant's eyes and his mouth got tighter
under the rough brown beard. He laid the calf on the ground.
"You look after him, Buck," and he stumped off in his bearlike
roll.

They were already stopped at the end of Grant's lane, though
the constable was pulling at the mule's halter. Jeeter leaned back
mildly, waiting for Grant to come.

Hank Pellet was in plain distress. He kept stroking the mule
with an affectionate hand, but he looked broken-hearted and
ashamed when Grant stepped up. The constable looked a bit
sheepish, too. He tugged again at the mule's halter and then he
looked around as if he was surprised.

"Morning, Cap'n Grant."

Grant had on his old drill coat, and the constable made a
half-hearted attempt to salute.

"Where you taking the mule?" Grant asked.

"Three Corners," Constable said, looking at the ground.

Hank Pellet broke out, "He's going to sell him again, Cap'n.
I can't see it to save me."

"How's that?" Grant asked the constable.

"There's still some dollars owing to Aaron Powers."

"But I bought that mule myself. Twice over now I've bought
him. I drove him away my own property. Can't I loan a mule to
a neighbor without having him led off for sale once a week?"

"Lawyer's orders," the constable said as if he was ashamed
of it. He pulled a set of papers from his pocket.

Grant squinted at them. "No continued change of possession,"
he read. The frown deepened on his face. "What's that mean?"

"Well, Cap'n, I've been trying to figure it out myself. It
sounds like as long as Hank owes money to Aaron Powers, he's
going to keep on losing his mule. The mule is sold, and then

they find Hank has got that mule again, so the lawyer says there's no continued change of possession and he serves papers on the critter. Myself, I'm getting downright tired fetching this mule."

Grant puzzled at it again, squinting at the papers in the morning light. His face got heavier and heavier. Finally he gave it up. "I guess it's according to the law," he said doubtfully. He handed the warrant back to the constable. "When are you going to sell him?"

"Tomorrow."

Constable tugged again at the halter. Jeeter seemed satisfied now, and he followed the constable down the road.

Hank Pellet kept twisting a handful of wiregrass in his fingers. "Cap'n Grant, they say this here's a free country, but it appears to me like the law is a noose around my neck. If I'd had a rifle this morning, I'd shot that sheriff the minute he clumb into my cornfield."

Grant shook his shaggy head. "A man's got to accept the law. You go on home and I'll get the mule tomorrow."

The next day at Three Corners nobody would bid on Hank Pellet's mule, and the animal was knocked down to Grant for a dollar. He led the mule back to Hardscrabble Farm and tied him up in the stable. Then Grant went out in the barnyard and began to whittle. Buck toddled out there and played with the shavings for a while, but his father didn't have any mind for him. The calves and the colts came nosing around, but Cap Grant wasn't saying a word or looking up from that job in his hands. He had whittled a tether stake down to a fine point before he got the business figured out.

The next morning he led Jeeter over to Hank Pellet's place. But when he turned the mule over to Hank, he also gave him a folded paper.

"This," he said, "is a letter of authority. Now you keep this letter on your person and go over to Jefferson County and trade this mule for another mule, for me." He emphasized "for me" as though Constable Kinney and Aaron Powers and the St. Louis lawyer and the county judge were all there, witnessing.

"Why have I got to trade him, Cap? You wouldn't find a better mule than Jeeter in all the kingdom."

"The reason is," Grant said, sounding like a judge, "there's got to be a continued change of possession."

"Yes, but it does seem a shame to trade Jeeter for some contrary Jefferson County mule that can't follow a corn row. I've seen their mules over there, and it does seem a shame."

Cap Grant puzzled about that for a minute while Jeeter winked his big black eyes and switched his tail like a pump handle. "Yes, he's a good mule." He lowered his voice. "Well, mules look pretty much alike. You take him over to Jefferson County and see if you can't trade him for a mule just about like him, with a mane cut off shorter maybe and a tail docked a little."

Hank Pellet frowned and studied. "You mean . . ."

But Grant was already stumping away. At the fence he called back, "Don't forget to take that letter of authority."

Hank Pellet put an old blanket on Jeeter's back and rigged up a rope bridle and rode him over to Jefferson County, and in the evening he came back to Hardscrabble Farm riding a big black mule with a ragged tail and a bristly mane.

"Here's your mule, Cap," he said, jumping down off the animal's back.

Grant looked the mule over carefully, and the animal sniffed at him in a friendly way and nosed around him until Grant got a green apple out of his pocket. "Looks like you made a fair trade," he said. "This is a mighty good mule for a Jefferson County mule."

Then Grant wrote out a lease of the mule for one cent a month to Henry Pellet, and both he and Hank signed the lease, and Grant made another copy of it so they both could keep one.

Hank climbed back on the mule's back. "Come on, Jeeper." he said.

Grant looked up pretty sharp for a man that usually moved so slow. "What's that mule's name?"

"Jeeper," Hank said happily. "On the way home I got to thinking, and I decided to call him Jeeper because he ain't so very much different from that other mule named Jeeter that I traded him for."

Grant said, "I think maybe you'd better give him a more different name."

Hank thought a minute. "How about calling him Cap? I had a good horse once by that name, and he's really your mule, Cap'n. You bought him enough times."

"How's that?" Grant said sharply.

"I mean you bought the one I traded him for. You think Cap would be a proper name?"

"I guess that would be all right."

Hank chirked proudly, "Come on, Cap," and he rode down the lane.

As Hank Pellet used to tell the story, he always added, "Cap Grant never asked me for the rent on the mule. He was satisfied. You know how it was in Virginia when he said, 'I mean to fight it out on this line if it takes all summer!' Well, that might of surprised Jeff Davis, but it didn't surprise me. I remembered how he said he was going to have that mule if he had to buy him once a week all summer. I always knew Cap Grant was an uncommon man."

16. Morgan's Race

On the misty morning of July 8, 1863, Captain James H. Pepper was piloting his steamboat *Alice Dean* past the dim hills of Indiana. War had blockaded the Mississippi, but Union gunboats patrolled the Ohio, where a busy commerce was moving. Captain Pepper was bound for Cincinnati with mixed cargo from Mound City, Illinois. As he passed the village of Brandenburg, Kentucky, he saw through the mist another steamer, idle in midstream, seemingly in distress. Soon he recognized the big Anderson and Louisville packet, *J. J. McCombs*. As he steered alongside for assistance he heard the stamp of horses and saw a solid press of men at the rails. Quickly they took his mooring line and made the steamers fast. While he was asking what was needed, the dusty, sweat-stained men swarmed aboard.

They needed his vessel, in the service of the Confederacy, and now they had it, along with the *Dean*, which they had commandeered at the Brandenburg landing. Morgan's cavalry was about to invade the North.

General John Hunt Morgan, bold, brilliant, unpredictable, was already known for his swift strokes into enemy country far from his base of supply. At the Battle of Shiloh his slashing cavalry had taken five hundred prisoners. In the summer of 1862 he knifed into disputed Kentucky, and six months later he dealt the Federal forces a stinging blow. In that Christmas raid, ten days after his marriage to a belle of Murfreesboro, he destroyed vital railroads, bridges and supplies and captured two thousand prisoners, with a loss of two men killed and twenty-four wounded. Cool, daring, chivalrous, he was a leader whose men would follow anywhere. Now they were following him across the Ohio. They could not capture or subjugate the North, but they could spread confusion and alarm, engage five times their number in pursuit, and hearten the South with a foray into enemy country.

On the Kentucky landing men, horses, mules, wagons, artillery came aboard—horses of all shapes, size and color, men in broadcloth, tow cloth and homespun—and the two captive steamboats churned across the river. A burst of gunfire came from the Indiana shore. As the mist lifted, the Rebel officers saw through their glasses Hoosier militiamen firing from houses and haystacks and hauling up a cannon slung on a pair of wagon wheels. When Morgan's artillerymen got their three-inch Parrott guns on target, the militia retired, leaving their lone cannon pointing idly across the river.

While the captured transport pushed on toward Indiana, a new vessel steamed around the lower bend, the improvised Federal gunboat *Springfield*. The misty sun shimmered on her sheeting, a puff of pale smoke spouted from her bow and a shell came flying. Again Morgan's ordnance men sighted their long-range Parrotts. After a few exchanges the *Springfield* turned tail and disappeared downstream.

All the long hot afternoon the two captive steamers shuttled across the river. Dusk was darkening the hills when the last men of the first brigade landed on the hostile shore. While they fanned out, cutting telegraph lines, burning bridges, foraging in deserted farm kitchens and barnyards, the second brigade embarked. In its century of frontier commerce the Ohio had never carried freight like this: horses, mules, men, carts, wagons, caissons, cannon, ambulances. At midnight, with her boilers seething and lights jiggling on the water, the *Alice Dean* brought the last load across. The crew were given a few minutes to take what they could—clothing, bedding, some scraps of food from the pantry—before the boats were burned and set adrift. Captain Pepper watched his vessel go up in flames in the summer night. He had a long walk to Cincinnati, where the stevedores were waiting for his cargo.

The boats burned quickly. As darkness came back to the river, Morgan rode after his men, who were making their first camp at Frake's Mill, six miles inland. He must have wondered what the next days would bring.

The odds against him were overwhelming. He had some twenty-five hundred men, a dozen mounted cannon and some wagonloads of ammunition and medical supplies, and he was already beyond the reach of Southern support or reinforcement. "When we were across the great river," wrote Basil Duke, his second-in-command, "we would stand face to face with the hostile and angry North—an immense and infuriated population, and a soldiery outnumbering us twenty to one would confront us. Telegraph lines, tracing the country in every direction, would tell constantly of our movements; railways would bring assailants against us from every quarter; and we would have to run this gantlet, day and night, without rest or one moment of safety, for six hundred miles." This Churchillian passage does not exaggerate Morgan's hazardous situation.

The first resistance came at the old Indiana capital of Corydon, where Hoosier militiamen were waiting behind rail barricades. The raiders charged head-on, then from the flank, and the militia took to flight. While women peered from the windows, Morgan's cavalry pounded on, over the Salem road. Outriders swept the side roads, gathering horses from every barnyard and pasture.

Men could stay in the saddle twenty hours a day, but horses gave out. Behind them the raiders left exhausted animals in exchange for the horses they "pressed." Hobson's Union Cavalry was in pursuit, twenty-four hours away. Without fresh horses he could not close the gap.

Every town and village had its hour of history as the raiders neared. In Vernon dusk fell while a makeshift company of Home Guards waited, and through the insect-buzzing darkness came a great splashing from nearby Finney's Ford. At the sound the Guards were up and running. Half of them fell over the twenty-foot embankment above the creek, where a herd of cattle was splashing through knee-deep water. This was the Battle of Finney's Ford, remembered with wry Hoosier humor ever since. While the defenders were tumbling down the ravine, Morgan's columns were in the next township, doubling back northward to Dupont.

At every settlement the raiders raised their spirits by plunder and looting. They were war-hardened men in enemy country, a rich region untouched by conflict, and they remembered the plundered province of the South. In senseless greed and glee they collected trophies—shoes, clocks, parasols, musical instruments, tablecloths, rolls of muslin and calico. Men stuffed their shirts with gloves, ribbons, stockings. They used shawls for horse blankets, tied booty to their saddles and trailed streamers in the dust. One grimy trooper, Basil Duke remembered, carried a bird cage with three canaries; another gloated over an empty chafing dish; a third rode through the summer heat with seven pairs of skates around his neck. With more reason they gathered bread and pies in empty kitchens (Indiana women had a practice of preparing food in large quantities, and Morgan's men arrived on baking day) and stripped gardens and orchards along the route. At Dupont, Indiana, they captured a wagonload of beer and then raided a packing plant. They rode away with two thousand hams slung from their pommels.

Most families fled, leaving their doors open, when the raiders drew near. But at Dupont cross-grained Old Sally Truesdale hung two Union flags from her gateposts and sat on the porch with a furled umbrella. When a file of troopers pulled up and reached for the flags, old Miss Sally flew at them. The horses reared away and the Rebels rubbed their red-rimmed eyes. "Horse thieves! Robbers! Murderers!"—her high voice followed them down the road. The flags were still flying when she went back to the porch.

On his march Morgan met thousands of militia, but they hardly hindered his advance. Untrained, unled, confused by the enemy's feints and thrusts, they waited for attack while the enemy swept around them. Then they got into action, putting out fires that were crackling around bridges, depots, lumberyards and even wooden water tanks. At Versailles, Indiana, Morgan's men came upon a mass meeting of militiamen who were considering how to defend the town. The cavalry broke up their deliberations and swept on. At Sumansville Rebel outriders passed a trainload of militia in boxcars, moving toward Cincinnati and unaware of Morgan's presence.

It was a summer invasion, with an enemy suddenly present and soon past, and it brought more excitement than destruction. In the rich summer country living was easy; there would be no hunger and desolation after the enemy was gone. The raiders suffered from sleeplessness but not from hardship. They gorged on the plenty along the way and turned their exhausted horses into ripening fields of grain. The defending militiamen found food laid out for them in every town. They feasted and then marched off, trigger-happy, to meet the foe. At Lawrenceburg, Indiana, the advance guard of a regiment rounded a hill and mistook their own right flank for the enemy. Five were killed and seventeen wounded in that skirmish. Meanwhile there was a scurrying of the populace to bury heirlooms and secrete their horses. Horses hidden in the woods were always found by Morgan's scouts, but a minister in Madison successfully hid his horse in the church basement and a woman rolled up the carpet and kept her horse in the parlor.

Before cutting telegraph lines along his line of march, Morgan had his men monitoring the defender's messages and sending out false reports. He knew his pursuer's movements, but no one knew his. Rumors were thick as dust: Morgan was headed for New Albany and Jeffersonville to burn Federal army stores; he was racing toward Indianapolis to burn the State House; he was marching on Cincinnati, where reinforcements would join him from the South.

In Cincinnati Sunday, July 12, was a day of alarm. The mayor asked all citizens to assemble in their wards, prepared to defend the city. From Columbus Governor Tod telegraphed a proclamation to the Cincinnati press, calling out the militia in thirty-two southern Ohio counties. General Burnside proclaimed martial law. Under his orders the city was divided into four districts, with headquarters at the Broadway Hotel, the Burnet House, the orphan asylum, and the Finley Methodist Chapel. Meanwhile Morgan was at the door. While Cincinnatians were arming themselves with old flintlocks and barrel staves, his brigade burst into Harrison, twenty miles away, where they looted all the shops in town.

Anticipating a massing of force in Cincinnati, Morgan began maneuvers to confuse the defenders. He sent detachments north, south and east, setting fires and burning bridges, but he made the most show of marching toward Hamilton, twenty-five miles north of Cincinnati. From Hamilton came word that Morgan was about to attack, and in Cincinnati headquarters released captives of the raiders were reporting Morgan's own word that Hamilton was his target. That night, July 13, the weary raiders made a forced march around the northern edges of Cincinnati. Morgan with his guides kept a steady pace through Glendale, Sharonville, Montgomery and Batavia. But the rear brigade had trouble. Dazed with exhaustion, choked with dust, groping through darkness on strange roads, they repeatedly lost the way. At road junctions they lighted paper flares to study the drift of dust and to search for froth and slaver left by the brigade ahead. At every pause men slid from the saddle and red-eyed officers prodded them awake. Troopers slept on the march, riding like dead men, with eyes closed and feet braced in the stirrups. Morgan was tireless and alert to every danger, but scores of his men fell out on that night march.

At daybreak the dusty column crossed the Little Miami Railroad and halted to feed their horses. Dawn cheered and wakened them, and with a sense of triumph they saw the long low roofs of Camp Dennison, a Federal training base. While outriders skirmished with the pickets, the long file surged past in the sunrise, leaving a rosy pillar of smoke from a burning corral of government wagons. Buoyed by this effrontery, they raced on to Williamsburg, twenty-eight miles east of Cincinnati. In thirty-five hours they had covered ninety miles, and the tight place was behind them. They hawked up the dust and hummed,

> I'll bet ten cents in specie
> That Morgan wins the race . . .

while tethering their horses and lighting cooking fires. Then they fell asleep in the long evening shadows.

Behind them came a growing pursuit—General Hobson was on Morgan's route, starting up the dust almost as soon as it had settled; companies from Camp Dennison were boarding railroad cars for points ahead of Morgan's march; and Judah's troops were crammed into steamboats that would head off the racing columns from the river. But Morgan could still maneuver. One column feinted, dashing down to the river at Ripley; then they pounded north over the plank road to Mt. Orab and cut sharply east to join the main force at Sardinia. Again his dusty outriders passed for Federal troops and spread false word of Morgan's movements. By now there were fifty thousand Ohio militia around him, but they could not block his way. One sweating regiment felled trees across the Batavia road where the raiders had already passed. At Chillicothe one militia company mistook another for invaders; they burned a bridge for their own protection.

The raiders raced on, through Georgetown, Piketon, Jackson, Pomeroy. There Morgan was again on the banks of the Ohio—nine long days after the crossing into Indiana. But pursuit was closing in. His goal was the fording place at Buffington Island, twenty miles farther, where he could get his brigades across to West Virginia. Squads of Federal troops waited in the side roads and Hobson was pressing on his rear. For five miles his route led through a valley with Federals firing from the hills. They ran that gantlet, reaching the town of Chester in the heat of noon. There Morgan halted to let his stragglers come up and to gather his wagons and ambulances.

It was a needful halt and a dear one. As a result the raiders did not reach Portland, the landing abreast of Buffington Island, till after dark. Already Federal troops occupied the hills guarding the ford. In the dusty darkness Morgan pondered. Should he fight through to the riverbank and try a night crossing? The Federal troops had come up the river in transports; now gunboats were lurking beyond the dark mass of Buffington Island. Morgan wanted to save his wounded as well as his fighting men, his supply wagons, ambulances and artillery. He would wait for daylight.

Under the summer stars the raiders slept and the river murmured in the willow fringes, the insect buzzing rose and fell, a horse coughed and a man muttered in a dream. Morgan passed among his pickets, waiting for dawn. He did not know that at midnight the Federals had withdrawn from the hills and he might have crossed in safety.

The gray-green morning brought a rattle of rifles. General Judah's advance company had arrived, ahead of a force of ten thousand. Morgan had waited too long. The invaders were caught in the wooded valley which funneled toward the river. Before they could rally their horses, the Union cavalry came charging. Morgan's Parrott twelve-pounders were quickly captured and his wagon trains surrounded. A great dust grew in the north; Hobson's horsemen were racing down the Chester road.

With spent horses and dwindling ammunition the raiders faced two superior forces. Then gunboats churned the river and their shells came flying.

The first tin-clad to appear was the *Allegheny Belle*. At her single gun crouched lanky young Nathaniel Pepper, the son of the captain of the *Alice Dean*, which had gone up in smoke at Mauckport, Indiana, ten nights past. Like an avenger he hurled shells into the raiders' chaotic camp.

While Morgan rallied twelve hundred of his men, the rest were in confusion. Plunder trailed from rearing horses, wagons locked together, howitzer teams lunged in the raining cross fire. Through this chaos Morgan moved his column to the north end of the valley and onto open ground. Behind him Duke's milling brigade was surrounded; seven hundred men were captured, including Morgan's younger brothers Charlton and Dick. While they were prodded aboard the steamer *Starlight* Morgan was racing through the dust.

After twenty miles' hard riding they reached the river again, near Blennerhassett Island. It was not a chosen crossing, but Morgan led the men in, swimming their tired horses in the broad current. Three hundred got across and another hundred were drowned. Morgan was in midstream when a gunboat barred the way. He splashed back to his eight hundred men on the Ohio shore. At Berlin crossroads Colonel Ben Runkle's two thousand militia waited. The skirmish there cost the raiders a few casualties and three priceless hours. They fled on eastward, toward the Muskingum. Pursuit was closing. On the night of July 22 they were surrounded on three sides. In the summer darkness Morgan moved his exhausted men along a shelving hillside; they raced away before daylight revealed their abandoned camp. They reached Eagleport on the Muskingum just ahead of two hurrying steamboats crowded with the Eighty-sixth Ohio Regiment. These pursuers watched the last of the raiders splashing their horses onto the far side of the river. Landing a mile above the village, the Eighty-sixth struck the road in time to give them one volley at long range. Lines of dust in the morning sky showed Morgan bearing away to the northeast. Soon a curtain of dust came up behind, the advance guard of Hobson's cavalry, and the foot-slogging Eighty-sixth gave over. Ahead, on the dusty roads of Morgan County, Morgan's weary men fled on.

Ahead of their flight a grotesque alarm spread through Columbiana County. It was still a comic opera. A boy hunting squirrels in the woods set off a swiftly widening rumor of raiding columns. The husband of a woman in childbirth, riding for the doctor, sent the Home Guard for their shotguns and local women to burying heirlooms in their gardens. At the dust of cattle on the road a farmer crawled into a pigpen and lay down with the litter of pigs behind a brood sow. Another farmer crept into the scratchy safety of a shock of wheat. In Marietta frantic citizens took up the floor of their bridge over the Muskingum. Near Mc-Connelsville a militia force with two brass cannon took aim on a barn that the colonel thought might be harboring Morgan. They demolished the barn and returned to their base without a casualty. At Ashtabula, on the shore of Lake Erie, people waking to the daybreak clangor of the courthouse bell assembled guns, blankets, canteens and powder horns, though no one knew whether they were preparing for flight or an expedition.

Somehow Morgan kept his exhausted column marching. Hundreds of stragglers fell out, but a hard core pounded on. In another day he might have watered his horses in Lake Erie, but that would have been a dead end. His only hope was to reach an upper ford of the Ohio an hour ahead of his pursuit. But near the village of Salineville in rolling Columbiana County the Ninth Michigan Cavalry caught up. The raiders turned to fight. In a brief resistance 30 were killed, 50 wounded and some 500 taken prisoner. While the prisoners were marched onto railroad cars (where they fell into a bottomless sleep) for the hot ride to Camp Chase at Columbus, the word of Morgan's capture went ahead. It set off bells, bugles and bonfires throughout the Ohio and Indiana. The raid had given the South a brief and misleading sense of triumph; it unified and deepened military resolution in the North. And after the war was over, it left in the Ohio Valley a relished folklore of adventure, alarm and final capture of the enemy. Here is the difference between the war experience of the North and the South. The first Northern reports of Morgan described him as a destroyer, thief and murderer, the leader of a "wretched gang" of plunderers and horse thieves. A Northern writer described his final capture, in a buggy drawn by two white horses. "He lashed them furiously, hoping to escape. But Major Way, on his fleet horse, overhauled him and seized the reins. . . . In the buggy were found Morgan's rations, containing a loaf of bread, two hard-boiled eggs, and a bottle of whisky." This was written by a Connecticut journalist in 1864. Since then Morgan has been adopted by a romantic Ohio Valley folklore. His bullet holes are preserved in weatherboarding of farmhouses, along with tales of his courage, honesty and honor. An Ohioan who saw him at age ten eventually wrote of him as a leader whose character was "not without traces of a noble nature." In this rich and secure heartland an unscarred people could forgive the vanquished and cherish his mistaken valor in their own comforting folklore.

After their capture Morgan and his officers were confined, under orders of the War Department, in the Ohio State Penitentiary. Four months later they delivered themselves in a dramatic escape and made their way back to Kentucky. The rest of the raiders, taken at the Battle of Buffington Island and in the final surrender at Salineville, were sent to confinement on Johnson Island in Sandusky Bay in western Lake Erie. From this least onerous of military prisons they almost escaped. But that is another story.

17. Thunder in the North

From the lofty Perry Monument at Put-in-Bay, the Lake Erie islands lie tranquil and timeless on the water. There are the three Bass Islands in a chain (the southern one is generally called Put-in-Bay and the northern, Isle St. George), the green Garden Island, the coiled and sleeping Rattlesnake, and the little mounded Ballast—where Commodore Perry weighted his men-of-war with crushed limestone. Across an eight-mile channel lies shield-shaped Kelley's Island, with the sun white on the old quarries and ribs of surf along its ledges. Farther west, Cedar Point throws its curving arm around Sandusky Bay. There on Johnson Island in 1864 three thousand Confederate officers were prisoners of war.

On the islands the wind smells of grass and distance. Sheep browse among the little tented cedars and pheasants feed on wild sumach that has crept into the ragged vineyards. From the monument on a summer day the world lies wide, with the smoke of Detroit on one horizon and the glint of Cleveland on the other, and over the lake pass the long ships laden with iron ore for the Midwest mills. Strong currents of change have washed the islands which remain unchanged. On Kelley's Island are signatures from the deep past—great grooves of the glacier in its limestone outcrop and picture-writing of the Indians on the shore. When seas break white above the reefs and the gulls fly over, it is as innocent as an undiscovered country. Yet the islands have seen the Midwest's most dramatic episodes of war.

In the tense summer of 1813, with the British commanding Lake Erie and the Detroit River, General William Henry Harrison marched his army northward through Ohio. He broke a British siege on the Maumee, near present Toledo, and prepared to proceed against Detroit. But that required command of the lakes, which were patrolled by British gunboats. On the forest shores of Erie, Pennsylvania, Commodore Oliver Hazard Perry, with a crew of Rhode Islanders, was building a fleet. He had five vessels in the water by the end of May, but it was midsummer before he got them rigged, armed and over the sand bar to the open lake. Eluding the British patrol, he sailed west and anchored his fleet in Sandusky Bay. From there he sent word to Harrison, camped with his army at Fort Seneca, thirty miles inland.

On the rainy morning of August 19 Harrison rode with two of his generals, Lewis Cass and Duncan McArthur, to Sandusky harbor. With them went old chief Tarhe the Crane and twenty friendly Wyandots. Dinghies took them out to Perry's flagship, *Lawrence*. Tarhe and his warriors climbed over the vessel, marveling at the ranked cannon, the heavy bulkheads, the web of rigging on the lofty masts. That night Harrison talked alone with young Commodore Perry. He suggested Put-in-Bay, between South and Middle Bass islands, as a protected anchorage, and he agreed to send Perry some badly needed men.

Back at Fort Seneca Harrison called for volunteer seamen. Some river boatmen stepped forward and a larger number of Kentucky sharpshooters who had never seen a mainsail or a capstan. A week later Perry received a hundred recruits. From the Put-in-Bay anchorage he trained his glasses on the head of the lake, waiting for the British fleet to come out of the Detroit River.

At noon on September 10, under a cloudless sky, a rumble of thunder came to Harrison's troops on the Lower Sandusky road. For two hours the thunder rolled and men looked toward Lake Erie with questioning eyes. A great battle had begun and ended; the blank sky told them nothing more. Two days later a long-oared boat pulled up the Sandusky River and a naval officer leaped ashore. He mounted a horse and pounded to Fort Seneca. At headquarters he saluted General Harrison and delivered Perry's scribbled message: "We have met the enemy and they are ours—two ships, two brigs, one schooner and one sloop." With 4,500 men Harrison began to march. The way was open for re-capture of Detroit and pursuit of the British into Canada.

Half a century later another warfare came to the tranquil islands. In 1864 Confederate agents were plotting a Northwest Uprising—to deliver Rebel prisoners from Northern camps, to burn the cities of the lakes and put the Copperheads in power. What now looks like fantasy was as real as a Lake Erie hurricane a hundred years ago.

In 1861, when Lincoln asked for an army, the Western states had responded with a rush of volunteers. Ohio alone could have filled his call for seventy-five thousand men. But recruiting was reluctant in 1862. The bloody battle of Shiloh had shocked and sobered the Northwest, where a growing party of Peace Demo-crats—"Copperheads" to their opponents—wanted to abandon the "Abolition War" and save the Union by a vague and wishful reconciliation. In the chill spring of 1863 Union military fortunes were at an ebb and Copperhead sentiment was rising. Clement L. Vallandigham, former Congressman from Ohio, urged every resistance to the Federal war program. To silence him General Burnside, military commander in Cincinnati, issued "Order 38," calling for the arrest of treasonous dissenters, and Vallandigham was taken at midnight from his home in Dayton. He was con-fined in Cincinnati's luxurious Burnet House, which he referred

to as "a military bastille." President Lincoln, seeing that martyr-
dom could only strengthen Vallandigham's cause and enlarge his
following, ordered him released to the Confederacy. A special
train took him, with his Union army escorts, to Tennessee. In a
memorable midnight scene he was delivered to General Rose-
crans. Then he proceeded in a wagon through the streets of
Murfreesboro, past the sleeping camps of ten thousand Federal
troops, to General Braxton Braggs's headquarters. "Guard after
guard," wrote the correspondent for the Cincinnati *Gazette*,
"picket after picket, sentinel after sentinel was passed, the magic
countersign opening the gates in the walls of living men which,
circle behind circle, surrounded the town of Murfreesboro. The
men on guard stood looking in silent wonder at the unwonted
spectacle, little thinking that they were gazing on the great
copperhead on his way through the lines."

A few weeks later Vallandigham went to Bermuda on a Confederate blockade runner, and from there he sailed to Canada.
From the Niagara River he looked across at his country. Above
the roar of the great Falls, he was aware of another tumult; he
had become the subject of the noisiest political campaign in
Ohio's history. A frenzied convention in Columbus, with fifty
thousand Peace Democrats milling over the State House grounds,
named him their candidate for governor. During the campaign
Vallandigham moved to Windsor, on the Detroit River. While
he paced a hotel room, looking out at the Federal gunboat *Michigan* on patrol in the river, a tense and bitter struggle cleft Ohio,
a struggle that was watched by North and South alike. In the
army camps at Chattanooga Federal and Rebel soldiers daily followed the Ohio elections, shouting the news across their picket
lines. On the rainy midnight of October 13 the final word came—
Vallandigham was overwhelmingly defeated by rugged Republican John Brough—and shouting rang from every tent in the
Union army. Ohio was still on the side of the federal government.

With this defeat the Peace Democrats gave up hope of political
control in the Northwest, but the plot of a Northwest Uprising

still smoldered. Vallandigham, a brave, stubborn and mistaken man, still argued a political theory of state's rights. On a June night in 1864 he left Windsor in disguise and took the train to Hamilton, Ohio, where he spoke to a party gathering charged with electing delegates to the National Democratic Convention. He warned his followers against "unlawful armed resistance to the Federal or State authorities," while also warning the regime in power that "there is a vast number, a host whom they cannot number, bound together by the strongest and holiest ties, to defend by whatever means the exigencies of the time shall demand, their natural and constitutional rights as free men."

Meanwhile Confederate agents were conspiring with his followers to seize control of the Northwest. Into Chicago for the Democratic Convention poured a hundred thousand Copperheads. They came on foot, on horseback, crowded into carts, buggies and farm wagons, hanging onto the side of trains. Soon the city was a vast whispering gallery, murmuring with rumor and conspiracy. Arms had come from Canada in stacks of boxes labeled "hymn books" and "prayer books." A few thousand armed men, the leaders believed, could storm Camp Douglas (the Stephen A. Douglas estate, on which the Little Giant was buried, had become a barracks-walled compound crammed with Confederate prisoners) and release its five thousand captives. They were hardened men, with only a twelve-foot board fence around their seventy-acre prison. One determined rush, synchronized with an attack from outside, would batter down the walls. Then they would swarm over Chicago, with thousands of Copperheads swelling their ranks. Some would seize a train and hurry to Camp Morton in Indianapolis, where another store of arms waited in boxes labeled "Sunday-school books," and another deliverance would be accomplished.

It was not a wholly unrealistic plan: the smoldering Sons of Liberty numbered three hundred thousand, two-thirds of them in Illinois, Indiana and Ohio, and a few thousand well-led men could have touched off a vast explosion. But alert Federal officers had already strengthened the garrisons at the prison camps, and tense days passed without violence. At last Uprising Day was set for August 29, when the great convention would assemble. On that day the conspirators were in dispute about the number of Federal troops at Camp Douglas and uncertain of their own plan of action. There was will enough among the Sons of Liberty, but having a military objective without a military organization, they could not find a way. All they accomplished in Chicago was the nomination of General George B. McClellan for the Presidency on a platform of immediate ending of the war.

But there came a night of action, a few weeks later, in the quiet waters of Lake Erie. Here the trigger was pulled and the plot came near fulfillment.

The three hundred wooded acres of Johnson Island, in Sandusky Bay, were once a fishing camp of the Wyandots and a place where they brought their captives after a successful episode of war. In 1861, long after the Wyandots had departed, the federal government leased the island for use as a military prison. It held some three thousand men, and in 1864 many of Morgan's junior officers were confined there. Because of rumors that Confederate sympathizers in Canada might attempt a rescue of the prisoners, the Federal gunboat *Michigan*, the first iron ship in the U.S. Navy, was stationed there.

The prisoners on Johnson Island were fortunate. They lived in a roomy eighteen acres surrounded by a board stockade. The parade ground sloped slightly toward the shore; behind it stood the ranked barracks. The men had athletic contests on the trampled ground; they held minstrel and musical shows in the mess hall; they bathed in the lake, a hundred at a time, escorted by their friendly guards. They could carry pocket knives and they did a lot of whittling, carving finger rings and watch-charms from gutta-percha buttons and making flutes and whistles from twigs of willow. One of the camp teamsters supplied whisky, until he was caught and drummed off the island with a sign I SOLD WHISKY TO THE REBELS around his neck. He was put aboard the boat and marched through the streets of Sandusky, to the jeers and laughter of the townspeople. The war was no grimmer than this on the Lake Erie shore.

But across the lake in Canada, watching the water with restless eyes and coughing into a stained handkerchief, was a somber young Virginian who had become a confidential agent for the Confederacy. John Yates Beall, a brooding, soberly dressed man of twenty-eight, had been invalided out of the Southern army with a bullet in his side and a tubercular lung. He had not long to live, but he had bold intentions. He meant to capture the U.S.S. *Michigan*, to deliver the prisoners from Johnson Island and to create havoc along the Lakes. Allied with him were Captain Charles Cole, once of Morgan's Cavalry, and the shadowy Captain Thomas H. Hines, who lurked behind the whole Northwest conspiracy. These men had been busy. After scouting the Federal garrisons and arsenals in Buffalo, Cleveland, Chicago and Milwaukee, identifying the Copperhead leaders in Sandusky, and gaining a warm social acquaintance with the master of the *Michigan*, they saw success ahead.

When the steamer *Philo Parsons* left Detroit on the night of September 18, 1864, a quiet-voiced traveler asked the captain if he could call for a couple of passengers at Sandwich on the Canadian side of the river. The obliging captain made the stop, where John Yates Beall and a companion came aboard. At Amherstburg, ten miles farther, where the river widens into Lake Erie, a file of men came up the gangway, two of them carrying a heavy trunk. This was not unusual; in 1864 many fugitives were traveling to and from Canada. The *Parsons* churned out into Lake Erie, her smoke rosy in the sunrise.

In the bright September morning passengers lounged in the saloon and on the decks—all but two men in a stateroom who were taking guns and ammunition from the battered trunk. On the lake rim grew the long low wooded line of the Bass Islands. The ship steamed around North Bass—Isle St. George on the old lake charts—with its broad sheep meadows and its rusting vineyards. Then it swung across the channel toward the south shore of Kelley's Island, where it stopped to unload passengers and freight. While the helmsman was steering away from the dock, the mate heard a dry hacking cough behind him. He looked around at a pointed pistol. In his quiet voice John Yates Beall said that the captain was a prisoner, the ship was a prize of the Confederacy and the crew were captives of war. One of the conspirators took the wheel and the *Parsons* steamed back to Put-in-Bay to debark the prisoners. Ahead appeared the broad-beamed *Island Queen* on its run from Sandusky to Toledo. At Beall's order the *Parsons* swung across her bow and drew along-side. While puzzled Captain Orr asked what was wanted, Beall's men threw grappling hooks aboard the *Queen* and made the two vessels fast. On their new prize the raiders found thirty-five fur-loughed Federal troops homeward-bound to Toledo. Unarmed, they gave no resistance. After putting his prisoners ashore at Put-in-Bay, Beall scuttled the *Island Queen* off Ballast Island. Then, under the midnight stars, he steered the *Parsons* toward Sandusky Bay, where the U.S.S. *Michigan* lay off Johnson Island.

According to plan, the gunboat should now be in possession of the Rebels. Captain Cole, in the guise of a rich oil man from the new boom town of Titusville, Pennsylvania, had become a friend of the *Michigan's* officers; he had already been their guest on a lake cruise. In return he entertained the naval men in a hotel banquet room in Sandusky. He was given the run of Johnson Island, where he had talked freely with the prisoners. Soon he had ten accomplices doing guard duty on the island and two more serving as enlisted men on the gunboat. On this appointed night Captain Cole was to give a dinner for the officers on board the *Michigan*. The wine was drugged. Cole had merely to wait for his victims to fall asleep and then to watch for the appearance of his colleagues on the *Parsons*. He would deliver the gunboat to them without a shot.

Now the *Parsons* crept near, winking signal lights, but no answer came from the *Michigan*. Pacing the *Parsons*'s bridge with his quiet coughing, Beall could only wait and wonder. At last he steered across to the Canadian shore, debarked his men and set fire to the ship. In the gray dawn he watched it burn to the water.

If things had gone as planned, a bigger smoke would now be darkening the lake. Twenty-five hundred prisoners on Johnson Island would be released. They would cut telegraph lines out of Sandusky, seize a railroad train and head for Columbus to release the Confederate prisoners there. Meanwhile, joined by northern Ohio Copperheads, raiders would be destroying the lake cities. That morning, according to the schedule, Toledo, Sandusky and Cleveland would be burning.

The plot was both audacious and careful, but Federal officials were not as blind as the Confederates supposed. By some counter-intelligence activity the fifth column was intercepted. One version has Cole dressing in his hotel room prior to the banquet aboard the *Michigan* when Federal officers broke in. Another version has him on the ship, going on deck at midnight to signal the *Parsons* when he was arrested. Cole was confined on Johnson Island as a prisoner and then was sent to Fort Lafayette in New York harbor, where a court-martial sentenced him to death as a Confederate spy. In his prison cell he signed a confession, took an oath of amnesty and was released. The rest of his life is unknown.

A week before Christmas, 1864, John Yates Beall was arrested by Federal police in the railroad station at Niagara Falls. Sentenced to death by court-martial, he was hanged at Fort Columbus on Governor's Island, New York, on a bleak February afternoon in 1865.

To Johnson Island a few months later came news from Appomattox. The prisoners were released, the guards discharged, the barracks boarded up. The long war was over.

At that time a big bearded man was living like a hermit in a shack on the shore of South Bass Island. He had come there like a fugitive, though he could not have been a soldier: he had a withered left arm and a pale, shriveled hand like a limp turkey's foot. When the war was over, his name became known. He was Owen Brown, the youngest son of John Brown of Harper's Ferry.

On the tranquil island he had troubled memories. He had been with his father and his brothers and the huddle of desperate men in the farmhouse on the Ferry Road, waiting for the hour to strike. It was a tense vigil, week after week, while the Maryland neighbors grew suspicious. What kind of farming went on at the Kennedy place, with no one working in the fields? How could Smith wear as many shirts as hung on the line when his daughter did the washing? What kind of tools or implements did they bring in long dark boxes, heavy as iron?

At night in the valley darkness the men came out of hiding. They paced like horses in the barnyard, looking across to the lights of Harpers Ferry, living the action over and over, raiding the arsenal a hundred times before the first shot rang in the Ferry streets. They were waiting for fifty promised men, but the weeks passed and no one came. So new plans were drawn— a handful of men must do the work of a brigade. Each had his swift and vital mission, to cut off the railroad and the telegraph, to seize the arsenal and paralyze the town. Guns would be moved from the farmhouse to the school building by the canal lock; couriers would ride through the hills and soon the liberated slaves would come streaming down the valley roads. That liberation would race like a wind through all the South.

On Sunday, October 15, 1859, the men filed down the creaking steps from the farmhouse attic. They ate a silent supper. John Brown reached for his rifle. "Men, get your arms," he said. "We will proceed to the Ferry."

Owen Brown was to stay at the farm where the freed slaves would gather. The morning wore on. Gunfire rattled across the river and a few slaves shambled down the Ferry Road. Where were the multitudes? All day Owen Brown waited, and at dusk the word came. John Brown's men were beaten and surrounded, trapped like animals in the arsenal and the enginehouse. That night a dozen slaves crept back to their masters and Owen Brown fled through the hills toward Pennsylvania. There was a price on his head, but he slept in thickets and hid his withered hand under a knapsack while passing through the towns. He was bound for Canada, but when his father was hanged at Charles Town, West Virginia, his flight ended. He had found refuge on South Bass Island, where he lived in peace. In the prison cell in Charles Town, John Brown had written: *I give to my son Owen Brown my double spy Glass & my Rifle Gun (if found). It is Globe Sighted and new. I give also to the same Son Fifty Dollars in consideration of his terrible sufferings in Kansas & his crippled condition from his childhood.*

In time the war faded into memory, and the G.A.R. held a summer encampment at Put-in-Bay. From his shack, where he had a board of bright little butterflies, each one pinned up with its name beneath it—*Red Admiral, Tiger Swallowtail, Hobomok Skipper, Olive Hairstreak*—Owen Brown heard their drums and bugles. While stars glimmered in the water he heard them singing, "Tenting tonight, Tenting tonight, Tenting on the old campground"; and sometimes the morning wind brought their marching song: "John Brown's body lies a-moldering in the grave . . ." It followed him all his life.

Now the National Guard has an artillery range at Camp Perry on the lake shore. On summer days a faint thunder rolls across the islands, like an echo of battles long ago.

18. A Brakeman, a Carpenter and the Hillside Tomb

In the fall of 1864 William S. Porter, from the sleepy southern Illinois town of Jerseyville, was mustered out of service with the Forty-first Illinois Infantry. He was just sixteen but the war had left a man's lines in his face. A few days after his discharge he became a brakeman on the Chicago and Alton Railroad—riding on top of the train, setting hand brakes and couplings. From the swaying roof of boxcars and coaches he watched the prairie roll past, in sunlight and starlight, all the way from Chicago to St. Louis.

Late in April, 1865, Bill Porter dropped off a train at Bloomington, Illinois, and reported to the superintendent. In the office he found a dozen young brakemen, weathered and wind-burned like himself. They were ordered to Chicago, on special duty. They rode the cushions there.

On the Chicago lake front, at Twelfth Street and Michigan Avenue, Bill Porter joined a special train—a baggage car and nine coaches, all draped in black. The first seven coaches carried a New York military company in dress uniforms. The final car was occupied by an official party, including General Joseph (Fighting Joe) Hooker, Secretary Edwin M. Stanton, Governor Richard Yates, Captain Robert Lincoln, the late President's oldest son, and Lincoln's long-time friend Supreme Court Justice David Davis. The next to the last car was heavily draped in mourning, with crepe rosettes framing each of its twelve windows. On its side was the presidential seal. Sentries wearing the blue campaign cap, white gloves and black arm bands stood rigid at both vestibules. Inside the car on a raised dais was a small coffin containing the body of twelve-year-old Willie Lincoln, who had died three years before in Washington and was now to be buried with his father in Springfield. There was room on the dais for a larger coffin, but now that space was empty. The coffin had been taken to the Chicago Courthouse where an endless stream of people passed it, night and day. Bill Porter had time to get some new overalls before his job began.

In its solemn twelve-day journey from Washington the train had been visited by thousands of silent people and seen by millions. In a dozen cities plumed horses and military companies marching to muffled drums had escorted the coffin from the funeral train. Abraham Lincoln's body lay in state in the Pennsylvania capitol at Harrisburg, in Independence Hall in Philadelphia, in the City Hall in New York—while vast hushed crowds filed past. In Syracuse thirty thousand came through a midnight downpour to pay their tribute to the assassinated President. At Cleveland the coffin lay in a black-draped tabernacle in the Public Square. At Columbus eight hearse-horses clattered over the planking of High Street between silent ranks of people, and the coffin was carried between the black-draped pillars of the State House. In the rotunda fifty thousand people, two and a half times the city's population, moved past the open casket. Indianapolis was thronged with citizens from every county of Indiana. In a steady rain a hundred thousand awaited their turn to walk past the President's coffin.

Abraham Lincoln's death in the hour of military triumph prevented exultation in the North. Rejoicing swiftly changed to sorrow, and the whole nation felt the massive tragedy of the war. In place of victory banners every town and city hung out emblems of grief. Instead of martial music there was the tolling of bells and the somber boom of cannon.

From Washington Walt Whitman followed in his mind the President's return to the heartland.

> Over the breast of the spring, the land, amid cities,
> Amid lanes and through old woods, where lately the violets
>   peep'd from the ground, spotting the grey débris,
> Amid the grass in the fields each side of the lanes, passing the
>   endless grass,
> Passing the yellow-spear'd wheat, every grain from its shroud
>   in the dark-brown fields uprisen,
> Passing the apple-tree blows of white and pink in the orchards,
> Carrying a corpse to where it shall rest in the grave,
> Night and day journeys a coffin.

In Chicago on the evening of May 2 the funeral cortege formed at Washington and La Salle streets, outside the Cook County courthouse. Eight sergeants carried the coffin to the hearse, drawn by eight black horses, each accompanied by a Negro groom, and the procession moved west on Madison Street with an echoing *clip-clop* of hooves on the pavement. Fifty thousand persons followed the military guard. Acres of people stood outside the Union Station while the coffin was carried into the catafalque car. The long coffin was set down beside the small one. Night had fallen when Bill Porter freed the brakes on the funeral coach and the train began its journey to Springfield.

When the lights of Chicago dwindled, there was the huge dark prairie under the stars. It was a slow run and the train hardly swayed on the long straight track. Lights and voices filled the cars ahead, but the funeral coach was dark and still.

Sometimes in Springfield on Sunday mornings Willie and Tad went with their father to his office while their mother went to church. Willie brought his kitten. They clattered up the board stairs and into the long room with its desk, bookshelves and paper-strewn table. They piled up books and toppled them over, they made a quiver of arrows out of pencils and a spittoon, while their father lay on the battered couch, playing with the kitten. Willie was the older by three years, a bright, happy, imaginative boy who could make up games and stories. Little Thomas was a bubbler and a wriggler—"Tadpole," his father called him. When carriages passed outside, coming from church, they went home, cutting through the pasture to the sand-colored house at Eighth and Jackson streets.

In the White House in Washington Willie and Tad kept kittens, goats, rabbits and a little dog named Jip that often sat in the President's lap at mealtimes, watchful for morsels. They had a doll named Jack, dressed like a soldier, and in their play Jack drew a death penalty for sleeping on picket duty. The boys dug Jack's grave in the shrubbery, but before the burial a White House gardener had an idea that the President might pardon him. The boys appealed and got a reprieve, written on Executive Mansion notepaper. "The doll Jack is pardoned. By order of the President. A. Lincoln."

Willie and Tad ran through the White House halls, bursting into the President's office in the midst of conferences. If the door was closed, they rapped three shorts and two longs (the number 3), a signal they had learned in the war telegraph office. "I've got to let them in," Lincoln would say. "I promised never to go back on the code."

During the winter of 1862 Willie lay languid and bright-eyed with fever. At midnight Lincoln came in his old dressing gown and sat by the bedside, smoothing the burning forehead with his big hand. In the waning light of a gray afternoon Willie died. That evening John Nicolay found Lincoln lying on the floor of his study trying to console sobbing little Tad. A few months later fire broke out at night in the White House stables. Lincoln ran out, asking for the horses, but was stopped by secret service men. From a bedroom window he watched the flames die down. Willie's pony was in the ruins.

By midnight the funeral train was dark and the rails clicked steadily under the wheels. In the catafalque there was darkness within darkness, two coffins on the dark dais in the dark car rolling homeward over the dark prairie.

In the fall of 1864 sixteen-year-old Edmond Beall of Alton, Illinois, went to work as a carpenter for the Chicago and Alton Railroad. In the last week of April, 1865, he reported to Superintendent Chafee, who had charge of all bridge and carpenter work on the railroad, for special duty. With a dozen other carpenters he was sent to Springfield to drape the Lincoln house in mourning.

Ed Beall was a rangy youth with a long reach, and it fell to him to hang the black "droopers" from the eaves above the second story of the house. On the steep rooftop his comrades paid out a rope and Ed slid down, head first, until he could reach over the edge. When his hammer sounded, an upstairs window opened. Mrs. Lucian A. Tilton, wife of the railroad official who had rented the Lincoln house, instructed him to set the black rosettes just eight feet apart. Lying there with his head hanging into space, the boy could not precisely judge that distance, and he said so. Mrs. Tilton soon reappeared with a two-foot rule taken from Lincoln's old desk. When the job was done, Ed Beall tucked the ruler under his belt and was hauled back up the roof. For years afterward the Lincoln ruler was a prized keepsake in his house in Alton.

While the carpenters were at work on the eaves and cornices, hundreds of visitors gathered at Eighth and Jackson streets. They stripped the new-leafed shrubbery for souvenirs. They hacked off splinters of the Lincoln picket fence and dug bricks from the wall. Photographers hawked tintypes of the house, barn and garden. Two enterprising men showed the crowd the Lincoln family horse, Old Tom, and took a collection for their pains. Old Tom was sold when the Lincolns left for Washington; for five years he had been a familiar dray horse on the streets of Springfield. Now the two speculators had bought him for a reported $500 and were planning to take him on an exhibition tour of the country.

From the Lincoln residence the carpenters moved on to the Illinois State House. They draped the building in black velvet and built a catafalque for the coffin in the Assembly Hall.

Meanwhile the crowds were growing. Every train into Springfield was crammed with visitors and endless lines of wagons came over the Sangamon County roads. Horses, mules, traps, carts, buggies, wagons and a multitude on foot choked the dusty streets. Old residents pointed out the Lincoln landmarks—the site of Lincoln's first law office; the room where the first County Court convened; the plain Butler house, where bachelor Lincoln had lodged; the Edwards mansion, where he was married; the Globe Tavern, where he had taken his bride to live; the pasture where he grazed his horse and cow.

In Washington the distraught Mary Todd Lincoln had been unable to decide where her husband should be buried. The citizens of Springfield proposed to erect a tomb on the spacious wooded Mather Place, site of the present Illinois capitol, on Second Street between Monroe and Edwards. Mrs. Lincoln demurred, and while the funeral train was crossing Indiana, she came to a decision. The burial should be in the Oak Ridge Cemetery on a prairie knoll beyond the northern edge of Springfield.

On the first of May Ed Beall and the other carpenters climbed onto lumber wagons and creaked out to Oak Ridge to build a speakers' stand and a platform for a three-hundred-voice choir. Day and night the saws and hammers sounded under the oak trees where leaves had just begun to bud. On the morning of May third their work was done.

From Chicago the railroad officials sent orders over the line. At every creek and river the bridges were guarded by watchmen. Regular trains were sent onto sidings an hour before the funeral train would pass. Two locomotives, No. 40 and No. 57, were assigned to the special train. Both were wood-burners with balloon stack, iron jacket, brass dome, brass sandbox and brass bell-frames—all polished like the sun. Both were decorated from the cowcatcher to the rear draw-bar with flags and bunting intertwined with crepe. Under the headlight each engine carried a crayon portrait of Lincoln in a five-foot wreath of flowers. No. 40 served as a "pilot" engine, going ahead to test the safety of the track. Veteran engineer Jim Cotton was at the throttle of No. 57.

With its own slow clangor lost in the tolling of church bells, the train stopped at Joliet, Wilmington, Bloomington, and Lincoln, where acres of people stood in silence. The train crept through villages where people had waited in the midnight hours with lanterns, flags and torches. At every crossroad families stood bareheaded in the fitful light of bonfires. At last sunrise warmed the prairie and from the top of the train brakeman Porter saw the glint of water through the wooded bottoms of Salt Creek. The next downgrade carried across the Sangamon, and Springfield showed in the distance.

After all night on his carpenter job at Oak Ridge Ed Beall climbed onto an empty lumber wagon and jolted in to Springfield. The streets were filled with horses, vehicles and people on foot—all pressing in toward the C & A depot. Three blocks north Ed jumped off the wagon and shouldered through the crowd. His workman's badge got him past the guards and onto the observation platform. He was there when the pilot engine, puffing pale woodsmoke, its brasswork gleaming under the black shroud, panted past the station. Then, while the buzzing crowd fell silent, the funeral train crept past—the black-dressed engine, the coaches with sentries at the vestibules, the catafalque car with its emblems of office and of mourning. When the train stopped, the crowd surged forward. Ed Beall saw pickpockets at work below the platform. From the rear coach stepped General Joe Hooker, a straight, brisk-striding man with a face as red as an Indian's. Fighting Joe broke his stride when he saw a pickpocket reaching for a spectator's wallet. One of his brisk feet shot out and sent the thief sprawling.

Eight tall sergeants carried the coffin to the hearse, and the honor guard fell in behind. Drums throbbed and the procession moved through the bright May morning to the State House. Ed Beall followed the casket in and took his position at the top of the stairs. He divided the crowd that came, six abreast, sending them in two files past the dais where the coffin rested.

All that day and that night the lines moved through the Assembly Hall. These were the folk from Lincoln's own country—from Petersburg, Jacksonville, Beardstown, Towanda, Metamora, Charleston; people who had known Lincoln the ax-man, the boatman, the surveyor, people from the Eighth Circuit towns who had known Lincoln the lawyer, who had heard his drawling stories in the tavern and his arguments and summations in the courtrooms.

Among that endless line of mourners was lean, long-faced William H. Herndon. He had first seen Lincoln on a horseback trip along the Sangamon, when Lincoln was piloting the steamer *Talisman* over the ruined dam at New Salem. He had gone stump-speaking with Lincoln, had ridden with him on the circuit court, and had been his law partner for twenty-one years; their names were still together, "Lincoln & Herndon," on the office door now hung with crepe. During all that time they were "Billy" and "Mr. Lincoln," and now Bill Herndon stood with his own thoughts above the open coffin. "We who had known the illustrious dead in other days," he wrote, "and before the nation laid its claim upon him, moved sadly through and looked for the last time on the silent upturned face of our departed friend."

All night long the streets were thronged with people, as though no one could sink to rest, and church bells tolled hour after hour through the darkness. It was a warm windless May night, and the morning of May 4 brought a burning sunrise in a cloudless sky. It was the beginning of a blazing day—the hottest day ever known in Illinois, old residents said. By midmorning hundreds were prostrated and Mayor Dennis of Springfield was carried away from the crowded State House square.

At noon a salute of twenty-one guns boomed through the hot still air and the final funeral procession formed. At the head was General Hooker and his staff, then Brigadier General Cook, Brigadier General Oakes, huge Justice Davis, whom Lincoln had appointed to the Supreme Court, Governor Yates of Illinois and his staff, the governors of other states, members of Congress, and a multitude of others. In the procession was Old Tom, sweating under a caparison of black velvet, led by two perspiring grooms.

At Oak Ridge Bishop Matthew Simpson of the Methodist Church, a warm friend of Lincoln's in Washington, gave a eulogy and the massed choir sang in the blaze of sun. The coffins of Lincoln and his son Willie were placed in the hillside tomb. That small room was cool and dim, and it smelled of evergreens strewn on the stone floor.

Slowly the crowd dispersed. In the trance of heat Springfield grew quiet as the country town to which Lincoln had come nearly thirty years before. The Congressmen went back to Washington. The governors returned to their capitals. By train, wagon, horseback and on foot a multitude of people journeyed homeward. And from their assignment with history young Ed Beall went back to repairing boxcars and Bill Porter caught a freight train on the Chicago and Alton run.

19. The Presidential Chair

In the winter of 1862 the fear and sorrow of the time afflicted a fiction writer, even in quiet Concord, Massachusetts. So Nathaniel Hawthorne put away his romance and gave himself to reading newspapers and listening to the click of the telegraph, like the other villagers. Finally he took the train for Washington, to see for himself what war was doing to his country. The result was a dry, discerning essay in the *Atlantic Monthly*, a discourse on the war and the shadow that it cast across America's future. He had no doubt that the Union would survive, but it would not be the nation he had known.

Hawthorne found the capital overrun with office seekers, wirepullers, inventors, editors, railway directors and mail contractors, until his own identity was lost among them. Through the smoke and voices of Willard's Hotel he glimpsed the future of his country—"one bullet-headed general will succeed another in the presidential chair; and veterans will hold the offices at home and abroad, and sit in Congress and the State legislatures, and fill all the avenues of public life." He saw the old America receding, the

Bostonian empire ended and the Virginia dynasty closed, while new populations surged onto the prairies and the Western valleys dominated national politics.

The romancer was a realistic prophet. Soon the generals were in the presidential chair—Grant, Hayes, Garfield, Harrison, all Ohio-born—with Major McKinley, also of Ohio, to follow. In their years of office Hawthorne's hinterland would become the heartland of the nation.

"Forty years of failure" was the story of Grant's life in 1861. He looked older than that, a slow, silent, bearded man stacking hides in his father's tannery in Galena, Illinois. Cashiered from the army, he had failed at business, trade, and farming. Bad luck and bad management had followed him like his own shadow.

When Lincoln called for volunteers, Cap Grant was the only man in Galena who knew how to drill a company. He followed the recruits to Springfield, hoping for an army commission; he had to settle for a clerk's desk in the office of the adjutant general. He went to St. Louis to see General Frémont, but nothing came of that. He waited two days in Cincinnati for a futile appointment with General McClellan. He wrote to the Secretary of War, and got no answer. There seemed to be no place for a washed-up army man. Then Governor Yates of Illinois, needing to replace the incompetent commander of the Twenty-first Illinois Volunteers, happened to remember the ex-army man from Galena. Forty years of failure were ending.

Seven years later the Republican delegations streamed into Chicago with one name on their banners. They were meeting not to select a candidate but to announce one. That formality was preceded by a "Soldier's and Sailor's" convention, an early-day American Legion, which marched the streets of Chicago and then noisily nominated Grant in their mock caucus. A day later eight thousand people crowded into Crosby's Opera House, where General Logan, speaking for the Illinois delegation, nominated Ulysses Simpson Grant. There could be no other candidate, and the General was named by acclamation.

In Washington, at his desk in the War Department, Grant received the news without comment or emotion. Four months later in Galena, having had no part in his campaign, Grant heard the news of his election. He was the calmest man in town.

A great general had been called upon to be a President, and so his name became attached to an age whose material greed and cultural confusion were no more of his doing than the "General Grant architecture" was of his designing. Grant had lived in army barracks, a farm cabin and a Galena cottage. During his presidency the federal government erected the most unlovely of all public buildings, the State, War and Navy building adjoining the White House grounds. A classic simplicity distinguished the Executive Mansion, and other capitol buildings had copied the columned and domed dignity of Republican Rome. But the structures of Grant's period were cluttered, pretentious, and heavy with false ornamentation. Outside, the State building was vastly vulgar; inside, it was a labyrinth of passageways and swinging doors. Here was a monument to the Gilded Age that Hawthorne had predicted and Mark Twain pilloried.

In the midst of greedy turmoil and ostentation, Grant was silent, letting his personal simplicity speak for him, if it could. He dismissed the military guard and lived quietly in the White House with Dent and Grant relatives settling in for lengthy stays. Julia Dent Grant was a simple, kindly woman, always generous and loyal to her husband and easily flattered by politicians who through her sought presidential favors. Grant had shrewdly measured his military adversaries, but he could not judge his so-called friends. He became their victim and the victim of his own limitations. He could not grasp the complexities of business and politics in the hectic years of reconstruction.

Grant's older son, Frederick, was making a dubious record at West Point, and Ulysses, Jr.—"Buck"—was starting in at Harvard when the General went to the White House. From college Buck plunged into banking. He had the restless expectations of the Gilded Age, and in financial matters he was given his father's trust and deference. Eventually Grant's own fortune was lost in his son's failure.

In bankruptcy Grant lost even his swords and military medals. To pay his debts he wrote his *Personal Memoirs*, which became one of the most successful books ever published in America. In its chapters he looked past the scandal and rancor of his administration to the great struggle for the Union. With surprising passion the silent man recalled his campaigns in Tennessee and the Wilderness. Even when cancer struck, he kept on with the *Memoirs*. From all parts of the country came notable visitors, none more welcome than the Confederate generals Forrest, Longstreet, Hancock. As President, Grant had held on to a stubborn vision of a wholly united nation. When the Southern leaders came to his mountain cottage in the Adirondacks, in the last season of his life, he could see his hope fulfilled.

Inauguration date, 1877, fell on Sunday, and the inaugural ceremonies were postponed for a day. Grant's term would be over before the new President was installed. Like a soldier, Grant was concerned over that brief gap in command. On Sunday afternoon in the Red Room of the White House, in a small, secret ceremony, Rutherford B. Hayes took the oath of office. Another Ohio general had become commander in chief of his nation.

Grant was born in a two-room cabin in the hamlet of Point Pleasant on the Ohio River. Hayes, beginning one step higher, was born in a two-story house in Delaware, Ohio, on the Whetstone River, which the Indians had called the Olentangy. His father had died before he was born, and his widowed mother longed for her native Vermont. But on a visit there she missed the energy and expansiveness of the Midwest. She returned to Ohio, to rear her son in the new country. As a boy Hayes once said, "I have an aversion to Yankees." He signed himself R B H, BUCKEYE.

At Kenyon College in the woods of central Ohio, Hayes lived in an attic room of gothic Old Kenyon and became the most popular man in his class. From there he went to Harvard Law School, where he read French, Latin and philosophy along with torts and contracts. This Buckeye youth had a roving mind, open in all directions.

As a young lawyer Hayes began practice at Lower Sandusky, now Fremont, Ohio, and then moved to Cincinnati, where he slept in his office to save expense. In lively, cosmopolitan Cincinnati he enjoyed social and professional success. Soon he was a family man, busy with local politics and public affairs. He was a likely candidate for Congress when war interrupted his career.

Serving in the Twenty-third Ohio under Rosencrans, Hayes's natural leadership soon carried him to command of his regiment. Wounded at South Mountain, he was urged by his family to return to civil life. But he chose to stay in uniform. A bold and resourceful soldier, he conducted rescue raids behind Confederate lines and hurried his troops northward to intercept Morgan's raiders at Gallipolis, Ohio. War strengthened Hayes's will and character, and it brightened his future. Commissioned brigadier general, in 1864 he was elected to Congress while still in the field. After a term in the House of Representatives he campaigned for the governorship of Ohio. Two terms in that office brought him national attention. He was a vigorous and enlightened governor, improving the state welfare program and helping to establish The Ohio State University and the state geological survey.

With political astuteness Hayes declined to run for the Senate against the austere and able John Sherman—an earlier Bob Taft —but he ran again for Congress while campaigning for Grant's second term. Two years later he was again elected governor of Ohio—an office which he resigned for a greater one. In 1876 Hayes had been proposed by John Sherman and James Garfield as a presidential nominee. His liberalism, his party loyalty and his rank of general in the war all made him an attractive candidate, even after Bob Ingersoll's eloquent nominating speech for Blaine. The Republican convention of 1876 was held in Cincinnati, where Hayes had warm friends and a committed press. After seven see-saw ballots he was the convention's man. In the campaign that followed Hayes made few appearances, but no candidate ever had such a roster of stump speakers. His name was carried up and down the country by Carl Schurz, James G. Blaine, James A. Garfield, Bob Ingersoll and Mark Twain.

In the closest of all American elections it appeared that Hayes had lost to Samuel J. Tilden, the Democratic candidate, but the Republican organization disputed the returns from Oregon and three southern states. In that impasse Congress set up an electoral commission which first decided for Tilden and then reversed itself. By a margin of one vote the electors declared Rutherford B. Hayes the nation's President.

As chief executive Hayes withdrew the last Federal troops from the South, bringing an end to the so-called Reconstruction. He undertook civil service reform, asserting a firm hand after the laxness of the Grant Administration, as his wife brought temperance rules to the White House after the Grant indulgence. Weathering a storm of business and labor troubles, Hayes ended his term in a season of prosperity. He was an esteemed leader when he left the presidential chair—he had previously expressed opposition to a second term for any President—retiring to tranquil Spiegel Grove in Fremont, Ohio.

In 1831 barely a fifth of Ohio was cleared and cultivated. But canal boats were creeping from Lake Erie to the Ohio River and the first Ohio railroad was being laid between Dayton and Sandusky. In that year James Abram Garfield was born in a farm cabin near Cleveland. His father, who had dug some miles of the Ohio Canal, died two years later. Growing up on a thirty-acre farm, "Jim Gafill" (the Western Reserve was then as Yankee as Cape Ann) did a man's work between terms in a frontier schoolhouse.

As a broad-shouldered, six-foot youth of seventeen, Garfield strode in to Cleveland to become a Great Lakes sailor. Boarding a topsail schooner, he found a drunken crew in the fo'c'sle and a surly captain in the cabin. Back on the waterfront, feeling less adventurous already, he heard a familiar voice shouting across the canal basin. It was his cousin, Amos Letcher, canal boatman. Amos was looking for a mule-driver, and soon Garfield was on the towpath, taking a load of copper ore, on the barge *Evening Star*, to Pittsburgh. He brought back coal on the return trip and collected wages of $14 a month. His canal career ended in October when he went home, shaking with malarial fever. He had spent just two months on the canal, but his biographers would never forget them.

After some schooling at a local academy and schoolteaching at slightly less than his towpath pay, Garfield turned toward college in the East. He wrote to Yale, Brown and Williams. It was a sentence from President Mark Hopkins: "We shall be glad to do what we can for you," that took him to Williamstown in the great hills of the Berkshires. He arrived in time to hear an address by Ralph Waldo Emerson, a lecture he quoted from all the rest of his life. After two happy years he was graduated from Williams with high standing in scholarship and debate.

Back in Ohio he became a teacher, soon promoted to principal, in the institute which later became Hiram College. From that academic chair he was elected to the Ohio Senate, where war found him in 1861. Appointed lieutenant colonel of volunteers, he quickly rose to colonel. At Middle Creek, Kentucky, he won one of the first Union victories and was given a brigade. His staff work with the Army of the Cumberland won him a reputation for courage and judgment. After two years in uniform he was a major general, and then, in 1863, he was elected to Congress as a Representative from Ohio. Garfield had been fortunate in war, and he would be fortunate in politics until an assassin blocked his way.

After eight successive terms in Congress Garfield was a party leader in the House. During a time of widespread scandal he did not escape charges of corruption, but he surmounted them. In 1886 he served on the electoral commission which awarded the presidency to Hayes. Four years later he was elected to the Senate, a chair he never filled. Instead of taking his Senate seat in 1881, he became President of the United States.

Garfield's presidency was as nearly accidental as his brief career on the towpath. John Sherman of Ohio was seeking the Republican nomination in 1880, and Garfield went to Chicago as Sherman's manager. His able conduct on the convention floor kept him in the foreground while Sherman was deadlocked with rival candidates. On the thirty-sixth ballot the avalanche broke loose and Garfield was the man. He had lost the nomination for his candidate and won it for himself.

In the campaign that fall the disgruntled Republican leaders in the East finally made a Western trip, appearing at Garfield rallies in Ohio, where Mark Hanna was learning political strategy. It was Hanna who got Grant and Conkling to stop off at Mentor to pay a call on Garfield. After the "Treaty of Mentor" the Republicans had a solid front. Victorious in November, Garfield resigned his place in the Senate, which went then to John Sherman. It was a neat reversal of fortunes.

Garfield's administration began with a horde of office seekers, from whom he escaped long enough to read the newly published *Ben Hur*, as a multitude of Americans were doing. One of the unsuccessful applicants intercepted him a few months later in the Washington railroad station. The assassin's bullet lodged in Garfield's back and was never located.

For eleven weeks the President lay in bed, his fever rising and falling in the hot Washington summer. He died in September, 1881. A martyr's death made a hero of him, and twelve Garfield biographies appeared within two years. One of them, *From Log Cabin to White House*, quickly went through seven editions in London, and *From the Towpath to the White House* was read all over the United States. The log cabin myth, an idealization of the frontier period then ending in America, was never more alive than in the year of Garfield's death.

Grant, Hayes and Garfield all came from Yankee families who had gone west to the new country. Benjamin Harrison had a Virginia ancestry which included a signer of the Declaration of Independence and a governor of Virginia. His grandfather, William Henry Harrison, went west as a youth of eighteen, marching over the mountains and flatboating down the Ohio with a company of recruits for Governor St. Clair's army. He became aide-de-camp to Anthony Wayne, governor of the huge Indiana territory, and a short-term President of the United States with whom the log cabin myth began.

The log cabin ascribed to "Old Tippecanoe" was actually a fourteen-room house, surrounded by gardens, orchards and fruitful fields, at North Bend on the Ohio River. Ben Harrison grew up on an adjoining farm, whose western acres touched the boundary of Indiana. He was both a Buckeye and a Hoosier. As a youth of seventeen he went to Miami University at Oxford, Ohio; its Old Main building, where he studied Greek and logic, was renamed Harrison Hall in the twentieth century. He was graduated in 1852, four classes ahead of Whitelaw Reid, who would be his running mate on the Republican ticket in 1892. A stocky, studious, sober youth, he stood on the platform under the campus trees and gave his Senior Oration on "The Poor of England." According to a classmate he was a protectionist from age nineteen. He wanted to save his country, by means of high tariff, from the poverty of other lands.

Within a few years in Indianapolis, Ben Harrison was a rising young lawyer, growing with the Western country. Then came the news from Fort Sumter. In war as in law, Harrison applied himself with diligence and system. Commissioned second lieutenant of Indiana Volunteers, he rose to the command of his regiment. He was breveted brigadier general in 1865.

Back home in Indiana, he took up his sober career—as lawyer,

Sunday-school superintendent, speechmaker for the Republican party and public causes. In 1880, after a defeat for the governorship of Indiana, he was chairman of the Indiana delegation that helped to nominate Garfield for the Presidency. He declined a post in Garfield's cabinet to run for the Senate. As a Senator he sided with Indians and homesteaders against the Western railroads; he stood for railroad regulation and a protective tariff. Though his opponents labeled him cold and distant, his old troopers called him "Little Ben" and cheered his support of pension legislation.

In 1884 there was talk of Harrison for President, but Harrison was not ready. In 1888 his nomination came on the eighth ballot. That summer he instituted the "front-porch campaign," receiving delegations that paraded to his brick and stone mansion on North Delaware Street in Indianapolis. Meanwhile a literary Hoosier general, Lew Wallace, having written *Ben Hur*, turned to Ben Harrison, producing a campaign biography that showed the human side of the Republican candidate.

As President, Harrison gave new impetus to the rising current of American expansion and imperialism. He hastened the opening of Oklahoma Territory to settlement and helped along statehood for Utah. He launched a new navy of steel ships and an enlarged merchant marine. Forgetting the landlocked horizons of his youth, he became concerned with islands in the Caribbean and the Pacific. One of his last acts as President was to approve a treaty annexing Hawaii.

Harrison did not want a second term—he never could relax in the presidential chair—but his friends persuaded him to run again. With his long-time friend Whitelaw Reid he was defeated, while economic shadows deepened into the panic of 1893. It was an uneasy office that he left, returning to the staid Hoosier capital. There he took up his law practice while newspapers echoed the clamor of the Populists and free-silver men. Though lukewarm to Hanna and McKinley, he took an active part in the campaign of 1896, when McKinley and Bryan were contesting for the presidential chair.

In 1867 erect young William McKinley (he was just twenty-two, a major of Ohio Volunteers, when the war ended) left the village of Poland, Ohio, for the county seat of Canton. In that year the first cargo of iron ore from Minnesota was unloaded in Cleveland harbor, the beginning of a trade that would make Canton a steel town and that would heap up fortunes for Ohio iron merchants. One of them would use his wealth and power to put McKinley in the White House after the most violent political campaign in American history.

Hanna and McKinley, whose names would become insepa-rable, met in 1876 on opposite sides of a Canton courtroom, when McKinley was defending a group of coal miners involved in labor trouble with the firm of Rhodes & Company. Young Mark Hanna had married the daughter of Daniel P. Rhodes, a Cleveland coal and iron baron. Soon the Rhodes firm would be M. A. Hanna & Company. Wherever Mark Hanna moved in, he took over.

Rhodes & Company had recognized a newly formed union which was protesting a cut in miners' wages following a break in coal prices which came with the panic of 1873. In April of 1875 James Ford Rhodes, who would become a pre-eminent American historian, presided at a conference of miners and owners. His brother-in-law, Mark Hanna, was spokesman for the employers. Arbitration failed and violence developed at a mine near Canton. When Governor Hayes sent a company of Ohio militia, the defiant miners set fire to several properties of Rhodes & Company. The troops arrested some miners and restored order; soon the strikers returned to work at lowered pay. Defense of the miners was conducted by William McKinley. He won the case, and the life-long admiration of the loser, Marcus Alonzo Hanna.

Burly, bluff, broad-shouldered, his Irish mouth ready to roar with rage or laughter, Hanna could be stubborn and magnani-mous by turns. In a Hanna mine on Lake Superior one of the mine mules was called "Mark"; he was as obstinate as a mule could be. But the secretary of the miners' union said that Mark Hanna was the most intelligent and considerate of all the operators. He was a *personal* businessman, close to his associates and close to his employees. He could talk to stevedores on the red-stained ore docks, to sailors on ships whistling through the Soo River, to miners in the open pit and the deep drifts underground. During the Cleveland streetcar strike Hanna's tram cars kept rolling. He listened to his workmen and talked to them, one man to another. "You mean working men?" he once asked a Philadelphia banker who had referred to the "lower classes." "Or do you mean criminals and that kind of people? Those are the lower classes."

In the 1880's the Midwest was burgeoning with new business. Men of New England ancestry, the Mathers, Hannas, Pickands, Nortons, Bradleys, brought Yankee shrewdness and energy to this industrial arena. They made Cleveland the capital of the iron-ore trade and they hastened the transformation of Ohio from a wheat state to a state of smoking mills and furnaces. The Western country changed the Yankee settlers as they changed the new land. It relaxed their Puritanism and enlarged their interests and undertakings; it made Yankee farmers into Ohio merchants, bankers, industrialists and politicians.

The Hanna company had its hands deep in a dozen enterprises —coal mines, iron mines, steamship lines, docks, blast furnaces, street railways, oil refineries, newspapers, banks, theaters. Their Globe Shipbuilding Company launched the first steel freighters on the lakes. The Hanna fleet carried coal to the north and brought back iron ore. The firm sold iron ore and converted it to pig iron in their own furnaces. They reaped profit from every activity—mining, transporting, manufacturing, selling. In this integrated business Mark Hanna built up one of the great fortunes of the Gilded Age.

While business seesawed in a period of boom and panic, Hanna pondered the vast new energies at work in the heart of America. He saw that all business was linked together—mining, transportation, manufacturing, finance—and then he saw something more. He saw that all business was linked to politics. It is a commonplace now, but it was a discovery in the nation that was hurrying away from a simple rural civilization to a complex industrial order. Business was harnessed to politics. Politics could be controlled like a machine. The machinery was powered by money. It was simple, logical and revolutionary.

Mark Hanna became the first big businessman in politics. He steamed into politics with the system and drive of a railroad or a shipping magnate. When his friend McKinley sponsored a tariff bill in Congress, Hanna, an ardent protective tariff man, became McKinley's ardent supporter. In 1890, when McKinley was defeated for re-election to the House of Representatives, Hanna thrust him into the race for the governorship of Ohio. The year 1891 was a season of general Republican defeat, but McKinley won hands down. Four years later, billing his friend as "advance agent of prosperity," Hanna oiled the machinery that would make McKinley the Republican candidate for the presidency.

The Hanna-McKinley team was a combination of unlike men who perfectly complemented each other. Hanna was impulsive, outspoken, hot-tempered, profane. McKinley was dignified, formal, guarded, a devout Methodist and a supporter of missionary schools for heathen children. Hanna had bold imagination. McKinley was logical, conscientious and hard-working. In the heat of argument Hanna pounded the table, his brown eyes yellowed with anger. McKinley calmly put his position into words. Hanna was rumpled, McKinley looked always like a man on the way to church. Said William Allen White, who as a young reporter saw them in all kinds of action, "Hanna had everything that McKinley lacked."

The odd thing is that the burly businessman idolized the careful politician. McKinley was not Mark Hanna's man, as the Hearst papers insisted; he was the object of Hanna's lasting admiration and affection. Hanna was the stronger man, but he put

McKinley into power. For a time it seemed that Hanna was the more important: "The President," it was frequently said, "is lunching with Mr. Hanna." But McKinley was an independent President, and irascible Mark Hanna is remembered because of the unruffled man at his side.

When McKinley's nomination was secured, Hanna loosed a blizzard of folders, placards, posters and campaign literature across the country. For the first time in history a political organization hit the nation with a barrage of advertising. Campaign workers passed out millions of McKinley buttons, gilded elephants, blue-and-gold emblems. It was Hanna's circus. "He has advertised McKinley," said Teddy Roosevelt, "as if he were a patent medicine." In a hundred cities brass bands, parades and stump speakers agitated the summer days, while special trains brought daily delegations to McKinley's front porch in Canton.

McKinley had been nominated in the Exposition Hall at St. Louis in mid-June, 1896. A month later, on a hot July day in Chicago, a tall young Nebraskan in a long black coat and a black string necktie stilled the stormy Democratic convention with his silver voice: "You shall not press down upon the brow of labor this crown of thorns, you shall not crucify mankind upon a cross of gold."

All of William Jennings Bryan's thirty-six years had led him to that hour and that eloquence—his Bible-nurtured youth in Illinois, his debating triumphs on a prairie college rostrum, his decision to become a preacher and his compromise on law, his unseasoned success in prairie politics. As a college orator, practicing in a grove outside of Jacksonville, Illinois, he scared the inmates of the state insane asylum. Carried west by the currents of the 1880's, he charmed the prairie farmers of Nebraska. During two terms in Congress he remained unaware of the clamoring issues around him; he followed the Populist uprising without understanding it. When defeated for the Senate in 1894, he became an itinerant lecturer, proclaiming the silver gospel.

In the 1890's the silver mines of the West were idle and farm prices were ruinously low. To cure both ills with one medicine the free-silver men demanded that silver be purchased at the bullion price of forty-eight cents an ounce and coined as a dollar. This was the silver gospel, and it sounded like salvation to the farmers of the West. Bryan, with no knowledge of banking, of financial credit, of international exchange or of the folly of fiat money, first hypnotized the Populists and then the National Democratic Convention. His Chicago speech was barely twenty minutes long, but for four months it reverberated across the nation.

So began the delirious presidential campaign of 1896, with one Midwestern candidate voicing the doctrines of industry—McKinley stood for a protective tariff and the gold standard—and another shouting the frantic faith of the Populists. The economic issue dividing the parties was easily converted into a class and sectional issue. Gold meant the East; silver meant the West. Gold was the weapon of capitalism; silver was the defense of the poor. Gold was the greed of Wall Street; silver was the hope of the prairies. To the simple followers of Bryan, and of the purblind powerful Hearst press, the campaign was a struggle of rich against poor, East against West, bankers against farmers, Wall Street against the common man.

McKinley, guileless, kindly and upright, the devoted husband of an invalid wife, the lover of brass bands and saddle horses who hid his cigar from the camera so as not to corrupt the young, was no target for hatred. But there was a target beside him, and the fire fell upon Hanna. He was cartooned as a leering moneybags, a mud figure daubed with a dollar sign, an obese glutton feeding on the flesh and blood of the poor. For four months in 1896 the Hearst papers poured upon Mark Hanna the most brutal villification and caricature.

Of all accounts of the campaign, the one that will be remembered longest is not journalism but poetry. In "Bryan! Bryan! Bryan! Bryan!" Vachel Lindsay chanted of the candidate who sketched a silver Zion. It was a natural subject for the Springfield poet who shared the Great Commoner's prairie simplicity and Biblical fervor. They had the same zeal for salvation and the same west-wind charm.

"It was eighteen ninety-six, and I was just sixteen"—the right age for dreams, parades and fireworks. Young Lindsay never forgot the day when Bryan came to Springfield and Altgeld rode with him through the town, all bunting, flags and sunshine, to the old State House yard and the unfading shadow of Lincoln. All Sangamon County was there, the villages deserted while carts, buggies, buckboards and farm wagons rattled in to Springfield. By noon the streets were jammed for the parade against the power of gold.

In a cloud of nostalgia and rhetoric Lindsay recalled the campaign twenty-five years later. He saw it as the plutocrats against democracy, bank vaults against the golden wheat fields, the folklore of the West against the ways of Tubal Cain. In Bryan's voice were "things Mark Hanna never dreamed of"—the hopes of prairie-schooner children, the *Tipi-ti-yi-yay* songs of Texas cowboys, the rustle of aspen groves in Colorado valleys. And while Bryan spoke in Springfield, a tornado swirled across the prairie a hundred miles west. It was a portent of something, "a sign on high."

Lindsay described the campaign almost like a prize fight. July, August saw Wall Street shaken and stunned by the prairie avenger from Nebraska. September, October, and the whole East was down for the count. "Then Hanna to the rescue, Hanna of Ohio . . . Rallying the bucket-shops . . . Rallying the trusts . . . Pouring out the long green to a million workers, Spondulix by the mountain-load, to stop each new tornado . . ."

Election night in November brought Bryan's defeat—"defeat of western silver, defeat of the wheat"—and victory for the plutocrats with dollars in their eyes. McKinley was elected by the largest popular plurality yet recorded.

"Where is McKinley?" Lindsay asked twenty-five years later, "respectable McKinley, The man without an angle or a tangle . . .

Where is McKinley, Mark Hanna's McKinley, His slave, his echo, his suit of clothes?" Lindsay should have known better by that time. The Hearst papers lampooned Hanna as a greasy organ-grinder with McKinley on a leash like a monkey, dancing to his tunes. But after the election McKinley gave orders and Hanna accorded him a proper deference. Of course they stood on common ground. Hanna wanted to align the Republican party with the business interests. McKinley believed that industry served the national prosperity. But the President made his own decisions.

Hanna declined an appointment to McKinley's cabinet, but when Senator Sherman of Ohio became Secretary of State, Hanna was appointed to the vacancy in the Senate. A year later he won the office by election. In the campaign he slowly learned how to be his kind of public speaker, using his own colloquial voice and finding his own relationship with his hearers. His repeated theme was the responsibility of government to encourage business and to see that prosperity was distributed fairly throughout the nation.

As President, McKinley fulfilled his pledge to establish the gold standard, and he judiciously maintained tariff protection for American industry. He was a good man—honest, kindly and a friend of all—a President who sought to do the will and seek the welfare of his people.

In the year 1901 the new century was full of promise. The Wright brothers from Ohio were testing glider wings on the sands at Kitty Hawk and planning to build a flying machine. The first automobile show had opened in Madison Square Garden. By "Hertzian waves" the inventor Marconi signaled the letter s across the Atlantic. Thomas Edison was making motion pictures with his Vitascope. The liner *Celtic* with nine decks above the water had arrived in New York Harbor. The New York Central railroad was tunneling under Park Avenue and the Flatiron Building was climbing twenty stories into the sky.

In Buffalo the Tower of Light, 409 feet high and faced with

35,000 electric lamps, blazed every night over the grounds of the Pan-American Exposition. There Buffalo Bill's Wild West Show played to a packed arena, with General Miles sharing a box with notorious Chief Geronimo, who, according to the papers, had just been converted to Christianity. Everything looked fair in that summer of 1901 when President McKinley, shaking hands with a line of people between the Fountain of Abundance and the Court of Lilies, was shot point-blank by a young anarchist who did not believe in government, marriage or religion. McKinley believed in all three. He thought of his office, and of his wife ("Be careful how you tell her—oh, be careful") and he was whispering the Lord's Prayer when they gave him ether to remove the bullet from his abdomen. The bullet was not found.

For a week the nation waited with alternating hope and fear while the President rallied and then weakened. Thomas Edison sent a new X-ray machine with a trained operator. It could not be used; the President was in a stupor. In the twilight of September 13 he came back to consciousness, murmuring, "Good-by—good-by all." A few hours later he was dead.

To Mark Hanna, Mc Kinley's death was both a personal and a political blow. No one outside the White House had held such power as his, power which he used to hurry the headlong growth of America's great new corporations. "The old nations of the earth creep on at a snail's pace," said Andrew Carnegie; "the republic thunders past with the speed of an express." Hanna was in the locomotive, but he belonged to the century that was ending.

The new President, Theodore Roosevelt, was a man twenty years younger, with a wholly different political philosophy. He believed that the business of government, regardless of the corporations, was to serve the public welfare and to promote justice among all citizens. Hanna and Roosevelt were two strong men, alike in courage, candor, energy and will, but there was a gulf between them. Hanna saw the first signs of defeat before his sudden death, of typhoid fever, in Washington on a chill February day in 1904.

William McKinley held public office most of his life, and to all but two of his positions, as schoolmaster and army officer, he was elected. William Howard Taft held public office most of his life, but he was elected only once, and he regretted that.

Civic leadership began in the Taft family soon after Alphonso Taft, a rangy Vermont lawyer, came West to Cincinnati in 1839. He became Judge of the Ohio Superior Court and was one of the founders of the Republican party in 1856. He served as Secretary of War under President Grant and as ambassador to Vienna and Moscow. At home he helped to establish the University of Cincinnati, where his son William Howard Taft took a law degree after his graduation from Yale.

Before he was thirty stalwart Will Taft had made a dual reputation as athlete and scholar. He played football and baseball at Yale, and according to a Cincinnati legend, he turned down a contract as catcher with the Cincinnati Reds. He loved law more than baseball, and at twenty-nine he was appointed to the Ohio Superior Court. Four years later he stepped up to the Federal Circuit Court, where he served both McKinley and Roosevelt with clear-eyed legal decisions unvexed by the turmoil of politics. In 1899 he declined to be considered for the presidency of Yale University, saying that he was not qualified. Instead he went to the Philippines, where as Civil Governor he brought order and progress to the islands and took a greater liking to the Filipinos ("our little brown brothers") than he ever had for the American populace. When he returned to the United States in 1904 he had a record of effective administration. As Secretary of War under Theodore Roosevelt he clearly analyzed problems for the President's decision. A seasoned and judicious man with no political debts or entanglements, he was Roosevelt's choice as a successor in the presidential chair.

So, on a warm June day in 1908, a big, beaming man stood on

the steps of a gracious mansion on Cincinnati's Pike Street—now the Taft Museum—and accepted nomination for the presidency.

Roosevelt won the election for Taft and then went off to the wilds of Africa, leaving Taft to the fortunes of politics. In the White House Taft consented to conservative Congressional leadership despite a clamor of liberal public opinion. Blind and deaf to the popular revolt, he smiled his jovial smile and traveled around the country, half persuading himself that he was winning the people over. Surrounded by conservative advisers, he never understood that a tide of liberalism was rising across the land, though he found his office increasingly irksome. When Roosevelt returned with his hunting trophies, he quickly saw Taft's failure and disavowed him. "Taft means well," he said, "but he means well feebly." If the President's cautious supporters could not see that, the nation did. When Taft was renominated in 1912, he carried just two states, Utah and Vermont. With no regret, the unhappiest of Presidents heaved himself up from the presidential chair and went to Yale as a professor of constitutional law.

Eight years later the Republican party brought forward another Ohio man, a politician this time, whose failure was of another kind than that of upright, aristocratic William Howard Taft. President Harding appointed him Chief Justice of the Supreme Court, an ideal place, above the hurly-burly of democracy, for the ponderous man who could deal with ideas but could not cope with public opinion.

From the democratic Heartland had come the illogical belief that a background of poverty and simplicity was the best qualification for a President. It began with the folklore of the log-cabin candidate, Old Tippecanoe—though William Henry Harrison had a classical education and an aristocratic family tradition. It had a confirmation in the character of Abraham Lincoln, and it was invoked in the campaigns of Garfield, the mule-driver on the Ohio Canal, and of McKinley, the herd-boy who warmed his bare feet in the grass where the cows had lain. It collapsed in the case of Warren G. Harding, the country editor.

In Iberia, Ohio, Warren Harding left a rural academy before graduation. He went to the county seat of Marion, learned printing, and as a youth of twenty bought the weekly Marion *Star*, circulation five hundred, for $300. The paper and its proprietor grew with the town. Harding married a banker's daughter, joined the Masons and the Elks, played a tuba in the town band, supported the local causes and saw his paper, converted to a daily, grow to a circulation of ten thousand.

As a state senator at the turn of the century he became acquainted with Harry M. Daugherty, fledgling lobbyist and politician. Harding was a complacent, prosperous, party-minded man who believed in party government and subordinated his own opinions, when he had any, to the party program. He was a team player. His voice was like his tuba in the Marion band, deep, mellow, resonant and faithfully following the score. He got along well with the Ohio gang. He rose in politics as a speech-maker and figurehead for the Ohio Republican Committee. In 1912 he nominated Taft at the Republican National Convention. Two years later, guided by Daugherty, he was elected to the U.S. Senate.

In the strenuous war years Harding found the Senate "a very pleasant place." He drank and played poker with his friends while he encouraged the Anti-Saloon League and supported the Volstead Act. He followed the party line, opposed high taxes on war profits, and dismissed the League of Nations as "an empty thing, big in name, . . . that will ultimately disappoint all of humanity that hinges its hope upon it."

Theodore Roosevelt, still vigorous and magnetic, was the leading prospect for Republican nomination in 1920. His sudden death, in 1919, left the party without leadership. Into the vacuum moved a group of oil men—Albert B. Fall, Harry F. Sinclair, Edward L. Doheny—and the Ohio Republican Committee.

The oil industry had its first roots in Ohio in the 1870's, with John D. Rockefeller and Henry Flagler employing four thousand men in their Standard Oil refinery and sending carloads of kegged kerosene to light the lamps and lanterns of America. By 1920 oil was a vaster industry; it was energy and fuel driving the American industrial machine. It also drove the Republican convention. In the hot June days in Chicago the delegates seesawed and deadlocked between General Leonard Wood and Governor Frank O. Lowden of Illinois. On the tenth ballot the oil men had their candidate, Warren Gamaliel Harding.

Harding's front-porch campaign was likened to McKinley's— again the Ohio town decorated, brass bands at the station, a friendly, handsome man waving a straw hat under the maple trees. While another Ohio man, Governor James M. Cox, carried the torch of Woodrow Wilson, Harding campaigned on a platform of "normalcy." Denouncing the League of Nations, but vaguely supporting a nonexistent "agreement among the nations to preserve the peace of the world," he asked for no risk and no sacrifice. A disillusioned and leaderless majority put him into power.

As President, Harding named some good men to his cabinet, Hughes, Hoover and Mellon, along with some to whom he was indebted. In the White House he was a likable, well-intentioned man from Main Street who suddenly found himself surrounded by graft and corruption. Scandals were developing in the Veterans Bureau, the Office of the Alien Property Custodian, and the Departments of Justice, the Navy and the Interior. The gravest charge concerned the lease of naval oil-reserve lands by private interests in the oil industry and the exerting of influence by the "Ohio gang" over the Department of Justice. To postpone the showdown, Harding made an official visit in the summer of 1923 to Alaska, but the scandal followed him. He was a harried, bewildered, sleepless man, nearing collapse, before a case of ptomaine poisoning prostrated him. He died of bronchopneumonia in San Francisco on the second day of August.

Harding was not a villain but a victim, a victim of his rapacious friends and of the nation that had thrust him into an arena for which he was wholly unprepared. The Harding Memorial in Marion, where he was the friendly, handsome editor with a hand in every local undertaking, is less a monument to a man than to the office he could not fill.

IV

AN UNFINISHED COUNTRY

From America's rich gestating center south of the Great Lakes, one seems merely to overhear the world while one broods on the permanent functions of the earth. And yet that center is not central. Like the human heart, the Middle West is to one side of the median line.

—JACQUES BARZUN

20. The Haymarket Tragedy

A hundred years ago prairie farmers drove into the west side of Chicago with heaped hay wagons and groaning loads of grain. They came in on Randolph Street and pulled up at an open oblong place, like a village market square, between Halsted and Desplaines. It was four blocks north of the river, with yellow lumber wharves and the masts of schooners showing in the distance. In the "Square" the farmers sold their hay, oats and corn to Chicago's livery-stable men. It was a busy, cheerful place with a rich smell of horses, mules and sweated harness and pigeons fluttering in the manure-strewn street.

But everything changed in Chicago. In the great fire of 1871 the blocks just west of the river, where the fire began, were the first to be destroyed, and when Chicago rose from its ashes, an industrial district spread over the near west side. This region became the home of many thousands of immigrants who swelled Chicago's population from 300,000 to 1,000,000 in the next two decades. In the same years the city expanded northward and southward and onto the inland prairie, spreading over an area of two hundred square miles. The great influx of people was an endless tide of immigrants, German, Bohemian, Scandinavian, Irish. Fully half the city's population was foreign-speaking in the 1880's, and most of the immigrants were workmen. They put in a ten-hour day of manual labor, except for periods of industrial shutdown, in machine shops, lumberyards, railroad shops and freight houses, foundries, steel mills and stockyards. Already a railroad center, Chicago was rapidly becoming a center of many kinds of manufacturing. In this new Chicago, industry lined Halsted and Desplaines streets and the old "Haymarket" was darkened by factories and warehouses. On a spring day in 1886 that rural name became a word for bloodshed and violence of class warfare.

Thousands of German workmen had left the Old World to escape social, political and economic tyranny. They came to the growing cities of the American Midwest, hoping to enjoy justice and opportunity. When they found widespread unemployment, a bare subsistence wage, long hours and inhuman working conditions, they began to organize radical associations and to ally themselves with national and international labor movements. The International Working People's Association, organized in London in 1881, quickly established itself in Cleveland, Cincinnati and Louisville, as well as in Chicago, which became its dynamic center. In the shabby streets west of the Chicago River were published five organs of the International: the daily *Arbeiter-Zeitung*, the Saturday *Vorbote*, the Sunday *Fackel*—all in German; the *Alarm*, in English; and the Bohemian *Boudoucnost*. Circulation of these radical labor papers ranged from 3,000 to 12,000 copies.

The winter of 1886 was long and bitter. Week after week icy winds blew from Lake Michigan and stinging snow swept the city streets. Though Chicago's industrial production was growing, labor-saving machinery had cut into the working force. In that season thousands of men walked Halsted and Canal streets looking for work—streets ringing with iron hoofs and iron-rimmed wagon wheels. All the horses in Chicago were employed, all were fed and cared for, not one horse went hungry; but thousands of men were idle and in want. With agitation for the eight-hour working day strikes spread through factories and freight houses. Street meetings were dispersed by police on the charge of impeding traffic. When the meetings moved to vacant corners, the police followed, charging disturbance of the peace. Amid a growing tension, the labor press called for solidarity and resistance.

Chief editor of the German publications was thirty-year-old August Spies, who had come to America as an orphan youth of seventeen. In Chicago he read Marxist and Socialist literature, and soon threw himself into the radical labor movement. Growing disillusioned about the sufficiency of political action, he reluctantly turned to doctrines of violence. A vigorous, sturdy, idealistic man, fluent in both German and English, he was a natural leader of his less articulate countrymen. The *Alarm* was edited by Albert R. Parsons, whose American ancestry led back to the second voyage of the *Mayflower* and included a distinguished New England jurist and a general in the Revolutionary War. Born in Alabama of originally Northern parents, Parsons had joined the Confederate army at the age of thirteen. Before he was twenty he had founded a newspaper in Texas. He came to Chicago in the 1870's, and there began the study of Socialism. In 1884 he became editor of the high-voiced *Alarm*. He was an emotional and tireless speaker. A third leader in this group was Samuel Fielden, a Lancashire Englishman who had come to the United States in 1868. For years he drove dray horses through the teeming Chicago streets. Less intellectual than the others, Fielden had a brooding earnestness that often verged on melancholy. This mild, middle-aged man, with hulking shoulders and bushy black beard, contained smoldering emotions. His deep voice thundered in street meetings. Michael Schwab, a reporter on the *Arbeiter-Zeitung*, was a scholarly-looking man, thin, tall, slightly stooped, with long black hair and beard and deep-set eyes peering through iron-rimmed spectacles. Adolph Fischer, who had come to America as a youth of fifteen, was a typesetter on the German papers. His pleasant, easy-going manner belied the violence of his beliefs and his fearless devotion to them. George Engel, heavy, slow-spoken, seemingly phlegmatic, looked like a German bartender. But he burned with a slow fire. These were the men whose names would go down in history because of the events in Haymarket Square on a spring night in 1886.

Certain saloons, club rooms and meeting halls on Desplaines and Lake streets were meeting places of the socialist and anarchist groups. In drab rooms over mugs of beer men sat reading Marx, Engels and Lassalle and talking quietly of the clash to come, the classes warring for the future of the world. In bare second-story halls, before rows of half-filled benches, men talked in various languages and accents of the "robber rich" and the hungry poor, of the proper function of the state, the spirit of the American Constitution, the tyranny of the press, the brutality of the police, and the necessity of revolution. Then they took up a collection for destitute workmen and widows, knowing that collections were not enough. There was a ferment working in the gray streets around Haymarket Square.

Zepf's Hall, above Zepf's saloon, near the corner of Desplaines and Lake, half a block from the old Haymarket, was the center of the underground resistance. One can readily picture the place. On the wall beside the stairway leading up from the street was a chalked sign:

EDUCATIONAL MEETING TONIGHT
All Welcome

By eight o'clock the room was nearly full, workers crowding onto the benches in the bad light. Sam Fielden sat at the bare table in front, still in his long shabby overcoat that smelled of horses and harness, and beside him were Adolph Fischer and Michael Schwab. The habitually restless Fischer got up and chalked on the wall:

ALARM   VORBOTE
Get Your Copies Here

and he dragged up a bench with two stacks of paper on it. At the table Schwab ran his fingers through his unkempt hair and peered through his spectacles at an open book. He was reading "The Masque of Anarchy."

> As I lay asleep in Italy
> There came a voice from over the sea. . . .
> What art thou, Freedom? . . .
> For the labourer thou art bread,
> And a comely table spread
> From his daily labour come
> In a neat and happy home. . . .
> To the rich thou art a check,
> When his foot is on the neck
> Of his victim. . . .
> Thou art Justice—ne'er for gold
> May thy righteous laws be sold . . .

His mind went for a moment to Percy Bysshe Shelley, living at Villa Volsavano amid the serene old olive groves of Tuscany, not knowing that what he wrote would send men to the barricades in Chicago, a name he never heard.

> Rise, like Lions after slumber
> In unvanquishable number,
> Shake your chains to earth like dew
> Which in sleep has fallen on you—
> Ye are many—they are few.

He frowned and riffled the pages, and out fell a worn circular. He peered at an underlined passage: *No assembly of the Knights of Labor must strike for the eight-hour system on May first under the impression that they are obeying orders from headquarters, for such an order was not, and will not be, given. Neither employer or employee are educated to the needs and necessities for the short hour plan.*

As Fischer stood up and made some announcements, Fielden looked over the room. There were some new faces in the back rows. Some converts, perhaps, from his street meetings. And of course some plainclothes police. There would be a report at the precinct station soon after the meeting was over. Fischer ended by introducing the speaker—our comrade and fellow worker, Sam Fielden.

Fielden began quietly, with a review of scattered strikes in the west side factories, the lumberyards, the stockyards. The walk-outs had failed to bring a reduction in the working day because the workers had not acted in unity. The workers had power if they would learn to use it. They had the only power in the world, the power to produce the things that people need. And they had power to overthrow the greedy, blind, inhuman capitalistic system, to make a new system that would be fair to all. At this point his hulking shoulders leaned forward and his voice deepened. He began to talk about money, the myth of money, the printed paper that won't feed a man who is hungry or warm a man who is cold. The things produced by human toil are real, but money is a myth. Why is the myth perpetuated? So that a few bankers and politicians can control millions of work-men and grow rich on the goods they produce. These men own the newspapers, not these—pointing to the little stacks of *Alarm* and *Arbeiter-Zeitung* on the bench—but the big newspapers that control the huge unthinking public. They own the courts and the legislature and the police force, and they call it a govern-ment. They say a man must work ten or twelve hours for a dollar and a half a day, and out of every dollar of the owner's profit the workman gets just fifteen cents. The time had come for the workmen to overthrow that system.

All winter revolutionary voices had sounded in Zepf's Hall, Grief's Hall, Florus Hall, Neff's Hall. Spring brought new strikes, increasing demonstrations and a sense of crisis.

In the last days of April strikes spread among railroad and gas company workers, iron-mill workers, lumber shovers, stockyards men and plumbers—all demanding an eight-hour day. Despite the hesitation of the Knights of Labor—saying that the time was not ready for a nation-wide struggle—the Chicago groups planned a massive demonstration for May first. There was already enacted in Illinois a law declaring: "Eight hours of labor, between the rising and the setting of the sun, in all mechanical trades, arts and employments, and other cases of labor and service by the day, except farm employments, shall constitute and be a legal day's work, where there is no special contract or agreement to the contrary." This vague statute allowed employers to dictate an "agreement to the contrary." But now the workers were clamoring for reform.

Saturday, May 1, began with a strange silence. Forty thousand Chicago workmen were on strike. Plants and factories were lifeless, with the fire dead in the boilers and no steam to blow the six o'clock whistle for the men who would not come. With teamsters and freight handlers on strike, the streets were nearly empty; silence hung over the big terminals on Lake and Canal streets. By midday the city was alive and restless, with thousands of men forming into processions—German marching associations, Bohemian, Swedish and Irish brotherhoods, labor unions and socialist societies. Hundreds of furniture workers and mill hands paraded under banners which credited their employers with establishing the eight-hour day. An army of ten thousand lumbermen marched behind a blood-red flag. A thousand freight handlers made the rounds of the big freight depots, calling out other men to join them.

All afternoon, in huge meetings in the parks and on the lake front, speakers in English, German, Bohemian, Swedish, and Norwegian proclaimed the cause of labor. Detectives moved through the crowds, listened to the speeches and to the muttered comments of the listeners, and reported to headquarters. The police waited for violence, but no violence came. The sun sank over the city, and through the spring twilight the demonstrators went peacefully home. The crisis, it seemed, had passed.

But on Monday, May third, a sullen crowd gathered on the Black Road beside the big McCormick Reaper plant. Along with the striking McCormick workers hundreds of members of the

Lumber Shovers Union had gathered to hear a speech by August Spies. Black Road ran along an open field bordered by a railroad siding. On the track stood an empty freight car. From that high platform Spies discussed the shortened working day and urged labor solidarity in the face of the employers' threats and lockouts. While he was speaking, a bell rang in the McCormick works and a shift of nonunion men came out of the factory. Spies's crowd turned upon them, attacking the "scab" workmen with sticks and stones. In the midst of the melee two hundred police arrived. They charged in, swinging clubs and firing revolvers. In a few bloody minutes six strikers were dead or dying and scores were wounded.

Back in his littered office Spies wrote a rapid-fire account for the next issue of his newspaper. Then, still in a heat of protest, he composed a circular for immediate distribution.

WORKINGMEN!   To ARMS!

Your masters sent out their bloodhounds—the police—they killed six of your brothers at McCormick's this afternoon. They killed the poor wretches because they, like you, had courage to disobey the supreme will of your bosses. They killed them because they dared ask for the shortening of the hours of toil. They killed them to show you "free American citizens" that you must be satisfied and contented with whatever your bosses condescend to allow you, or you will get killed!

You have for years endured the most abject humiliation; you have for years suffered immeasurable iniquities; you have worked yourselves to death; you have endured the pangs of want and hunger; your children you have sacrificed to the factory lords—in short, you have been miserable and obedient slaves all these years. Why? To satisfy the insatiable greed and fill the coffers of your lazy thieving masters! When you ask him now to lessen your burden, he sends his bloodhounds out to shoot you, to kill you!

If you are men, if you are the sons of your grandsires, who have shed their blood to free you, then you will rise in your might Hercules, and destroy the hideous monster that seeks to destroy you.

To arms, we call you, to arms!

YOUR BROTHERS

A thousand of these circulars, in both English and German, were passed out at labor meetings that night.

While Spies was distributing the "revenge circular," Adolph Fischer in the printing shop was setting up a handbill, in both English and German, to announce a meeting, arranged by delegates of several labor unions, for the next night.

ATTENTION WORKINGMEN!
GREAT
MASS-MEETING
TONIGHT AT 7 O'CLOCK
AT THE
HAYMARKET
RANDOLPH STREET, BETWEEN DESPLAINES & HALSTED
Good speakers will be present to
denounce the latest atrocious act of
the police, the shooting of our fellow-
workmen yesterday afternoon.
WORKINGMEN ARM YOURSELVES AND APPEAR IN FULL
FORCE!
THE EXECUTIVE COMMITTEE

The evening of May 4 was overcast, the gray daylight almost gone as the meeting hour came. Something like a thousand men gathered in the street as darkness fell—a far smaller number than the leaders had expected. Somehow the May Day zeal had evaporated. This was a dull, dispirited assembly, of no consequence. The speakers' platform was a battered truck wagon, standing halfway down the block where an alley led off from Desplaines Street. (Every word spoken from that makeshift platform would go into the record of history; it would be studied by lawyers, judges, governors; it would be read and discussed in distant countries and in years to come.) Above the wagon loomed the dark walls of the Crane Brothers' elevator factory.

There, an hour and a half after the announced hour of the meeting—they had waited vainly for a larger crowd to gather —August Spies began speaking in German. He blamed the capitalistic press for misreporting the violence on Black Road and misrepresenting the cause of labor. He spoke of forty to fifty thousand men locked out of their employment because they refused to submit to the will of a few greedy men. He closed by rebuking the capitalistic press for saying there were no Americans among the strikers. Every honest American, he declared, was on their side.

The next speaker was Albert Parsons. He began by asking the men for patience and order. With his ten generations of American ancestors behind him, he promised justice and a fair hearing from the American people. Now was the time to make a clear statement of the workers' grievances. The world should know that workmen and their families had been shot down by Chicago police. What lay behind this violence? He proceeded in a clear and forceful speech to outline the struggle for reform and the necessity of an eight-hour working day. He denounced the capitalistic press, attacked the banks, explained how Socialism would correct the abuses of Capitalism and called for solidarity among the working class in fighting for their rights.

At the edge of the crowd stood Carter Harrison, mayor of Chicago. That afternoon he had been urged to proclaim a ban on street meetings. But he was not so alarmed as to deny the rights of free speech and free assembly. Now, hearing the familiar socialist argument and exhortation, he was satisfied with his decision. Chicago would have a peaceful night. When Parsons finished speaking, a chill wind gusted through the street, bringing a drizzle of rain. The crowd began to scatter. No more than five hundred were left when the mayor turned up his coat collar and started back toward the center of the city. On the way, just a block from the assembly, he passed the Desplaines Street police station, where a reserve force had been summoned for an emergency. The mayor stopped there briefly, telling the captain that he expected no trouble. Then Harrison went home.

But the meeting was not over. In the drizzle the thinning crowd was restless. Some men pressed against the dark buildings for shelter and more began drifting toward the saloons on Randolph and Lake streets. They stopped when a new voice came through the rain. On the wagon bed stood big, bushy-bearded Sam Fielden, the English Socialist, shouting about the organized force mobilized against the workingmen, who must now crush that force and overthrow their oppressors. In the McCormick fight men had been shot down by the law in the protection of property. This showed that it was the capitalistic law, the enemy of the working people. The wind came colder, and the speaker's voice reached after the restless men on the edges of the dwindling crowd. The law had nothing to offer workingmen but enslavement. Workmen must destroy the law, kill it, stab it. This was the worker's task, no one else would do it for him. He deserved nothing better than enslavement unless he would make an effort to lift himself from oppression.

A few of the men wandering away into Desplaines Street were detectives. At ten o'clock they came into the precinct station with word that the crowd was growing excited. Inspector Bonfield, a notorious strikebreaker and cracker of workmen's skulls, ordered his two hundred reserves to form into four divisions. Marching toward Crane's Alley, they took up the center of Randolph Street, pressing the crowd back on either side. Captain Ward pushed through to the speakers' wagon with his ranks behind him. "I command you," he said, "in the name of the people of the State, to immediately and peaceably disperse."

From the wagon Fielden replied, "We are peaceable."

Among the agitators the German word *Ruhe* had been chosen as a signal of uprising; it had appeared that day in the black-bordered "Letters" heading in the *Arbeiter-Zeitung*. *Ruhe* meant "peace," and now Fielden had answered the police with the trigger word. Whether it was mere coincidence would never be known, but the next instant a small dark hissing object, thrown from the shadows of Crane's Alley, arched over the head of Captain Ward and fell among the second division of police. An explosion shook Haymarket Square, hurling a score of policemen to the ground. The next minute Bonfield's rear ranks were firing revolvers into the crowd, and according to police statements, workmen returned the fire. But most of the crowd was already in flight through the streets and alleys. When the gunfire stopped, there rose the cries of wounded and dying men. The violence had occupied a few minutes; it would reverberate for many years.

The next day Chicago was a stunned city and *Haymarket* was suddenly a somber and fearsome word. As a result of the bombing and shooting one policeman was dead and seventy were wounded; six of them would soon die. One workman was dead and nearly a hundred were injured. As anger and fear gripped the city, Mayor Harrison prohibited all meetings and processions. Newspapers over the nation denounced anarchists and socialists and vilified all German immigrants. No one knew, or would ever know, who threw the bomb, but the press agreed that the agitators were responsible. They must be charged with murder.

To match the hysteria of the press the Chicago police went into frantic activity. Twenty-four hours after the riot, Spies, Fielden, Schwab and Fischer were arrested and in jail. Police squads raided fifty socialist clubs, saloons and meeting halls and rounded up hundreds of suspects. By the middle of May thirty-one men were indicted for murder. Eight of them eventually stood trial on the charge that the murder was the result of a planned conspiracy under control of the men who edited and published the radical papers *Alarm* and *Arbeiter-Zeitung*. Trial began in the third week of June.

The eight defendants were August Spies, Samuel Fielden, Michael Schwab, Adolph Fischer, George Engel, Oscar Neebe, Louis Lingg and Albert Parsons. Parsons had left Chicago on the night of the bombing. He went north to Waukesha, Wisconsin, near Milwaukee. Having shaved his heavy mustache and dyed his hair, he was safe from discovery. But on June 21 he walked into the Chicago courtroom and took his seat with the other prisoners; he would share their trial and their penalty. The next three weeks were spent in selecting a jury. After two months of newspaper hysteria and horrific rumor, it was impossible to find twelve men who had formed no opinion as to the guilt of the anarchists. The chosen jurymen—six of them in their twenties, most of them white-collar workers, all but one native-born American—hoped to render a fair verdict, though it was obvious that they had prejudged the prisoners. This seemed no obstacle to Judge Gary, who proceeded with the trial in an atmosphere heavy with animosity. No evidence connected any of the charged men with the throwing of the bomb; half of them had not even attended the Haymarket rally. It was a case of Society vs. Anarchy—Society seeking revenge upon men who had questioned its authority and shaken its order.

During the trial the prosecution exaggerated the anarchist "conspiracy" into fantastic dimensions. It charged that a stock of bombs was assembled at Neff's Hall—the anarchist arsenal—to be used at the Haymarket mass meeting, where twenty-five thousand striking workmen were expected. At the same time other agents were to take bombs to various quarters of the city, where they would blow up police stations and destroy patrol wagons. Still other men were to start fires in the city and bomb the fire department. What the prosecuting lawyers described was a maniacal plot to annihilate Chicago. Only the police intervention at Haymarket Square, they concluded, saved the city from devastation.

Returning to the fact that police had been killed while performing their duty, the judge instructed the jury: they must hold responsible not merely the bomber, but those who abetted, assisted and encouraged the throwing of the bomb. The trial was over and the case was in the hands of the jury on August 19. They reached a decision that night.

On the morning of August 20 a thousand people thronged the streets around the Criminal Court Building. Inside, the prisoners were brought into the courtroom. They watched the jury take its place. As the clock struck ten the foreman read their verdict. The eight defendants were found guilty as charged. Seven of them were sentenced to death; the eighth, Oscar Neebe, to fifteen years' imprisonment. When word went outside, a roar of approval rose from the street.

The jury had been but three hours in reaching its verdict, and most of that time was spent in discussing the case of Oscar Neebe. The evidence against him was that he owned two dollars' worth of stock in the *Arbeiter-Zeitung*, he was a member of the International Working People's Association, and when his house was searched without warrant, police found a pistol, a sword, a breech-loading gun and a red flag. Neebe was thirty-six, born in New York of German descent. He had been active in the trade-union movement. It was observed during the trial that the testimony against him would not justify a five-dollar fine, and Mayor Harrison had advised withdrawing the charge. The jury decided to protect society from this dangerous man for at least fifteen years.

In answer to the question if there were reasons why sentence should not be pronounced upon them, the eight men responded in terms of their individual temperament and character. Parsons spoke for eight hours, in two sessions, giving a detailed history of the working class in America and of the labor movement. Spies, thinner now, his triangular face accentuated by his pointed beard, defended anarchy as a philosophy which opposed all force and coercion, and he declared that these ideas could not be crushed by sending men to the gallows. Fielden went from autobiography to the evils of capitalism, his part in the Haymarket rally and his innocence of any crime. Cold-eyed young Louis Linng concluded a scornful address by stating: "I am the enemy of 'order' today . . . and as long as breath remains in me. . . . I despise you. I despise your order, your laws, your force-propped authority. Hang me for it!" Neebe's speech was the shortest, the quietest, and the most disturbing to his hearers. He concluded:

> Well, these are the crimes I have committed. They found a revolver in my house and a red flag there. I organized *Trade Unions*. I was for reduction of the hours of labor, and the education of the laboring man, and the re-establishment of the *Arbeiter-Zeitung*—the workingmen's newspaper. There is no evidence to show that I was connected with the bomb-throwing, or that I was near it, or anything of that kind. So I am only sorry, your honor—that is, if you can stop it or help it—I will ask you to do it—that is to hang me

too; for I think it is more honorable to die suddenly than to be killed by inches. I have a family and children; and if they know their father is dead, they will bury him. They can go to the grave and kneel down by the side of it; but they can't go to the penitentiary and see their father, who was convicted of a crime that he hasn't had anything to do with. That is all I have got to say. Your honor, I am sorry I am not to be hung with the rest of the men.

No event since the Civil War had so excited the American nation, and the vast majority of the American people approved the outcome of the trial. Yet voices of protest were heard on both sides of the Atlantic. In America William Dean Howells, Robert G. Ingersoll, Charles Francis Train, General Roger A. Pryor and other liberal spokesmen asked the governor of Illinois to commute the death penalty. In London William Morris, George Bernard Shaw, and the Besants spoke in defense of the anarchists; on a Sunday afternoon three weeks later sixteen thousand members of the workingmens' clubs signed a protest against the execution of the labor leaders. Members of the French Chamber of Deputies and of the Paris Municipal Council appealed to Governor Oglesby of Illinois to spare the lives of the condemned men.

In October in Judge Gary's court a motion for a new trial was overruled and the execution date was set for December 3. However, under a stay of execution, the case was reviewed by the Illinois Supreme Court. Here, before the largest attendance in the court's history, veteran attorney Leonard Swett, Lincoln's comrade on the prairie circuit forty years earlier, argued for a reversal on the ground that the State's theory of conspiracy was untenable. But after long deliberation the court sustained the original verdict. A final appeal was made to the United States Supreme Court. Though it did not approve the principle of punishing men because of their opinions, for a crime which they were not shown to have committed, the effect was the same as if the principle had been approved. Affirming the legality of the trial, the Supreme Court denied a writ of error.

The new date of execution was November 11, 1887. On the

tenth of November Governor Oglesby commuted the sentences
of Fielden and Schwab to life imprisonment. Parsons declined a
similar commutation, since it did not extend to all the condemned
men. Later that day sardonic young Louis Linng committed
suicide in his cell by exploding in his mouth a small bomb that
had been smuggled into the prison. His defiant words to the
court—"Hang me for it!"—could not be carried out. On the
gray morning of November 11 Spies, Parsons, Fischer and Engel
were put to death. Six thousand silent marchers followed their
bodies to the Waldheim Cemetery on South Desplaines Street
beside the sluggish Des Plaines River; there ten thousand
watched the burial and heard memorial addresses in German and
English. Meanwhile Fielden, Schwab and Neebe were facing the
empty future in the state prison at Joliet.

Six years passed. Slowly the "anarchist scare" subsided, and
into the governor's office in Springfield came John Peter Altgeld.
With hysteria forgotten, a painful social conscience became concerned about the Haymarket penalties. In 1893 a monument was
placed over the five graves at Waldheim Cemetery—a bronze
figure of Justice crowning with laurel leaves a fallen worker. In
that same year a petition signed by sixty thousand citizens of
Illinois, asking for pardon of the three prisoners, was brought to
the governor. In his characteristic way Altgeld, himself an experi-
enced lawyer and judge, made a thorough study of the records.
His decision was to pardon the condemned, and to condemn the
procedure that had convicted and imprisoned them. The first
step would have appeased the public. When it was followed by
the second step—an eighteen-thousand-word excoriation of the
judge, the prosecution and the jury—society was outraged. Upon
Altgeld from every corner of the country came torrents of
vituperation. "The storm broke," wrote his young legal assistant,
Brand Whitlock, "and the abuse it rained upon him broke his
heart, but I never again heard him mention the anarchist case."

When they left their prison cells, Fielden, Schwab and Neebe
ceased to be public figures. They vanished into private life and

their names were forgotten. But the Haymarket remained a name for warfare in the heart of America, and a symbol of the never-ending struggle for economic and social justice.

On the site of the riot the city erected the Statue of the Chicago Policeman—a mustached, helmeted bronze figure with a belted coat and an upraised hand: "In the name of the people of Illinois, I command peace." Originally placed in the intersection of Desplaines and Randolph streets, it was moved in the 1950's when the Expressway replaced the old Union Street. All the old streets and buildings are gone, and so, perhaps, are the fears and hatreds. Now the monument stands a block from the site of the tragedy, above the Northwest Expressway, where travelers speeding in from the International Airport might think it a memorial to the traffic policeman who was stationed there before Randolph Street bridged the twelve-lane throughway.

21. Writing from the Heartland

I would have to tell the tales of my own people.
—SHERWOOD ANDERSON

The first Chicago writers—the first to write about Chicago—were visitors from afar: Harriet Martineau from London, Charles Joseph Latrobe from England and Switzerland, James Shirreff from East Lothian in Scotland, Charles Fenno Hoffman from New York, Margaret Fuller from Boston. They all wrote of it as an outpost, a crude, sprawling settlement with astonishing energy and an instinctive sense of the future. Three generations later an English magazine, the London *Nation*, published H. L. Mencken's famous article "The Literary Capital of the United States." It was Chicago that Mencken hailed, the city that at the turn of the century had produced Henry B. Fuller, Frank Norris and Theodore Dreiser. He went on to name the serious novelists of the new generation "who have sprung from the Middle Empire that has Chicago for its capital"—Garland, Anderson, Miss Cather, Mrs. Watts, Tarkington, Wilson, Herrick, Patterson. If he could have looked ahead a few years, he would have added Hemingway, Wescott, Hecht, Edna Ferber, Farrell, Halper, Algren.

306

Here was a burst of energy to compare with the other energies that had impelled Chicago's growth in industry and merchandising. And Mencken went on with a further observation: "The new poetry movement is thoroughly Chicagoan; the majority of its chief poets are from the Middle West; *Poetry,* the organ of the movement, is published in Chicago." A poetical flowering had come to the prairie, producing Masters, Lindsay, Sandburg, Sara Teasdale, Sarett, Neihardt, and sending to the East young Eliot and MacLeish. Of these names three inevitably fall together because of their attachment to Illinois backgrounds and of the central place of Illinois scenes and subjects in their writing. They are the prairie poets—Masters, Lindsay, Sandburg. They appeared almost on the same morning under the same springtime prairie sun.

THE PRAIRIE POETS

The Spoon River flows into the Illinois from the north, and just fifteen miles downstream from that confluence the Illinois is joined by the Sangamon, winding in from the southeast. Put the two valleys together—broad, shallow, barely discernible valleys in the prairie land—and there is the Spoon River country, that is to say, the country of *Spoon River Anthology.* Edgar Lee Masters lived from his first to his twelfth year at Petersburg on the Sangamon; his next ten years were spent in Lewistown, near the Spoon. His one good book of poetry (out of many) grew from these backgrounds of his youth. He blended the two towns into his fictitious village of Spoon River, and he put people from both river valleys into his graveyard on the hill.

Spoon River Anthology was a new kind of book from a plodding poet, and successful lawyer, of middle age. When he began to write the epitaphs—harsh, bitter, wistful, wondering, recriminating, regretful—the lives of an entire community came crowding into his mind.

The weak of will, the strong of arm, the clown,
   the boozer, the fighter—
All, all, are sleeping on the hill.

Spoon River Anthology is a book about the dead, but it was the one passionate conception of Masters's literary life.

In one of the unforgettable epitaphs Masters summarized the false poetic quest of his early years. "Petit," the village poet, had rhythms in his head, little rustling rhythms, *tick, tick, tick*, like the seeds in a locust pod at the end of summer. Those rhythms set him to writing timid, pale and repetitious ballads about the vanished snows of yesteryear and the fading rose of love. Echoes of Villon, Tennyson and Swinburne occupied Petit all his life, and only from the grave came the realization of what he had missed: "Life all around me here in the village." In their own voices one could reveal the courage, constancy, heroism, failure of the village lives, against the ever-changing patterns of woodland, meadow and shadowed riverbank. Petit was blind to it all his life long, but Masters saw it, suddenly, at the age of forty-five.

Young Edgar Lee Masters lived in his two prairie towns at the right time. There were still some early settlers—old Bill Piersol who had traded with the Indians, and the Revolutionary soldier "John Wasson," who came by ox cart to Spoon River and cut the buffalo grass on the prairie and helped build the old Concord Church on the ridge. In his boyhood Masters saw them sitting under the trees in the town square. He heard the rich local anecdotes and the scandals of the courthouse; his father was a leading lawyer of the county. The town inventor who repaired watches while dreaming of the engine he would build; Seth Compton, whose circulating library was sold at auction on the public square; his father's friend old William H. Herndon, who sat in a farmhouse window in the winter sunset, remembering his years with Lincoln; Anne Rutledge, who lay buried in the old Concord Cemetery; William Cullen Bryant (the poet's nephew), who died at twenty-four of a gunshot in a hunting accident and was buried in the Lewistown cemetery with a figure of a woman on a marble shaft marking his grave—all these waited for use in *Spoon River Anthology*.

Most of the two hundred fourteen poems in the *Anthology* can be traced to actual persons in Petersburg or Lewistown. A few of them were still living when Masters put them underground. Ragged, mud-stained "Dow Kritt" was still walking around Lewistown with his shovel on his shoulder when he spoke from the grave:

> . . . I did not need to die to learn about roots:
> I, who dug all the ditches about Spoon River.

Simple-minded Charley Metcalf—he would never read *Spoon River Anthology* or anything else—was still living in the livery stable, sleeping in a stall, talking to the horses, when Masters gave his memories to "Willie Metcalf."

> I could crawl between the legs of the wildest horses
> Without getting kicked—we knew each other.
> On spring days I tramped through the country
> To get the feeling, which I sometimes lost,
> That I was not a separate thing from the earth.

Doctor Strode was still making his village rounds, satchel in hand, and returning to his office with its collection of stuffed birds, gophers and snakeskins when Masters put him in the cemetery as "William Jones." He knew the weeds in the fence rows and the mollusks on the shore, and he corresponded with naturalists across the Atlantic. In his grave he asked to be covered with shells from Spoon River.

Spoon River was named for its abundance of fresh-water clams, a favorite food of the Indians. They used the clam shells as spoons, and white men gave that name to the stream; the Indians had called it "Amaquon." "Lucinda Matlock," a portrait of the poet's own grandmother Lucinda Masters,

> Rambled over the fields where sang the larks,
> And by Spoon River gathering many a shell . . .

Ancient earthworks and burials, including the famous Dickson Mound, are found along the Spoon. A spell of the past lies upon this gentle valley.

For Masters, Spoon River was both a town and a region, the combined valleys of the Spoon and the Sangamon. His people sleeping on the hill were drawn from the seven counties that are drained by the two meandering rivers. The *Anthology* contains allusions to actual towns in both valleys. To the valley of the Spoon belong the villages of Ipava, Summum, Bernadotte and London Mills; on or near the Sangamon are Chandlerville, Winchester, Mason City, Clary's Grove and Atterbury. The two actual towns, Petersburg and Lewistown, which blend into the imaginary Spoon River are not mentioned in the poems.

So local is *Spoon River Anthology* that it becomes universal. Its two hundred fourteen lives make up a microcosm. The graveyard contains two doctors, one dentist, six lawyers, four preachers, seven prostitutes, four storekeepers, a photographer, two poets, the town drunkard, the village atheist, several teachers, about an equal number of farmers and tradesmen, a gambler, a revivalist, a piano tuner, a night policeman, two fiddlers—one of them blind—an editor who lost his job because he wrote about the Haymarket anarchists, a boy who ran away with the circus, an inventor, a livery-stable man, some politicians, and a stonemason who carved gravestones for the dead. Many of them lived to old age, and none died early, though three were victims of accident, and two of suicide. Masters examined the full pattern of life, and his irony did not include the death of the very young.

Running through the lives are certain events that link and interweave them. Ten people in the *Anthology* are affected by the failure of the bank. The Haymarket riot and the Spanish-American War alter village lives. Gatherings in the Opera House have diverse influence upon various villagers. Disputes over land boundaries involve bankers, lawyers and farmers. Furtive alliances come to light in the candor of the grave.

A recurrent theme among the epitaphs is the shaping of personal belief by occupation. Asks "Dixon," the unworldly piano tuner:

Is there no Ear round the ear of a man, that it senses
Through strings and columns of air the soul of sound?

. . . .

Surely the concord that ruled my spirit is proof
Of an ear that tuned me, able to tune me over
And use me again if I am worthy to use.

The "Widow McFarlane," weaver of carpets for the village, had found a fateful truth:

For the cloth of life is woven, you know,
To a pattern hidden under the loom—
A pattern you never see!

"Tom Beatty," the gambler, could see no difference between himself and the county lawyers:

For I tried the rights of property,
Although by lamp-light, for thirty years,
In that poker room in the opera house.
And I say to you that Life's a gambler
Head and shoulders above us all.

. . . .

And he gives you seventy years to play:
For if you cannot win in seventy
You cannot win at all.

In "Webster Ford" Masters wrote an epitaph for a poet, presumably himself, since he had used that pseudonym with his early *Songs and Sonnets;* as a youth Webster Ford saw visions when other boys saw fox fire. In "Theodore the Poet" Masters reached outside the Spoon River country and portrayed his friend Dreiser. But the picture fits Masters better than the brooding novelist. As a boy Theodore sat for hours on the weedy banks of the Spoon, waiting for the crayfish to come out of his mud burrow and wondering what that lowly creature knew and what he wanted from existence. Later the poet watched for men and women to come out of their burrows of fate amid great cities, and wondered what kept them crawling so busily through the sand when the water fails in dry seasons. In *Spoon River Anthology* he saw into those lives with a burning insight which he never found again. From New York in 1925 he wrote to Harriet Monroe, the famous editor of *Poetry*: "That man is fortunate who lives where his father lives and where he knows everyone. . . . I believe my spiritual home is Petersburg, Illinois, where my grandparents lived. But it is all changed of course. I couldn't stand it there." He both loved and loathed the prairie town.

Spoon River Anthology was a new kind of poetry in 1914, and its phenomenal popularity is proof that it spoke to a new age. It contained troubling insights: the restless frontier energies with no frontier tasks remaining, uneasy inklings of the new Freudian psychology, a new candor that would look *for* rather than away from the violation of traditional restraints. Three generations earlier the prairie had been called the Garden of the World. And what had the garden produced? Rich crops of corn and wheat, fat hogs and cattle, drab towns and slack lives, occasional rebellion amid smugness, hypocrisy and frustration, a slow erosion of character. In a prose work, *The Sangamon*, Masters told how gunsmith Robert Bishop came to Petersburg after long whaling voyages off the coast of Chile and Peru. His son Jay inherited the gun shop, with old pistols, swords and ship models in the window, and lived into the twentieth century. In a matter-of-fact tone Masters tells how an outhouse collapsed and dropped him into the pit, where he died of suffocation. "That may be a symbol," he concludes, "of what many little towns do to many citizens who walk the village square and pine for a different life."

And yet the strong voices from the Spoon River graveyard sound above the bitterness and repining. "It takes life to love Life," observed Lucinda Matlock, aged ninety-six; and though Petit was blind to it, there was life in the village that could start vibrations in a poet's mind and in his language. The *Anthology* is both harsh and haunting. All its people have some secret—of guilt, defiance, protest, loneliness, longing or exaltation. The liberated ones are those who feel a kinship with the earth. "Fiddler Jones" found words for it:

> The earth keeps some vibration going
> There in your heart, and that is you.

The star-struck Alfonso Churchill, laughed at as "Professor Moon," saw man as part of a scheme of things that embraces far-off Spica and the spiral nebulae. And William Jones, collector of seed pods and river shells, lived in wonder, worshiping earth and heaven.

Masters was never a public figure, even when his book was a best seller on both sides of the Atlantic. Few of his readers ever saw him—a round-faced, solemn-looking, owl-eyed man. But his friend Vachel Lindsay was a professional troubadour, seen and heard by many more people than ever saw his poems in print. Those who did read him came to the books by way of the man. In the early years, when it was still all wonderful to him, he rose to every audience, and he raised them with him.

I first heard Lindsay when I was a high-school youth, in the years of his first fame. Decatur, Illinois, is thirty-five miles from Springfield. To the Decatur High School came "the Springfield poet," and for one who had supposed that poetry belonged to Cambridge, England, and Cambridge, Massachusetts, it was exciting to hear of a poet in the next city. Nothing in my youth remains more vivid than that chill November evening when we passed the globe-lighted entrance and trooped noisily into the high-school auditorium, I, at least, wondering whether the poet would look anything like other Springfield, and Decatur, men. When he came onto the platform, he looked less than other men, shorter than our school principal who introduced him, his hands and feet restless as he sat waiting. He could have been a Macon County farmer, thick features, big nose and ears, a neck too long for a short man, a shock of hair falling down his forehead. He looked "dressed up," as though he was not used to the clothes he was wearing.

The next thing I remember is a tingling. On his feet the poet was a charged and changed man, pacing the stage, tossing his head, his great voice filling the darkened room like the sound of the sea in a shell. I believe they turned off the lights, though it may have been the darkness of Africa. He was chanting a new poem, "The Congo," and it filled the room with pictures: tattooed cannibals dancing beside the river, a Negro revival singing of Jacob on the golden stairs, witch doctors shaking the voodoo rattle and calling on the fearful gods of the jungle. And weaving through it all, the great golden river curving through the blackness of Africa. As I walked home that night, the familiar streets were strange and the words still echoed around me.

> Then I saw the Congo, creeping through the black,
> Cutting through the forest with a golden track.

It seemed a far cry from Illinois. But a few years later when I lived in Springfield, on South Fifth Street across from the Lindsay home, I learned that "The Congo" and "General Booth" and "The Chinese Nightingale" came from there, as much as did the bronzed lank man who walked the streets at midnight, the prairie-bred Lincoln. "General William Booth Enters Into Heaven" came to Lindsay as he stood night after night at the Salvation Army street meeting on the Springfield courthouse square. "The Congo" with its jazz and revival rhythms was suggested by the singing and dancing of Negro waiters around the woodpile behind the old Leland Hotel. "The Chinese Nightingale," though it pictured Chang at his ironing board while San Francisco was sleeping, came from the Chinese laundry in Springfield near "the railroad yard and the clock-tower bright" of the Illinois Central station. As a fifth-grade boy Lindsay had won a prize for an essay on "The Resources of Sangamon County." Later he would find a poet's resources there.

When he tramped his way to Florida and New Mexico, and when he made the lecture circuits, chanting his jazz prophecies in every corner of the country, he was always a man from the Midwest, naïve, zealous, visionary, evangelistic. Whipped up by his own excitement, he wrote too fast and too much, and he was too quickly satisfied with the words that came. Hardly one of his poems could not be improved by many lesser poets, who never could have conceived them. He had a grab-bag mind, undisciplined and disorderly but crammed with startling colors. He never could decide whether to condone or condemn the headlong energy of commercial America.

> While smoke-black freights on the double-tracked railroad,
> Driven as though by the foul fiend's ox-goad,
> Screaming to the West Coast, screaming to the East,
> Carry off a harvest, bring back a feast,
> And harvesting machinery and harness for the beast . . .

As an art student in Chicago, twenty-two years old, he wrote on the flyleaf of his Bible: "The man who is not a fanatic is as useless as a tombstone." He was alive and excited, and he saw poetry all around him.

He ranged from Babylon to Santa Fe, from St. Francis to Mark Twain, from Johnny Appleseed to John L. Sullivan, but always Springfield was his center. For a dozen years—his one sustained endeavor—he worked on *The Golden Book of Springfield,* an account of his dream city in the year 2018, two centuries after Illinois' statehood. Among other things that book was a vision of world government. In 1918, for a victory anthology of verse, Lindsay wrote not of victory but of universal brotherhood.

> Sew the flags together.
> Do not tear them down.

The dream began in Springfield, but it was not to end there. "Reader, in your town many like these [in *The Golden Book*] are brooding alone over unaccountable vistas of the future of their city, that have come to them in battle or by the fireside or in the storm. They have found themselves standing momently at cross streets of vision, before they felt their hearts to be as dust again. Call them together. Blow ashes into flame. Start a brotherhood of your own. Live in the new city that is revealed to you, as we are living in our City and in the streets of our Tomorrow."

It was Lindsay's conviction that art must begin at home, and his best poems are rooted in the prairie. In "Bryan, Bryan, Byran, Bryan" he recalled his own youth and the crusading Nebraskan in the summer when the world was to be set free. It was 1896 and he was just sixteen when Bryan came to Springfield "in a coat like a deacon, in a black Stetson hat." On that brave day the eager farmers and villagers stirred up dust on all the county roads.

> When Bryan came to Springfield, and Altgeld gave him greeting,
> Rochester was deserted, Divernon was deserted,
> Mechanicsburg, Riverton, Chickenbristle, Cotton Hill,
> Empty: for all Sangamon drove to the meeting . . .
>
> .   .   .   .
>
> The State House loomed afar,
> A speck, a hive, a football,
> A captive balloon!
> And the town was all one spreading wing of bunting,
>   plumes, and sunshine,
> Every rag and flag, and Bryan picture sold,
> When the rigs in many a dusty line
> Jammed our streets at noon,
> And joined the wild parade against the power of gold.

The Lindsay home on Fifth Street was next door to the Governor's Mansion. From his window the poet looked into the gardens where Altgeld had walked in the loneliness of his decision. In 1896 he had marshaled the Democratic party in support of the Populist candidate Bryan, and he had walked in that garden when the newspapers of America were vilifying him for pardon of the Haymarket anarchists. When he died, his name was shadowed by that reproach, and the nation was eager to forget the man who had rebuked its hatred and injustice. But Lindsay, standing in his study window, remembered.

> Sleep softly . . . eagle forgotten . . . under the stone,
> Time has its way with you there, and the clay has its own.
> Sleep on, O brave-hearted, O wise man, that kindled the flame—
> To live in mankind is far more than to live in a name . . .

In that room Lindsay awoke one stormy midnight with a vision of the wild prairie—he had been writing about it in *The Golden Book of Springfield*. It was a midsummer storm, a sudden, crashing cloudburst after a day of humid heat. The house trembled and shook as the thunder came. In white flickers of lightning he rushed to the doorway and found the city vanished. In that stormy vision his house had become a log hut beside a prairie stream and over the dark land came ghosts of Indian hunters astride bear, elk, deer, long-horned cattle and white bronchos. They rode in endless lines to the West—"the blue was their home." Then out of the dark earth rose the ghosts of the buffaloes, the great dark mass of the stampede thundering over the prairie.

> Buffaloes, buffaloes, thousands abreast,
> A scourge and amazement, they swept to the West.

The storm passed, the city reappeared, and the dazed poet wandered back to bed. There is no silence deeper than the hour following a prairie thunderstorm. In that stillness a cricket in the governor's garden—it, too, had been dazed and shaken—tried its voice on the night, and a last sigh of wind spoke to the poet on the edge of sleep.

> "Dream, boy, dream,
> If you anywise can.
> To dream is the work
> Of beast or man.
> Life is the west-going dream-storms' breath,
> Life is a dream, the sigh of the skies . . ."

Outside, in the governor's trees, the summer locusts began their buzzing and the cricket called, "Good-night . . . good-night."

Lindsay was thirty-five when he saw the ghosts of the buffaloes. He still had the dreams of youth, but they were dreams of an America that had vanished or was vanishing. A strain of West-going runs through the poems. The troubadour tramps west on the Santa Fe Trail; Bryan smashes Plymouth Rock with boulders from the West; after planting orchards in the midland clearings, Johnny Appleseed went on—

> "To the farthest West he has followed the sun,
> His life and his empire just begun."

In 1924 Lindsay himself moved to the West, settling for five years in Spokane, Washington, and living beyond his means in the Davenport Hotel. There, in 1925, he married a young English teacher from the Lewis and Clark High School. He exclaimed about the majesty of Mount Rainier and the sublimities of Glacier Park, but no poetry came. His heart was still on the prairie. To newspaper articles in Spokane he signed himself, "A Citizen of Springfield, Guest of Spokane." Amid recurrent depression and illness he wrote to his brother-in-law, Paul Wakefield, in 1928: "If we can hold out another year we will probably have the money and courage to move. . . . I want to go *home*." He came home to Springfield, with a wife and two children, in 1929.

He had just two years left, downhill years in which he struggled with poverty, illness and the despairing realization that the wellspring of his poetry had gone dry. He made long, exhausting lecture tours, worrying about money, spending money foolishly, drugging himself with movies, trying to rise to new audiences, to take over the school auditorium, the luncheon club, the college chapel with his shout and whisper and his once-bright dreams. Now he could hardly whip himself through "The Congo," "General Booth" and "The Santa Fé Trail." After thousands of readings they had lost all meaning for him. He came home tired in mind and body.

In the old familiar house on Fifth Street where he had written with racing hand in years past, he sat all night staring at blank paper, and no words came. In his filing cabinet were hundreds of notes and jottings, a mine of poems to be. He pulled out a page that read "Mentor Graham." Once, he remembered, he had a burning idea about the testy, impatient, meticulous man who spent his life with makeshift people but found one mind hungry for learning—the man who taught grammar, history and logic to Abe Lincoln in New Salem. Now the paper was dead.

The hot Illinois summer dragged by, and he thought that when the autumn came, when days grew crisp and dusk came early, he would write again. But autumn brought desperation and despair.

At last, at midnight on December 4, 1931, he drank poison.

Springfield had smiled indulgently at Lindsay, thought him harmless and amusing and no doubt admirable in his way, and never gave back a trace of the faith and love he lavished on his city. But with his death came a realization that a greatness had been there and was gone. Springfield took a first fame from Lincoln; now it had a second fame from Lindsay, and one could recall Nathaniel Hawthorne's irony: "It is not the warrior or the monarch that survives, but the despised poet, whom they may have fed with their crumbs." Lindsay was buried on a slope of Oak Ridge, near Lincoln's tomb, and there was a sudden run on Lindsay's books in Coe's and Barker's bookstores. The Springfield Rotary Club stood for a moment's silent tribute. The City Council expressed respect for Lindsay's achievement and regret at his passing. The Illinois legislature passed a resolution recognizing the loss of one who saw beauty where the world ignored it.

In 1935 Lake Springfield had spread over four thousand acres, a lovely many-armed lake impounded from the waters of Sugar Creek, which is a tributary of the Sangamon. Lindsay's last published words were a lifeless newspaper letter in support of the creating of Lake Springfield. "It will provide in tremendous quantities one of the city's most vital practical necessities, Water." He was too tired and empty to recall his youthful slogan: "Fair streets are better than silver; green parks are better than gold." After his death the city grew southward to this lake lying in the prairie swales, and over one of its narrows was built the Vachel Lindsay Memorial Bridge. At one end a stone pedestal supported a bust of Lindsay by Adrien Voisin.

It is a long-familiar irony, as old as poetry:

> Seven wealthy towns contend for Homer dead,
> Through which the living Homer begged his bread.

The poet loves the world, and the world spurns the poet till his time is past. Now the Lindsay house is preserved as a memorial, but at Lake Springfield the bust of Lindsay is almost swallowed in rank shrubbery and people around the lake are not sure which is the Vachel Lindsay bridge. If you ask at the State House information desk or the chamber of commerce, they can tell you. But they still miscall him Vatchel (like *satchel*), as they did when he lived among them.

"He looked at the sober glow in the southern sky: the forges of South Chicago. Through the window came the sad, acrid odors of fall. . . . All that had flourished would sink to decay, but still that throbbing light would keep on; vast structures would swing up from the earth; poets would chant their faith in iron, forgetting the preceding generations in favor of the hard fruit of the soil—flanges, rivets, mandrels." So a novelist, George Davis, in *The Opening of a Door*, sensed what matters and endures in ever-changing Chicago.

His words were already fulfilled when he wrote this prophecy in 1930. Carl Sandburg, the son of a Swedish immigrant blacksmith, had chanted:

> Lay me on an anvil, O God.
> Beat me and hammer me into a crowbar.

Yet this faith in iron was also a faith in man.

> A bar of steel—it is only
> Smoke at the heart of it, smoke and the blood of a man.

The world had discovered from his first two volumes, *Chicago Poems* in 1916 and *Cornhuskers* two years later, that there are several Sandburgs: the tough, slangy, strident poet of the Windy City, the poet of prairie reverie, the dismisser of preceding generations (". . . the past is a bucket of ashes") and the brooding biographer of Lincoln. He could be cryptic and sardonic like Masters, expansive like Lindsay, and pure Sandburg, as in the Chicago poem that made his voice known to the world.

The year 1914 was a literary phenomenon in Illinois. Within a few months appeared *The Congo and Other Poems*, published in New York; the first installment of *Spoon River Anthology*, published in Reedy's *Mirror* in St. Louis; and in Chicago's *Poetry: A Magazine of Verse*, a group of Sandburg's poems, including one which immediately became famous. It began:

Hog Butcher for the World,
Tool Maker, Stacker of Wheat,
Player with Railroads and the Nation's Freight Handler;
Stormy, husky, brawling,
City of the Big Shoulders . . .

And it sustained that personification with undiminished intensity and power.

Bareheaded,
Shoveling,
Wrecking,
Planning,
Building, breaking, rebuilding . . .

Galesburg, Illinois, was a town formed by a religious community and named for its gaunt Presbyterian parson, George Washington Gale. Its aim was the founding of a manual-labor college which would train ministers for the frontier. But in the 1850's the Burlington Railroad men took over, and a swarm of Swedish laborers came in. The abolition zeal of the Yankee founders made it an important station on another railroad, the Underground route of fugitive slaves smuggled up from the Ohio River in farm wagons heaped with hay. In 1858 the Knox College campus in the heart of town became the scene of a Lincoln-Douglas debate, and after Lincoln's death a bronze plate at the north front of Old Main Hall was inscribed with words he had spoken there. "He is blowing out the moral lights around us, when he contends that whoever wants slaves has a right to hold them." These were the first words of Lincoln that Sandburg ever read.

Carl Sandburg was a Galesburg boy, and a Galesburg as well as a Chicago man. His schooling ended at thirteen, and he worked on a milk wagon, in a brickyard, and as a barber shop porter and bootblack. Then at eighteen, a gawky blue-eyed youth with a mop of corn-colored hair, he started a three-year vagabondage, wandering through the midland country. He worked on a Mississippi River steamboat, on a railroad section gang in Missouri, in the Kansas wheat fields, as a coal-heaver in Omaha and a dishwasher in Denver. All this gave the youth a sense of his own country; it gave the future poet the stuff of *Cornhuskers* and *Slabs of the Sunburnt West*. After brief soldiering in the Spanish-American War and three years of college in Galesburg, he went to Chicago, wrote ads for a department store, and joined the staff of a small Socialist newspaper called the *Day Book*. In 1914, while reporting a waitress' strike, he interviewed the lawyer for the union and so became acquainted with Edgar Lee Masters, who was then writing the first of his Spoon River poems.

Say Chicago, and you think of Sandburg. He was a Windy City man. He had first gone to Chicago at eighteen, seeing the city for three days on $3.50. Walking was free, and to him the ringing city streets were a kaleidoscope:

> I walked miles and never got tired of the roar of the streets, the trolley cars, the drays, buggies, surreys, and phaetons, the delivery wagons high with boxes, the brewery wagons piled with barrels, the one-horse and two-horse hacks, sometimes a buckboard, sometimes a barouche with a coachman in livery, now and again a man in a saddle on horseback weaving his way through the traffic—horses, everywhere horses, and here and there mules—and the cobblestone streets with layers of dust and horse droppings. I walked along Michigan Avenue and looked for hours to where for the first time in my life I saw shimmering water meet the sky. Those born to it don't know what it is for a boy to hear about it for years and then comes a day when for the first time he sees water stretching away before his eyes and running to meet the sky.

That wonder at the lake- and prairie-bordered city never left him. He reveled in its crudity and swaggering power. He loved its polyglot harsh voices—voices crying through the summer twilight and the winter dusk in Greek, Bulgarian, Bohemian, Polish and in English which no Englishman could understand. He found beauty and mystery in the fog stealing from the lake, the smoky sunset over the Calumet marshes, the electric signs that made Chinese writing in the river. Walking through the Loop, ringed in the roar of the Elevated trains and in the larger circle of lake and prairie silence, he felt his way back to the city's beginning.

> Out of prairie-brown grass crossed with a streamer of wigwam smoke—out of a smoke pillar, a blue promise—out of wild ducks woven in greens and purples—
> Here I saw a city rise and say to the peoples round the world: Listen, I am strong, I know what I want.
> Out of log houses and stumps—canoes stripped from tree-sides— flatboats coaxed with an axe from the timber claims—in the years when the red and white men met—the houses and streets rose.
>
> A thousand red men cried and went away to new places for corn and women: a million white men came and put up skyscrapers, threw out rails and wires, feelers to the salt sea: now the smoke- stacks bite the skyline with stub teeth.
>
> In an early year the call of a wild duck woven in greens and purples: now the riveter's chatter, the police patrol, the song-whistle of the steamboat.

The Chicago poems reach out in all directions. They give a feeling of the great prairie and the great lake running away in long horizons, and of the wind sweeping in unhindered from the great plains that slant up toward the Rocky Mountains. Sandburg is alive to landscape as a musician is alive to an orchestral composition. He interweaves the city and the country. In "Prairie" he follows the picture of pearl-gray haystacks in the gloaming with the clanking wheels and hissing pistons of the overland limited passing under the walls of the city. In Lindsay there is a contest between the village and the city, the farm and the factory. But Sandburg's wide embrace encloses both.

All his landscapes, even the most lonely, are for people. They belong to people, and the people in them provide their meaning. Sometimes he is airy and empty:

> The people is the grand canyon of humanity
> and many many miles across.
> The people is pandora's box, humpty dumpty,
> a clock of doom and an avalanche when it turns loose.

But when he turns from the abstraction to flesh and blood and the sound of voices, the lines are suddenly alive:

> Drove up a newcomer in a covered wagon: "What kind of folks live around here?" "Well, stranger, what kind of folks was there in the country you come from?" "Well, they was mostly a low-down lying, thieving, gossiping, back-biting lot of people." "Well, I guess, stranger, that's about the kind of folks you'll find around here."

"Poetry," he wrote, "is an art practiced with the terribly plastic material of human language." Human language is the language of life, the strong, plain, common, careless language of the people. For him it never could grow stale.

THE HOOSIER TRADITION

Hoosier is a word of doubtful origin. One theory traces it back to an Indiana prizefighter named Aaron Short who, upon flooring his opponent, cried, "Hurrah for the Hoosier," meaning the formidable "husher" who could hush all comers. Other inferences point to the Anglo-Saxon *hoo*, meaning a rustic person; the pioneer's wary greeting to newcomers, "Who's yer?" the Southern term "hoozer" for a lanky, tobacco-spitting backwoodsman; a canal foreman, Sam Hoosier, who preferred to hire shovelmen from the Indiana side of the river. On his visit to Indianapolis in 1852 Louis Kossuth, the Hungarian patriot, was told that it came from *hoosa*, the Indian name for corn.

Whatever its origin, the name has had a lasting appeal for Indiana people and has acquired a quite enviable aura. For more than a hundred years it has continued to mean friendliness, neighborliness, an idyllic contentment with Indiana landscape and life. A certain Kentucky man named Pritchard, it is said, had moved to Indiana in his youth and was pleased with everything he found there. A friend once asked how old he was. "If I live till next October," he said, "I will be fifty years old."

"Ah, Pritchard," said the friend, "you are older than that. I have known you for nearly forty years."

"Well," said Pritchard, "I did live for twenty years in Kentucky, but I never counted that." He was a genuine Hoosier.

The first literary use of the term came in 1833, when John Finley's poem "The Hoosier's Nest" appeared in an Indianapolis newspaper.

> I'm told in riding somewhere West
> A stranger found a Hoosier's Nest . . .

The traveler was treated to the warmest hospitality in that well-appointed cabin in "blest Indiana."

> One side was lined with divers garmints,
> The other, spread with skins of varmints;
> Dried pumpkins overhead were strung
> Where venison hams in plenty hung;
> Two rifles placed above the door,
> Three dogs lay stretched upon the floor—
> In short the domicil was rife
> With specimens of Hoosier life.

In the next hundred years *Hoosier* became a familiar literary name. Edward Eggleston wrote *The Hoosier Schoolmaster* and *The Hoosier Schoolboy*. Maurice Thompson wrote *Hoosier Mosaics*. Meredith Nicholson wrote *The Hoosiers* and *A Hoosier Chronicle*. Even the fugitive Theodore Dreiser, back for a season in Indiana, wrote *A Hoosier Holiday*. With an unexplainable aptness, the name attached itself to local folkways. It had a power of suggestion which helped to define and to perpetuate the tradition. If the word had not been there, fewer Indiana books would have been written.

Of course, there could be no translation of *Hoosier*. *The Hoosier Schoolmaster* was first published in France in 1871—it appeared serially in *La Revue des Deux Mondes*—under the title *Le Maître d'Ecole de Flat Creek*. When it was issued in America, a year later, its picture of backwoods people in southern Indiana in the 1850's had an immediate and almost universal appeal. The first Indiana novelist had appeared.

A few years later an Indiana man came home from the wars

in Mexico. Sitting under a beech tree in the quiet town of Craw-fordsville, Lew Wallace wrote *Ben-Hur*, a tale of ancient Judea and Rome which became the best seller of its generation. In the same town twenty years later, Maurice Thompson showed that a Hoosier novelist need not look so far away. In *Alice of Old Vincennes* he told the story of George Rogers Clark's capture of the old post on the Wabash, a book that was soon being read all over America.

Meanwhile a carefree youth was driving his buckboard through the Indiana country, traveling the farming counties as a barn painter and a pedlar of patent medicine. He heard the wind in the corn, the creak of the windmills, the song of meadow larks and blackbirds in the sloughs; and soon Indiana had its poet. James Whitcomb Riley made Hoosier scenes and homely Hoosier people familiar to the world. A lifelong bachelor, he wrote about "An Old Sweetheart of Mine," and no single poem in America ever became so popular.

The turn of the century was a tranquil time. The frontier period had ended and the bright new century was at hand, with no sign of the wars and revolutions it would bring. Indiana in the heartland was a center of repose. A generation later Theodore Dreiser, forgetting his dark deterministic fiction, remembered an inexpressible charm in the Indiana of his youth, a kind of wistfulness that accompanies the dreams of unsophistication. "Contrasted with the neighboring states of Ohio, Michigan, and Illinois," he wrote, "Indiana pales as a center of manufacture. Ohio can boast quite ten centers to its one. In passing from any of these states into Indiana one is reminded of the difference between Holland and Germany and France, the one with its canals, its windmills, and level fields dotted with simple homes, the other with its plethora of cities and factories and, in the old days, its ever present army. The one is idyllic and the other almost disturbingly real and irritatingly energetic." Nowhere did the moon shine so bright as on the Wabash, nowhere was such contentment as lay over the Indiana fields when the frost was on the pumpkin and the fodder in the shock. And nowhere were people so agreeable and kindly as in the crossroads towns. This Indiana seemed as fixed as paintings on the wall. People played croquet on village lawns. Children skipped ropes, rolled hoops and pulled wagons. Families passed in surreys, buggies and phaetons. Farmers drove to town in wagons heaped with harvest. In Meredith Nicholson's *A Hoosier Chronicle* a contented old lady summed it up. "It's all pretty comfortable and cheerful and busy in Indiana, with lots of old-fashioned human kindness flowing round."

From this happy country at the turn of the century came an outpouring of fiction. Some of it was remote and romantic— Charles Major's *When Knighthood Was in Flower*, George Barr McCutcheon's *Graustark* and Meredith Nicholson's *The House of a Thousand Candles*. More of it was native—George Ade's racy, rustic *Fables in Slang* and *People You Knew*, Gene Stratton-Porter's saccharine *Song of the Cardinal* and *Freckles* and Booth Tarkington's gently realistic *The Gentleman from Indiana*. Remote or familiar, romantic or rustic, they all had the Hoosier magic. No group of novelists from a single state ever had such popular success. It was Indiana's day.

Right at the turn of the century appeared another Indiana novelist who was rarely called a Hoosier. Theodore Dreiser's somber *Sister Carrie* was printed in 1900 but withheld from circulation because of its supposed immorality. Born on the immigrant side of the tracks in industrial Terre Haute, Dreiser left Indiana at sixteen. Like the fictitious Carrie Meeber, he felt the pull of Chicago—that dark, magnetic center of the iron webs that hung on the wall of every railroad station in the Middle West. Yet Dreiser did not forget the innocence of Indiana. He came back from the larger world and found the old simplicities still there and wrote about them like a Hoosier.

By 1920 the Hoosier tradition was declining, and by 1930 it was all but gone. But in 1948 it came to life again. In *Raintree County*, Ross Lockridge, Jr., from an old Indiana family and nurtured on Indiana folklore, wrote the most Hoosier novel of all.

Raintree County is an eclectic scene, a miniature Indiana. Its town of Waycross is on the National Road (James Whitcomb Riley came from Greenfield on the old pike); its Great Swamp is like the Limberlost; and the mystical raintree comes from New Harmony, where Robert Owen's scientists had planted it in 1825. The Shawmucky River is a subject of piety like the Wabash, and the *Illustrated Historical Atlas of Raintree County* shows it as the center of the earth. "There was an illustrated title-page, colored fullpage maps of the County and each of its twelve townships, and smaller maps of the principal communities, including Waycross. At the back were unfolding maps of Indiana, the United States, and the Eastern and Western Hemispheres."

Raintree County was a fascinating anachronism. It brought together all the Hoosier strains—a long sense of the tradition of town and family, a gallery of village characters, a loving re-creation of the local scene, and a mystical dream of beauty, wisdom and love under the tree of golden rain. The novel was a 1,060-page reaching back to the past, the only way to find the vanished Hoosier tradition.

For Indiana was not outside the quickening currents of America but directly in their path. On the dusty Pumpkin Vine Pike outside of Kokomo in 1894 Elwood Haynes had cranked his horseless carriage and driven three miles without a stop—the first automobile in America. On Memorial Day in 1911 the annual motor race began at the Indianapolis Speedway, with an Indianapolis-made Marmon winning the first trophy. In the 1920's two Indiana sociologists, Robert S. and Helen Merrell Lynd, searched for a representative American community. It could not be a New England town, a Southern town, or a town in the Rocky Mountains. It must be, they felt, "in that common-denominator of America, the Middle West," near the center of population, which was then in west central Indiana. They chose the agricultural-industrial city of Muncie, named for the Munsee Indian tribe that once had lived there; the Lynds called it Middletown. The finding of a symbolic Middletown in a Hoosier community signalized the end of an era. When Indiana ceased to be unique and became typical, the Hoosier tradition was past.

FROM WINESBURG TO MALABAR FARM

Brooding over his own identity and the society he belonged to, Sherwood Anderson wrote: "I might drift here and there about America, but at heart I would be, to the New Yorker, a man from beyond the mountains, an Ohio man to the end. . . . To the end of my life I would talk with the half-slovenly drawl of the Middle-Westerner, would walk like such a Middle-Westerner, have the air of something between a laborer, a man of business, a gambler, a race-horse owner, an actor."

In the 1880's, the years of Anderson's youth, Ohio was the place where financial and industrial energies of the East met the open lands of the interior. Heavy industry was spreading along the forty-first parallel. In the Lake Erie cities blast furnaces were melting Lake Superior iron ore and lumber mills were converting Michigan timber into wagon wheels, railroad cars, and cross-arms for telegraph poles. In Cleveland the cooperage factory of the Standard Oil Company daily turned twenty acres of oak forest into the endless stream of barrels that were carrying kerosene to every corner of the country. Yet there was still a simple, rural life in Ohio, untouched by the new industries. As a boy Sherwood Anderson belonged to the rural Ohio, as a man he made a dramatic flight from the commercial Ohio. As a writer he brooded over them both and over the dilemma of a people caught between the two.

Anderson was born in 1876 in the country town of Camden, in the southwestern corner of the state. His father was a harness-maker, having learned that trade while serving in the Seventh Ohio Cavalry during the Civil War. In Camden on Saturday afternoons young Sherwood Anderson stood at the intersection of two country roads, the present U.S. 127 and Ohio 752, selling the weekend edition of the Cincinnati *Enquirer* to mud-stained farmers. He was more ambitious and industrious than his easy-going father. When the harness business failed in 1884, the family moved two hundred miles north to the town of Clyde. Here the ex-harnessmaker worked in a farm-machinery factory, making the shift from craftsmanship to manufacturing that later disturbed Sherwood Anderson the writer. But the elder Anderson soon turned to more informal trades. He became a sign painter and housepainter, though he often quit in the middle of a job.

Clyde, Ohio, traces its origin to a young army officer in the War of 1812 who took a liking to a campsite in Sandusky County. Before breaking camp he drove a stake into the ground and said, "At this spot I shall build my future home, which shall be the nucleus of a thriving town." Eight years later he came back, scoured the woods for his weathered stake, and found smoke sifting up from a squatter's cabin. With a barrel of whisky he bought off the squatter and took possession. In eight more years a settlement began and the town of Clyde was plotted. After the Civil War it had a small fame as the birthplace of James B. Mc-Pherson, general in the Union Army, who was killed in the Battle of Atlanta. It would have a wider fame as the original of "Winesburg, Ohio." For this town the pen was to be more important than the sword.

Clyde was a pleasant town in the midst of fruit and berry farms. In Anderson's stories its horizons are softened by a smoky haze which suggests the overcoming of the simple agricultural life by new forces of industry and trade. Here in his later boyhood Sherwood Anderson worked at the race track, the fair grounds, and in a bicycle factory. At twenty he left the village for the city, becoming a laborer in a Chicago warehouse. A brief term of service in the Spanish-American war was followed by a year at Wittenberg Academy in Springfield, Ohio. Then he returned to Chicago and began a business career as a writer of advertising copy. Ten years later he was in Elyria, Ohio, a settled family man with a mail-order paint company of his own. He was succeeding in business but troubled in mind. He walked in the woods along the Black River and began to write amorphous stories about the small-town people he remembered. "When you are puzzled about your life," he later confided, "you can throw imagined figures through situations in which you have been involved."

In 1912 came the crisis and the rebellion, the dividing point in Sherwood Anderson's dual life. A nervous breakdown resulting in a temporary amnesia put an end to his life as a businessman. In his own account, he came to the end of the road on the morning before Thanksgiving Day. Abruptly, in the midst of dictating a business letter, he told his secretary: "My feet are cold and wet. I have been walking too long on the bed of a river." Then he turned and left the office, to which he would never return. "I laughed as I walked lightly toward the door," he recalled years later, "and out of a long and tangled phase of my life, out of the door of buying and selling, out of the door of affairs." He was thirty-six years old. His former life was ended and his new one not yet begun.

Having cut himself off from business and family, he went to Chicago in December, 1912. While advertising copy paid the bills, he fumbled with stories about people in small towns of the Middle West. He spent a winter alone in a hut in the Ozark Mountains of Missouri, writing a novel there and destroying it. Back in Chicago he fell in with a group of newspapermen, critics and poets—Floyd Dell, Ben Hecht, Maxwell Bodenheim, Carl Sandburg and others—who spent evenings together in a Bohemian quarter on Fifty-seventh Street near Jackson Park. Art lives upon discussion, and Anderson took encouragement and direction from the passionate exchange of ideas in the smoky candlelight. Years later he recalled that ferment. "It was a time when something blossomed in Chicago and the Middle West. . . . Something which had been very hard in American life was beginning to crack, and in our group we often spoke of it hopefully. And how exciting it was! Something seemingly new and fresh was in the very air we breathed."

One night Anderson entertained this group in his own room on Cass Street. Ben Hecht came—it was his first meeting with Anderson—and found his host sprawled in a chair between two candles which darkened his rumpled hair and shadowed his eyes. This is the way Hecht remembered it:

> I became aware that this rugged-seeming man was a gentle, almost womanish fellow. There was a tremor to his lips, and his large handsome face seemed to flutter when he spoke, as did his voice. . . . One hand reached out and waved rhythmically at us, in a gentle, patronizing fashion. His voice caressed us and I heard a fine writer speak for the first time.
>
> "I was going to read you a book I've written called *Windy McPherson's Son*," he said, "but it's a very long manuscript and kind of heavy to hold. So I'll read you some stories I've written about a town called Winesburg, Ohio. They're not really stories. They're just people."
>
> We waited silently as our host moved a candle nearer his penwritten pages.
>
> "Down the street ran George Hadley . . ." Sherwood Anderson began reading.

Between 1916 and 1919 Anderson published three fumbling books. Then came a sure one. He had added to the *Winesburg* stories and introduced them with "The Book of the Grotesque," a thematic fable describing how each person grasped a single, separate truth, called it his truth and tried to live his life by it, and thus became a misshapen man, a grotesque, while the isolated truth he had embraced became a falsehood. When *Winesburg, Ohio* was published in 1919, it reminded some readers of *Spoon River Anthology*. In the spring of 1915 a friend had given Anderson a copy of the Masters poems, which he read all night. A few months later he began working freshly on the Winesburg book— a group of sketches unified by a small-town setting and by the author's feeling of pity and understanding for his lonely, distorted people.

Winesburg, Ohio is a study of lives flowing past each other, sometimes crying out in darkness with no answer or reaching out vainly for something to cling to. Many of the episodes occur in twilight or darkness, a darkness which intensifies the theme of isolation. There are the twisted, loveless women; the fiercely religious men without love of God or man; the shy, silent boy who feels an outcast in the town; the man who scribbled thoughts on scraps of paper and threw them away; the man who ran at night over the low hills beyond the town, crying out to God in the empty spaces; the man who shut himself in a bare room and talked with imaginary people; the telegraph operator who sat alone all night in the grass in the station yard; the stoop-shouldered farm hand who could never tell what he thought or what he wanted. Isolation and loneliness surround these people in a village where everyone knows all the rest. Wing Biddlebaum did not think of himself as in any way a part of the town where he had lived for twenty years; to Louise Bentley it seemed there was a wall that cut her off from everyone else; and the enviable George Willard, the newspaper reporter, walked in the darkness detached and apart from all the life around him. At night these figures pass through the village streets, fighting their silent, unseen battles. Some of them have the pathetic delusion that the train to Cleveland promises escape. But it is themselves, not Winesburg, that is their trouble. They are not suffering from persecution but from humanity. While Anderson was depicting an Ohio village, he was also looking with kindness and humility into the secret places of human nature.

Winesburg, Ohio is a combination of the simplicity and subtleness that make up a recognizable Middle Western tradition. In the twenty books he was yet to write, Anderson would approach but never quite equal its insight and understanding.

It is just fifty miles from Clyde, Ohio, to Mansfield, the seat of Richland County. But Winesburg and "the Town" of Louis Bromfield's novels might belong to different countries. In the last decades of the nineteenth century Mansfield changed from a quiet market town to a restless industrial city. (Its brass, iron and steel mills are magnified in the Bromfield novels, where it became a city like Akron or Youngstown.) But Louis Bromfield also re-membered Mansfield's idyllic past.

One of the legendary figures of Richland County was Johnny Appleseed. On a spring day in the early years of Mansfield a circuit rider tied his horse to a sapling and began preaching to the village loafers. As he warmed to his subject, he pointed a bony finger at Williams's Tavern, calling God's attention to all who frolicked in dens of sloth and drunkenness. He waved a hand past the log courthouse and over the roofs of the town, condemning land-grabbers and townsite speculators, all men who in their greed and grasping lost their immortal souls. Where, he demanded, is the barefoot Christian, traveling to Heaven? While he waited for an answer a rustling came from a thicket. From behind a fallen log two bare feet waved in the air and a voice cried, "Here he is!" Up jumped a ragged man with dark hair falling to his shoulders. He carried a deer-hide pack on his shoulder. No one in Mansfield was surprised to see Johnny Appleseed jump out of a thicket in the public square. He passed through Richland County every season.

Other legends recalled the wandering Eleazer Williams, sup-posedly the lost Dauphin of France, the exiled son of Louis XVI and Marie Antoinette. For years this strange and simple man lived among the Indians, who knew him as Lazare. He had come to New England as a French-speaking boy, with only a bundle of clothing and a dazed memory of mobs and torches. A preacher named Williams took him in, but the boy soon wandered off and found a home with Indians and French traders. Being simple-minded, he was respected and protected by the Indians, who were always charitable toward that affliction. His wanderings took him to the great forest of Ohio when he sometimes roamed the trails with ragged Johnny Appleseed.

Bromfield cherished a family tradition of his Great Aunt Mattie, blind from the age of thirty, who had talked with these two barefoot pilgrims.

Sherwood Anderson once commented on the ignorance of frontier people which had in it a kind of childish innocence, and he lamented the loss of that innocence when a hard, prag-matic knowledge came into the lives of both townsmen and countrymen. Bromfield, so much more worldly, saw that same hardening of mind and heart. In his novels he contrasted the old house on the hill, with its outdated simplicity and charm, with the huge impersonal money-making mills. The mills were darken-ing the town and blighting the countryside. Again, in the opening chapter of *The Farm* he pictured the symbolic meeting of three men in the wilds of Midland County—the Maryland Colonel with his dream of making a Jeffersonian paradise "if men were good and wise enough," the Jesuit priest who was reluctantly leaving the Sandusky Indians for a new mission in Mexico, and the Yankee pedlar with no other feeling than an avidity for profits. In 1815 the French influence in Ohio was ending; the future belonged to the farmer and the merchant. In the century of change which he chronicles in *The Farm*, Bromfield shows how the Colonel's idealism lost out to the business philosophy of the pedlar. Silas Bentham had come into the wilderness leading a mule "so heavily laden that there was no place left for the man to ride." After a hundred years of commercial progress, the novel concludes, there was no place left in the new country for human dignity and independence.

As a novelist Bromfield had a sense of timely themes, and he enjoyed a large success. Before he was thirty he had won a Pulitzer prize, along with popular acclaim, for his "panel" novels, which portrayed the older simplicities of Ohio life giving way to the commercial values of "the Town." A visit to France in 1925 lengthened into a stay of a dozen years, interrupted by visits to the United States and India. In 1933 appeared *The Farm*, his most lasting and substantial book, a hundred-year chronicle of a family in the Western Reserve. Less fiction than a narrative of social change, *The Farm* had been epitomized a decade earlier in a paragraph in his novel *Possession:*

> The Town had known four stages in its development. In the beginning there had been but a blockhouse set down in a wilderness. Before many years had passed this was succeeded by a square, filled

with farmers and lowing cattle, and heavy wagons laden with grain. Then, in turn a community, raw and rankly prosperous, which grew with a ruthless savagery, crushing everything beneath a passion for bigness and prosperity. And now, creeping in towards its heart, stealthily, and as many solid citizens believed, suspiciously, there came a softness which some called degeneration—a liking for beauty of sound, of sight, and of color.

The Colonel, progenitor of the family whose fortunes are followed in *The Farm*, came into the wild land in 1815. The narrative ends in 1914, a somber time when an independent way of life had passed into the crushing interdependence of industry and war.

The family in *The Farm* was untouched by business. Their dreams had nothing to do with money, and they were deeply attached to the land they had lived upon. Bromfield sees idealism and integrity in their way of life, and in the next breath he declares that these virtues passed out of existence at the turn of the century. Beneath this oversimplification lies the plain fact that Jeffersonian individualism could not persist in the social and economic complexity of the new century.

In 1938 gathering war clouds in Europe sent the Bromfields back to America. In Ohio Louis Bromfield searched the back roads of Richland County for the scenes of his boyhood on his grandfather's farm. "As the car came down out of the hills and turned off the Pinhook Road the whole of the valley, covered in snow, lay spread out before us with the ice-blue creek wandering through it between the two high sandstone ridges where the trees, black and bare, rose against the winter sky. And suddenly I knew where I was. I had come home!"

In this "Pleasant Valley" he bought three half-wild adjoining farms, totaling six hundred and forty acres. With the help of a young partner he outlined a project of the rebuilding of depleted soil, remodeling of old farm buildings, developing of strong strains of livestock, preserving the woodlands and restoring native pastures, raising the water table and producing a wide range of field, orchard and garden crops. So began Malabar Farm, named for a hill district in India where the Bromfields had spent a memorable season.

It was a big, bold, imaginative plan, and, thanks to Bromfield's writing, it became a well-publicized one. Alternating between fields and desk, he wrote four books about Malabar Farm, books which helped to support the project which they described. Bromfield lived on a large scale, entertaining conservationists, governors, and motion-picture people, and visited by as many as twenty thousand persons a year. Some of the visitors were farmers; more were laymen attracted by the fame of Malabar Farm and its proprietor. The farmers admired Bromfield's contoured fields, his prize cattle and his rich, rolling pastures, but they concluded that the farm supported the writer less than the writer supported the farm. Bromfield cheerfully confessed that his project needed help from other sources. "I earned much money by writing, and in the background there was always Hollywood when the money ran short. As [my associate] George once suggested, there should be plaques on each of the buildings announcing that 'Twentieth Century Fox is responsible for the building of this sheep barn,' or 'Metro Goldwyn Mayer provided the money for remodeling this cattle-feeding barn.' 'United Artists, in payment for a short story, built this cottage.' "

The heart of the plan at Malabar Farm was a way of life, independent, in harmony with earth and sky and seasons, rooted in the Ohio countryside. That was fully accomplished before Louis Bromfield's sudden death in 1956. In his last years he called himself a farmer rather than a writer. But the two went well together. As the weathered lines had deepened in his face, his writing achieved deepening insights into man and nature. With a wondering "reverence for life," he loved all that was around him, from the big Angus bull in his pasture to the bright-eyed field mouse that nested in the radio beside his bed. At Malabar he achieved what had eluded all the troubled and fragmentary people of Winesburg: "a sense of belonging, of being a small and relatively unimportant part of something vast but infinitely friendly."

22. Miracle on the Farm

On the left- and right-hand side of the road,
Marching corn—
I saw it knee high weeks ago—now it is head high—
tassels of red silk creep at the ends of the ears.
—CARL SANDBURG

For a century the prairie has been cornland, long rows of ribboned leaves in June, a sea of tasseled stalks in August, tawny harvest fields in October. The source of all meat, poultry and dairy products, that ocean of corn is the basis of America's abundance. Corn was the Indian's staple before American history began. It has always been the New World's most important food crop.

When farming began on the prairie, the wild grasses were replaced by a tame grass. Corn is a giant grass that in four months grows taller than men and horses. It is a plant that has no rival in the world in its power to capture and store the basic energy

338

of the sun. When explorers came to the New World, they found the cornfields of the Indians, but they did not find corn growing wild. The origin of the corn grass is a mystery. With its seeds imbedded in a cob and swathed in layers of husk, corn cannot sow itself. Somewhere, probably in Central America twenty thousand years ago, it attached itself to man, and the human generations have kept it alive and spreading ever since. American Indians grew corn in forest clearings, in river bottoms, and on the floor of cliff-walled canyons. In Massachusetts and Virginia the English colonists quickly learned to grow Indian corn; they could not have survived without it. Emigrants brought seed corn over the Appalachian barrier to the Ohio valley. It flourished in the deep soil under the hot sun of the heartland. It was at home on the prairie as fish are at home in the sea.

By 1860 north central Illinois was a corn country. When Henry Wallace, two of whose descendants would serve the nation as Secretary of Agriculture, came from Pennsylvania to study at the Monmouth Theological Seminary, he found Illinois a cornucopia of corn. "It seemed," he wrote, "as if the state were literally full of corn. It was piled up in rail pens without covering, around the houses and other buildings, and sometimes in the fields. . . . The next winter I spent a Sabbath in the country, and sat by a stove burning corn for fuel. . . . The town itself was full of corn, corn everywhere."

Still more corn was coming, and Henry Wallace's descendants would have a hand in it. In the 1920's an Iowa story writer, Ruth Suckow, told of an old farmer who declared, "Yes, they talk about changing everything. This new machinery and all. But as far as I can see no one has yet found how to make the corn grow any way but from first planting the seed, and then getting it watered by the rains and warmed by the sun, tasseling out and being cut." At that moment Henry C. Wallace and other men were finding ways to produce a new kind of corn that would yield prodigious crops under almost any conditions of soil and climate.

Like everything else in America farming has changed profoundly in the twentieth century. Fields first plowed by oxen, then by horses, now are plowed by tractors that haul gang plows across the land. Sometimes their motors throb all night and their headlights sweep the furrows. Corn once planted by hand is dropped by many-row planters that apply fertilizer along with the seeding. Once cultivated by hand hoe, then by riding plows, the young corn is now tended by tractor-drawn cultivators. Once the cornhusker walked beside his horses in the frosty weather, corn ears thumping the bangboard and a yellow harvest growing in the wagon bed.

> The cornhuskers wear leather on their hands.
> There is no let-up to the wind.
> Blue bandannas are knotted at the ruddy chins.
>
> .   .   .   .
>
> The frost loosens corn husks.
> The sun, the rain, the wind loosen corn husks.
> The men and women are helpers.
> They are all cornhuskers together.

When Sandburg wrote about it, cornhusking was a long, laborious task, week after week in the withered winter fields. Now it is done by mechanical pickers that chew up the stalks and drop the ears into the harvest wagon. A motorized corn-picker harvests an acre in thirty minutes; twenty years ago an acre of corn was a long day's work.

These twenty years have brought more progress in food production—measured by a farm, a man or an hour—than was made in the past twenty centuries. Like the threshing ring, the harvest bee, and the old pitchfork haying, cornhusking has become folklore. Horse-plowing and hand-husking are becoming spectacles and contests—the heartland rodeo.

Behind the changes in corn production lies a modern miracle. A present-day traveler in the Midwest, passing through miles of cornland, may read at the fence corners a sign: "Funk's Hybrid," "DeKalb Hybrid," "Pfister's Hybrid," or "Pioneer Hybrid." Whatever name it bears, it is a small sign, no bigger than the scoop of a corn shovel. But it is the name of the miracle that has produced mountains of surplus food in the world's best-fed nation. Hybrid corn has vastly increased corn production while diminishing corn acreage—an acreage that still surpasses that of wheat, oats and cotton combined. It has made corn resistant to disease, drought and parasites and has produced stalks and ears that are sturdy enough to be harvested by machinery. It developed in the heartland in the twentieth century and it has spread to countries around the earth.

The Indians never understood the secret of pollenization. They worshiped the corn god and kept their seed through hungry winters and entrusted it to the warming earth of spring. They gave corn to the white men. Generations of farmers saved their best ears for seed, and by degrees they improved the strains, so that in four hundred years they had a sound, regular-kerneled corn that on the rich prairie would yield fifty bushels an acre. That slow patient process of selection led to the show-corn of agricultural fairs half a century ago. Show-corn was automatically seed corn. If kernels from the biggest and most shapely ears did not produce show-corn in turn, and did not yield consistently, no one asked the reasons why. No one had yet made studies of corn heredity.

Then came the miracle workers, the corn breeders who in a decade improved corn as much as it had been improved in four centuries of civilized agriculture. Hybrid corn, which now produces 98 percent of the nations's crop, was the result. It was achieved by a few college and government agronomists working in laboratories and experiment stations and a few practical farmers working in test plots in their own fields. All were building upon the basic discoveries of the geneticists. By groping experiment and a patient prolonged process of trial and error the corn breeders learned that controlled fertilization could produce pure strains, and that pure strains could be interbred so as to eliminate the weaknesses and concentrate the virtues of the corn plant.

Corn grows fast. In the American Corn Belt the first green

blades push up from the damp earth in mid-May. By August the corn stands head-high, its ribboned stalk crowned with tassels. Each tassel branch has hundreds of spikelets, and each spikelet is laden with microscopic pollen. Halfway down the stalk appears an ear shoot with a tuft of pale green or reddish silk, hungry for pollen. Any windblown pollen will stick to the silk, each fertilized strand of which will form a kernel on the sheathed cob. This was nature's way, a casual, careless open pollenization, where an unparticular silk would catch the dust from any of uncounted thousands of tassels.

The corn breeders replaced chance fertilization by controlled fertilization, shielding the cornsilk from all pollens except the one they selected. Their first object was to purify the corn strain, creating an inbred plant; the first step was to cover both tassel and silk and to fertilize it by hand, applying to the silk the pollen shed by the tassels of the same plant. This "selfed" corn, the initial inbred, was unimpressive. It produced gnarled ears and irregular kernels. When these kernels were seeded and the new plant was again "selfed," and the process repeated for several successive seasons, the breeders were purifying a strain which seemed of dubious value. With stunted stalks, runty, twisted ears and crooked rows of kernels, the inbred corn seemed a long step backward; a Corn Belt farmer would have thrown those patiently achieved ears to his hogs while he saved his big shapely ears for seed. But the magic was coming. When two inbred strains were crossed, the pollen from one fertilizing the silk of another, the resulting hybrid was a sound, strong, high-yielding corn. Or it could be. The hybrid might have the virtues of both parents and the defects of neither, or it might have the collective defects with no virtues. In the first case the hybrid was saved for further development; in the second—and much more common—case, it was discarded. In any event the hybrid-corn men were making nature over. Their aim was to eliminate corn's weaknesses and combine its virtues into a superplant which the chance processes of nature could never develop.

After years of inbreeding came the single hybrid corns, and then came the double cross. So the breeders produced a corn into which they gathered the best traits of four pure strains. It sounds simple, but to find the ultimate combination was like searching through a huge corncrib for a single distinctive ear. Thousands of hybrids were worthless, perpetuating the inferior qualities of the parent strains. It required prolonged research to uncover the few great hybrids.

In the 1920's, still unknown to the millions of farmers who were raising corn as generations had done before them, a few men in the experiment stations kept on making new inbreds and crossing and recrossing them into hybrids. They studied their ear-to-row plantings, kept their meticulous records, pondered the performance of new strains in many conditions of soil, climate and moisture, in many infestations of rot, rust and blight, and in contest with grasshoppers, corn borers, rootworms, chinch bugs, ear worms, army worms. They analyzed stalks, cobs and kernels, and while their eyes were on the test tubes and balances, their minds were in the future. They were using the fullness of biological science to create a new plant, a mass of heredity born out of the laws of genetics. Their work went on in scattered places—in a Connecticut Experiment Station, in a Nebraska Experiment Station, in a small corn plot in a Des Moines garden, in laboratories at Ames, Iowa; Champaign, Illinois, and West Lafayette, Indiana; in a test field on Tippecanoe Creek near the Wabash, where a few men won a victory in corn as important as General Harrison's victory over the Shawnee a hundred and ten years earlier.

Look at one place and one man in this campaign for better corn—the Funk Farms near Bloomington, Illinois, and the twenty years' research of J. R. Holbert. In 1913 Jim Holbert, a student at Purdue University, wrote to Gene Funk at Bloomington, asking for a summer job as a farm hand. Funk was a leading corn seedsman with a long family tradition on the Corn Belt prairie. The Funk family had come to the New World from

Bavaria in 1733 in search of political and religious freedom. Ninety years of westward migration took them successively to Pennsylvania, Virginia, Kentucky, Ohio and Illinois, where the journeys ended. Isaac and Absolom Funk were pioneer settlers of central Illinois; they gave their name to Funk's Grove, two thousand acres of dense woodland in McLean County. Two other brothers settled in northern Illinois. For seven years after his arrival Isaac Funk possessed no wagon; he carried corn on horseback fifty miles to Springfield. By 1840 he had a wagon, along with a huge spread of prairie land, but he had decided to walk his corn to market. He bought young cattle from Missouri and Texas, fattened them on his corn and drove the herds a hundred and twenty miles to the stockyards in Chicago. The wagon went along, loaded with feed corn for the eleven days of travel. In 1859 two of Isaac Funk's bulls were taken to a cattle show in Boston. They weighed nearly two tons each and measured fifteen feet from nose to tip of tail. By 1857 Isaac Funk owned 25,000 acres of Illinois land and was selling $65,000 worth of cattle every fall. His descendants improved the strains by selective breeding, a process which led them eventually to scientific grain-breeding and the development of hybrid corn.

To the Funk Farms, already famous for supplying seed to Corn Belt farmers, came young Jim Holbert in 1913. He spent days in the fields, detasseling corn for simple crosses; at night he studied monographs on corn culture and reports on experimental breeding. Gene Funk talked to his young friend, telling him about the long search for better corn, the seedsman's goal of a corn with deeper roots, stronger stalks and greater yield, corn that would resist drought, disease and parasites. Two years later, having completed his college course, Jim Holbert returned to Funk Farms with a plan for a program of corn breeding. Gene Funk had tried inbreeding a decade earlier; the strain got poorer and poorer until he gave it up. But he was willing to support a new attempt. With the confidence of the young, Holbert meant to develop hundreds of hybrids, one of which would be a magic corn bringing together stamina, yield, and resistance to weather damage and disease.

That fall Jim Holbert worked longer than the cornhuskers in McLean County's big fields. From dawn to dark he tramped the withered corn rows, inspecting every stalk and ear of corn in hundreds of acres. Across the field came the thump of the bangboard and farmers ordering their teams *Gee-up—whoa!* through the tattered corn. Other men were husking, Holbert was searching for harvests of the future. By January he had culled from millions of ears of corn two thousand choice specimens. Then he searched through corncribs for ears of exceptional weight and disease-free kernels. By mid-February he had collected five thousand prime ears of corn. For weeks he made painstaking germination tests in small frames of earth in a greenhouse. He discarded 3,000 ears and saved 2,000 to begin inbreeding.

That spring he plowed isolated seeding plots and made 2,000 ear-to-row plantings. In July he tied paper bags onto the tassels, and when the pollen was shed, he inverted the bags of pollen on the silk of the ear shoot on the same stalk. When he harvested his corn in October, he found that barely 1 per cent was better than average open-pollenated corn. Germination tests that winter reduced his superior strain to the corn from just twelve ears.

In the following summer his project seemed ruined when a battering July storm flattened most of his test field. But he carried on, the next year, with corn that had stood up. That, too, was a discouraging summer, with prolonged drought starving his experimental corn. He did not yet realize that these adversities were on his side; by eliminating inferior strains, they were leaving him with the heredity he was seeking.

During the years of the First World War corn acreage was increased and corn diseases were spreading. To combat corn disease the United States Department of Agriculture established field stations in the Corn Belt, one of them being located on the Funk Farms. Here government and academic scientists worked together, and Jim Holbert had the best of counsel. He purified his inbreds and then crossed them into single hybrids. Most of them were worthless, but certain ones proved resistant to chinch bugs, others withstood the corn borer, still others resisted root-pruning insects. He went on, year after year, crossing strains in search of the strongest combination. There were ancient enemies of grain. Two thousand years ago on each twenty-fifth of April the Romans burned sacrifices to Robigus, the rust god, to keep ruin from their fields; now a corn breeder in Illinois was developing a grain impervious to diseases older than history. Finally, in 1925, Holbert made his first double cross, bringing together four inbred lines. The result was a fulfillment of his stubborn dream. In 1929 a writer in *The Country Gentleman* told the world that "The Day of Super Corn-Crops Has Come."

But farmers are by nature conservative. It would take more than some reports from a test field to persuade them to buy seed corn when they had whole cribs full. With little more notice than before, Holbert went on with his hybrids. Then came the drought seasons of the mid-1930's, when the dust of the plowed plains hung like a threat over the Corn Belt and the fields withered in midsummer. In 1936 temperatures in central Illinois rose to 95 degrees on the last day of June, to 102 on July third, then to highs of 110 for an unbroken week. At Bloomington on July fifteenth the thermometer showed 115 degrees. After a month of this furnace heat with no rainfall, crop damage was reported across the Corn Belt. McLean County had no real moisture until the middle of August. Then came a soaking all-night rain, too late to save the fired corn—except for the deep-rooted hybrids, which began an astonishing recovery. That year the average corn yield in McLean County was twenty-five bushels. One of Jim Holbert's fields produced 101.3 bushels an acre.

The next year, 1937, saw the closing of the Federal Field Station at Funk's Farms. The corn men had accomplished their mission—high-yielding hybrids resistant to both drought and disease. Now the strains were developed and demonstrated, and the big seed companies were ready to provide hybrid seed corn to hundreds of thousands of farmers. Holbert remained with the Funk company. As a director of research he traveled from Canada to the Gulf of Mexico, studying the performance of new hybrids which were extending the range of corn and increasing its yield.

The most publicized of the corn breeders was a dirt farmer from El Paso, Illinois, a man derided by his neighbors until he suddenly grew rich and famous. Written about in newspapers and magazines, interviewed on radio and newsreels, he became known afar as the tenant farmer who made a fortune. But the real drama in his life was the development of Pfister's hybrid corn.

Leaving school at the age of thirteen, wiry Lester Pfister worked as a farm hand, planting, plowing and husking corn on Woodford County land that his grandfather had broken with an ox team. He was not content to be a routine farmer. In the early 1920's he began testing strains of open-pollenated corn. Dissatisfied with the results, he tried seed corn from his neighbor George Krug, who every winter sorted over the harvest in his crib to find the heaviest, most solid and disease-free ears, and who had improved his corn by continued selective planting. Starting with 388 ears, Pfister inbred the best plants of Krug corn. Working alone, he used up 100,000 paper bags and made 50,000 hand pollenizations. In five years he was down to a few puny ears inbred so long that their good traits were fixed. Then he began crossing the pure strains. Many were worthless. He let the weaklings die and kept on with the corn that showed promise. After ten years he grew his first double-cross hybrids. Depression brought hardship to his neighbors in the 1930's, but Lester Pfister was already deep in debt. Year after year his farm had been neglected while he tied paper bags on corn tassels and made ear-to-row plantings in his test field. For fifteen years of work all he had to show was a few hundred ears of his own hybrid corn, and they did not have the qualities he was seeking. He was threatened with eviction from his farm, but officials of the St.

Louis Land Bank thought there was promise in his corn breeding and extended his mortgage. Pfister then exchanged hybrids with Jim Holbert at Funk's Farms and produced a new corn—which marched straight and strong across the field, bearing at precisely the same height on each plant big, heavy ears rich in protein, starch and oil. He had produced a great hybrid.

By 1937 Lester Pfister was swamped with orders for seed corn. He licensed other farmers to produce Pfister's hybrid under his supervision. By 1943 he was selling annually a million dollars' worth of seed to Corn Belt farmers. Now he has a Woodford County farm of over a thousand acres, including the land that his grandfather had broken from wild prairie.

For unrecorded centuries seed corn came from the field crop, and until a generation ago farmers picked out superior-looking ears as corn was being shoveled from wagon to crib, or from crib to the feeding pen. Now seed corn is grown in isolated fields, where no stray pollen can invade the selected strain. These fields would puzzle a farmer of the past. They are planted with two rows of one strain to six of another. Tassels are removed from the six adjacent rows—seven thousand tassels to an acre—leaving pollen from the double row to fertilize the silk of the detasseled plants. On the detasseled corn the hybrid seed is grown. Until recently all the work was done by hand. Now the big seed companies have detasseling machines, invented by Lester Pfister, which ride through the field on oversize wheels and mow the stalks at tassel height.

Corn harvesting remained hand labor when most other farm tasks had been mechanized. After tractor-drawn plows, planters, harrows, hay-balers, and reapers had replaced horse-drawn implements, Corn Belt farmers had to keep their horses for corn harvesting. It was man and team together in the frosty season. Inventors failed to develop a corn-picking machine until the hybrids came. Hybrid corn stands upright, all winter long if need be, and it carries its ears at a uniform height on the stalk. Its solid ears do not badly shell and shatter in the rough handling of the machine. So the last team of horses disappeared from hundreds of thousands of farms, and the corn-picker came. Three-quarters of a million of them were in use in 1960. It was the latest step in a progress that had made the American farmer the most efficient food producer in the world.

Corn went to Europe in 1493 and was immediately grown in the royal gardens of Spain. Fifty years later it was growing in all the countries of central Europe, though it did not spread to the northern lands. Thirty years ago in Arvika, Sweden, I saw a single corn plant in the center of a hotel garden. The gardener was proud of it—a spindly stalk four feet tall with a sparse tassel and an ear like popcorn. It was an exotic plant in that far northern place, and the frost would get it soon. Now, if he is still growing corn, the Arvika gardener can have a better specimen. Hybrids have been developed for cooler climates and shorter growing seasons.

Since World War II the Corn Belt miracle has reached around the world. Hybrid corn has become an important crop in Rumania, France, Belgium and Holland. It is becoming established in Greece, Italy, Egypt and other Mediterranean countries. To the American seed companies come inquiries and orders in labored English from every country between Portugal and Indonesia. Henry Wallace has said that the Food and Agriculture Organization of the United Nations, with an expenditure of less than $100,000 on its hybrid corn program in Europe, has increased the value of corn yields by $50,000,000 a year. The success of this program led Khrushchev to introduce hybrid corn into Russia. The new corn has been America's best ambassador abroad.

In the heartland the agronomists and seed men go on searching for better hybrids. The new goal of two hundred bushels an acre is still in the future, but for a farmer who uses proper seed and fertilizer it is now as easy to produce a hundred bushels an acre as fifty. There are no real hazards, since corn breeders can vary the seed to meet changing conditions of climate, insects and disease.

In the past harvesting machinery was adapted to the crop, but now corn can be adapted to machines. Soon American farmers will be using a "corn combine" which picks, husks and shells the corn in a single operation in the field. Then the corncrib will disappear, the rudy-chinned cornhusker will drop back farther into the past, and the Department of Agriculture will be confronted with a bigger mountain of surplus food production. When political science catches up to the corn men, that cornucopia will spill out to hungry peoples. And as the plant breeders' miracle reaches around the world, it carries a hope of sufficiency for the growing populations of men.

23. New Times on the Ohio

From the weedy landing at Warsaw, Kentucky, a putt-putt ferryboat crosses the Ohio River to Indiana. There used to be a sign hung on a pole on the landing: "Ring here for ferry till you get answer. Then give signal. 1 tap for foot passenger, 2 taps for vehicle. Jeff Webb, Mgr." Now you call the pilot by an automobile horn. So progress comes to the Ohio.

Three miles downstream from Warsaw, five hundred and thirty-one miles from Pittsburgh, there is another change. Twelve massive piers of the Markland Dam stride across the river, holding twelve huge electric-powered gates; eventually the dam piers will support a highway bridge that will put the Warsaw ferry out of business. But the dam is really a navigation work, creating a pool of water that reaches upstream to New Richmond, Ohio, ninety-six miles away. Markland Dam is not yet completed, but the locks beside it are in operation. Through the main lock pass barge tows three times as big as a football field, loaded with coal, steel, oil and chemicals. With its thirty-five-foot lift, the Markland lock replaces five outmoded locks between Warsaw and New Richmond.

The Markland project is one of six major navigation works now under construction on the Ohio. It is part of a twenty-year program, to cost a billion dollars, in which nineteen high-lift locks and dams will create a superwaterway over the entire nine hundred and eighty-one miles from Cairo to Pittsburgh.

From the steamer *Criterion* on her way to Cincinnati in February, 1828, Mrs. Frances Trollope admired the changing shores of the Ohio River—the more so after her monotonous journey up the featureless forest-framed Mississippi. "I imagine that this river," she wrote of the Ohio, "presents almost every variety of scenery; sometimes its clear wave waters a meadow of level turf; sometimes it is bounded by perpendicular rocks; pretty dwellings, with their gay porticos are seen, alternately with wild intervals of forest, where the tangled bear-brake plainly enough indicates what inhabitants are native there. Often a mountain torrent comes pouring in silver tribute to the stream, and were there an occasional ruined abbey, or feudal castle, to mix the romance of real life with that of nature, the Ohio would be perfect." Nothing else in America pleased her this much.

If the testy Englishwoman could travel the Ohio today—on the Greene Line's big pleasure packet *Delta Queen*—she would find real life plentifully mixed with that of nature, though she might not use the term romance for the parade of manufacturing plants and smoking chimneys. In the present century the Ohio Valley has become one of the great industrial districts of the world.

The river that Mrs. Trollope knew was a highway into the heartland. It brought explorers and surveyors to the wilderness. It carried the frontier armies in fleets of flatboats—men, horses, wagons, arms, ammunition and supplies—to the border wars with the Indians. Then began the great migration of settlers in the valley and the freighting of their commerce. For a generation after the Revolution the trade was moved in man-powered scows, heavy flatboats floating down the river, keelboats drifting down-stream and laboriously poled against the current. In 1811 the first Western steamboat appeared, and for seventy years the Ohio was churned with paddle wheels. At mid-century the Cincinnati Public Landing saw eight thousand steamboat arrivals every year, an average of one boat an hour, day and night, around the calendar.

Railroads came to the interior in the 1840's, and for a while the steamboat men tried to rival them. Engineers tied down the safety valve and crammed their fires with cordwood. But on the shore, tooting his whistle while he pulled past, the locomotive engineer waved a friendly derisive greeting. New steamboats were built for speed and power and new fast river schedules were advertised. But the race was already won by the iron horse on rails. Railroads were not confined to the serpentine river course; they were not halted by fog and ice, by flood and drought; they made direct runs in all weather.

After the Civil War came a brief revival of river traffic. The expanding 1870's and 1880's brought a surge of population and commerce, and the river had a share. But new railroads were webbing the central states, and steamboats belonged to the past. In 1875, when Mark Twain recalled his river years in the *Atlantic Monthly*, his title was significant: "Old Times on the Mississippi." At the turn of the century the big boats were rotting at the landings, grass grew up in cobblestone levees, cities turned their backs on the river that had given them life. The Ohio was empty and forgotten, rolling between its shores as timeless and unburdened as in the savage past.

It took a world war to rediscover the rivers. With mountains of war goods to be moved, the American railroad system was overwhelmed. Millions of tons of merchandise piled up at the terminals. To break that jam the government turned to the rivers, outfitting old steamboats and barges, integrating local carriers into a system. The newly established Federal Barge Lines moved the war goods, and rediscovered a forgotten principle: water is more efficient than wheels. A mule can pull a one-ton wagon, or a forty-ton canal barge. The rivers were a natural highway, ready to carry vast burdens of commerce. One towboat could do the work of a dozen locomotives, and a barge cost a whole lot less than a string of coal cars.

When the war was over, the rivers were still flowing but the railroad rolling stock was depleted and the roadbeds were in disrepair. The Transportation Act of 1920 kept the government in business on the rivers; it also called for channel improvements and terminal construction. In 1924 the barge lines became a part of the enlarged Inland Waterways Corporation. Its purpose was to open the way for private carriers on the rivers.

Just a hundred years earlier, in 1824, custody of the Ohio and Mississippi had been assigned to the Corps of Engineers of the U.S. Army. At that time the engineers surveyed the river and spent a $75,000 appropriation in pulling snags and submerged trees out of the Ohio channel. In following years they dynamited some ledges and deepened channels that were regularly silted by sand bars. This was the river program for half a century. Then in 1875 the engineers made a thorough survey of the Ohio, projecting sixty-eight dams which would ensure a six-foot depth from Pittsburgh to Cairo. The first dam was built at Davis Island, five miles below Pittsburgh. It immediately stabilized Pittsburgh harbor, providing navigation at all seasons. But with the rapid spread of railroads at the end of the century there was no need to canalize the Ohio. A few dredge boats kept a shallow channel open for the dwindling local traffic.

In the 1920's, with revived river commerce, the 1875 program was dusted off and Congress began substantial appropriations for river improvements. While freight volume on the Ohio grew from 10,000,000 tons in 1923 to nearly 20,000,000 in 1925, the work went on. A great clatter rose at more than forty points on the river. Revised plans called for dams to provide a nine-foot pool of water and locks to accommodate barge tows six hundred feet long. The project was completed in 1929. At Cincinnati President Hoover dedicated a bronze tablet and hundreds of towboat whistles roared up and down the man-made river.

Now, for the first time since its creation, the river was controlled and regulated. The Ohio has generally steep shores, with
a rapid run-off of rain and snow water. People in Cincinnati can
remember floods that filled the lower streets and rose to the roofs
of shops and houses; they can also remember a knee-deep river
when boys waded across to Kentucky. After 1929 floods could
still occur—there was an awesome eighty-foot depth at Cincinnati in 1937—but no one would walk across the river again.

Of the forty-six dams on the Ohio all but four were movable.
Their timber wickets folded, like a cribbed fence, onto the river
bed in times of high water and boats passed over them without
using the locks. When the river was "in pool," boats were lifted
and lowered at the dam in navigation locks. In normal stages of
water the river had been made into forty-six lakes, each beginning and ending at a dam, with a slight westward current.

On this man-made river commerce doubled and redoubled.
Low-cost efficient transportation attracted new industries to the
valley, and the new industries poured an increasing trade into
the river barges.

In 1811 Zadok Cramer, publisher of the annual *The Navigator*,
which was the early riverman's bible, made a prediction:

> "Now the immense forests recede, cultivation smiles along [the
> Ohio's] banks, towns every here and there decorate its shores, and
> it is not extravagant to suppose that the day is not very far distant
> when its whole margin will form one continued village. The reasons
> for this supposition are numerous—the principal ones are, the im-
> mense tracts of fine country that have communication with the Ohio
> by means of the great number of navigable waters that empty into
> it; the extraordinary extent, fertility and beauty of the river bottoms,
> generally high, dry, and with few or no exceptions remarkably
> healthy, and the superior excellence of its navigation, through means
> of which the various productions of the most extensive and fertile
> parts of the United States must eventually be sent to market.

Now the prophecy is fulfilled; to hundreds of terminals in
scores of towns and cities the river carries a massive tonnage of

raw materials. Yet to a traveler on the river the most surprising and exhilarating discovery is shores that are mysterious and wild, as though Indians might be watching from the thickets. Though there are miles of industry on the Ohio, the characteristic river scene is wilderness. Sycamores and willows crowd down to the water, dense islands divide the silent current, timbered hills face green and level bottoms. You remember what Mark Twain said, referring to the Mississippi in Marquette's time: "The river was an awful solitude then. And it is now, over most of its stretch." Even now there is solitude on the rivers.

Then the spell is broken. The next bend brings the new age into view, with its hills of coal beside huge generating plants, its tall-stacked mills producing steel, chemicals, cement, plastics, textiles, ceramics, aluminum, titanium, zirconium, vanadium—things that Zadok Cramer never heard of. The valley has been changing ever since the flatboats steered

> All the way to Shawneetown
> A long time ago.

But the greatest changes are in progress now. Since 1950 fifteen billion dollars have been invested in Ohio Valley industry, and the river is being reshaped to the needs of an ever-growing commerce.

In Zadok Cramer's time no one could see the wealth beneath the valley's surface, or foresee the industrial use of coal, salt, salt brine, limestone and clay. One of the first to comment on the generosity of nature along the Ohio was an unexpected man— Ralph Waldo Emerson, on a philosophic lecture tour of the interior. Emerson, James Russell Lowell said, had a Greek head on Yankee shoulders. The Greek in him saw the beauty of the great valley, the Yankee saw its material promise. In 1851, in a letter to Thomas Carlyle in London, he wrote of the upper Ohio Valley: "Every acre of land has three or four bottoms; first of rich soil; then nine feet of bituminous coal; a little lower, fourteen feet of coal; then iron, or salt; salt springs, with a valuable oil called petroleum floating on their surface. Yet his acre sells for the price of any tillage acre in Massachusetts." Actually, though it was not known in Emerson's time, the upper Ohio runs through a bed of rock salt and coal. Coal men now say that the Pittsburgh Number Eight seam is the river channel. In a two-handed gift to the region, geography provided a route of transport along with the vast Appalachian coal beds.

Coal was just coming into commercial use in the mid-nineteenth century. The pioneer coal shipper on the Ohio was another Yankee, Samuel Pomeroy, who mined it by the bushel; in 1832 he loaded a thousand bushels of coal onto a log raft and sent it down the river. Until the 1850's the town of Pomeroy was the only coal port on the river. But when charcoal forests were depleted, coking coal came into demand for the blast furnaces where local iron ore was converted into pig iron. When that ore was exhausted, a richer iron ore came down the Lakes from Michigan and Minnesota, and the steel industry developed in the Ohio Valley because of its limitless supplies of coal and limestone. So the mills rose on the riverbank, at Pittsburgh, Weirton, Steubenville, Wheeling, Ashland, Portsmouth, Cincinnati and Louisville. The valley's oldest industry, it is still growing. Two billion dollars were spent on expansion of Ohio Valley steel plants in the 1950's.

Since Emerson's observation, the valley's oil, salt and salt brine have come into industrial use. Along with coal these resources have become the basis of a widely various chemical industry. Hundreds of plants now convert them into scores of products, plastics, resins and medicines. These are products of the new technology of the mid-twentieth century, and they have given the Ohio Valley a new vigor and vitality. Meanwhile a still newer development has brought the region onto the verge of tomorrow, making the river, as it was a century and a half ago, a road to the future. The region's newest product is atomic energy.

In the 1950's the Atomic Energy Commission located two gaseous diffusion plants on the river, one at Paducah, Kentucky, and one at Waverly, just above Portsmouth, Ohio. The Waverly plant, operated by the Goodyear Atomic Corporation, comprises three half-mile-long buildings, each one housing ninety thousand instruments for monitoring the production of enriched uranium 235. The mammoth plant at Paducah is run by Union Carbide. A processing plant at Fernald, Ohio, operated by the National Lead Company, refines uranium ore for the Atomic Energy Commission. On the edge of Cincinnati the Evendale plant of the General Electric Corporation operates a Nuclear Propulsion Laboratory where men have developed an atomic aircraft engine—a billion-dollar project that was on the verge of fulfillment when it was declared expendable in the spring of 1961. At Miamisburg, Ohio, in the shadow of a giant Indian mound, are the Mound Laboratories, operated for the Atomic Energy Commission by the Monsanto Chemical Company. In no other district in the world are so many men and machines at work with the atom; and probably nowhere else than in Ross, Ohio, at the mouth of the Miami River, is there an "Atomic Motel."

To meet the requirements of these and other industries, electric power production in the Ohio valley increased from 6.5 per cent of the national total in 1939 to nearly 13 per cent in 1960. Electric generating plants on the Ohio now consume over twenty million tons of coal annually. The low cost of barged coal makes it possible to produce electric energy at one-third less cost than the national average.

Past the power stations, with their multiple stacks as tall as a sixty-story building, move the river tows. A third of them carry coal; a third, oil; and the rest, steel, chemicals, alumina and other cargoes. Though not in a coal-mining district, Cincinnati, midway on the river, has become the largest coal distribution center in the world. Huge tows bring coal from West Virginia and Kentucky, and five Cincinnati railroads haul long lines of gondolas to inland markets and to Great Lakes ports. In recent years an average of forty million tons of coal has been barged on the Ohio. Some of it goes to distant places—to Chicago, Minneapolis,

Alabama, Tennessee, and to river towns in Wisconsin and Minnesota. Coal tows bound downstream meet up-bound tows of oil
—the two great sources of power passing on the river. Millions
of tons of Venezuela crude oil come up the Mississippi to Ohio
Valley refineries. Some of it is used in Ohio Valley steel plants,
whose products move on barges as far as the Gulf of Mexico and
the ports of Texas. Empty flat-top oil barges carry automobiles
at an easy eight miles per hour to cities on the lower Mississippi.
In recent years the glamorous St. Lawrence Seaway, opening the
Great Lakes to ocean commerce, has caught the world's attention. But the unsung Ohio carries three times the tonnage of the
dramatic seaway. This immense water-borne trade has led some
men to predict a new Ohio River–Lake Erie canal which would
link the commerce of the seaway and the river. Engineers are
now studying the cost and the capacity of a rubber belt con-
veyor, stretching from Lake Erie to the Ohio, to carry coal to the
lake and iron ore and limestone to steel mills on the river.

The new river trade is moved by powerful diesel towboats
which push strings of twenty steel barges with twenty thousand
tons of cargo—a load that a whole fleet of the old river packets
could not carry. A deep diesel horn echoes from the hills that
once heard the steam whistle and the pilot's bell, an electric steering lever does the work of the old big pilot wheel. On the towboat radar screens and electric sounding machines have replaced
the old pilot's instinct and the leadsman's cry. It is a loss in pic-
turesqueness (*M-a-r-k three! Quarter less three! Half twain!
Quarter twain! Mark twain!*), but a gain in power, safety and
dependable transportation. The barges are lashed together by
cables ("wires" on the river), chains and ratchets, and the towboat shoves them like a single object around the endless curves
and bends of the river. It is a simple, efficient, economical system,
moving in a single cargo a tonnage that would fill five hundred
freight cars. While barges are left to be unloaded or reloaded, the
towboat moves on. The costly power unit with its operators is
separate from the load-bearers, as the tractor truck on the high-

way is detachable from its trailer van. Parallel techniques are at work on the highways and the river. The towboat-barge combination is as far ahead of the picturesque steamboat as the tractor-trailer is ahead of the Conestoga wagon.

But the river did not change with its changing commerce. A boat entering the Ohio from the Mississippi moves through forty-six successive locks, at average intervals of twenty-one miles, and is lifted up these seven-foot steps on its voyage to Pittsburgh. Every three hours—a diesel's speed is about eight miles an hour—a towboat must pass its barges through the lock alongside the dam. The old locks are six hundred feet long, too small for the larger tows. The tow must then be divided, prodded through the lock, and reassembled. Traffic piles up at the busiest locks and transport is delayed by the frequent barriers. Today's commerce has outgrown the facilities provided forty years ago.

A dramatic new Ohio River is now in prospect, after a decade of careful planning. By 1950 it was evident that a new waterway was needed—a river with fewer and higher-lift dams, with larger locks, with deeper channel. One of nature's gifts to the valley was the deep-cut river course. In its 981 miles the Ohio falls 427 feet—a slight grade compared, for example, to that of the Miami River, which falls 600 feet in 160 miles. A new system of dams projected by the Corps of Engineers will climb 427 feet with 19 high-lift dams. There will then be much longer intervals, averaging fifty-two miles, between the locks. The locks will be 1,200 feet long, large enough to take the biggest tows. The new dams will ultimately provide a minimum depth of 12 feet, allowing a third more cargo in each barge and permitting the operation of bigger, more powerful towboats. It is estimated that these improvements will reduce the cost of barge traffic by 50 per cent, thus lowering the cost of electric power and of hundreds of industrial products.

Since 1953 the U.S. Congress has appropriated nearly two hundred million dollars for the new river, a substantial start on a replacement program that will cost a billion dollars. The nineteen projected high-lift dams, beginning at Cairo and ending at Pittsburgh, are Mound City, Dog Island, Uniontown, Newburg, Cannelton, McAlpine, Markland, New Richmond, Greenup, Gallipolis, Racine, Belleville, Willow Island, Opossum Creek, Pike Island, New Cumberland, Montgomery Island, Dashields, and Elmsworth. Some of these names are echoes from the old wilderness river, but each one will be a link in a modern waterway that carries more tonnage than the Panama Canal. The first appropriations put men and machines to work on the Greenup dam, just below the industrial concentration of Huntington, Ashland and Ironton, and on the New Cumberland dam, just above Steubenville. Other starts have been made at Louisville, Markland, Pike Island and New Richmond—where the dam has recently been renamed for Captain Anthony Meldahl, an old-time riverman whose contemporaries knew him as "Captain Tony." Completion of these works, scheduled for 1962, will provide deep water and long pools throughout the entire central reach of the river. In nearly four hundred miles, from below Louisville to the upper pool of Gallipolis dam, the big tows will pass through four commodious locks in place of the thirteen obsolete locks beside the old low-lift dams. This is the busiest part of the Ohio, on which passes the greatest river-borne tonnage in the world. It is expected that the entire project will be completed by 1980. Then the Ohio will be a superwaterway, with free-moving traffic like that on the new overland throughways. On this new river a ton of cargo will be moved the thousand miles from Pittsburgh to Cairo at the cost of moving it twenty miles by road or rail.

As hundreds of millions of dollars go into river improvements, a controversy grows: Should there be tolls on river transport? The railroads, hard-pressed by competition from air, highway and river, argue that barge traffic should help pay the cost of river works. The opposition refers to the historic Ordinance of 1787 regarding the settlement of the Northwest Territory: "The navigable rivers leading into the Mississippi and St. Lawrence, and carrying places between the same, shall be common water-ways, and forever free, as well to the inhabitants of the said territory as to the citizens of the United States, and those of any other states that may be admitted into the Confederacy without any taxing, impost, or duty therefor." It further argues that cheaply delivered coal produces low-cost electricity, which in turn generates industrial production resulting in business for the region's railroads—business that would not exist except for the low-cost transportation on a free waterway. The coal reserves of the valley are enormous—a century of mining has hardly dented the vast Appalachian coal beds—and low-cost coal is the key to the region's industrial growth. The imposing of river tolls, many industrialists declare, would halt the progress of the valley's economy.

River frontage was once sought by farmers who wanted a view of the frontier's great highway and their own flatboat landing. Now river sites are sought by an increasing number of industrial companies. Recently the Upper Ohio Development Council has taken large groups of businessmen on air and boat trips over 130 miles of the river between Marietta and East Liverpool, Ohio. They saw 20,000 acres of level river-front locations, ranging from 20 to 8,000 acres, sites where future industries can draw upon the valley's resources of water, coal, salt and a plentiful supply of labor. Meanwhile new chemical plants are spreading on the upper river, just above the huge complex of chemical industry on the Kanawha, and in the first railroad construction in half a century the Pennsylvania Railroad plans a new line along the river north from Marietta. Aluminum, the newest industry on the Ohio, is attracted by the economy of river transportation and the low cost of electric power, as well as by nearness to the aluminum-consuming market. Three giant smelters, at Ravenswood, West Virginia, Clarington, Ohio, and Evansville, Indiana, are now under construction. They will have capacity to produce one fourth of the nation's aluminum.

At many points, along Blennerhassett Island below Marietta, or between Point Pleasant and Gallipolis, or around the big bend beyond Madison, the river dreams and drowses between serene green shores. But soon comes the deep, deliberate throbbing of diesels and the big tows pass—acres of coal, oil, steel, limestone, sulphur, gravel. From the lofty windows of the Ohio Valley Improvement Association in the Carew Tower in Cincinnati you do not hear the throbbing but you see the long tows creeping around the great arc of the river. Sometimes four or five are in sight at once, with a hundred thousand tons of cargo on the move.

Around and past the ponderous tows race the pleasure craft. In the Cincinnati area there are twenty-eight thousand outboard motorboats and several thousand inboards. Now the Ohio is a clean stream; after years of contaminating the river, the valley cities have built waste disposal systems, and in pool stage the river runs clear. Recreation flourishes like industry on the improved river.

A generation ago the valley cities had forgotten the river except in calamitous times of flood. On the weedy bank rose the flood wall—these are the only walled cities in the New World—a haunt of old men, vagrants, a few shanty-boat people, fishermen and boys. But a change came after World War II. In a dramatic renewal project Pittsburgh made a gleaming new recreational and commercial district on the historic "point" where the Allegheny and Monongahela rivers join to form the Ohio. Downstream, other cities and towns rediscovered the river. With new inland reservoirs and conservancy districts retaining water in the tributary valleys, the flood danger diminished. The clean, clear modern river could be enjoyed by its people.

In pioneer Cincinnati, Fort Washington, like everything else in the burgeoning Queen City, faced the river. There Anthony Wayne assembled his troops and marched northward to secure the heartland for an American future. But Fort Washington was razed long ago, and the city climbed up to the level bench of land between the river and the hills. The lower streets became slums. Here Lafcadio Hearn wandered through Rat Row and

Sausage Row, and in the Bucktown taverns Stephen Foster heard the wild songs of the rivermen. By the end of the century the lower streets were abandoned to lofts, warehouses and wholesale markets. Fifty years later the grim old buildings were replaced by the spacious Fort Washington Way, with its complex of green-bordered freeways.

Now the Cincinnati riverfront is partly old and partly new. Near the new Kosmos Cement Works is the old Cincinnati Hay and Grain Company, which once supplied the livery stables of Second Street. Its dim entry is banked like a barn with bales of hay and straw; bagged oats and corn are piled to the roof. No one seems to do business there except the sparrows pecking at cracked corn on the sidewalk. CINCINNATI INSURANCE Co. is carved in granite over a doorway that leads to a storeroom piled with fruit crates and vegetable baskets. On the long steep cobbled levee acres of automobiles are parked, slanting in the sun. The levee leads down to a wharf shed labeled GREENE LINE STEAMERS. This is the home berth of the *Delta Queen*, the last pleasure packet left on the river; the *Queen* makes annual excursions to New Orleans and St. Paul and numerous week-long trips on the Ohio and the Tennessee. Beside the big *Delta Queen* are Johnston's *Party Boat* and the smaller Johnston's *Veranda*, ready for charter at any time. The Valley Yacht Club is nearby, directly across from the few old houses that recall the gracious past of Covington.

At the corner of Front Street and Broadway, once the center of Cincinnati, the old buildings have been replaced by a green river-front park. It lies directly opposite the mouth of the Licking and was the site of the tiny settlement which a schoolmaster-surveyor named: *L* for "Licking"; *os* for "mouth"; *anti*, "across"; *ville*, "city"—linking Latin, Greek and French syllables into Losantiville, which name Governor St. Clair changed to Cincinnati when he arrived in 1790. The first party of twenty-six settlers had landed here, beaching their boats in the shelter of Yeatman's Cove. Now Yeatman's Cove Park is a pleasant place between the swift motor traffic of the Fort Washington Way and the ponderous towboat commerce on the river.

A rediscovery of the river points to the future and also to the past. The historic Yeatman's Cove was long forgotten until the Cincinnati Park Board reclaimed the memory of the first landing of settlers in the middle Ohio Valley. Now the Cincinnati Planning Commission proposes to extend the memorial park to include the Public Landing and thirty-five acres along the river and to erect a replica of Fort Washington and a transportation museum. This will be a meaningful redemption of the river front, recalling for future generations one of the great stories of the American past.

24. The Fourth Seacoast

In the shortening days of November, 1959, twenty-six ocean freighters loaded cargo in Chicago harbor. The winches worked overtime, rattling under cluster lights while the night wind sharpened. Below decks the engineers had steam building in the boilers and on the bridge the captains studied navigation charts and weather maps. The twenty-six captains spoke nine different languages, but they all had the same worry. They wanted to reach salt water before the freeze-up in the St. Lawrence. It was the end of the first season of the Great Lakes–St. Lawrence Seaway, which had opened the heartland to the commerce of the world.

Once the soldiers of Fort Dearborn had watched the empty lake for the yearly schooner from Detroit and Mackinac. Now Chicago cargoes were loading for Sweden, Holland, Scotland, Argentina and Japan. After four years of blasting and dredging, of building dams, gates and navigation canals, the Lakes were unlocked. An eighth sea had been added to the earth's geography, and a fourth seacoast to the United States.

Beside the Chicago Art Institute on Michigan Avenue stands a sculptured fountain designed by Lorado Taft. Wretchedly placed, between the avenue traffic and the walled and sunken railroad tracks, it is almost out of sight of people who might admire it and of the water it symbolizes. It is the Fountain of the Great Lakes, representing them as five sisters who proudly hold their vessels of flowing water. Above the rest stands Lake Superior, pouring a crystal stream into the shell of Huron. Michigan stands beside her, the two receiving the falling water and sending it on to the gentle figure of Erie, who stoops to fill the shell of Ontario. This last sister is half turned from the others. She looks away, with hand lifted; her currents do not belong to the interior but flow toward the St. Lawrence and the tidal ocean.

The fountain suggests a profile of the Great Lakes, the vast basins spilling over, one into another, their outflow dropping six hundred feet to sea level in the St. Lawrence. At points in this long waterway there is the roar of falling water. It sounds at Sault Ste. Marie, at Niagara, and at the Long Sault of the St. Lawrence beyond the mouth of Lake Ontario. In the twentieth century each of these places has become a site of hydroelectric power, with the rushing water harnessed to generating turbines. The Great Lakes contain half the fresh water in the world, enough to cover the entire United States to a depth of fifteen feet. Through the St. Lawrence sweeps the outflow from the heartland, water pouring past the Long Sault at an average rate of 240,000 cubic feet a second. *Tick-tock*—and a quarter of a million feet of water has surged on toward the sea. This is the power aspect of the Seaway, the harnessing of a tremendous energy that had gone unused for ages.

The sites of hydroelectric power were obstacles to navigation. Until the mid-nineteenth century Lake Superior was cut off from the lower lakes by the mile-long rapids of the St. Mary's River. The first canal was opened there in 1855. Since then navigation works at the Soo have been repeatedly enlarged, while more than three billion tons of iron ore have been shipped down the lakes to steel plants in the heartland. Niagara Falls, the barrier between Lake Erie and Lake Ontario, was by-passed by the Welland Canal, repeatedly enlarged by its Canadian builders. Canada also built a 115-mile system of canals and locks along the St. Lawrence rapids. For many years these Canadian canals, with a 14-foot channel and 270-foot locks, carried a commerce of small vessels. A 27-foot channel and giant locks, large enough for ocean liners, are now provided by the dramatic seaway.

By a generous gift of geography the Lakes offered a transporation route in the midst of huge natural resources. The northern shores were ringed in timber. For fifty years fleets of white-sailed schooners delivered building lumber to erect cities, to pave the first plank roads, to lay the railroad beds, to build the farmhouses and the big square barns on the prairies. Other vessels carried copper from the rich mines of Lake Superior, limestone from the quarries on Lake Huron and Lake Erie, oil from the wells of Pennsylvania.

But the greatest cargoes were iron. At the beginning of the age of steel, when some men were still fevered by the search for gold and silver in the western mountains, Andrew Carnegie made a quiet comment: "Gold is precious, but iron is priceless." Iron ore was being imported to the United States from Sweden in 1845 when a surveying crew on the rough south shore of Lake Superior found their compass needle swinging wildly. They lost their bearings for a time, but they found the first iron outcrop that led to the rich deposits of the Marquette range. Soon prospectors came into those old blunted hills. They built stone ovens and burned the northwoods maple to make charcoal. They set up small forges and fused the ore and manufactured iron in that wilderness. With a six-horse team they hauled it twelve rough miles to the port of Marquette. They shipped their iron to the Soo, portaged it around the falls, reloaded it into vessels for Lake Erie. It was a slow, arduous and costly business. So the pioneer iron men concluded they must ship raw ore to the lower Lakes, where coal was plentiful and the market for finished iron was at hand. Their conclusion was in line with history. In half a century that became the largest single commerce in the world.

So in 1853 they shipped the first iron ore, in barrels, across Lake Superior. There was no open waterway, but commerce could not wait. They portaged it in creaking wagons around the St. Mary's rapids. They reloaded it in wind-borne schooners for the port of Cleveland. When it arrived there, men stared curiously at the rusty red rock that was so much heavier than granite. Inevitably the Soo canal was opened, and on an August day in 1855 the brig *Columbia*, with her sails slack from the yardarms, passed through the locks. On her deck she carried, in little mounds like refuse, 132 tons of red iron ore. It was the first bulk shipment of iron ore down the Lakes. In 1943, less than a century later, 80,000,000 tons of iron ore passed through the great new locks of the canal.

That lake-shipped ore went into railroad tracks and locomotives. It went into harvesting machines and barbed-wire fences. It went into bridges and the hulls of steamships. It was strung across the continent on telegraph poles. It went into motorcars and airplanes. It went into axes, saws, and hammers, into bolts, nails and hinges, into razor blades and hairpins, into the girders of skyscrapers and the armor plate of dreadnoughts. As the demand for iron ore grew greater, new sources of supply were uncovered. Lake Superior was found ringed in iron hills. The Marquette range, the Menominee, the Gogebic, the Vermilion, finally the giant range Mesabi—with its vast ore bodies lying just underneath the ground—poured out their age-old ores to build America.

The seaway is new, but Lakes commerce has gone to sea for more than a century. In 1844 the brigantine *Pacific*, with Ohio wheat heaped in her hold, made sail off the Cleveland breakwater and set her course for Liverpool. In 1847 the schooner *New Brunswick* sailed from Chicago to Liverpool laden with 18,000 bushels of wheat. During the gold fever of 1849 the barque

Eureka sailed from Cleveland out the St. Lawrence and around Cape Horn to California; she carried fifty-nine passengers to the excitement of the Sierras. In 1850 the first Lakes steamship reached salt water; the propeller *Ontario* made the long run from Buffalo to San Francisco. In 1854 a Norwegian-American lake captain sailed his brig *Scott* from Lake Michigan to his native town of Stavanger, Norway. Two years later the schooner *Dean Richmond* delivered Chicago wheat in Liverpool after a seventy-seven-day voyage. In 1857 the first European vessel, the English brigantine *Madeira Pet*, sailed into the Great Lakes with a cargo of iron, glass, paint and earthenware. The *Pet* loaded hides in Chicago and barrel staves in Detroit for delivery in Liverpool. Her cook and four seamen had deserted in Detroit and Chicago, but her voyage was celebrated on both sides of the Atlantic. The *Chicago Magazine* saw the safe arrival of the *Madeira Pet* as the inauguration of a European commerce to the Prairie State of Illinois.

In 1859 forty-nine vessels cleared the Lakes for foreign ports, and in 1860 there were nearly as many bound down the St. Lawrence and across the Atlantic. Then the Civil War halted the foreign trade, which would not revive until the twentieth century. After the war the growing lake traffic in lumber, limestone and iron ore kept the lake fleets at home. With this enlarged trade ships grew beyond the dimensions of the St. Lawrence canals, and the sea route was all but forgotten.

The turn of the century brought a new interest in Lakes-to-ocean shipping. In 1901 some Chicago grain merchants built five small steamers to the scale of the Canadian canals and sent cargoes of wheat direct to northern Europe. Their ships were too small for a profitable trade and the venture was not repeated. But Midwestern farmers and merchants began to urge construction of an enlarged seaway.

For fifty years the talk went on. Wheat growers declared that by direct shipment grain could be delivered to European ports as cheaply as to New York and Boston. Wisconsin paper men argued the need of economical imports of pulp and pulpwood. Manufacturers saw an increased export of farm machinery by direct shipment to Europe. New canals around the St. Lawrence rapids, an enlarging of the Welland Canal and dredging of the rivers that link the Great Lakes would bring the Atlantic fifteen hundred miles inland.

Meanwhile a foreign trade was squeezing through the old St. Lawrence canals. In the 1920's small freighters from England, Holland, Denmark, Norway and Sweden became familiar in Great Lakes harbors. In 1930 Canada built the new Welland Canal—the fourth enlargement of this waterway—with tiered locks carrying thirty feet of water on the sills, and Lake Ontario was open to the biggest vessels on the Lakes. Proponents of the seaway pressed for a joint U.S.–Canadian construction of controlling dams on the St. Lawrence and a series of deep-draft navigation locks and canals.

Opposition came from the Eastern railroads, shipping and harbor interests on the East Coast, and Great Lakes shipping companies that did not like the prospect of fleets of foreign vessels in their home waters. It was a confusing argument, with a welter of statistics supporting contradictory theories of a seaway's effect upon domestic and foreign trade. One view saw Boston's docks deserted while foreign rubber, wool and pulpwood were unloaded in Great Lakes ports; the other view pictured a boom for Boston, with New England shoes, machinery, fish and leather products going from Boston to the interior by way of the St. Lawrence. The same divergent views foresaw Buffalo languishing after a lost grain trade or gaining new activity in the production of steel, chemicals and metal alloys.

No doubt the argument would be sounding now had not a new situation developed in the steel industry. During World War II massive quantities of iron ore were shipped to the Midwest blast furnaces. Under the assault of war production great ore beds were depleted. Even in the huge Mesabi pits steam shovels began biting bottom. Seeing that the old direct-shipping ores were running out, mining companies began upgrading lean ores and pelletizing the iron content of taconite rock. But these measures could not supply all the needs of the enlarging mills. For the first time the American steel industry began looking for foreign ores.

High-grade ores were uncovered in Chile, Peru, Brazil and Liberia. But a dependence on these sources would compel the steel industry to move from its traditional Midwest center— Pittsburgh, Youngstown, Cleveland, Toledo, South Chicago— to coastal districts, so as to avoid the expensive rail-haul of raw materials. For a time it seemed that the Midwest steel industry had no future.

Then came reports of iron ore in Labrador, huge formations just beneath the frozen muskeg, near the mouth of the St. Lawrence River. Said one mining geologist after his first Labrador exploration, "I have looked at the new Mesabi."

Drilling crews went into the Labrador bush. Engineers projected mining sites, railroads and a big shipping dock at Seven Islands on the Gulf of the St. Lawrence. At the same time powerful new voices urged construction of a seaway which would assure the future of the Midwest steel industry. It was estimated that iron ore from Labrador would become 30 per cent of the future seaway traffic.

Early in 1954 Congress enacted legislation providing for joint construction with Canada of navigational and hydroelectric power works on the St. Lawrence, and on a summer morning a few months later the first dynamite rumbled above the ancient roaring of the rapids. Plans called for a channel 192 miles long and 27 feet deep, including 45 miles of canals and seven high-lift locks. In four and a half years the work was completed.

On April 25, 1959, the seaway was open. The first ocean vessel to pass through was the Dutch freighter *Prins Wilhelm George Frederick*. Dressed in all her pennants, with a fresh gray hull and cream superstructure, she steamed past Montreal and into the canal alongside the main stream of the St. Lawrence. A mile farther, with the engine room telegraph at "Dead Slow," she crept into the St. Lambert lock, leaving a smear of gray paint on the approach wall. The currents were hard to judge. The first American ship through was the Grace Line steamer *Santa Rosa*, inaugurating a general cargo trade between the Great Lakes and South America. At the formal opening on June 26 President Eisenhower of the United States joined Queen Elizabeth II of Canada on the royal yacht *Britannia*. As the *Britannia* steamed through the navigation channels, guns, sirens, trumpets and the bells of three hundred churches sounded over the St. Lawrence. During June and July a squadron of twenty-eight ships of the U.S. Navy, led by the heavy cruiser *Macon*, entered the seaway and voyaged on all the Great Lakes. The inland waters, spacious and irregular like a New World Mediterranean, reached halfway across the continent.

In this first season twenty million tons of cargo passed through the seaway. Nearly a third of it was iron ore from Labrador; another third was wheat and other grains exported from Canada and the United States. Coal, petroleum products, pulpwood and general cargo made up the rest. The trade was carried in the ships of seventeen countries.

Despite the flag-decked vessels, the booming of cannon and the ceremonial speeches, there was trouble on the seaway. Pilots ran ships aground in channels they had not had time to learn. Lock men blundered, and bewildered captains cursed them in a dozen different tongues. Salt-water ships smashed navigation lights, lost their bearings and anchored in midstream, creating a new hazard for themselves and everyone else. Traffic piled up at the Welland Canal. At one time ninety ships were lined up at the approaches; some waited fifty hours for passage through. These delays were especially irksome for lake captains and expensive for their companies; delay is more costly on an American ship, where ordinary seamen are paid $400 a month, than on a British steamer under the Liberian flag, with Chinese seamen drawing fifty cents a day.

With the seaway a new term came to the inland Lakes.

"Salties" were ocean-going ships, most of them under foreign flags, and they looked like intruders to the crews of lake vessels from Cleveland and Chicago. The "lakers" knew the traffic rules and the channel lights. They were accustomed to quick passage through the canals and prompt despatch from their terminals. Now the blundering salties were in the way. They ran aground in the Detroit and St. Clair rivers. They collided with lake freighters and with each other. They made the lake lanes hazardous. The German S.S. *Betelgeuse*, with a cargo of beans for England and scrap iron for Italy, rammed the new bridge at Bay City on Lake Huron and then went aground in the Saginaw River. On the way to Detroit for a Coast Guard inquiry she collided with the Canadian freighter *Algoosa* near Corsica Shoal. The Greek *Polaris* collided with the Swedish *Torsholm* in the St. Lawrence, and a few weeks later struck a railroad bridge at Manitowoc, Wisconsin. The damage halted railroad traffic, but the *Polaris* kept going. Her captain was anxious to get back to the comfort of salt water. More than a few "salties" were dented and scarred when they steamed out the St. Lawrence.

The first season was the hardest. Since then the seaway pilots have learned the channels and lock-tenders have mastered their machinery; salt-water ships have come equipped with tension winches, controllable pitch propellers and stern anchors for maneuvering in the canals. New navigation markers and lock-gate fenders have been installed. New mooring walls and improved lock controls in the Welland Canal have eased that bottleneck. The second season brought increased tonnage through the canal in fewer ships. The trend toward larger vessels, both domestic and foreign, will continue.

An unseen but essential part of the seaway is the deepening of connecting channels in the Great Lakes and of the inland harbors. The new 27-foot channel opens the way for bigger freighters at little increase in running costs. From the Lakes shipyards has come a new class of freighters 730 feet long with cargo capacity of 25,000 tons. At the same time foreign shipbuilders are designing vessels for the seaway trade. The Fjell-Oranje Line of Rotterdam has already put into service two big combination freight-passenger ships which carry a hundred tourists between Europe and the American Midwest. These are the first ocean liners to sail on regular schedule through the Detroit River, under the long Mackinac Straits Bridge and into Chicago harbor. There will be more liners by the year 1968, when the trade is to reach the seaway's capacity of 50,000,000 tons.

Some ships have locked through the seaway on a one-way passage. The steamer *Monrovia* from Liberia ran aground and sank in Lake Huron. Another Liberian freighter, *Francisco Marizan*, piled up on a reef off the south coast of South Manitou Island in Lake Michigan. Her crew was saved by the Coast Guard, but the ship was a total loss. After plodding past the Detroit skyline, the rusty Greek freighter *Theodoras A* was halted by a U.S. Marshal in Lake St. Clair and seized for debt. The crew abandoned her there and the ship was sold to the Lorain Sand and Gravel Company. The steamer *Hemlock* of the Interlake Steamship Company, after half a century in the iron-ore trade, was towed down the St. Lawrence across the Atlantic and through the Mediterranean. Her destination was a scrap yard in Genoa. Another Lakes veteran, the *Calumet*, was loaded with scrap iron and towed to a breaking yard in England. In November, 1960, the Dutch ocean-going tug *Zealand* towed the old lake freighter *Harry R. Jones* to Europe for dismantling. The *Jones*, loaded with scrap iron, joined her cargo on the scrap pile.

For the handling of grain, coal and iron ore the lake ports have the most efficient machinery in the world. But seventeen-ton electric shovels cannot handle Scotch whisky and Ceylon tea. The seaway trade requires new docks and terminals, as a new commerce comes into the iron and coal ports. Ashtabula Harbor, midway along the Ohio shore of Lake Erie, is the greatest bulk tonnage port on the lakes. When the big ore freighters steered in, in the spring of 1960, they found two new piers and a freight storage warehouse ready to handle mixed cargo from abroad.

New dock facilities were under way in Erie, Conneaut, Fairport and Lorain. Milwaukee had a spacious new pier and outer harbor terminal. In Chicago new cargo machinery was installed in the great Navy Pier and a big ocean ship terminal was taking shape along dredged channels in Lake Calumet on the southern edge of the city.

By 1960 the port of Cleveland had doubled its capacity for foreign cargo and big new terminals were operating in Toledo. Into these Lake Erie harbors came ships from many countries. In their holds were Italian marble, Swedish glassware, Dutch nails, Spanish olives, Italian anchovies, French wine, Brazilian coffee, chrome ore from Norway, cheese from Portugal, apricots from Spain, twine from Holland, lacquered trays and boxes from Japan. When their cargo was discharged, they began loading the products of the heartland's fields and factories; flour for Egypt, lard for Italy, soybeans for Turkey, home freezers for Brazil, frozen turkeys for Holland, trucks for Burma, steel bridge girders for Iran. While the Malayan *Pindar* was unloading a first shipment of crude rubber from Singapore, the British *Manchester Pioneer* took on a hundred thousand gallons of latex for the manufacture of foam-rubber products in England. At the same time the Finnish *Peter* was loading sheet steel for London and the Swedish *Laholm* was putting hatch covers on a cargo of glass building blocks for delivery in Malmo.

Winter is a seaway problem. The eight-month navigation season leaves lake crews and vessels idle for a third of the year; it creates traffic jams each spring and fall, and it compels the movement of cargo by land when the channels are locked in ice. Officials in Cleveland and Toledo are talking of a free port where merchandise of all nations could be stored, assembled and processed without payment of duties and taxes. A free zone at one or more lake ports would create a reservoir of cargo to counteract the seasonal activity of the seaway. There is also talk of keeping the seaway open all winter. The open stretches of the Lakes do not freeze over, and the connecting channels might be kept ice-free by means of surmerged air lines which would force the warm water upward. A more immediate measure is to extend the navigation season by using ice-breakers and ice-diversion jetties.

In September, 1960, the Georgian Bay Line's S.S. *South American,* long familiar on the upper Lakes, carried 359 passengers through the Welland Canal, over Lake Ontario and through the seven locks of the seaway to Montreal and Quebec. It was the first time a Great Lakes passenger ship had sailed to tidewater. But these were not the first tourists through the seaway. Scheduled passenger service between inland ports and Europe has used the seaway since its opening, and each year more freighters carry passengers to far parts of the world. The gangway at Chicago leads to Italy, Argentina and Japan. With the seaway's commerce Midwestern isolation has gone beyond recall.

The marine news in the Lakes cities lists the ships up-bound and down-bound on the lakes, ships named for the officials of the steel corporations. Now, along with *Samuel Mather, Arthur B. Homer, Charles M. Schwab* and *Edward L. Ryerson* from Duluth, Chicago and Buffalo are the *Maria Louisa* from Helsinki, the *Tsuneshima Maru* from Yokohama, the big new *Solvikin* from Oslo, the *Akash* from Calcutta, the *Vares* from Trieste, the *Roonagh Head* from Glasgow, the *Van Yung* from Formosa. Over the waters that La Salle and Tonty paddled come ships from all the world.

On the steamship *Inverness* from Glasgow a young ship's officer stands on the bridge wing, watching the shoreline pass. He sees a restless, youthful country, without ruins or antiquities, with few signs of any past. Civilization came here with a rush; there are still remnants of wilderness along the shores. It is clear that this land has been good to its people. It gave them a dependable climate, invigorating but not severe, with ample moisture and a long growing season, and a rich soil that would produce more than its people could consume or market. Beneath the soil were minerals and fuels, the making of many industries. In the harbors grain spills out of huge storage bins, factories overflow with goods, warehouses bulge with merchandise. Here for the first time in history a people contend with overproduction. The problems of this region are not hunger and want; its problems are riches.

Ashore the seaman from Glasgow finds streets choked with motor traffic, multilane highways slicing through industrial districts, suburbs spreading into the countryside. There is a frequent saying here, "Take it easy"; but no folk phrase could be more contradicted by its people. Change obscures continuity in this restless region. It is a land grown populous and prosperous and still unsatisfied. "I tell you the past is a bucket of ashes," said one of its poets. Tomorrow is another day.

Bibliography

The historical literature of the three states north of the Ohio River is varied and extensive. Works of large scope are the six-volume *History of Ohio*, edited by Carl Wittke (Columbus, 1941–1944); the two-volume *History of Indiana*, by Logan Esary (Ft. Wayne, 1924); and the ten-volume *Centennial History of Illinois* (Springfield, 1917–1920). More concise but general works are *A History of Ohio*, by Eugene F. Roseboom and Francis P. Weisenberger (Columbus, 1953); *Historic Indiana*, by Julia Henderson Levering (New York, 1916); and *The Story of Illinois*, by Theodore Calvin Pease (Chicago, 1925). R. C. Buley's two-volume *The Old Northwest* treats the region between the Ohio River and the Great Lakes during the frontier period. Detailed source material appears in the *Indiana Historical Collections*, 39 vols. (Indianapolis, 1916–1959), and the *Illinois Historical Collections*, 32 vols. (Springfield, 1903–1945), and the 70 vols. of Ohio Archaeological and Historical Society publications. Henry Howe's *Historical Collections of Ohio* (Cincinnati, 1847), revised and enlarged to two volumes (Columbus, 1889–1891), contains first-hand observations and reports of many localities in Ohio. These general works have been consulted countless times, along with the more specific works indicated by chapters.

CHAPTER 2   PRAIRIE GIBRALTAR

LEGLER, HENRY E., *Chevalier Henri de Tonty*. Parkman Club Publication, No. 3 (1896).
MURPHY, EDMUND ROBERT, *Henry de Tonty*. Baltimore, 1941.
PARKMAN, FRANCIS, *LaSalle and the Discovery of the Great West*. Boston, 1869.
KELLOGG, LOUISE PHELPS, *Early Narratives of the Northwest, 1634–1699*. New York, 1917. Contains Tonty's Narrative and Hennepin's Narrative, and the "De Gannes Memoir." The memoir, clearly the work of Tonty's cousin Desliette, offers the best account of the Illinois country and the Illinois Indians.
Illinois Historical Collections, Vol. XXIII.
Michigan Historical Collections, Vol. XXXIII.

CHAPTER 3   THE SMOLDERING FIRES

DARLINGTON, W. M., ed., *Christopher Gist's Journals*. Pittsburgh, 1893.
DOWNES, RANDOLPH G., *Council Fires on the Upper Ohio*. Pittsburgh, 1940.
HANNA, CHARLES A., *The Wilderness Trail*, 2 vols. New York, 1911.
LAMBING, A. A., ed., *Céloron's Journal*. In *Ohio Archaeological and Historical Publications*, Vol. 29 (1920).
PARKMAN, FRANCIS, *Conspiracy of Pontiac*, 2 vols. Boston, 1883.
PECKHAM, HOWARD H., *Pontiac and the Indian Uprising*. Princeton, 1947.
THWAITES, REUBEN GOLD, *Early Western Travels*, Vol. 1. Cleveland, 1904.
———, *Jesuit Relations*, Vol. 69. Cleveland, 1896.
WAINWRIGHT, NICHOLAS B., *George Croghan: Wilderness Diplomat*. Chapel Hill, 1959.

CHAPTER 4   A PRIEST AND A COMMANDER

BAKELESS, JOHN, *Background to Glory*. Philadelphia, 1957.
ENGLISH, WILLIAM HAYDEN, *Conquest of the Northwest, 1778–1783, and Life of George Rogers Clark*, 2 vols. Indianapolis, 1896.

Illinois Historical Collections, Vol. VII. *George Rogers Clark Papers*. Springfield, 1912.
KENTON, EDNA, *Simon Kenton*. Garden City, 1930.
LAW, JUDGE [JOHN], *The Colonial History of Vincennes*. Vincennes, 1858.
Transactions of the Illinois Historical Society, 1905. Springfield, 1906.

CHAPTER 5   THE BIG LAND OF LITTLE TURTLE

BOND, BEVERLY W., JR., *The Foundations of Ohio*. Columbus, 1941.
DOWNES, RANDOLPH C., *Council Fires on the Upper Ohio*. Pittsburgh, 1940.
GILPIN, ALEC R., *The War of 1812 in the Old Northwest*. East Lansing, Mich., 1958.
HILL, LEONARD U., *John Johnston and the Indians*. Piqua, Ohio, 1957.
McDONALD, JOHN, *Biographical Sketches*. Cincinnati, 1838.
OGG, FREDERICK A., *The Old Northwest*. New Haven, 1919.
YOUNG, CALVIN, *Little Turtle, the Great Chief of the Miami Nation*. Greenville, Ohio, 1917.

CHAPTER 6   ESCHICAGAU—THE LONELY STATION

CURREY, J. SEYMOUR, *The Story of Old Fort Dearborn*. Chicago, 1912.
GILPIN, ALEC R., *The War of 1812 in the Old Northwest*. East Lansing, Mich., 1958.
KINZIE, JULIETTE, *Wau-bun, The "Early Day" in the Northwest*. New York, 1856.
PRUCHA, FRANCIS PAUL, *Broadax and Bayonet: The Role of the United States Army in the Development of the Northwest*. Madison, 1953.
QUAIFE, MILO M., *Chicago and the Old Northwest*. Chicago, 1913.
ROOSEVELT, THEODORE, *The Winning of the West*, 4 vols. New York, 1889–1896.

CHAPTER 7   SIMON KENTON'S PRISONER

ANTRIM, JOSHUA, *History of Champaign and Logan Counties*. Bellfontaine, Ohio, 1872.

History of Champaign County, Ohio. Chicago, 1881.
HOWE, HENRY, *Historical Collections of Ohio.* Cincinnati, 1847.
KENTON, EDNA, *Simon Kenton.* Garden City, 1930.
McCLUNG, JOHN A., *Sketches of Western Adventure.* Maysville, Ky., 1832.
McDONALD, JOHN, *Biographical Sketches.* Cincinnati, 1838.
McFARLAND, ROBERT W., "Simon Kenton." In *Ohio Archaeological and Historical Publications,* Vol. 13 (Jan. 1904).

CHAPTER 8   THE FOREST OF THE WEST

BAKELESS, JOHN, *The Eyes of Discovery.* Philadelphia, 1950.
HALL, BAYNARD RUSH, *The New Purchase.* New York, 1843.
LILLARD, R. G., *The Great Forest.* New York, 1947.
PAULDING, JAMES K., *Westward Ho.* New York, 1832.
RICHTER, CONRAD, *The Trees.* New York, 1940.
———, *The Fields.* New York, 1946.
———, *The Town.* New York, 1950.
WILKEY, MAJOR WALTER, *Western Immigration.* New York, 1839.

CHAPTER 9   "THIS UPSTART VILLAGE"—CHICAGO

Chicago City Directory, 1844.
KINZIE, JULIETTE, *Wau-bun, The "Early Day" in the Northwest.* New York, 1856.
LATROBE, CHARLES JOSEPH, *The Rambler in North America.* New York, 1835.
POWER, RICHARD LYLE, *Planting Corn Belt Culture.* Indianapolis, 1953.
SHIRREFF, PATRICK, *A Tour through North America.* Edinburgh, 1835.

CHAPTER 10   THE GRAND PRAIRIE

ATWATER, CALEB, *Writings.* Columbus, 1833.
BIRKBECK, MORRIS, *Letters from Illinois.* London, 1818.
BOGESS, ARTHUR CLINTON, *The Settlement of Illinois, 1788–1830.* Chicago, 1908.
FARNHAM, ELIZABETH W., *Life in Prairie Land.* New York, 1846.
HOFFMAN, CHARLES FENNO, *A Winter in the West.* New York, 1835.

PECK, J. M., *A New Guide for Emigrants to the West*. Boston, 1836.
POGGI, EDITH MURIEL, *The Prairie Province of Illinois*. University of Illinois, 1934.
POOLEY, W. P., *Settlement in Illinois, 1830–1850*. Madison, 1908.
SCHOOLCRAFT, HENRY ROWE, *Travels in the Central Portions of the Mississippi Valley*. New York, 1825.
TILLSON, CHRISTIANA HOLMES, *A Woman's Story of Pioneer Illinois*. Chicago, 1919.
WEAVER, J. E., *The North American Prairie*. Lincoln, Nebr., 1954.

CHAPTER 11   HOOSIER, YANKEE AND THE WESTERN MAN

HILL, RALPH NADING, *Yankee Kingdom*. New York, 1960.
HOLBROOK, STEWART H., *Yankee Exodus*. New York, 1950.
MATHEWS, LOIS KIMBALL, *The Expansion of New England*. Boston, 1909.
PECK, POOLEY, TILLSON, works cited in Chapter 10.

CHAPTER 12   MEN OF MANY NATIONS

BERNARD, HARRY, *Eagle Forgotten, The Life of John Peter Altgeld*. Indianapolis, 1938.
"*Journal of Ebenezer Mattoon Chamberlain*." In *Indiana Magazine of History*, Vol. XV (1919).
MELVILLE, HERMAN. *Redburn*. London, 1922.
PULSKY, FRANCIS AND THERESA, *White, Red and Black: Sketches of American Society in the United States*, 2 vols. New York, 1853.
ROBERTSON, PRISCILLA, *Revolutions of 1848*. Princeton, 1952.
WITKE, CARL F., *We Who Built America*. New York, 1940.
———, *Refugees of Revolution*. Philadelphia, 1952.
———, *The Irish in America*. Baton Rouge, 1956.
ZUCKER, A. E., *The Forty-Eighters*. New York, 1950.

CHAPTER 13   THE IRON ROAD

ACKERMAN, W. K., *Early Illinois Railroads*. Chicago, 1890.
CALKINS, ERNEST ELMO, *Genesis of a Railroad*. Illinois State Historical Library Publications, No. 42. Springfield, 1935.
GATES, PAUL WALLACE, *The Illinois Central and Its Colonization Work*. Cambridge, Mass., 1934.

HARLOW, ALVIN F., *The Road of the Century*. New York, 1947.
JENKS, L. H., *The Migration of British Capital to 1875*. London, 1927.

CHAPTER *14* THE PRAIRIE LAWYER

DUFF, JOHN J., *A. Lincoln, Prairie Lawyer*. New York, 1960.
HERNDON, WILLIAM H., *Herndon's Lincoln*, 3 vols. Chicago, 1889.
HILL, FREDERICK TREVOR, *Lincoln the Lawyer*. New York, 1906.
KING, WILLARD L., *Lincoln's Manager, David Davis*. Cambridge, 1960.
PRATT, HENRY EDWARD, *David Davis, 1815–1886*. In *Transactions of the Illinois State Historical Society*. Springfield, 1930.
THOMAS, BENJAMIN P., *Lincoln's New Salem*. New York, 1934, 1954.
WHITNEY, HENRY CLAY, *Life on the Circuit Court with Lincoln*. Caldwell, Idaho, 1940.

CHAPTER *15* CAP GRANT'S MULE

CRAMER, JESSE GRANT, ed., *Letters of Ulysses S. Grant*. New York, 1912.
GRANT, ULYSSES SIMPSON, *Personal Memoirs of U. S. Grant*, 2 vols. New York, 1885–1886.
LEWIS, LLOYD, *Captain Sam Grant*. Boston, 1950.
ROSS, ISHBEL, *The General's Wife*. New York, 1959.
SCHARF, JOHN THOMAS, *History of St. Louis City and County*. Philadelphia, 1883.
WILLIAMS, BYRON, *History of Clermont and Brown Counties, Ohio*. Milford, Ohio, 1913.

CHAPTER *16* MORGAN'S RACE

ABBOT, JOHN STEVENS CABOT, "Pursuit and Capture of Morgan." In *Harper's Magazine*, Vol. XXXI (August, 1865).
Aunt Emily Ford Correspondence, Jackson, Ohio, July 23, 1863. In Ohio State Historical Library, Columbus.
DUKE, BASIL W., *History of Morgan's Cavalry*. Cincinnati, 1867.
McFARLAND, R. W., "*The Morgan Raid in Ohio*." In *Ohio Archaeological and Historical Publications*, Vol. XVII (July, 1908).
REID, WHITELAW, *Ohio in the War*, 2 vols. Columbus, 1893.

WEBER, L. J., "Morgan's Raid." In *Ohio Archaeological and Historical Publications*, Vol. XVIII (January, 1909).

CHAPTER 17 THUNDER IN THE NORTH

GRAY, WOOD, *The Hidden Civil War: The Story of the Copperheads*. New York, 1942.
HARPER, ROBERT S., *The Ohio Press in the Civil War*. The Ohio Historical Society, for the Ohio Civil War Centennial Commission, 1961.
HORAN, JAMES D., *Confederate Agent*. New York, 1954.
PEEKE, HEWSON LINDSLEY, *History of Erie County*. New York, 1916.
RANDALL, EMILIUS O., and RYAN, DANIEL J., *History of Ohio*, vol. IV. New York, 1912.
REID, WHITELAW, *Ohio in the War*, 2 vols. Columbus, 1893.
ROSEBOOM, EUGENE H., *The Civil War Era*. Columbus, 1944.
Trial of John Yates Beall by a Military Commission. New York, 1865.

CHAPTER 18 A BRAKEMAN, A CARPENTER AND THE HILLSIDE TOMB

BEALL, EDMOND, "Recollections of the Assassination and Funeral of Abraham Lincoln." In *Journal of the Illinois State Historical Society*, Vol. V (1913).
Harper's Weekly Magazine, Vol. IX (1865).
MORRIS, B. F., *Memorial Record of the Nation's Tribute to Abraham Lincoln*. Washington, 1865.
PORTER, WILLIAM S., "The Lincoln Funeral Train." In *Journal of the Illinois State Historical Society*, Vol. IX (1916).
SWEET, W. W., "Bishop Matthew Simpson and the Funeral of Abraham Lincoln." In *Journal of the Illinois State Historical Society*, Vol. VII (1914).
TARBELL, IDA M., *The Life of Abraham Lincoln*. New York, 1917.

CHAPTER 19 THE PRESIDENTIAL CHAIR

BARNARD, HARRY, *Rutherford B. Hayes and His America*. Indianapolis, 1954.
BEER, THOMAS, *Hanna*. New York, 1929.
BOWERS, CLAUDE G., *The Tragic Era*. New York, 1929.

CALDWELL, ROBERT GRENVILLE, *James A. Garfield, Party Chieftain*. New York, 1931.

CROLY, HERBERT, *Marcus Alonzo Hanna*. New York, 1912.

FORAKER, J. B., *Notes on a Busy Life*. Cincinnati, 1917.

GARLAND, HAMLIN, *Ulysses S. Grant*. New York, 1898.

GRANT, ULYSSES S., *Personal Memoirs of U. S. Grant*, 2 vols. New York, 1885–1886.

HESSELTINE, WILLIAM B., *Ulysses S. Grant, Politician*. New York, 1935.

KOHLSAAT, HERMAN H., *From McKinley to Harding*. New York, 1923.

LEECH, MARGARET, *In the Days of McKinley*. New York, 1959.

WALLACE, LEW, *Life of Benjamin Harrison*. Philadelphia, 1888.

WHITE, WILLIAM ALLEN, *Masks in a Pageant*. New York, 1928.

CHAPTER 20   THE HAYMARKET TRAGEDY

BROWNE, WALDO E., *Altgeld of Illinois*. New York, 1924.

CHRISTMAN, HENRY M., ed., *The Mind and Spirit of John Peter Altgeld*. Urbana, Ill., 1960.

CULP, DOROTHY, "The Radical Labor Movement, 1873–1895." In *Papers in Illinois History*. The Illinois State Historical Society, Springfield, 1938.

DAVID, HENRY, *The History of the Haymarket Affair*. New York, 1958.

HARRIS, FRANK, *The Bomb*. New York, 1909.

MASTERS, EDGAR LEE, *The Tale of Chicago*. New York, 1933.

McCONNELL, SAMUEL P., "The Chicago Bomb Case: Personal Recollections of an American Tragedy." In *Harper's Magazine*, Vol. 168 (May, 1934).

SCHAACK, MICHAEL J., *Anarchy and Anarchists*. Chicago, 1889.

WHITLOCK, BRAND, *Forty Years of It*. New York, 1925.

CHAPTER 21   WRITING FROM THE HEARTLAND

BROWN, MORRISON, *Louis Bromfield and His Books*. Fair Lawn, N. J., 1957.

CHANDLER, JOSEPHINE CRAVEN, "The Spoon River Country." In *Journal of the Illinois State Historical Society*, Vol. XIV (1921).

DUFFEY, BERNARD, *The Chicago Renaissance in American Letters*. East Lansing, Mich., 1954.

HOWE, IRVING, *Sherwood Anderson*. New York, 1951.

MENCKEN, H. L., "The Literary Capital of the United States." In *The Nation*, London, April 17, 1920.

SANDBURG, CARL, *Always the Young Strangers*. New York, 1953.

SCHEVILL, JAMES, *Sherwood Anderson*. Denver, 1951.

Shane Quarterly, *The*, "Vachel Lindsay Number." Vol. V, Indianapolis, 1944.

CHAPTER 22   MIRACLE ON THE FARM

CATES, SIDNEY, "The Day of Super Corn Crops." In *Country Gentleman*, March, 1929.

CAVANAGH, HELEN M., *Funk of Funk's Grove*. Bloomington, Ill., 1952.

CRABB, A. RICHARD, *The Hybrid Corn-Makers*. New Brunswick, N. J., 1948.

UNITED STATES DEPARTMENT OF AGRICULTURE, "Corn Production." Farmer's Bulletin No. 2073 (September, 1960).

WALLACE, HENRY A., AND BROWN, WILLIAM L., *Corn*. East Lansing, Mich., 1956.

Yearbooks of the United States Department of Agriculture.

CHAPTER 23   NEW TIMES ON THE OHIO

BANTA, R. E., *The Ohio*. New York, 1944.

[CRAMER, ZADOK], *The Navigator*. Pittsburgh, 1814.

HARTLEY, JOSEPH R., *The Economic Effects of Ohio River Navigation*. Bloomington, Ind., 1959.

OHIO VALLEY IMPROVEMENT ASSOCIATION, *News Letters*, 1959.

———, *The Ohio Valley Story*, Cincinnati, 1959.

SPORN, PHILIP, "The Ohio Valley as a Dynamic Industrial Area." Cincinnati, 1960.

Summary Report on the Economic Potentialities of the Upper Ohio Valley. Battelle Memorial Institute, Columbus, n.d.

TROLLOPE, FRANCIS, *Domestic Manners of the Americans*. London, 1832.

CHAPTER 24   THE FOURTH SEACOAST

Annual Reports of the Lake Carriers' Association. Cleveland.

BULLOCK, FREDERICK J., *Ships and the Seaway*. Toronto, 1959.

Great Lakes Seaway Journal, May, 1959. First issue of monthly news Journal.

Heartland, The, Great Lakes–St. Lawrence Association, 1951.

HIGBEE, EDWIN C., "Cleveland and the St. Lawrence Seaway." Cleveland, 1960. Manuscript in Cleveland Public Library.

HILLS, T. L., *The St. Lawrence Seaway*. London, 1959.

IRELAND, TOM, *The Great Lakes–St. Lawrence Deep Waterway to the Sea*. New York, 1934.

MABEE, CARLTON, *The Seaway Story*. New York, 1961.

MALKUS, ALIDA, *Blue-Water Boundary*. New York, 1960.

Index

ABOUT THE AUTHOR

Walter Havighurst was born in Wisconsin and grew up in central Illinois. He attended Ohio Wesleyan University and graduated from the University of Denver.

After several years of graduate study and service in the Merchant Marine, Mr. Havighurst in 1928 became a member of the Department of English at Miami University in Oxford, Ohio, where he has remained ever since.

Walter Havighurst's interest has long been focused on the region between the Ohio River and the Great Lakes, and has resulted in the writing of many books about it, including *The Long Ships Passing, Wilderness for Sale,* and *Land of the Long Horizons.*

About *The Heartland* he writes: "Much of the material for this book was gathered on the road and on the scene, in places like Starved Rock and New Salem, Illinois; New Harmony and Vincennes, Indiana; and Piqua and Marietta, Ohio. But there was a good deal of book work too, and I took a lot of notes in the State Historical Libraries in Columbus, Indianapolis and Springfield. Some final research was done in Paris, where the first maps of the American interior are preserved in the Ministry of the Marine, and in the British Museum, where I found some fresh details on the British regime in the Mississippi Valley.

Set in Linotype Janson
Format by Stanley Wheatman
Manufactured by The Haddon Craftsmen, Inc.
HARPER & ROW, PUBLISHERS, INCORPORATED

WINNEBAGOS

LAKE MICHIGAN

Hennepin's capture ✗

● Galena

Rock River

SAUKS AND FOXES

Du Page R.

Des Plaines R.

1803 Ft. Dearborn (Chicago)

Fort Miamis 1679 ■

New Buffalo

Fort St. Joseph

River

KICKAPOOS

Fort St. Louis, 1682

ILLINOIS & MICHIGAN CANAL

Kankakee R.

Mississippi

● Bishop Hill

(Starved Rock)

Spoon River

Lake Peoria 1819

△ Illinois Village

CHICAGO R.R.

1811 Tippecanoe ✗

Maur

ERIE CANAL

MIAMIS

River

■ Fort Crèvecoeur 1679

● Bloomington

Sangamon R.

Fort Ouiatenon ■

WABASH & ERIE CANAL

INDIA

● New Salem

ALTON &

● Urbana

Indianapolis

Illinois River

Springfield ●

Embarrass R.

ST. LOUIS,

● Decatur

National Ro

ILLINOIS

ILLINOIS

● Alton

Vandalia ●

Kaskaskia River

ILLINOIS CENTRAL R.R.

Terre Haute

St. Louis ●

Cahokia, 1700

● Belleville

Missouri River

● Prairie du Rocher

Fort Sackville (Vincennes) 1705

Salem ●

Fort de Chartres ■

New Harmony

Wabash R.

Corydon ●

N Al

PIANKESHAWS

Kaskaskia 1695

Shawneetown

Evansville

Cairo ●